Growth, Crisis and the Korean Economy

Since the 2008 global financial crisis, policymakers as well as academicians have been seeking to fathom why subsequent recoveries remain tenuous. Other outstanding issues that they have been trying to understand include: why do some economies grow faster than others? How should exchange rate volatility be understood and what factors make an economy more likely to fall into an exchange rate crisis? What policies need to be taken during tranquil periods, and how should they be changed once the crisis is triggered? As a partial effort to meet such interests, this book provides insights into these issues.

This book examines growth and convergence (Part I), exchange rate volatility and the Asian crisis (Part II), and the global crisis (Part III). In addition, the book also draws lessons from South Korea's experiences – a country which has undergone three different crises and brisk recoveries (Part IV). The book also includes some practical and policy-oriented analysis. This is a truly comprehensive book bringing together varied topics and diversity under one common theme – economic growth and crisis.

Dongchul Cho is Chief Economist at the Korea Development Institute (KDI) and Professor at the KDI School of Public Policy and Management. He is also serving as a member of National Economic Advisory Council to the President. Before he joined the KDI in 1995, Dr. Cho was Professor of Economics at Texas A&M University. He graduated from Seoul National University and holds a PhD in Economics from the University of Wisconsin-Madison. His major areas of interest are macroeconomics and international finance.

Growth, Crisis and the Korean Economy

Dongchul Cho

Routledge
Taylor & Francis Group

LONDON AND NEW YORK

First published 2015
by Routledge
2 Park Square, Milton Park, Abingdon, Oxon OX14 4RN

and by Routledge
711 Third Avenue, New York, NY 10017

First issued in paperback 2017

*Routledge is an imprint of the Taylor & Francis Group,
an informa business*

British Library Cataloguing in Publication Data
A catalogue record for this book is available from the British Library

Library of Congress Cataloging-in-Publication Data
Cho, Dongchul.
  Growth, crisis and the Korean economy / by Dongchul Cho.
    pages cm
  1. Economic development—Korea (South) 2. Korea (South)—
Economic policy—1988– 3. Korea (South)—Economic
conditions—1988– 4. Financial crises—Korea (South) I. Title.
  HC467.96.C42757 2015
  330.95195—dc23
  2014040813

ISBN 13: 978-0-8153-5069-9 (pbk)
ISBN 13: 978-1-138-79274-6 (hbk)

Typeset in Galliard
by Apex CoVantage, LLC

Contents

Figures

Tables

Part I
Growth and convergence

1   Industrialization, convergence, and patterns of growth*

1.   Introduction

The long-run behavior of national growth rates has long been of great interest because it sheds light on future income disparities across countries as well as the prospective income of individual countries. Recently, the interest has been further stimulated, for the neoclassical growth model (Cass, 1965; Solow, 1956) and new endogenous growth models (Lucas, 1988; Romer, 1989) yield sharply different predictions: while the neoclassical growth model predicts that countries with similar preferences and technology will converge to similar levels of per capita income, endogenous growth models predict that there will be no such tendency.

In this regard, a substantial body of empirical study has examined whether the regression of the growth rate on the level of income per capita indeed produces a negative coefficient as predicted by the neoclassical model. Evidence is mixed, however. In particular, the regression results are very sensitive to the selection of countries: typically, the results for relatively developed countries (DCs) are consistent with the convergence hypothesis (Baumol, 1986; Dowrick and Nguyen, 1989), but the results for the samples including less developed countries (LDCs) are rather in conflict with the convergence argument (DeLong, 1988; Romer, 1988). The goals of this chapter are: (1) to document a stylized nonlinear (humped) pattern in growth; (2) to demonstrate how an explicit recognition of this pattern helps reconcile the conflicting results on convergence (and the conditional convergence result, below); and (3) to suggest a potential explanation for the humped pattern from a view of industrialization.

Section 2 shows that there exists an economically and statistically significant hump in the growth rate of postwar cross-country data: on average, middle-income countries grew the fastest, high-income countries the next, and low-income countries the slowest. Thus, a negative correlation between growth rates and income per capita is observed when low-income countries are excluded from the sample, but no such correlation is found for a larger class of countries.

To find the factors that can explain the fast growth of middle-income countries, this chapter first considers the most widely used three explanatory variables in growth regressions: the investment-to-GDP ratio, the percentage of age group enrolled in secondary education, and the rate of population growth. Both parametric and nonparametric analyses show that these variables cannot explain the humped pattern: middle-income countries grew far faster than could be explained by these variables. In addition, the failure of the regressions to capture the humped pattern results in the conditional convergence results (Barro, 1991; Mankiw et al., 1992): the regressions tend to under-predict the growth rates for middle-income countries and over-predict for high-income countries, and the resulting positive/negative residuals for middle/high-income countries generate negative correlations between the growth rate and income per capita.

Section 3, therefore, examines another factor of growth – industrialization. It has long been argued that economies can exhibit a spurt in growth during the course of industrialization. Rosenstein-Rodan (1943) notes that industrialization of some leading sectors, which needs a large initial set-up cost, can "big-push" the rest of the economy to industrialize. Rostow (1962) also argues that economies can "take-off" when some social/economic preconditions (e.g. infrastructure such as railroads) are met. These big-push and take-off ideas have been explored both empirically (Chenery et al., 1986; Denison, 1967) and theoretically (Azariadis and Drazen, 1990; Cho, 1993; Murphy et al., August 1989, Oct. 1989).

In spite of rigorous models on industrialization, there remains a fundamental difficulty in assessing the empirical plausibility of the models – how to measure "industrialization"? This section uses the increase in the portion of the labor force employed in manufacturing production as a proxy variable for industrialization, although this is admittedly not the perfect proxy. Along with the proxy variables for capital accumulation, this variable appears to explain the pattern in growth suitably: high-income countries grew faster than low-income countries because high-income countries accumulated (both physical and human) capital faster, but middle-income countries grew even faster because of drastic industrialization. When the explanatory variables appropriately describe the humped pattern, one can hardly find the conditional convergence result. Further examinations suggest that the result appears neither a sheer coincidence nor the result of the reversed causation between the growth rate and the proxy variable for industrialization.

Regarding the convergence vs. divergence debate, the observation in this section seems most relevant to the argument of Baumol and Wolff (1988, 1155): "The results indicate that smaller groups of countries began to converge as early as, perhaps, 1860; that the size of the convergence club has since risen". That is, income per capita of a country in the early stage of industrialization does not converge to the levels of leading countries. Going through industrialization, however, the country can reduce the income differential from leading countries and eventually join the "convergence club".

Section 4 briefly discusses the patterns of growth from time-series data for the United Kingdom, the United States, and Japan over the past 100 years. Section 5 concludes, and the Appendix lists the sources of the data.

2. Convergence and humped pattern in growth

2.1 Convergence and the selection of countries

The simplest but commonly used convergence test is to check whether growth rates are indeed negatively correlated with initial levels of income per capita. Table 1.2 shows the results for 95 countries in the Summers-Heston (1988) data during the 1965–1980 period; see Table 1.1 for the descriptions of the variables.

Table 1.1 Descriptions of the variables in tables

GRO:	average annual compound growth rate of GDP per capita (%).
Y_0:	log-GDP per capita in 1965.
INV:	investment to GDP ratio (%).
EDU:	portion of age group enrolled in secondary education (%).
POP:	average annual compound growth rate of population (%).
EXP:	export to GDP ratio (%).
ΔEXP:	average annual increase in EXP (%).
P_M:	portion of the labor force employed in manufacturing production in 1965 (%).
P_S:	portion of the labor force employed in service production in 1965 (%).
ΔP_M:	average annual increase in P_M during the 1965–1980 period (%).
ΔP_S:	average annual increase in P_S during the 1965–1980 period (%).

See the Appendix for data sources.

Table 1.2 Regressions of growth rates (%)

Sample	Constant	Y_0	Y_0^2	R^2	Implied Max.	F
95 Countries	−2.64 (1.52)	.69 (.21)		.102		3.70 [.028]
48 LDCs	−6.24 (4.85)	1.22 (.76)		.053		
47 DCs	6.58 (3.26)	−.44 (.41)		.025		
95 Countries	−30.24 (11.87)	8.39 (3.29)	−.53 (.23)	.153	$2738	1.55 [.208]

See Table 1.1 for the descriptions of the variables. Numbers in parentheses (brackets) are standard errors (*p*-values). Column "Implied Max." reports GDP per capita value (in 1980 international prices) implied by the quadratic regression estimates at which the growth rate attains the maximum. Column *F* tests the null hypothesis that the parameters are the same across the subsamples (48 LDCs and 47 DCs). Countries were divided by the level of 1965 GDP per capita.

Summers-Heston data, 95 countries, 1965–1980

Results reported in this section are virtually identical to the results from the data for more countries and longer sample periods,[1] although this chapter uses a little restrictive sample due to the data availability of the variables considered below. The average annual growth rate of GDP per capita (*GRO* hereafter) for each country was regressed on 1965 log GDP per capita (Y_0 hereafter). The positive coefficient estimate (first regression) indicates that on average high income countries grew faster than low income countries, which is against the convergence hypothesis.

The result, however, differs substantially across two half-sized subsamples, 48 LDCs and 47 DCs, categorized by Y_0, the initial GDP per capita (second and third regressions): it is positive for the LDCs but negative for the DCs. An *F*-test rejects (at a 5 percent significance level) the null hypothesis that the regression coefficients are the same across the subsamples. In fact, there exists a significant concave pattern: when the quadratic term of Y_0 is included in the regression, it appears significant (fourth regression). The quadratic regression estimates imply that the growth rate attains the maximum around the countries with \$2,700 of GDP per capita (in 1980 international prices of the Summers-Heston 1988 data).

This nonlinearity in the pattern of growth is best revealed by nonparametric estimation. (For the argument in this chapter, readers who are not familiar with nonparametric estimation may simply regard it as a sophisticated moving average method.) Figure 1.1A plots *GRO* against Y_0 along with the result of the nonparametric kernel estimation (solid line) and the 95 percent confidence band (dotted

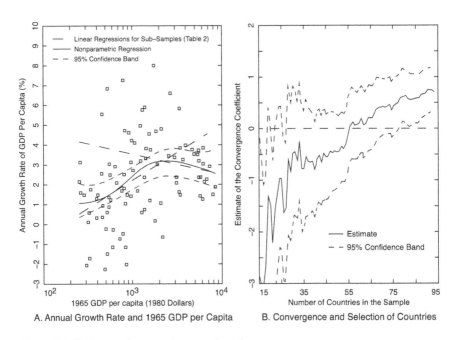

A. Annual Growth Rate and 1965 GDP per Capita   B. Convergence and Selection of Countries

Figure 1A–B Humped pattern in growth and convergence

lines).[2] Despite the wide dispersion, the weighted average of the growth rates (solid line) increases from 1 to 3.2 percent and then decreases to 2.6 percent thereafter. That is, middle-income countries grew the fastest, high-income countries the next, and low-income countries the slowest.

The implication of the concave pattern regarding the above linear convergence test is clear: the more low-income countries are included in the sample, the less likely the convergence result appears. Figure 1.1B confirms this proposition. I ranked the 95 countries in the order of Y_0 and performed the linear regression of GRO on Y_0 for the sample with 15 highest income countries. Then I ran the same regression for the sample with an additional next highest income country at a time. Figure 1.1B shows how the coefficient estimate increases with the number of countries included in the sample. Perhaps it is well known that there is strong evidence for the convergence across developed countries such as Organisation for Economic Co-operation and Development (OECD) countries, while there is no such evidence for a wider range of countries. In light of Figure 1.1B, the convergence result among developed countries may be considered as a local manifestation of the global humped pattern.

2.2 Conditional convergence and humped pattern in growth

Even for a wide range of countries, the growth rate appears to be negatively correlated with income per capita if some variables are controlled for to capture heterogeneities across countries. Barro (1991), Mankiw et al. (1992), and many others have found this result, called the conditional convergence.

Table 1.3A, Regression 1, reports the results of the regressions using the most commonly used three control variables: the investment-to-GDP ratio (INV, a proxy for a physical capital accumulation rate), the percentage of age group enrolled in secondary education (EDU, a proxy for a human capital accumulation rate), and the average annual rate of population growth (POP). The population growth rate does not appear significant at all in the first regression. This result may not be surprising, given the finding of Levine and Renelt (1992) that this variable is not robust in explaining the variations in the cross-country growth rate of income per capita. Since the population growth rate makes only negligible differences to the subsequent results (compare for example the results of Regressions 1 and 2 in Table 1.3A), this chapter mainly discusses the regressions that exclude this variable.

While the above control variables dramatically change the sign of the coefficient on Y_0 from .69 of the unconditional coefficient (the first regression in Table 1.2) to −.69 of the conditional convergence coefficient (the first regression in Table 1.3A), they fail to capture the concave pattern. The quadratic pattern remains almost untouched in the residuals of the regression (column Y_0^2), and the F-test (column F) still rejects the null hypothesis that the regression coefficients are the same across the subsamples, 48 LDCs and 47 DCs. As will be clearer in the next section, the conditional convergence result and the concave pattern are closely related to each other: when the explanatory variables suitably capture the

Table 1.3A Regressions of growth rates

No.	Const.	Y_0	INV	EDU	POP	EXP	ΔEXP	$ΔP_M$	$ΔP_S$	R^2	F	Y_0^2
1	2.98	−.69	.13	.037	.25					.336	2.57	−.48
	(2.49)	(.37)	(.03)	(.015)	(.28)						[.03]	(.19)
2	4.05	−.74	.13	.032						.330	3.37	−.55
	(2.19)	(.37)	(.03)	(.013)							[.01]	(.19)
3	3.96	−.71	.10	.030		.01	1.07			.405	3.19	−.42
	(2.09)	(.35)	(.03)	(.013)		(.01)	(.35)				[.01]	(.18)
4	.07	−.15	.07	.031	−.004	.01	1.02	2.85	.25	.539	.98	.01
	(2.21)	(.34)	(.03)	(.012)	(.24)	(.01)	(.31)	(.59)	(.52)		[.46]	(.17)
5	.06	−.12	.08	.030			1.08	2.84		.535	.63	−.01
	(2.01)	(.33)	(.03)	(.011)			(.31)	(.56)			[.70]	(.17)
6	−.05	−.14	.10	.033				2.90		.470	.90	−.11
	(2.13)	(.35)	(.03)	(.012)				(.59)			[.49]	(.18)
7	−.87		.10	.030				2.98		.469	.69	−.08
	(0.41)		(.03)	(.008)				(.55)			[.60]	(.18)
7-1	−1.12		.09	.043				3.25		.406		
	(.61)		(.04)	(.020)				(1.26)				
7-2	−.15		.11	.013				2.40		.402		
	(.77)		(.04)	(.012)				(.64)				

See Table 1.1 for the descriptions of the variables. Numbers in parentheses (brackets) are standard errors (*p*-values). Column *F* tests the null hypothesis that the coefficients are the same across the subsamples, 48 LDCs and 47 DCs in terms of 1965 GDP per capita. Column Y_0^2 reports the estimate of the coefficient on a quadratic term when the residuals are regressed on a quadratic function of Y_0. Regressions 7-1 and 7-2 are run for the 48 LDCs and 47 DCs, respectively.

high growth rates of middle-income countries, the conditional convergence result almost disappears.

2.3   *Does the expansion in export explain the hump?*

Since some export-oriented middle-income countries such as Singapore, Taiwan, and Korea have been growing remarkably fast, it is often suspected that the expansion in export may help explain the fast growth of middle-income countries. I used two proxy variables to measure the openness of one country, the export to GDP ratio (*EXP*) and the average annual increase in this ratio (Δ*EXP*). Regression 3 in Table 1.3B reports the result. *EXP* does not appear significantly correlated with *GRO*, which is also confirmed by the extensive study of Levine and Renelt (1992). On the other hand, Δ*EXP* appears significant in the growth regression and reduces the concave pattern in the residual to an extent. Yet, the quadratic pattern is still significant, and the *F*-test rejects the null of stable

Table 1.3B Regressions of variables on polynomials of Υ_0

Regressor	Dependent Variable							
	GRO	INV	EDU	POP	EXP	ΔEXP	ΔP_M	ΔP_S
Υ_0	.69	5.34	23.42	-.65	3.64	.13	-.16	.14
	(.21)	(.68)	(1.46)	(.08)	(1.77)	(.05)	(.03)	(.03)
Υ_0^2	-.53	-.51	2.81	-.34	-2.90	-.10	-16	-.03
	(.23)	(.74)	(1.57)	(.07)	(1.92)	(.06)	(.03)	(.04)

See Table 1.1 for the descriptions of the variables. Numbers in parentheses are standard errors. Each dependent variable was regressed on both linear and quadratic functions of Υ_0. The table reports the coefficient estimates of the highest order of the polynomials.

coefficients. The expansion of export seems a factor, but not the principal factor, that can explain the fast growth of middle-income countries.

3. Industrialization and the humped pattern

3.1 Industrialization as a source of growth

As mentioned in the introduction, industrialization has long been thought of as an important factor of growth. Regarding the pattern of growth in association with industrialization, the underlying argument of this chapter is guided by the model of Cho (1993) in particular. This dynamic optimization model decomposes the growth rate into two effects: (1) an effect from capital accumulation; and (2) an effect from industrialization. The model allows for agent heterogeneity in the sense that agents own different amounts of human and/or physical "capital" (the only production factor). Each agent has access to two technologies: a less productive traditional technology and a more productive industrial technology. Since the industrial technology requires a fixed cost, the agents stay in the less productive traditional sector until their capital exceeds a threshold level. The adoption of the more productive technology – industrialization – leads to a higher marginal return to capital, hence a larger savings rate. Thus, the capital accumulation effect is not only inexhaustible but accelerates as an economy develops (in accordance with the divergence view.) On the other hand, industrialization realizes the potential productivity of resources that have been employed in the traditional sector and thus brings about further increases in production. This effect of industrialization, in the aggregate, is determined by the distribution of capital across agents. This effect is not noticeable for underdeveloped economies in which few agents have reached the threshold level; it peaks for industrializing economies in which many agents are close to the threshold level; and it dies out for developed economies (in accordance with the convergence view) in which most agents have already passed the threshold level. As an economy develops, the aggregate growth rate (the sum of these two effects) is generally increasing with a possible hump in the middle of intense industrialization. Regarding the convergence vs. divergence debate, this model is consistent with the argument of Baumol and Wolff (1988) mentioned in the introduction.

Many researchers have regarded the rise in manufacturing sectors as the signal of industrialization, and this notion seems consistent with various models on industrialization if the manufacturing sectors can be viewed as industrial sectors with a fixed set-up cost. To measure how fast an economy industrialized during the sample period, therefore, I used the average annual increase in the portion of the labor force employed in manufacturing production (as opposed to agricultural and service production), ΔP_M. The increase in the portion was used because the growth rate of income per capita is associated with the rate of industrialization rather than its level. This variable is by no means the perfect proxy for the rate of industrialization. Yet, it seems that this is a reasonable proxy variable that is available for a wide range of countries.

A simple specification of the aggregate production function that is consistent with the following growth regressions is

$$Y_t = A_t\, K_t^\alpha\, H_t^\beta,$$

with

$$A_t = A_0 e^{gt}\{(1 - P_t) + (\gamma + 1)P_t\},$$

where subscript t denotes time, Y aggregate output, A the total factor productivity, K physical capital, H human capital, g the rate of technology progress, P the relative size of industrial sectors, and α, β, γ positive parameters. The assumption $\gamma > 0$ states that industrialization increases the total factor productivity A_t. Take the logarithm and then the first difference of the above production function, approximate $\log(1 + \gamma P) \approx \gamma P$ for a small P, and use INV and EDU as the proxy variables for the growth rates of K and H, and ΔP_M as the proxy variable for ΔP. Then the growth equation becomes

$$GRO = g + \alpha INV + \beta EDU + \gamma \Delta P_M.$$

Although this chapter invokes industrialization for the effect of ΔP_M on growth, the following empirical results are also consistent with other related hypotheses. For example, the hypothesis that manufacturing production such as "social overhead capital" (notably in transportation sectors) and machinery exhibits great external effects throughout the economy is consistent with $\gamma > 0$. Another hypothesis is that manufacturing production is subject to increasing returns to scale, while agricultural and service production exhibit constant returns to scale. Under this assumption, Panagariya (1988) shows that many stylized facts on growth can be explained. In this case, too, the rise in the relative portion of manufacturing production can bring about the increase in income per capita due to the increasing returns to scale.

3.2 Regression results

Regressions 4 through 7 in Table 1.3A report the results using ΔP_M as an additional explanatory variable. This variable appears to have a significant effect on the growth rate, while the corresponding variable for service production ΔP_S does not. Only the rise in manufacturing relative to agricultural and service production seems to help one country's growth. The effect of ΔP_M on GRO also appears robust with respect to different specifications (Regressions 4 through 7) as well as across the subsamples (Regression 7-1 for the 48 LDCs and Regression 7-2 for the 47 DCs).

Above all, ΔP_M greatly helps explain the fast growth of middle-income countries: the concave pattern left over in the residuals reduces to become virtually zero. As a result, the F-tests do not reject the null of the stable coefficients across the subsamples. Another interesting result is that the conditional convergence coefficient also substantially reduces (in absolute value) to become no more significant at all.

The contribution of each explanatory variable to the explanation of the linear or quadratic pattern of growth in each regression can be explicitly computed by combining the estimates in Tables 1.3A and 1.3B. Table 1.3B reports the regression results of each variable on the linear or quadratic functions of Y_0: each column reports the coefficient of the highest order of the polynomials (note that column GRO was copied from the corresponding cells of Table 1.2). Using as an example Regression 7 in Table 1.3A, consider the following relationship between the total derivative and partial derivatives:

$$dGRO/dY_0 = (\partial GRO/\partial INV)(dINV/dY_0) + (\partial GRO/\partial EDU)(dEDU/dY_0)$$
$$+ (\partial GRO/\partial \Delta P_M)(d\Delta P_M/dY_0).$$

Plugging the estimates in Regression 7 of Table 1.3A and the estimates in Table 1.3B, the right hand side is estimated:

$$(0.10)(5.34) + (0.030)(23.4) + (2.98)(-.16) = .53 + .70 - .48 = .75.$$

That is, when one country's income per capita is twice as high as another's (or when Y_0 is higher by a unit), INV, EDU, and ΔP_M are on average higher by 5.34, 23.4, and $-.16$ percent, respectively. Since one percent rises in these variables bring about 0.10, 0.030, and 2.98 percent increases in GRO, the growth rate of the high income country is expected to be higher by .75 percent. This indirect estimate through the explanatory variables is close to the direct estimate of the total derivative, .69 percent (column GRO in Table 1.3B). The difference between the direct and the indirect estimate, $-.06$ (= .69 $-$ .75), is left over in the residual of the regression, and insignificant (standard error .34). That is, most effect of the convergence conditional on INV and EDU is absorbed through ΔP_M (as much as $-.48 = (2.98)(-.16)$).

Similarly, the contribution of each explanatory variable in Regression 7 to the quadratic pattern in growth can be computed. While the roles of INV and EDU are negligible (.03 = $-.05 + .08 = (.10)(-.51) + (.030)(2.81)$), the contribution of ΔP_M ($-.48 = (2.98)(-.16)$) is substantial. Again, the difference between the direct estimate of the quadratic pattern −.53 (Column *GRO* in Table 1.3B) and the estimate through the explanatory variables −.45 (= .03 − .48) is left over in the residual, which is far from significant (column Y_0^2 for Regression 7).

In fact, the contribution of each explanatory variable to describing the pattern of growth can be best visualized using the nonparametrically estimated patterns of the explanatory variables in Figures 1.2A–F in the places of the

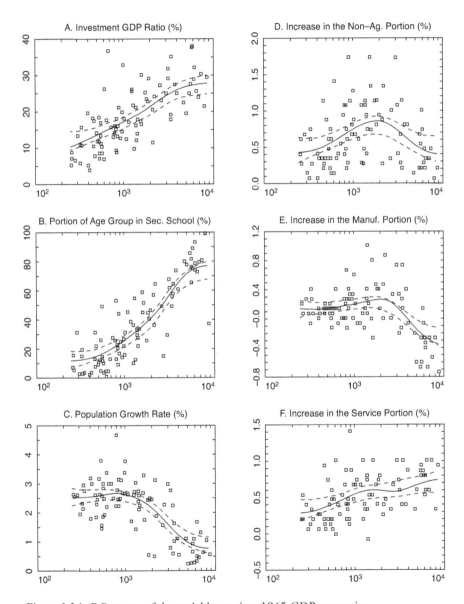

Figure 1.2A–F Patterns of the variables against 1965 GDP per capita

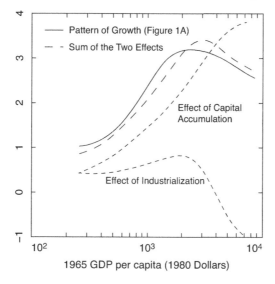

Figure 1.3 Decomposition of the patterns of growth

values in Table 1.3B. These figures plot each explanatory variable against Υ_0 in the same fashion as in Figure 1.1, and thus the results in Table 1.3B can be regarded as linear or quadratic approximations of these nonlinear patterns (solid lines in Figures 1.2A through 1.2F). Both *INV* and *EDU* (Figures 1.2A and 1.2B) rise monotonically with Υ_0 and show no sign of decline for developed countries. In contrast, ΔP_M (Figure 1.2E) peaks around middle-income countries and sharply declines for developed countries. Using the results of Regression 7 in Table 1.3A again, Figure 1.3 plots the estimated effect of the two capital accumulation rates,

$$-.87 + .10 \text{ \{solid line in Figure 1.2A\}} + .030 \text{ \{solid line in Figure 1.2B\}},$$

and the estimated effect of industrialization,

$$2.98 \text{ \{solid line in Figure 1.2E\}},$$

along with the directly estimated pattern of the growth rate in Figure 1.1. The vertical sum of these two estimated effects appears to well describe the directly estimated pattern of growth: high-income countries grew faster than low-income countries because high-income countries accumulated capital faster but middle-income countries grew even faster because of drastic industrialization.

In addition, this figure suggests the following interpretation regarding the conditional convergence result: when ΔP_M is not considered, the growth regression cannot capture the humped pattern and thus inevitably tends to under-predict the growth rates for middle-income countries and over-predict for high-income countries. The resulting positive/negative unexplained growth rates for middle/high-income countries produce the negative correlations with Y_0 – the conditional convergence result. When the humped pattern is suitably captured by ΔP_M, the conditional convergence result disappears. That is, the rate of industrialization ΔP_M "explains" why the total factor productivity grows slowly in high-income countries relative to middle-income countries.

3.3 Sheer coincidence?

Looking at the result in Figure 1.3, one can become suspicious that ΔP_M may be just one of many variables whose pattern with respect to Y_0 happens to coincide with the corresponding pattern of the growth rate unexplained by *INV* and *EDU*. It may be that ΔP_M has appeared significant in the growth regressions because of this coincidence in the patterns, rather than because ΔP_M along with *INV* and *EDU* has generated the pattern of growth as asserted above.

To see whether this suspicion is the case, I decomposed ΔP_M into $\Delta \hat{P}_M$ and $\Delta P_M - \Delta \hat{P}_M$, where $\Delta \hat{P}_M$ is the fitted value of ΔP_M obtained by regressing on a cubic function of Y_0^3 and then regressed *GRO* on these two decomposed variables along with *INV* and *EDU*. If the above significant correlation between *GRO* and ΔP_M results from a sheer coincidence in the patterns, it may be expected that the coefficient on $\Delta P_M - \Delta \hat{P}_M$ is near zero while $\Delta \hat{P}_M$ appears significant. But the result reported in the first line of Table 1.4 shows that both $\Delta \hat{P}_M$ and $\Delta P_M - \Delta \hat{P}_M$ have significant effects on *GRO* (other results in this table are discussed below). Furthermore, the effects of $\Delta \hat{P}_M$ and $\Delta P_M - \Delta \hat{P}_M$ on *GRO* are similar: the null hypothesis that the two coefficients are the same is not rejected (*p*-value .27). After the portion that generates the humped pattern in growth is purged, there remain enough variations in ΔP_M that confirm the significant effect of industrialization on the growth rate.

Table 1.4 Two-stage regressions of growth rate

Dep.Vbl.	Const.	INV	EDU	$\Delta \hat{P}_M$	$\Delta P_M - \Delta \hat{P}_M$	Y_0	P_M	P_S	R^2
GRO	−1.18	.10	.034	3.91	2.54				.476
	(.51)	(.03)	(.010)	(1.03)	(.69)				
GRO	−1.48	.11	.035	4.16					.395
	(.53)	(.03)	(.010)	(1.10)					
GRO	−1.44	.10	.038	4.41					.469
	(.46)	(.03)	(.009)	(.82)					
ΔP_M	1.07					−0.15	2.36	−1.61	.580
	(.34)					(.06)	(.34)	(.28)	

See Table 1.1 for the descriptions of the variables. $\Delta \hat{P}_M$ denotes the fitted value of ΔP_M. In the first and second regressions, $\Delta \hat{P}_M$ was obtained by regressing ΔP_M on the cubic function of Y_0, while in the third regression $\Delta \hat{P}_M$ was obtained by regressing ΔP_M on Y_0, P_M, and P_S. $\Delta P_M - \Delta \hat{P}_M$ is the residual of this regression. Numbers in parentheses are standard errors.

3.4 Reversed causation?

It seems that the close correlation between GRO and ΔP_M is not just a coincidence. However, a more serious challenge on the argument of this chapter arises from the recognition that the above cross-country regression results do not imply the direction of causation. Even if ΔP_M is simply a result of growth rather than its source, the regressions can yield statistically significant correlation coefficients. Admittedly, in addition, one country's industrial structure depends heavily upon the country's domestic demand.

Yet an informal examination of the regression results seems to suggest that the strong correlation between GRO and ΔP_M might not completely result from a reversed causation. It is commonly observed that the rise in domestic demand due to economic development is associated with not only the portion of manufacturing production but also the portion of service production.[4] If the above regressions only captured the pure reversed causation between GRO and the industrial structure, it might be expected that the coefficient on ΔP_S is also significant: but only ΔP_M appears significant (Regression 4 in Table 1.3).

A formal technique that helps avoid this causation problem is an instrumental variable estimation. The first regression in Table 1.4 already reported the result of the two-stage least square estimation using as instruments the polynomials of Υ_0, a certain exogenous variable. The coefficient on $\Delta \hat{P}_M$, exogenous variations with respect to GRO, was significant and similar to the coefficient on ΔP_M in the previous regressions. In fact, the test for the null hypothesis that the coefficients on $\Delta \hat{P}_M$ and $\Delta P_M - \Delta \hat{P}_M$ are the same is equivalent to the Hausman's (1978) specification test for endogeneity: the null of no endogeneity was not rejected. The second regression result of Table 1.4 appears to reinforce the argument of this chapter. When $\Delta P_M - \Delta \hat{P}_M$ is excluded, the estimate on $\Delta \hat{P}_M$ becomes even larger. That is, the endogenous variations in ΔP_M, if any, might have biased the coefficient toward zero rather than a positive number.

Instead of the polynomials of Υ_0, I also regressed ΔP_M on all the other variables considered in this chapter that are assumed exogenous. Only three variables, Υ_0, P_M, and P_S, appeared significantly correlated with ΔP_M. The result of the regression of ΔP_M on Υ_0, P_M, and P_S is reported in the fourth row of Table 1.4: a high ΔP_M is associated with a low Υ_0, a high P_M, and a low P_S. These three variables are observed in the initial year of the sample period, and thus they should be exogenous to the subsequent growth. The growth regression using the fitted value of ΔP_M from this regression also gives a similar result (the third row of Table 1.4).

4. Humped patterns in time-series data?

Are the humped patterns in growth rates also found from time-series data? For this question, I examined three countries: the United Kingdom, the forerunner of industrialization, the United States, the present world leader, and Japan, a latecomer to industrialization. For these countries over the past 100 years, the portions of the labor force employed in non-agricultural production were available, but data for the further breakdown into manufacturing and service production were not available to me. Thus this section briefly compares three available variables for the time-series data, *GRO*, *INV*, and $\Delta P (= \Delta P_M + \Delta P_S$, the annual increase in the portion of the labor force employed in non-agricultural production) with the corresponding variables in the postwar cross-country data.

Figure 1.4 plots the results of nonparametric regressions (solid lines) of the variables on time, along with the actual observations (dotted lines) for each country. As in the postwar data, *INV* rose with development from 8 to 18 percent in the United Kingdom and from 7 to more than 30 percent in Japan. The high value of *INV* after World War II in Japan – the main engine of the Miracle of Japan – may be regarded to an extent as exceptional, but the general increase also is observed from the prewar series. In the United States, however, this value was remarkably high in the late nineteenth century (approximately 20 percent, compared to 8 percent for the contemporary United Kingdom or Japan) and does not exhibit a subsequent rise.

The variable ΔP shows a concave pattern except for the United Kingdom in which more than three-fourths of its labor force was already employed in nonagricultural industry around 1870. In the United States and Japan as well as the "average" postwar countries, the peak in ΔP was achieved when 60–65 percent of the labor force is employed in non-agricultural production. The pace at the peak, however, is quite different between the prewar and the postwar samples. While only about 0.5 percent per annum around 1900 for the United States (Figure 1.4B, bottom), it is almost 1.2 percent around 1960 for Japan (Figure 1.4C, bottom), and about 0.85 percent for the postwar countries (Figure 1.2D).

The quantitative difference in ΔP may deserve attention because it can generate a qualitative difference in the pattern of growth rates. The faster its rate at the peak, the more likely the growth rate exhibits a hump in the middle of industrialization. In fact, the countries that attained the peak after World War II, the postwar countries and Japan, happen to reveal the humped patterns in growth rates,[5] while the United States does not. Several factors might be relevant to this pre- and postwar difference. First, the world war itself might have galvanized traditional agricultural societies to industrialize and "take-off". Second, the explosive expansion of foreign trade and the information industry after World War II might have made it relatively easy to imitate advanced technologies and industrial structures (Baumol, 1986).

Table 1.5 reports the regression results of the growth rates on *INV* and ΔP for the average values per annum of annual and semi-decennial data. Semi-decennial data are used to lessen the possible spurious effects of short term fluctuations.[6] Each regression allows for the first order serial correlation of the error term.[7] For the annual data, I performed the *F*-test that checks the stability of the coefficients across the pre- and post-1945 samples.[8] The coefficients on *INV* except for the United States appear fairly similar to the corresponding estimate for the cross-country sample. The small estimate for the United States results from the weak correlation between *GRO* and the large values of *INV* for the prewar series, which

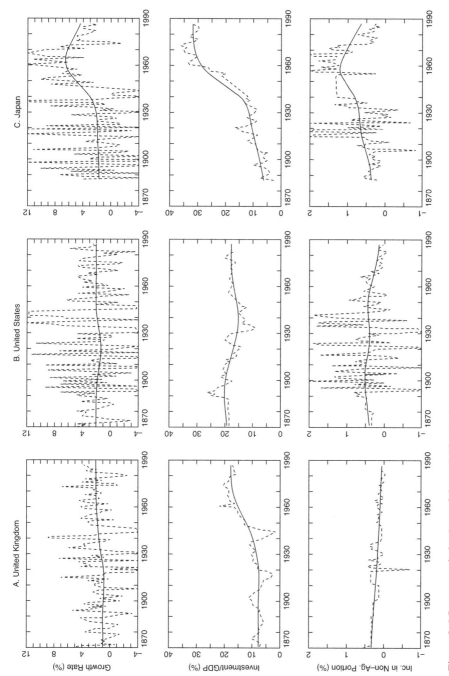

Figure 1.4 Long-run behaviors of the variables in time-series

Table 1.5 Regressions of growth rates, selected countries

Data	Constant	INV	ΔP	ρ	R^2	n	F
	A. United Kingdom (1871–1987)						
Annual	−2.50	.22	8.17	.22	.151	116	.38
	(1.01)	(.07)	(1.99)	(.09)			[.77]
Semi-Decennial	−1.77	.20	5.35	−.25	.297	23	
	(1.22)	(.07)	(3.23)	(.21)			
	B. United States (1871–1987)						
Annual	−1.80	.09	5.23	.14	.501	116	5.95
	(.02)	(.14)	(.50)	(.09)			[.001]
Semi-Decennial	.40	−.03	5.05	−.05	.715	23	
	(.02)	(.11)	(.71)	(.21)			
	C. Japan (1887–1940, 1954–1987)						
Annual	.14	.16	1.05	−.16	.184	87	2.67
	(.95)	(.05)	(.74)	(.11)			[.05]
Semi-Decennial	−1.37	.11	3.79	−.09	.866	17	
	(.58)	(.03)	(.67)	(.24)			

See Table 1.1 for the descriptions of the variables. Numbers in parentheses (brackets) are standard errors (*p*-values). Regressions are performed using the Cochrane-Orcutt method to allow for the first order serial correlation of the error term. Column ρ reports the estimate of the first order serial correlation coefficient, Column *n* sample size, and Column *F* the result of the *F*-test of the null that the coefficients are the same across the pre- and post-1945 samples. For the semi-decennial data, 1871–1877 period in the US and the UK was used as the first observation and 1887–1890 and 1954–1957 periods in Japan were treated as separate observations.

also causes the *F*-test to reject the null of the stable coefficients.[9] Close correlations between ΔP and *GRO* are also found in these regressions. The regressions using ΔP instead of ΔP_M are, however, likely to be affected by the reversed causation, and the results may have to be considered as tentative ones.

5.   Concluding remarks

Patterns of national growth rates against levels of per capita income seem to be best understood through the behavior of the relevant factors of growth. This chapter describes patterns of growth as the sum of patterns in the capital accumulation rates and patterns in the pace of "industrialization" with development. In conjunction with the time series behavior of the variables, the postwar cross-country data suggest the following interpretation: as one country develops, the rate of capital accumulation, and hence the growth rate of income, tends to increase in general, but drastic industrialization can generate a hump in the growth rate during the course of development.

In relation to the convergence results for postwar cross-country data, the analysis in this chapter seems of particular interest. The humped pattern in growth provides an explanation for the sensitive results of the unconditional convergence test with respect to the selection of countries. Also, the nonparametric analysis shows how the conditional convergence results are generated and how they can be explained by industrialization.

Concluding the chapter, I would like to clearly acknowledge the limitations of my results. Among those, the most serious limitations may be the legitimacy of the proxy variable for industrialization and the causation problem between this variable and the growth rate. I believe that further research (using micro data) can yield sharper results.

APPENDIX: DATA SOURCES

A. 95 countries, 1965–1980

I used the Summers-Heston (1988) data for GRO, Y_0, INV, POP, and the World Development Report (1988) for EDU (Table 30), EXP (Table 5), P_M and P_S (Table 31). The variables that denote the annual average increases (GRO, POP, ΔEXP, ΔP_M and ΔP_S) were computed by dividing the differences between the initial and the last year values of the relevant variables by 15, the sample period. See Table 1.1 for the definitions of the variables.

Since the data for P_M and P_S are available for each country in only two years, 1965 and 1980, all the other variables were also constructed for the sample period 1965–1980. Among the 121 countries of the Summers-Heston (1988) dataset, the following 25 countries are excluded due to either data availability or oil countries: Gabon, Gambia, Guinea, Lesotho, Rwanda, Swaziland, Angola, Afghanistan, Bahrain, Iran, Iraq, Kuwait, Oman, Saudi Arabia, Taiwan, United Arab Emirates, Yemen, Cyprus, Iceland, Luxembourg, Malta, Barbados, Guyana, Surinam, Venezuela, and Fiji.

B. Time-series data

B.1 *GDP per capita and the growth rate*

Annual GDP series were taken from Maddison (1982, Tables A6–A8) as far as available (1870–1979 for the UK and the US and 1885–1944, 1947–1979 for Japan). Population data were also taken from Maddison (1982, Tables B2-B4) to compute the annual GDP per capita. These series were extended to 1987 by the OECD (1989) data. The annual growth rates of GDP per capita were obtained by taking the log differences of consecutive years. Thus, the final series of the growth rate are 1871–1987 for the UK and the US and 1886–1944, 1948–1987 for Japan.

B.2 Share of investment in GDP

UK: For 1870–1965, the share of investment to GDP was computed from Feinstein (1972, Table 19), the gross domestic fixed capital formation (column 3) and GDP (column 8).

US: Kendrick (1961) reports the annual estimates of the national accounts for 1889–1953 and the annual averages for the decades of 1869–1878 and 1879–1888. The ratio of investment to GDP was computed by the gross domestic investment (Table A-IIa, column 5) and GDP (Table A-III, column 5). It was assumed that this value for 1869–1888 was the same as the annual average value for the corresponding decades.

Japan: For 1885–1940 and 1955–1969, Ohkawa and Shinohara (1979) report the annual estimates of gross capital (Table A42) and GDP (Table A12). The ratio of investment to GDP was computed by assuming that investment was the annual increase of gross capital. In this manner, the data for 1886–1940 and 1956–1969 were obtained. I dropped the first observation because it is unreasonably high (over 50 percent).

OECD data: All the above data were extended to 1987 by the OECD (1979, 1989) data. Gross fixed capital formation is taken as the relevant investment. The series of the OECD (1979, 1989) data go back to 1960 for the UK, 1952 for the US, and 1953 for Japan. The OECD data instead of the above were used where there was overlap.

B.3 Portion of the labor force in non-agricultural industry

UK: Feinstein (1972, Table 59) reports the annual number of persons employed by industry for 1920–1938 and 1948–1965. In line with the OECD definition, I took the sum of agriculture and forestry (row 1) and fishing (row 2) as "agricultural industry". For 1870–1919 and 1939–1947, this portion of the labor force was (linearly) interpolated from the decade data (Table 60), and thus the rate of the structural change is constant during the corresponding decades.

US: Kendrick (1961, Table A-VI) reports the number of persons engaged in the private farm and nonfarm sector for 1889–1953 annually. I interpolated the portion for 1870–1888 from the decade averages. For 1954–1970, the civilian labor force from the Bureau of the Census (1975, Series D11-25) was taken.

Japan: Ohkawa and Shinohara (1979, Table A18) reports the annual series of the number of gainful workers in agricultural and non-agricultural production for 1885–1840 and 1953–1970.

OECD data: The series were extended to 1987 by the OECD (1991) data.

Notes

* This chapter is reprinted from *Southern Economic Journal*, 1984, pp. 398–414.
1 For 108 countries during the 1960–1985 period, for example, the results are very similar.
2 The nonparametric kernel estimation estimates an unspecified (nonlinear) conditional expectation function. For general expositions, see (Silverman, 1986; Ullah,

1988). I used the standard Gaussian kernel among others and set the bandwidth equal to {the estimate of the regressor's standard deviation} times {the sample size to the minus one fifth} as suggested in the above references. The 95 percent confidence bands were obtained from 1000 iterations of the bootstrapping experiment.

3 A quadratic function or higher order polynomials produced very similar results.

4 For example, when P_M and P_S (the portions of the labor force employed in manufacturing and service production in 1965, respectively) are regressed on Υ_0 respectively, the coefficients are .10 for P_M and .17 for P_S.

5 Unlike the case of the postwar cross-country data, however, the argument that industrialization may have generated the hump in the growth rate in Japan seems vulnerable, since the hump was achieved right after World War II (the recovery period) and the slowdown after the Oil Shock was a worldwide phenomenon.

6 Constructing the semi-decennial series involves the judgmental problem of where to cut the periods. However, several trials showed that the regression results are very insensitive to arbitrary period cut-off. The results reported in the text were obtained from the series constructed by the principles: (1) take as one period the five years sequentially from the recent year; and (2) if the number of the remaining years is less than five, take it as one separate period.

7 I used the Cochrane-Orcutt method. The results were similar to the OLS estimation results.

8 For the semi-decennial data, the sample sizes are too small to conduct the F-test.

9 The estimates are $-.092$ for the prewar annual data and 1.60 for the postwar data, while the estimates for ΔP are 5.58 and 3.79, respectively.

References

Azariadis, Costas and Allan Drazen, 1990. "Threshold Externalities in Economic Development," *Quarterly Journal of Economics*, May, pp. 501–526.

Barro, Robert J., 1991. "Economic Growth in a Cross Section of Countries," *Quarterly Journal of Economics*, May, pp. 407–443.

Baumol, William J., 1986. "Productivity, Growth Convergence, and Welfare: What the Long-Run Data Show," *American Economic Review*, December, pp. 1072–1085.

—— and Edward N. Wolff, 1988. "Productivity Growth, Convergence, and Welfare: Reply," *American Economic Review*, December, pp. 1155–1159.

Bureau of the Census, 1975. Historical Statistics of the United States, Colonial Times to 1970, US Department of Commerce.

Cass, David, 1965. "Optimum Growth in the Aggregate Model of Capital Accumulation," *Review of Economic Studies*, July, pp. 233–240.

Chenery, Hollis B., Sherman Robinson and Moises Syrquin, 1986. *Industrialization and Growth: A Comparative Study*, Washington, DC, World Bank.

Cho, Dongchul, 1993. "Industrialization and Growth: A Heterogeneous Agents Model," Manuscript, Texas A&M University.

DeLong, J. Bradford, 1988. "Productivity Growth, Convergence, and Welfare: Comment," *American Economic Review*, December, pp. 1138–1154.

Denison, Edward F., 1967. *Why Growth Rates Differ*. Washington, DC: The Brookings Institution.

Dowrick, Steve and Duc-Tho Nguyen, 1989. "OECD Comparative Economic Growth 1950–85: Catch-Up and Convergence," *American Economic Review*, December, pp. 1010–1030.

Feinstein, Charles H., 1972. *National Income Expenditure and Output of the United Kingdom, 1855–1965*, Cambridge, Cambridge University Press.

Hausman, Jerry A., 1978. "Specification Tests in Econometrics," *Econometrica*, November, pp. 1251–1271.

Kendrick, Jhon W. 1961. *Productivity Trends in the United States.* Princeton, NJ: Princeton University Press.

Levine, Ross and David Renelt, 1992. "A Sensitivity Analysis of Cross-Country Growth Regressions," *American Economic Review*, September, pp. 942–963.

Lucas, Robert E. Jr., 1988. "On the Mechanics of Economic Development," *Journal of Monetary Economics*, 22, pp. 3–42.

Maddison, Angus, 1982. *Phases of Capitalist Development.* New York: Oxford University Press.

Mankiw, N. Gregory, David Romer and David N. Weil, 1992. "A Contribution to the Empirics of Economic Growth," *Quarterly Journal of Economics*, May, pp. 407–437.

Murphy, Kevin M., Andrei Shleifer and Robert W. Vishny, 1989a. "Income Distribution, Market Size, and Industrialization," *Quarterly Journal of Economics*, August, pp. 537–564.

———, 1989b. "Industrialization and the Big Push," *Journal of Political Economy*, October, pp. 1003–1026.

OECD, 1979. National Accounts of OECD Countries, Paris.

———, 1989. Labor Force Statistics, Paris.

———, 1989. National Accounts of OECD Countries, Paris.

———, 1991. OECD Main Economic Indicators, No.10, Paris.

Ohkawa, Kazushi and Miyohei Shinohara, 1979. *Patterns of Japanese Economic Development, A Quantitative Appraisal.* New Haven and London: Yale University Press.

Panagariya, Arvind, 1988. "A Theoretical Explanation of Some Stylized Facts of Economic Growth," *Quarterly Journal of Economics*, August, pp. 509–526.

Romer, Paul M., 1989. "Increasing Returns and Long-Run Growth," *Journal of Political Economy*, 95, pp. 1002–1037.

———, 1988. "Capital Accumulation in the Theory of Long Run Growth," in *Modern Business Cycle Theory*, edited by R.J. Barro, pp. 51–127. New York: Wiley & Sons.

Rosenstein-Rodan, Paul N., 1943. "Problems of Industrialisation of Eastern and South-eastern Europe," *Economic Journal*, June-September, pp. 202–211.

Rostow, Walt W., 1962. *The Stages of Economic Growth: A Non-Communist Manifesto.* Cambridge: Cambridge University Press.

Silverman, D.W., 1986. *Density Estimation for Statistics and Data Analysis.* New York: Chapman & Hill.

Solow, Robert M., 1956. "A Contribution to the Theory of Economic Growth," *Quarterly Journal of Economics*, 70, pp. 65–94.

Summers, Robert and Alan Heston, 1988. "A New Set of International Comparisons of Real Product and Price Levels: Estimates for 130 Countries," *The Review of Income and Wealth*, March, pp. 1–25.

Ullah, Aman, 1988. "Non-Parametric Estimation of Econometric Functionals," *Canadian Journal of Economics*, August, pp. 625–658.

World Bank, The, 1988. World Development Report, Washington, DC, World Bank.

2   The other side of conditional convergence*

The empirical evidence reveals conditional convergence in the sense that economies grow faster per capita if they start further below their steady state positions.

(Barro et al., 1993, abstract)

1.   Introduction

The most prominent purpose of the conditional convergence literature is to protect the traditional neoclassical growth model (see, for example, Solow, 1956)
from the tumultuous attack of the endogenous growth camp. Since Romer
(1986) and Lucas (1988), the recent endogenous growth literature has claimed
postwar cross-country growth experiences as the main evidence for the failure of
the neoclassical model. In particular, rich countries have grown, on average, faster
(or no slower, at least) than poor countries, which has been interpreted as being
in sharp conflict with the neoclassical model that predicts convergence of standards of living to a steady-state level.

However, more scrupulous empirical assessments have found that steady-state
levels may be substantially different across countries. Thus, a proper way to test
the neoclassical convergence is to examine the correlation between the growth
rate and the initial level of income per capita conditional on each economy's
steady state. Here the empirical results appear to support conditional convergence
(Barro, 1991; Mankiw et al., 1992; Barro and Martin, 1992; and many others).

This chapter presents a direct implication of this success that is contrary to what
we believe is a common conjecture rooted in the neoclassical growth model. The
common conjecture is that lower income countries converge to their steady states
from farther below, as is revealed not only in the quotation given at the beginning
of the paper but also in many articles, such as Romer:

> Countries starting from a low level of the capital labor ratio are assumed to
> accumulate capital more rapidly and catch up with the countries that start
> from a higher initial position. For example, countries like Germany and Japan
> that suffered large losses during World War II, or developing countries like
> Korea, are thought to have grown faster than the United States in the 1950s

and 1960s because of more rapid capital accumulation as they approached the capital-labor ratio in the United States.

(1987, p. 2)

This chapter follows the analysis of Mankiw et al. (1992) (MRW hereafter), which seems the most articulated model for conditional convergence. Using their data set, we found that, unlike this above common conjecture, however, the conditional convergence regression estimates imply that poor countries are converging *from farther above* to their steady-state income levels. Specifically, these countries' steady-state levels are only half of their income levels in 1960. With this result, one may find hardly any grounds for the policies such as the World Bank's investment in these poorer countries with the intent of pushing them towards their steady states.

2.   Initial positions, steady state positions, and growth rates

A standard manipulation of the human capital augmented Solow model in MRW yields the steady-state income per capita at time t, $y^*(t)$,

$$\ln(y^*(t)) = (\ln A(0) + g^t) - \alpha_1 \ln(n + g + \delta) + \alpha_2 \ln(s_k) + \alpha_3 \ln(s_h), \qquad (1)$$

where $A(0)$ is the initial level of technology, g is the exogenous progress rate of $A(t)$, δ is the common rate of depreciation of physical and human capital, n is the rate of labor growth, s_k and s_h are the fractions of income invested in physical and human capital, respectively. Taking an approximation of the model around the steady-state position y^* yields

$$d \ln(y(t))/dt = g + \lambda[\ln(y^*(t)) - \ln(y^*(t))], \qquad (2)$$

Where λ is the speed of convergence. Equations (1) and (2) lead to the regression equation:

$$\ln(y(t)) - \ln(y(0)) = gt - \gamma_1[\ln(y^*(0)) - \ln(y(0))] \qquad (3-1)$$

$$\gamma_0 + \gamma_1 \ln(y(0)) + \gamma_2 \ln(n + g + \delta) + \gamma_3 \ln(s_k) + \gamma_4 \ln(s_h), \qquad (3-2)$$

Where

$$\gamma_0 = gt - \gamma_1(\ln A(0)), \gamma_1 = -(1 - e^{\lambda t}) < 0, \gamma_2 = \alpha_1\gamma_1 < 0, \gamma_3 = -\alpha_2\gamma_1 > 0,$$
$$and \ \gamma_4 = -\alpha_3\gamma_1 > 0$$

To save space, we confine ourselves to the discussion of the results using the data for the 98 "non-oil" countries provided by MRW. Apart from the residual terms, the results are[1]

$$\ln((y(t) - \ln(y(0)) = -0.27 + 0.094\ln(y(0))$$
$$= 3.04 - 0.289\ln(y(0)) - 0.505\ln(n + g + \delta)$$
$$+ 0.524\ln(s_k) + 0.233\ln(s_h)$$

where time 0 and t denote year 1960 and 1985 respectively. That is to say, the coefficient on $\ln(y(0))$ is positive unconditionally,[2] but negative conditionally. We state this finding as:

> *Finding 1.* Economies converge conditionally, although they diverge unconditionally.

Noting that the growth rate is determined by the (log) distance from the steady state (Eq. (2)), the higher (unconditional) growth rates of rich countries, on average, imply the following alternative statement:

> *Implication 1*: Economies with higher income per capital are, in general, further below their steady-state positions, provided all the economies are below their steady states.

The steady state of each country can be computed from Eq. (1), if the relevant parameters are identified. Unfortunately, γ_0 in Eq. (3–2) does not identify $A(0)$ from g. To identify $A(0)$, we took a widely used a priori value of g, 2 percent per year (see, for example, Barro et al., 1993).[3] Using the estimates of regression (3–2) and noting that the sample period is 25 years, we can estimate the steady state of each country by using the following:

$$\ln(y^\star(0)) = \{\gamma_0 - (0.02)(25) + \gamma_2\ln(n + g + \delta) + \gamma_3\ln(s_k)$$
$$+ \gamma_4\ln(s_h)\}/(-\gamma_1) \qquad (3\text{–}2')$$

Figure 1 plots these estimates of y^* against current income y in 1960. Each point represents an individual country's steady-state level of income, y^*, the dotted line is obtained by regressing $\ln(y^*)$ on $\ln(y)$,[4] and the solid line (45° line) represents y. Consistent with the first part of Implication 1, the dotted line appears steeper than the solid line. Among 98 countries in the sample, however, a half of countries (49 countries) appear to be above their respective steady-state positions. Thus Figure 2.1 leads to the following statement:

> *Finding 2.* On average, relatively poor countries converge to their steady-state positions *from above*, while rich countries converge from below.

To make this statement clear, we divided the 98 countries into four groups in terms of the 1960 GDP per adult, and computed the (geometric) average GDP per adult for each group. Table 2.1 shows the results. Probably the most surprising result in this table is that the average GDP per adult in the "low income"

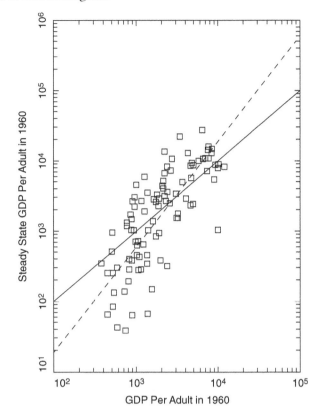

Figure 2.1 Current vs. steady-state positions, 98 countries

Table 2.1 Current vs. steady-state GDP per adult by income group

	Low Income	*Lower Middle Income*	*Upper Middle Income*	*High Income*
Number of Countries	24	25	25	24
GDP per Adult in 1960	$683	$1282	$2553	$7126
Steady State GDP per Adult	$333	$938	$3247	$8389

countries is approximately twice as high the corresponding value in steady states. In fact, Finding 2 appears more surprising, noting that it implies the following:

> *Implication 2*: In poor countries rather than rich countries, the current capital to (effective) labor ratio tends to be higher than the steady-state level, and thus this ratio *decreases* over time to converge to the steady states.

The usual name for poor countries, "less developed countries", seems a misnomer in this sense, because poor countries, in general, are already "over-developed" compared with their potential or steady-state positions.

While implication is simply a mirror statement of Finding 1, which is the main finding of the conditional convergence, Finding 2 (and hence Implication 2) relies on the particular specification and data of MRW.[5] In particular, the number of countries that are positioned above the steady-state levels depends heavily upon our assumption about g: a higher value of g implies more countries positioned above their steady-state levels.[6]

3.   Concluding remarks

This chapter derives a peculiar implication of conditional convergence. By combining the backbone idea of the neoclassical convergence (Eq. (2)) with the main finding of MRW (economies converge conditionally but diverge unconditionally), we are lead to state that lower income countries are far above their steady-state positions, while higher income countries are below their steady states. These results do not logically contradict the neoclassical growth model per se: they are the unexpected, but inevitable, implications to preserve the conventional neoclassical model.

Notes

* This chapter is reprinted from *Economics Letters*, pp. 285–290, 1996, which was co-authored with Stephan Graham.
1 These results can be found in tables III and V of MRW. See MRW for the details of the data. Briefly, GDP per adult is used for y, the rate of growth of the working-age population for n, the share of investment for s_k, and the percentage of the working-age population that is in secondary school for s_h.
2 This is a general finding for a wide set of countries (see, for example, Barro, 1991; Barro and Sala-i-Martin, 1992; and others), even though it is often reported that this coefficient estimate is not statistically different from zero for other sets of countries, excluding the poorest countries (e.g. MRW's "intermediate countries").
3 An anonymous referee suggested an alternative normalization to anchor the steady-state positions, which assumes the average steady-state (log) income across countries to be equal to the average actual income, This experiment yields almost identical results (the implied value of g is 1.8%).
4 The result is $\ln(y^*(0)) = -2.65 + 1.32 \ln(y(0))$, where the standard error of the slope is 0.12. Thus the slope is significantly greater than 1.
5 We have also used Summers and Heston's data (1988) and found consistent results.
6 Note that apart from random errors Eq. (3a) implies,

$$\{\ln(y(t)) - \ln(y(0))\}/t \gtrless g \leftrightarrow \ln(y^*(0)) \gtrless \ln(y(0)). \gtrless \ln(y(0)).$$

That is, countries with an annual growth rate less than g are the countries whose positions were above their steady-state positions.

References

Barro, Robert, 1991. "Economic Growth in a Cross Section of Countries," *Quarterly Journal of Economics*, May, pp. 407–443.

—— and Xavier Sala-i-Martin, 1992. "Convergence," *Journal of Political Economy*, April, pp. 223–251.

——, Gregory Mankiw, and Xavier Sala-i-Martin, 1993. "Capital Mobility in Neoclassical Growth Models," NBER Working Paper no. 4206, Cambridge, MA.

Lucas, Robert, 1988. "On the Mechanics of Economic Development," *Journal of Monetary Economics*, 22, pp. 3–42.

Mankiw, N. Gregory, Romer, David and Weil, David N., 1992. "A Contribution to the Empirics of Economic Growth," *Quarterly Journal of Economics*, May, pp. 407–437.

Romer, Paul M., 1986. "Increasing Returns and Long-Run Growth," *Journal of Political Economy*, 94, pp. 1002–1037.

——, 1987. "Crazy Explanations for the Productivity Slowdown," *NBER Macroeconomics Annual*, pp. 167–201.

Solow, Robert M., 1956. "A Contribution to the Theory of Economic Growth," *Quarterly Journal of Economics*, 70, pp. 65–94.

Summers, Robert and Heston, Alan, 1988. "A New Set of International Comparisons of Real Product and Price Levels: Estimates for 130 Countries," *The Review of Income and Wealth*, March, pp. 1–25.

3 An alternative interpretation of conditional convergence results*

1. Introduction

Almost a decade ago, Baumol (1986) asked whether relatively poor economies grow faster than rich economies, causing levels of per capita income to converge across economies. This question is interesting in its own right but becomes more so in relation to the recent debate between the traditional neoclassical growth model (Solow, 1956; and Cass, 1965, among others) and endogenous growth models (Romer, 1986; and Lucas, 1988, among others). While the assumption of diminishing returns to capital in the neoclassical model drives the model economy to converge to the steady state, there is no such tendency in most endogenous growth models because, in these models, marginal returns to aggregate capital do not diminish with capital accumulation.

Since Baumol (1986), a substantial body of empirical study has examined whether a regression of the growth rate on the level of income per capita indeed produces a negative coefficient as predicted by the neoclassical model. Evidence from postwar cross-country data is mixed.[1] First, data do not support neoclassical convergence per se for a wide range of countries.[2] If anything, relatively rich countries appear to grow faster than poor countries. However, when some additional variables (such as the investment-to-GDP ratio, the population growth rate, the school enrollment rate, measures of political and economic instabilities, and so forth) are included in the regression to control for heterogeneities across countries, the growth rate appears negatively correlated with the level of income. This is called "conditional convergence".

This chapter examines two of the most widely used control variables in conditional convergence regressions, the investment-to-GDP ratio and the population growth rate, and finds that these variables do not appear to be exogenous with respect to growth. The investment-to-GDP ratio rises and the population growth rate declines with income growth. The endogeneity of the control variables causes a negative bias in the commonly used regression coefficient for the conditional convergence test. The bias appears sufficiently important that the conditional convergence result is not found when alternative regressions are designed to avoid the bias.

Perhaps more important than the simultaneity bias is the interpretation of the conditional convergence regression result when the control variables are endogenous. Let $g = G(y, s(y), n(y))$, where g is the growth rate of GDP per capita, y is the log-GDP per capita, s is the investment-to-GDP ratio, and n is the population growth rate. The conditional convergence coefficient, though consistently estimated, only measures the partial correlation between y and g, or $\partial G/\partial y$. However, it seems that the convergence question should consider the sign of the total correlation including the indirect effects through the endogenous channels of the control variables, or $dG/dy = \partial G/\partial y + (\partial G/\partial s)(ds/dy) + (\partial G/\partial n)(dn/dy)$ The Summers-Heston data (1988) appear to show $\partial G/\partial y = 0$, $\partial G/\partial s > 0$, $ds/dy > 0$, $\partial G/\partial n < 0$, $dn/dy < 0$, and hence $dG/dy > 0$, indicating that economies tend to accelerate growth through the two endogenous channels, the rise in s and the decline in n. Stated differently, "starting behind" appears to hinder growth by generating a low value of s and a high value of n. This alternative interpretation sharply contrasts with the conditional convergence interpretation.

Section 2 explains the conditional convergence interpretation of the basic cross-country regression results. Section 3 presents evidence for the endogeneity of the investment-to-GDP ratio and the population growth rate. Section 4 discusses the simultaneity bias, Section 5 provides an alternative interpretation, and Section 6 contains concluding remarks.

2.   Basic results on convergence

Based on the neoclassical growth model, the following relationship between the growth rate and the level of income per capita can be derived:[3]

$$g_{i,t+1} = \delta + \delta(y_{i,t} - y_t^* + \eta_{i,t+1}^g, \quad \delta_y < 0), \tag{1}$$

where $g_{i,t+1} = y_{i,t+1} - y_{i,t}$, y_{it} is GDP per capita of country i in year t, y_i^* is the steady state level of country i, and $\eta_{i,t+1}^g$ is the error term that is uncorrelated across i and with regressors. The parameter restriction, $\delta_y < 0$, is the main implication tested in the convergence literature, which states that an economy positioned further below the steady state level tends to grow faster.

A frequently used cross-country growth regression can be formed by recursive substitutions of $y_{i,t}$ in equations (1) from $t = 0$ to $T - 1$:

$$\bar{g}_i = \lambda + \lambda_y(y_{i,0} - y_i^*) + \eta_i^g \quad \lambda_y < 0, \tag{2}$$

where the overbar denotes the average value during a relevant sample period, $y_{i,0}$ is the initial value of y_i, $\lambda = (\delta/T)\sum_{j=0}^{T-1}(1+\delta_y)^j$, $\lambda_y = \left\{(1+\delta_y)^T - 1\right\}/T < 0$, and $\eta_i^g = (1/T)\sum_{j=0}^{T-1}(1+\delta_y)^j \eta_{i,T-j}^g$. If $y_i^* = y^*$ for all i, that is to say, if the steady state levels were not substantially different across countries, the neoclassical model would imply unconditional convergence that $\bar{g}_i$ is negatively correlated with $y_{i,0}$.

If $y_i^* \neq y^*$, however, $\bar{g}_i$ is negatively correlated with $y_{i,0}$ only when y^* is controlled for. Approximate y_i^* by:

$$y_i^* = \theta + \theta_s\ \bar{s}_i + \theta_n\ \bar{n}_i + \eta_i^y \quad \theta_s > 0, \theta_n < 0, \tag{3}$$

where $\bar{s}_i$ and $\bar{n}_i$ are the sample averages of the investment-to-GDP ratio and the rate of population growth, and η_i^y is the error term that is uncorrelated across i and with regressors. This paper considers only the two control variables, s and n, because: (1) they are the key variables in the traditional Solow (1956) growth model (s as a proxy for the saving rate); (2) annual time-series data for a variety of countries are available from the same source as GDP per capita (Summers and Heston, 1988); (3) Levine and Renelt (1992) found the investment-to-GDP ratio to be the only "robust" explanatory variable among a large set of explanatory variables in cross-country growth regressions; and perhaps most importantly, (4) the analysis of these two variables can help illustrate similar effects of other control variables on the conditional convergence results.

Finally, substitute equations (3) for y_i^* in equations (2) to obtain a cross-country regression equation for the growth rate:

$$\bar{g}_i = \left(\lambda - \lambda_y\theta\right) + \lambda_y\ y_{i,0} - \left(\lambda_y\theta_y\right)\bar{s}_i - \left(\lambda_y\theta_n\right)\bar{n}_i + \left(\eta_i^g - \lambda_y\eta_i^y\right) \tag{4}$$

Using the data of Summers-Heston (1988) for 109 countries[4] during the 1960–1985 period, the first two rows in Table 3.1 show the results of the regressions of $\bar{g}_i$ on $y_{i,1960} (\equiv y_{i,60}$ hereafter) with and without $\bar{s}_i$ and $\bar{n}_i$. The basic finding of the conditional convergence literature is the sharp contrast between the signs of the coefficients on $y_{i,60}$: it is positive unconditionally, but negative conditionally. This result appears consistent with conditional convergence, and thus countries that have not yet attained their steady state levels are expected to have slower growth over time.

Table 3.1 Cross-country regressions, Summers-Heston data, 109 countries, 1960–1985

No.	Dependent variable	Constant	$y_{i,60}$	$\bar{s}_i$	$\bar{n}_i$	R^2
1	$\bar{g}_i$	−0.017 (0.014)	0.0052 (0.0020)			0.061
2	$\bar{g}_i$	0.033 (0.018)	−0.0049 (0.0024)	0.154 (0.025)	−0.344 (0.185)	0.348
3	$\bar{s}_i$	−0.175 (0.047)	0.0510 (0.0066)			0.352
4	$\bar{n}_i$	0.067 (0.005)	−0.0065 (0.0007)			0.433

Note: Variables are defined in Section 2. Standard errors in parentheses.

3.　Endogeneity of the control variables

The drastic deviation of the conditional from the unconditional estimate is generated by the strong correlations between the control variables and $y_{i,60}$. The plots of $\bar{s}_i$ and $\bar{n}_i$ against $y_{i,60}$ (Figures 3.1A and 3.1B) and the corresponding regression

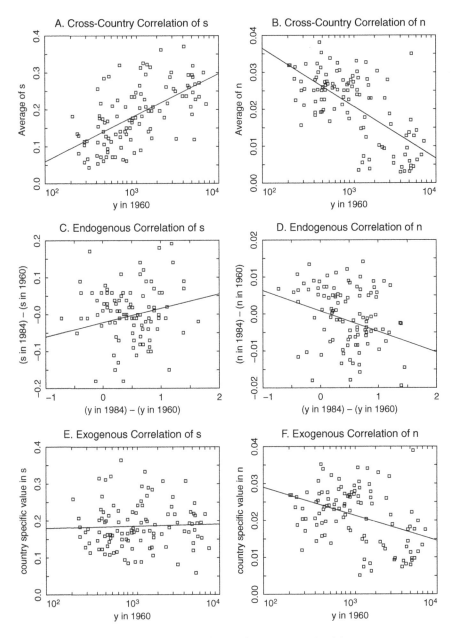

Figure 3.1A–F Control variables (*s* and *n*) and GDP per capita (*y*)

coefficients (the third and fourth lines of Table 3.1) readily confirm that a high $y_{i,60}$ is associated with a high $\bar{s}_i$ and a low $\bar{n}_i$. This is a well-known fact, and similar figures can be found even in standard textbooks. For example, Mankiw (1992, Chapter 4) presents similar plots (with the horizontal and vertical axes switched and the terminal value of y used) as evidence of the Solow (1956) growth model. That is, a country endowed with a high s and a low n has become rich as equations (3) predicts.

In contrast, there has also been a great deal of effort to understand these correlations in reverse. For example, many models in the development literature allow the subsistence level of consumption to explain why the saving rate rises with income growth, and various fertility models are motivated by the observation that the population growth rate tends to decline with income growth.[5] These models argue that y (hence g) is a major determinant, rather than just a consequence, of s and n. That is, s and n are endogenous with respect to income growth, so that a currently poor country will also be able to raise s and reduce n (hence increase g) if y increases sufficiently.

To formalize this idea, consider the following model:

$$g_{i,t+1} = \alpha + \alpha_y\, y_{i,t} + \alpha_s\, s_{i,t} + \alpha_n\, n_{i,t} + \epsilon^g_{i,t+1}, \quad \alpha_y \leq 0,\ \alpha_n < 0 \tag{5-1}$$

$$s_{i,t} = \beta_i + \beta_i y_{i,t} + \epsilon^s_{i,t}, \quad \beta_y \geq 0, \tag{5-2}$$

$$n_{i,t} = \gamma_i + \gamma_y y_{i,t} + \epsilon^n_{i,t}, \quad \gamma_y \leq 0 \tag{5-3}$$

where $\epsilon_{i,t}s$ are error terms that are uncorrelated mutually, across i and t, and with regressors. Equation (5-1) is similar to equations (4). Equations (5-2) and (5-3) show that each of s and n contains both an exogenous country specific effect and an endogenous effect.[6] The conditional convergence interpretation is critically based on the assumption that s and n are exogenous: $\beta_y = 0$ and $\gamma_y = 0$.

Panel A of Table 3.2 compares s and n in 1960 and 1984 in the three fastest and three slowest growing countries.[7] In 1960, the three fast-growing countries would not have been expected to grow faster than the three slow-growing countries: the fast growers had a slightly higher s but a slightly higher n as well. During the sample period, however, the fast-growing countries succeeded in raising s and reducing n, while s declined and n rose in the slow-growing (contracting) countries. In 1984, as a result, the fast-growing countries would have been expected to grow even faster.

These endogenous correlations between growth and the within-country variations of s and n can be tested by regressing $s_{i,84} - s_{i,60}$ and $n_{i,84} - n_{i,60}$ on $y_{i,84} - y_{i,60}$, respectively.[8] Figures 3.1C and 3.1D plot the variables and Panel B reports the regression results.[9] The within-country variations appear to be significantly correlated with the growth rate, and the estimates of β_y and γ_y (0.0409 and −0.0056) are only slightly smaller (in absolute values) than the corresponding values in Table 3.1 (0.0534 and −0.0065), suggesting that most of the cross-country correlations between y and s or n may come from the endogenous effects of y on s or n.

Table 3.2 Endogeneity of the control variables Summers-Heston data, 109 countries, 1960–1984

A. Slow- and Fast-Growing Countries (in Percent)

Country	$\bar{g}_i$	$s_{i,60}$	$s_{i,84}$	$n_{i,60}$	$n_{i,84}$
Chad	−2.83	5.4	3.9	1.7	2.4
Ghana	−1.70	13.1	7.7	2.6	3.2
Mozambique	−1.65	5.9	5.4	2.2	2.8
Korea	5.95	6.7	31.8	2.6	1.2
Hong Kong	6.62	20.9	19.0	3.3	1.1
Singapore	7.45	11.9	35.8	3.3	1.1

B. Endogenous Variations of the Control Variables, Sample Size 109

Dependent Variable	Constant	$y_{i,84} - y_{i,60}$	R^2
$S_{i,84} - S_{i,60}$	−0.0209 (0.0436)	0.0409 (0.0193)	0.035
$n_{i,84} - n_{i,60}$	0.0429 (0.0053)	−0.0056 (0.0018)	0.086

C. Pooled Annual Data Regressions with Country Dummies, Sample Size 2,725

Dependent Variable	Constant	$y_{i,t}$	R^2
$S_{i,t}$	109 Country Dummies	0.0462 (0.0041)	0.739
$n_{i,t}$	109 Country Dummies	−0.0032 (0.0005)	0.749

D. Country Specific Effects and Levels of GDP per Capita, Sample Size 109

Dependent Variable	Constant	$y_{i,60}$	R^2
$\hat{s}_i$	0.1692 (0.0436)	0.0020 (0.0061)	0.001
$\hat{n}_i$	0.0429 (0.0053)	−0.0031 (0.0007)	0.141

I also estimated equations (5-2) and (5-3) directly using pooled annual data, including 109 country dummy variables. The estimates of β_y and γ_y in Panel C (0.0462 and −0.0032) are similar to the estimates in Panel B: when y increases by a unit, s increases by approximately 4.62 percent and n declines by 0.32 percent.[10] The effects of the country dummies were also significant at a 1 percent level in both regressions (not reported). However, it is not the country-specific variations themselves but their correlations with $y_{i,60}$ that affect the estimate of the conditional convergence coefficient. If the country-specific variations are orthogonal to $y_{i,60}$, controlling for them has no impact on the coefficient of $y_{i,60}$, although there exist significant country-specific effects in s and n. The estimated country-specific effects are plotted against $y_{i,60}$ in Figures 3.1E and 3.1F and the corresponding regression results are reported in Panel D of Table 3.2.[11] The regression lines in these figures are much flatter than the ones in Figures 3.1A and 3.1B because substantial portions of cross-country variations are "explained" by the endogenous effects. While the country-specific variations in n are still significantly correlated with $y_{i,60}$, the country specific variations in s are almost orthogonal to $y_{i,60}$, which may indicate that a high investment-to-GDP ratio in a rich country is a result, rather than a cause, of a high level of GDP per capita in that country. This result is in accord with the recent finding of Carroll and Weil (1993) that growth causes the saving rate.[12]

4. Simultaneity bias and time aggregation

Unlike the neoclassical growth model, many endogenous growth models assume that there is no conditional effect of initial income on growth, specifically $\alpha_y = 0$ in equations (5-1). Under this null hypothesis, recursive substitutions of $y_{i,t}$ transform equations (5-1) into the same regression equation as equations (4):

$$\bar{g}_i = \alpha + \alpha_y\, y_{i,0} + \alpha_s\, \bar{s}_i + \alpha_n\, \bar{n}_i + \bar{\epsilon}_i^g, \quad \alpha_y = 0,\ \alpha_s > 0,\ \alpha_n < 0, \tag{6}$$

Unless s and n are exogenous with respect to y, however, the (OLS) least square regression is subject to a simultaneity problem caused by the correlations between the control variables, $\bar{s}_i$ and $\bar{n}_i$, and the error term, $\bar{\epsilon}_i^g$. To see the sign of the simultaneity bias, note from equations (5) that for $t \geq 1$:

$$y_{i,t} = (\alpha + \alpha_s\beta + \alpha_s\gamma)\sum_{j=0}^{t-1}\phi^j + \phi^t\, y_{i,0} + \sum_{j=0}^{t-1}\phi^j\left\{\epsilon_{i,t-j}^g + \alpha_s\epsilon_{i,t-j-1}^s + \alpha_n\epsilon_{i,t-j-1}^n\right\}, \tag{7}$$

where $\phi \equiv 1 + \alpha_y + \alpha_s\beta_y + \alpha_n\gamma_y > 1$ if $\alpha_y = 0$, $\alpha_s > 0$, $\beta_y > 0$, $\alpha_n < 0$, and $\gamma_y < 0$ For the sample period of $T \geq 2$,

$$\mathrm{Cov}(\bar{y}_i, \bar{\epsilon}_i^g) = (1/T^2)(1/(\phi-1))\{(\phi^T - 1)/(\phi-1) - T\}\,\mathrm{Var}(\epsilon_i^g) > 0, \tag{8}$$

and thus $\mathrm{Cov}(\bar{s}_i, \bar{\epsilon}_i^g) = \beta_y\mathrm{Cov}(\bar{y}_i, \bar{\epsilon}_i^g) > 0$ and $\mathrm{Cov}(\bar{n}_i, \bar{\epsilon}_i^g) = \gamma_y\mathrm{Cov}(\bar{y}_i, \bar{\epsilon}_i^g) < 0$. The asymptotic bias of the regression estimate, $\hat{\alpha}_y$, is then

$$\hat{\alpha}_y - \alpha_y \rightarrow -Cov(y_{i,0}, \bar{y}_i)\,\mathrm{Cov}(\bar{y}_i, \bar{\epsilon}_i^n) + \gamma_y^2\,Var(\hat{v}_i^s)\}\,/\Delta\ < 0, \tag{9}$$

where $\Delta > 0$ is the determinant of the variance-covariance matrix of the regressors (details of the proof are available upon request). Therefore, the estimate of α_y is biased downward in the regression of $\bar{g}_i$ on $y_{i,0}$ with the control variables $\bar{s}_i$ and $\bar{n}_i$.

To understand this bias intuitively, consider two countries (one poor and the other rich) and two years (1960 and 1984). The poor country had a low s_{60} and a high n_{60} because y_{60} is low, and thus could not grow fast during the 1960–1984 period. As a result, s_{84} and n_{84} were similar to s_{60} and n_{60}. The rich country, on the other hand, had a high s_{60} and a low n_{60}, and thus grew fast and generated an even higher s_{84} and a lower n_{84}. Comparing $\bar{s} = (s_{60} + s_{84})/2$ and $\bar{n} = (n_{60} + n_{84})/2$ (instead of s_{60} and n_{60}) with the growth rate for each country, it appears that the rich country did not grow as fast as it should have – the downward bias on $\hat{\alpha}_y$.

One way to detect this simultaneity bias is to trace $\hat{\alpha}_y$ with increasing T. Recalling $\phi > 1$ (see equations (7)), the downward bias increases with T (see equations (8)), and thus $\hat{\alpha}_y$ tends to decline.[13] Under the conditional convergence hypothesis in contrast, there should be no such trend. If anything, the coefficient estimate would increase because $\lambda_y = \left\{(1 + \delta_y)^T - 1\right\}/T$ in equations (4) approaches zero from below. Figure 3.2B plots the sequence of $\hat{\alpha}_y$ (solid line) and the

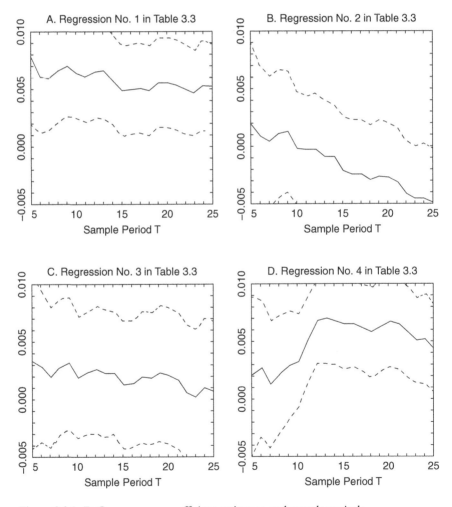

Figure 3.2A–D Convergence coefficient estimates and sample periods

Table 3.3 Alternative conditional convergence tests, dependent variable $\bar{g}_i$

No.	Estimation	s	n	Const.	$\Upsilon_{i,60}$	s	n	R^2
1	OLS			−0.017 (0.014)	0.0052 (0.0020)			0.061
2	OLS	$\bar{s}_i$	$\bar{n}_i$	0.033 (0.018)	−0.0049 (0.0024)	0.154 (0.025)	−0.344 (0.185)	0.348
3	2SLS	$\bar{s}_i$	$\bar{n}_i$	0.006 (0.024)	0.0006 (0.0031)	0.067 (0.039)	−0.169 (0.308)	0.096
	Hausman's Specification Test = 11.55 [0.000]							
4	OLS	$\hat{s}_i$	$\hat{n}_i$	−0.029 (0.017)	0.0042 (0.0019)	0.129 (0.028)	−0.217 (0.235)	0.228

95 percent confidence intervals (dotted lines) for $T \geq 5$ (from the 1960–1965 to 1960–1985 period). Figure 3.2A plots the unconditional regression coefficients for comparison. While no clear pattern is observed in the unconditional regression, a downward trend is apparent in the conditional regression.

A more direct test for the simultaneity bias can be performed using instrumental variables. Since the initial values of s_i and n_i are uncorrelated with $\bar{\epsilon}_i^g$, I used $s_{i,60}$, $n_{i,60}$, and $y_{i,60}$ as instruments. The third line of Table 3.3 reports the result of a two-stage least square (2SLS) estimation employing these instruments, with the first two lines copied from Table 3.1 for comparison (the fourth line is discussed below). The estimate of α_y (0.0006 with standard error 0.0031) is virtually zero, suggesting that the negative estimate in the conditional regression results from the simultaneity bias. Figure 3.2C plots 2SLS estimates of α_y for $T \geq 5$ to compare with the OLS estimates in Figure 3.2B. The 2SLS estimates are all greater than the corresponding OLS estimates and the downward pattern has almost disappeared.

By including the first-stage fitted values of $\bar{s}$ and $\bar{n}$ in the conditional convergence regression, I conducted Hausman's (1978) test for simultaneity bias. The null hypothesis of no simultaneity bias is rejected at a 0.1 percent significance level (see Table 3.3). This statistic value gradually increases as T increases, and so the null is rejected at 5 percent levels for $6 \leq T \leq 9$, at 1 percent for $10 \leq T \leq 12$, and at 0.1 percent for $T \geq 13$ (not reported). This result is consistent with the gradual deviation of the estimate in Figure 3.2B from the estimate in Figure 3.2C, which may indicate that the bias becomes more serious as T increases.

5. An alternative interpretation

So far as an increase in y raises s and decreases n, both of which contribute to the rise in g, it is the *total* endogenous effect (or general equilibrium effect) of y on g and not the conditional effect that is relevant to the convergence issue. The reduced form expression of g in equations (5),

$$
\begin{aligned}
g_{i,t+1} = \alpha &+ (\alpha_y + \alpha_s\beta_y + \alpha_n\beta_y)y_{i,t} + \alpha_s\beta_i + \alpha_n\gamma_i \\
&+ \left(\epsilon_{i,t+1}^g + \alpha_s\epsilon_{i,t}^s + \alpha_n\epsilon_{i,t}^n\right),
\end{aligned} \tag{10}
$$

yields the total effect as the coefficient of y, $\alpha_y + \alpha_s \beta_y + \alpha_n \beta_y$. To estimate this equation, the fourth line of Table 3.3 uses the estimates of the country-specific effects, $\hat{s}_i$ and $\hat{n}_i$, obtained from Panel C of Table 3.2 instead of $\hat{s}_i$ and $\hat{n}_i$. The coefficient estimate of $y_{i,60}$, 0.0042, is slightly smaller than the unconditional estimate but still positive and statistically significant.[14] This result suggests that the effects of genuine country-specific variations in s and n are not so big that the sign of the convergence coefficient is dramatically changed. Figure 3.2D shows the estimates from the same regressions for $T = 5$ through 25.[15]

One can also decompose this total effect by combining the estimates reported in the third line of Table 3.3 ($\alpha_y = 0.0006$, $\alpha_s = 0.067$, and $\alpha_n = -0.169$) and the estimates in Panel C of Table 3.2 ($\beta_y = 0.0462$ and $\gamma_y = -0.0031$). That is, a unit increase of y tends to increase g by 3.1 percent ($= \alpha_s \beta_y$) through a rise in s, by 0.5 percent ($= \alpha_n \gamma_y$) through a decrease in n, and by 0.6 percent (α_y) through other unidentified channels. This interpretation sharply contrasts with the conditional convergence interpretation that low-income economies, relative to their steady state levels, grow faster.

6. Concluding remarks

This chapter focuses on the endogeneity of the investment-to-GDP ratio and the population growth rate. When the indirect, yet endogenous, effects through the control variables are taken into account, the Summers-Heston data (1988) appear to show that relatively high-income countries grow faster by generating high investment-to-GDP ratios and low population growth rates.

While this paper examines only two control variables, the literature covers larger sets of control variables. Among them, the primary and secondary school enrollment rates are similar to the investment-to-GDP ratio. In cross-country data, they are positively correlated with both the level and the growth rate of income per capita. Various measures of political and economic instabilities are similar to the population growth rate. They are negatively correlated with both the level and the growth rate of income. Controlling for such variables in cross-country growth regressions would yield a smaller estimate of the coefficient on income per capita. Consequently, the estimate of this coefficient is very sensitive to the choice of control variables.

Apart from the sign of the income coefficient, however, the basic question this chapter addresses is how to interpret the strong correlation between the control variables and the level of income across countries. That is, were some countries endowed with, for example, high schooling rates and became rich as a result, or were high schooling rates generated in rich countries because those countries were rich? A suitable answer to this question seems essential for an appropriate interpretation of cross-country regression results.

Notes

* This chapter is reprinted from *Journal of Money, Credit, and Banking*, pp. 669–681, November 1996.

1 For the empirical results of the convergence regressions, see DeLong (1988), Dowrick and Nguyen (1989), Barro (1991), Barro and Sala-i-Martin (1992), Mankiw et al. (1992), Evans (1994), Evans and Karras (1994), Durlauf and Johnson (1995), Cho and Graham (1996), and so forth.

2 When the sample is restricted to developed regions such as OECD countries (Dowrick and Nguyen, 1989, among others) or US states (Barro and Sala-i-Martin, 1992, among others), the negative correlation is observed without control variables. In order to focus on the unconditional divergence and conditional convergence results, this paper does not discuss this "local" convergence result.

3 See Barro and Sala-i-Martin (1992) and Mankiw et al. (1992) for the derivation of this equation.

4 Among the 121 countries in the Summers-Heston data set, the data in 1960 are not available for seven countries: Burkina Faso, Afghanistan, Bahrain, Oman, United Arab Emirates, Yemen, and Indonesia. Following Mankiw et al. (1992), I further excluded five "oil countries": Gabon, Iran, Iraq, Kuwait, and Saudi Arabia.

5 See, for example, Becker and Barro (1988) and Becker, Murphy and Tamura (1990).

6 The specifications in equations (5-2) and (5-3) have at least two problems. First, the assumption of no serial correlation is in fact rejected by the annual data in both equations. Second, the linear specification of the endogenous effect should be interpreted as a local approximation because, for example, s cannot exceed one while y increases indefinitely. Even though these assumptions do not seem to be essential for the main results of this paper on long-run data, they do greatly simplify the analysis for the simultaneity bias in Section 4. For this reason, I retain the specifications in equations (5-2) and (5-3) in the text.

7 Given the definition of $n_{i,t} = \log\left(N_{i,t+1}\right) - \log\left(N_{i,t}\right)$, where $N_{i,tt}$ is population, $n_{i,84}$ is the last available observation.

8 These cross-country regressions can easily be formulated by manipulations of equations (5-2) and (5-3).

9 I included a constant in each regression, which did not appear significant.

10 I also executed various experiments to handle the serial correlation and linear specification problems pointed out in Footnote 6. A short summary of the experiments is that the significant endogenous effects of y on s and n remain robust with respect to various specifications (detailed results are available upon request).

11 I adjusted $\hat{\beta}_i$ by the difference between the "world average" of $s_{i,t}$ and the average value of $\hat{\beta}_i$, so that $\hat{s}_i$ maintains the world average of $s_{i,t}$. The same adjustment is made to convert $\hat{\gamma}_i$ into $\hat{n}_i$.

12 Carroll and Weil (1993) suggest that s is a function of g, rather than a function of y as in equations (5-2). This paper does not clearly address this issue. Long-run time-series data, however, exhibit increasing secular trends for most countries (with the United States as a possible exception: see Maddison (1982) and Cho (1994) for example). Carroll and Weil also find that y maintains significant explanatory powers in most of their regressions of s on g.

13 More detailed and formal discussions on the relation between T and the size of the bias is available upon request.

14 To a large extent, this result can be expected from the weak correlations between the estimated country specific effects and $y_{i,60}$, as shown in Panel D of Table 3.2 and Figures 3.1E and 3.1F.

15 The country-specific effects were repeatedly estimated using the data for the corresponding sample period.

References

Barro, Robert J., 1991. "Economic Growth in a Cross Section of Countries," *Quarterly Journal of Economics*, 106, May, pp. 407–443.

——— and Sala-i-Martin, Xavier, 1992. "Convergence," *Journal of Political Economy*, 100, April, pp. 223–251.

Baumol, William J., 1986. "Productivity, Growth Convergence, and Welfare: What the Long-Run Data Show," *American Economic Review*, 76, December, pp. 1155–1159.

Becker, Gary S., and Robert J. Barro, 1988. "A Reformulation of the Economic Theory of Fertility," *Quarterly Journal of Economics*, 103, February, pp. 1–25.

———, Murphy, Kevin M. and Robert Tamura, 1990. "Human Capital, Fertility, and Economic Growth," *Journal of Political Economy*, 98, October, pp. S12-S37.

Carroll, Christopher D. and David N. Weil, 1993. "Saving and Growth: A Reinterpretation," NBER Working Paper no. 4470, Cambridge, MA.

Cass, David, 1965. "Optimum Growth in the Aggregative Model of Capital Accumulation," *Review of Economic Studies*, 32, July, pp. 233–240.

Cho, Dongchul, 1994. "Industrialization, Convergence, and Patterns of Growth," *Southern Economic Journal*, 61, October, pp. 398–414.

———, and Stephen Graham, 1996. "The Other Side of Conditional Convergence," *Economics Letters*, 50, pp. 285–290.

DeLong, J. Bradford, 1988. "Productivity Growth, Convergence, and Welfare: Comment," *American Economic Review*, 78, December, pp. 1138–1154.

Dowrick, Steve, and Duc-Tho Nguyen, 1989. "OECD Comparative Economic Growth 1950–85: Catch-Up and Convergence," *American Economic Review*, 79, December, pp. 1010–1030.

Durlauf, S. and Johnson, Paul, 1995. "Multiple Regimes and Cross-Country Growth Behavior," *Journal of Applied Econometrics*, 10, October, pp. 365–384.

Evans, Paul, 1994. "How to Estimate Growth Regressions Consistently," Ohio State University, Manuscript.

——— and Georgios Karras, 1994. "Convergence Revisited," Ohio State University, Manuscript.

Levine, Ross and David Renelt, 1992. "A Sensitivity Analysis of Cross-Country Growth Regressions," *American Economic Review*, 82, September, pp. 942–963.

Lucas, Robert E., 1988. "On the Mechanics of Economic Development," *Journal of Monetary Economics*, 22, January, pp. 3–42.

Maddison, Angus, 1982. *Phases of Capitalist Development*. New York: Oxford University Press.

Mankiw, N. Gregory, David Romer, and David N. Weil, 1992. "A Contribution to the Empirics of Economic Growth," *Quarterly Journal of Economics*, 107, May, pp. 407–437.

Romer, Paul M., 1986. "Increasing Returns and Long-Run Growth," *Journal of Political Economy*, 94, October, pp. 1002–1037.

Solow, Robert M., 1956. "A Contribution to the Theory of Economic Growth," *Quarterly Journal of Economics*, 70, February, pp. 65–94.

Summers, Robert, and Alan Heston, 1988. "A New Set of International Comparisons of Real Product and Price Levels: Estimates for 130 Countries," *The Review of Income and Wealth*, 34, March, pp. 1–25.

Part II

Exchange rate and Asian crisis

4 The predictive ability of several models of exchange rate volatility*

1. Introduction

This chapter compares the forecasting performance of six models for a univariate conditional variance, using bilateral weekly data for the dollar versus the currencies of Canada, France, Germany, Japan and the United Kingdom, 1973–1989. The six models include a homoskedastic one, two generalized autoregressive conditional heteroskedasticity (GARCH) models (Bollerslev, 1986; Engle and Bollerslev, 1986), two autoregressions and a nonparametric one. We compare the out-of-sample realization of the square of the weekly change in an exchange rate with the value predicted by a model of the conditional variance, for horizons of 1, 12 and 24 weeks. The measure of performance that we focus on is mean squared prediction error (MSPE).

For 12- and 24-week ahead forecasts of the squared weekly change, it is difficult to find grounds to choose one model over another. But at a 1-week horizon, we find that GARCH models have a slight edge over the other models. The GARCH mean squared prediction errors tend to be slightly smaller, and regressions of realized exchange rate squares on their estimated conditional variances tend to find somewhat more evidence of predictive power. But statistical tests typically cannot reject at conventional significance levels the null that the MSPE from the GARCH models are equal to those of other models, and standard regression tests for bias and efficiency strongly reject the null that the GARCH conditional variance differs from the realized exchange rate square by a white noise error. It appears that GARCH models leave something to be desired, even at the 1-week horizon.

Other papers have compared univariate volatility models in related frameworks. Using monthly stock return data and a one-month ahead MSPE criterion, Akigray (1989) found GARCH models preferable to naive and autoregressive moving average (ARMA) ones, and Pagan and Schwert (1990a) found GARCH and ARMA models preferable to nonparametric and Markov switching ones. While we, too, find that GARCH models perform well, our results complement and extend these earlier ones in three ways.

First, and least important, we use exchange rate instead of stock price data. One would obviously like to know if what works with one type of data works with another as well. Second, we formally test for equality of *RMSPE*s across models, using a straightforward asymptotic technique that may be of general interest. Third, we consider not only one period but multi-period horizons as well. Since, in the end, we could not reject the null of equality of *RMSPE*s across models, and since we found no grounds for preferring one estimator over another at horizons of more than one period, our endorsement of GARCH models is more moderate than it would have been had we not performed these tests and examined these horizons.

Before turning to the analysis, a final remark seems advisable. The literature on conditional volatility has grown enormously in recent years (see Bollerslev et al., 1992, for an excellent survey), and it is simply not practical to simultaneously study every model that has been proposed. While we feel that we have chosen a representative set of models, we recognize that some readers might prefer a different set. We hope that such readers will nonetheless find it useful that our analysis leads us to speculate that successful models will allow for what standard tests suggest is movement in unconditional variances.[1]

Section 2 describes our data and models, Sections 3 and 4 our empirical results. Section 5 concludes. An Appendix available on request from the authors contains some results omitted from the paper to save space.

2.   Data, models, and estimation techniques

2.1   Data

Our exchange rates are measured as dollars per unit of foreign currency, between the U. and Canada, France, Germany, Japan and the United Kingdom.[2] The data are Wednesday, New York noon bid rates, as published in *The Federal Reserve Bulletin*. When Wednesday was a holiday we used Thursday data; when Thursday was a holiday as well we used Tuesday data. After an initial observation was lost due to differencing (see the following), the sample for each country included the 863 observations from March 14, 1973, to September 20, 1989. Figure 4.1, parts 1–5, plot the levels rather than differences of the series, with the vertical axis measured in cents per unit of foreign currency. Figure 4.1, parts 1–5 will be discussed further below.

Prior to our formal analysis, we took logarithmic differences of the series, and then multiplied by 100. That is, our exchange rate series is

$$e_t \equiv 100 * \ln(\text{exchange rate in week } t/\text{exchange rate in week } t-1),$$

and thus has the interpretation of percentage change in the level of the exchange rate. With a slight abuse of terminology, we will sometimes refer to our data as "exchange rates" rather than "percentage changes in exchange rates."

Table 4.1 contains some summary statistics on these data. Most standard errors and *p*-values in the remainder of the table also are robust to the possible presence of serial correlation and conditional heteroskedasticity and are computed as

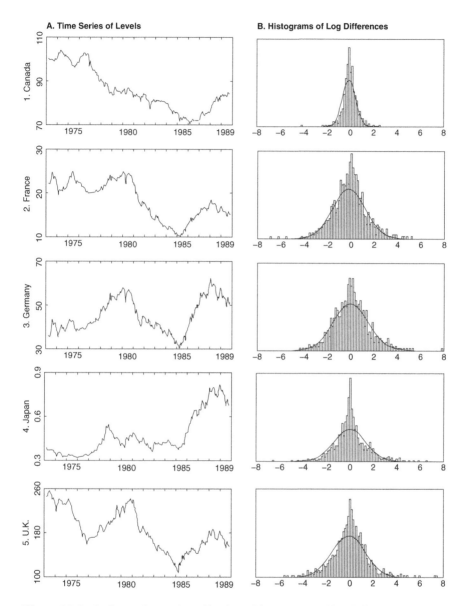

Figure 4.1 Basic data – time series of levels and histograms of log difference

described below. Table 4.1 is consistent with the results of many earlier studies (e.g., Baillie and Bollerslev, 1989; Diebold and Nerlove, 1989; Engle and Bollerslev, 1986)). Exchange rate changes appear to have zero unconditional means (line (1)), and, with the possible exception of Japan, appear to be serially uncorrelated (lines (5) to (7)).

Table 4.1 Summary statistics

		Canada	France	Germany	Japan	UK
Panel A. e_t						
(1)	Mean	−0.020	−0.044	0.042	0.068	−0.052
		(0.020)	(0.050)	(0.056)	(0.056)	(0.055)
(2)	Standard	0.552	1.408	1.466	1.361	1.406
	Deviation	(0.029)	(0.053)	(0.064)	(0.063)	(0.080)
(3)	Skewness	−0.423	0.103	0.480	0.385	0.261
		(0.455)	(0.245)	(0.203)	(0.233)	(0.270)
(4)	Excess	4.981	2.490	2.133	2.587	3.092
	Kurtosis	(2.636)	(0.846)	(0.900)	(0.715)	(0.857)
(5)	Modified	7.47	20.89	13.43	20.52	13.57
	L-B(10)	[0.681]	[0.022]	[0.200]	[0.025]	[0.194]
(6)	Modified	61.84	63.47	53.74	71.92	54.10
	L-B(50)	[0.122]	[0.096]	[0.333]	[0.023]	[0.321]
(7)	Modified	111.99	98.46	87.99	122.26	88.47
	L-B(90)	[0.058]	[0.254]	[0.540]	[0.005]	[0.526]
(8)	Min	−4.164	−6.825	−4.488	−6.587	−5.691
(9)	Q1	−0.313	−0.851	−0.850	−0.641	−0.773
(10)	Median	−0.030	0.000	0.023	−0.027	−0.034
(11)	Q3	0.272	0.675	0.855	0.606	0.708
(12)	Max	2.550	7.741	8.113	6.546	7.397
Panel B. e_t^2						
(13)	Mean	0.305	1.983	2.147	1.854	1.978
		(0.030)	(0.148)	(0.190)	(0.166)	(0.223)
(14)	Standard	0.809	4.196	4.395	4.001	4.446
	Deviation	(0.213)	(0.598)	(0.763)	(0.513)	(0.768)
(15)	L-B(10)	34.27	37.82	56.72	51.92	98.12
		[0.000]	[0.000]	[0.000]	[0.000]	[0.000]
(16)	L-B(50)	52.50	129.59	134.75	101.16	322.19
		[0.377]	[0.000]	[0.000]	[0.000]	[0.000]
(17)	L-B(90)	65.41	178.42	166.25	138.44	337.07
		[0.976]	[0.000]	[0.000]	[0.000]	[0.000]

Notes:
1. The variable e_t is the percentage change in the weekly exchange rate. The sample includes 863 weekly observations from March 14, 1973 to September 20, 1989.
2. In rows (1)–(4), (13) and (14), heteroskedasticity and autocorrelation consistent asymptotic standard errors are in parentheses.
3. Rows (5) to (7) and (13) to (15) contain Ljung-Box statistics of order given in the header to the row, modified in rows (5) to (7) to allow for possible conditional heteroskedasticity in e_t. The p-values of the asymptotic chi-squared statistics are given in the lower halves of the rows.

Exchange rate changes are also very fat tailed. This leptokurtosis may be seen in Figure 4.1, parts 1–5, each of which plots both a normal density whose mean and variance match sample estimates and a histogram of the data. More formal evidence is in panel A of Table 4.1. The standard deviation of exchange rate changes is about one percent per week (line (2)); the maximum and minimum changes in this sample of size 863 are generally five or more standard deviations away from the mean (lines (8) and (12)), and the interquartile range is much less than two standard deviations (lines (9) and (11)). Excess kurtosis is greater than two and is significantly different from zero at any conventional significance level for all countries except Canada (line (4)). With the exception of Germany, there is no evidence of skewness (line (3)).

Panel B of Table 4.1 contains some summary statistics on squared exchange rates. The means and standard deviations (lines (13) and (14)) are presented for convenience of interpretation of our empirical results; they are redundant in the sense that the point estimates can be deduced from the appropriate entries in panel A. Rows (15) to (17) in panel B suggest that, in stark contrast to the levels, the squares of exchange rates are highly serially correlated. This, too, is a result consistent with many earlier studies.

2.2 Models and estimation techniques

The in-sample evidence in Table 4.1 that e_t is linearly unpredictable is supported by the stronger results from other studies, some of which use out-of- as well as in-sample evidence, that there is not even any nonlinear dependence in the conditional mean of e_t. The most salient reference is Diebold and Nason (1990), who drew their data from exactly the same source as did we, but over the slightly shorter sample period 1973–1987. Despite much in-sample evidence of nonlinear dependence in the mean of e_t, they found little out-of-sample evidence of such dependence. Papers that come to similar conclusions using other data, sometimes with multivariate information sets, include Meese and Rogoff (1983) and Meese and Rose (1991). We, therefore, will limit ourselves to models in which the conditional mean of e_t is zero.

To define our models, some notation is needed. Let

$$h_{t,j} = \text{var}_t(e_{t+j}) = E_t e^2_{t+j}$$
$$= \text{(population) variance of } e_{t+j}$$
conditional on information generated by past e_s, $s \le t$; (1a)

$\hat{h}_{mt,j}$ = fitted conditional variance of e_{t+j}, according to model m
    (e.g., model m is GARCH(1,1), or homoskedastic), estimated
    using data on past e$_s$, $s \le t$; (1b)

$h_t \equiv h_{t,1}$, $\hat{h}_{mt} \equiv \hat{h}_{mt,1}$; (1c)

R = endpoint of first sample used in estimation of
    regression parameters; (1d)
T = endpoint of last sample used in estimation. (1e)

Note our dating convention: what we denote h_t corresponds to what is often called h_{t+1} or σ_{t+1} (e.g. Engle, 1982). For concreteness in interpreting (1b) and (1c), it may help to note that in the tables below we report results for $j = 1, 12$ and 24, corresponding to approximately to weekly, quarterly and semiannual horizons. To do so for a given horizon, we obtain for each model $T - R + 1$ fitted values $\hat{h}_{mt,j}, t = R,...,T$, for models $m = 1, \ldots, M$, where the number of models M in the tables below is 6. We then compute the root mean squared prediction error ($RMSPE$) for model m at horizon j as

$$[(T - R + 1)^{-1} \sum_{t=R}^{T} (e_{t+j}^2 - \hat{h}_{mt,j})^2]^{1/2}. \tag{2}$$

We focus on $RMSPE$ because mathematical expectations have minimum $RMSPE$, so a good statistical model for the expected value of exchange rate squares will tend to have forecast errors whose average squared value is small.[3]

Column (1) of Table 4.2 lists the models we estimated, column (3) the acronyms used in some subsequent tables.[4] Column (2) gives the formula for the

Table 4.2 Models

Column (1) *Model*	*Column (2)* *Formula for h_t*	*Column (3)* *Acronym*
Homoskedastic Model		
1. Homoskedastic	$h_t = \omega$	homo
GARCH Models		
2. GARCH(1,1)	$h_t = \omega + \alpha e_t^2 + \beta h_{t-1}$	(1,1)
3. IGARCH(1,1)	$h_t = \alpha e_t^2 + (1 - \alpha) h_{t-1}$	ig
Autoregressive models		
4. AR(12) in e_t^2	$h_t = \omega + \Sigma_{i=1}^{12} \alpha_i e_{t-i+1}^2$	e2AR
5. AR(12) in $\|e_t\|$	$h_t = (\pi/2)(E_t\|e_{t+1}\|)^2;$ $E_t\|e_{t+1}\| = \omega + \Sigma_{i=1}^{12} \alpha_i\|e_{t-i+1}\|$	|e|AR
Nonparametric Model		
6. Gaussian kernel	$h_{t,j} = E(e_{t+j}^2\|e_t);$ $\hat{h}_{t,j} = \Sigma_{t=1}^{N-j} w_{tN,j} e_{t+j}^2,$ $w_{tN,j} = c_{tN,j}/\Sigma_{s=1}^{N-j} C_{sN,j},$ $c_{tN,j} = \exp[-0.5(e_N - e_t)^2/b^2],$ $b = $ bandwidth defined in text	nonp

one-period ahead conditional variance, except for the nonparametric estimator for which the formula for the arbitrary j period ahead forecast is given. Since all the other models are linear, multiperiod forecasts can be obtained by the usual recursive prediction formulas. Consistent with the assumption that exchange rate changes have zero conditional mean, in such forecasts the changes were assumed to be conditionally uncorrelated at all nonzero lags (i.e., $E_{t-1} e_t e_{t+j} = 0$ for all $j > 0$)

The homoskedastic model (line (1)) simply set the conditional variance at all horizons equal to the sample mean of lagged e_t^2, s.

Two GARCH models were used (lines (2) and (3)). Both were estimated by maximum likelihood assuming conditional normality, using analytical derivatives, with presample values of h and e^2 set to sample means. Lee and Hansen (1991) and Lumsdaine (1989) show that the conditional normality assumption is not necessary for the consistency and asymptotic normality of the estimators.[5] We chose GARCH(1,1) and IGARCH from a larger set of possible GARCH models after (1) analysis of some in-sample diagnostics seemed to suggest GARCH(1,1) for Canada, Germany and the UK, IGARCH for France and Japan; and (2) a little experimentation with ARCH(1), ARCH(2), GARCH(1,2) and GARCH(2,1) models suggested that MSPEs from these models are comparable or worse than the two we chose to study.

We also studied two autoregressive models, both of which were estimated by OLS. One autoregression used e_t^2 (line (4)). It is included because GARCH models imply ARMA processes for e_t^2 (see Bollerslev (1986)); OLS estimation of such autoregressions, therefore, might perform comparably to more complicated GARCH estimation (although under the GARCH null, such OLS estimation is asymptotically inefficient). As in Schwert (1989a, 1989b), whose work is based on that of Davidian and Carroll (1987), the other autoregression used $|e_t|$ (line (4)). Schwert suggests the factor of $(\pi/2)$ because the variance of a zero mean normally distributed random variable is $(\pi/2)$ times the square of the expected value of its absolute value. For both autoregressions, the lag length of 12 was chosen because for all countries in-sample results indicated that such a lag length was more than sufficient to produce a Q-statistic that implied white noise residuals.

Finally, we also tried a nonparametric estimator (line (6)). It can be interpreted as working off the basic definition

$$E(e_{t+j}^2 \mid e_t) = \int_0^\infty e_{t+j}^2 \, f(e_{t+j}^2 \mid e_t) \, de_{t+j}^2,$$

Where $f(e_{t+j}^2 \mid e_t)$ is the density of e_{t+j}^2 conditional on e_t. See Pagan and Ullah (1990a, 1990b) for an excellent exposition. As in Pagan and Schwert (1990a) we used a Gaussian kernel, defined in column (2), with the bandwidth $b = \hat{\sigma}(R - j)^{-1/5}$, $\hat{\sigma}$ the sample standard deviation of e_t, $t = 1, \ldots, R - j$, $j = 1, 12,$ or 24. We did not try any other kernel. We did a little experimentation with some alternative fixed bandwidths and information sets, comparing *MSPEs*, but found that these yielded similar results.

There remain two questions before we can begin our model evaluation. The first is where to begin the out of sample exercise. We arbitrarily began our forecasts at the midpoint of the sample, and the first sample for which we fit any models included the 432 observations from March 14, 1973, to June 17, 1981. Because the final 24 weeks of the sample (April 12, 1989, to September 20, 1989) were used only for forecast evaluation, the last observation of our final estimation sample was April 5, 1989. (In the notation of (1d), $R = 432$ and $T = 839$.) For our one-week horizon, the predictions and realizations of e_t^2 spanned the 408 weeks from June 24, 1981, to April 12, 1989; the comparable 408-week period for the 12- and 24-week horizons may be obtained by shifting the one week dates forward by 11 and 23 weeks, respectively.

The other question concerned what sample should be used for estimation as additional observations were added beyond the June 17, 1981, date at which our first sample ended. In our initial work, we estimated each of our models on both: (1) rolling samples, in which the sample size used for estimation was fixed at 432, and what had been the initial observation as each additional observation was added; and (2) expanding samples, in which the sample size grew as additional observations were added. *RMSPEs* were quite similar for rolling and expanding samples, with those for rolling samples perhaps showing a slight tendency to be smaller (rolling *RMSPEs* were smaller in 63 of the 90 experiments [90 = 5 countries times 6 models times 3 horizons]). To keep the project manageable, we, therefore, decided to subject only the rolling estimators to detailed analysis.

2.3   Procedures for asymptotic inference

Most of our inference is based on asymptotic approximations described in the following. In addition to the usual reasons to be concerned about the finite sample accuracy of such approximations, there are grounds to be concerned about the applicability of regularity conditions typically underlying such approximations: exchange rate data may lack suitable higher order moments (e.g. Loretan and Phillips, 1992); one of our models uses a nonparametric estimator; more generally, the previous paragraph's observation that forecast quality did not deteriorate when we used rolling rather than expanding samples suggests that the usual conditions may not hold. Nevertheless, we conduct most of our inference using such theory, for two reasons. First, a small Monte Carlo experiment to double check one piece of our asymptotic analysis suggested that the asymptotic approximation is unlikely to be very misleading if some minimal conditions do hold, and, second, the computational cost of using bootstrap methods throughout is enormous, given the nonlinear search required to estimate GARCH and IGARCH models.

To explain the asymptotic procedures that we used: Let P be the sample size. Under suitable regularity conditions, it is well known that if g_t is a zero mean, covariance stationarity random vector, $P^{-1/2} \sum_{t=1}^{P} g_t \overset{A}{\sim} N(0, S)$, where $S \equiv \sum_{j=-\infty}^{\infty} \Gamma_j$, $\Gamma_j \equiv \mathrm{E} g_t g_{t-j}'$ (e.g. Hannan, 1973); White (1984) summarizes some parallel results that apply when data satisfy some mixing conditions but possibly are not stationary. Suppose that g_t is a function of an underlying vector of parameters of interest, say, θ, and that $\hat{\theta}$ is estimated by setting $P^{-1}\sum_{t=1}^{p} g_t(\hat{\theta}) = 0$. A straightforward Taylor series argument yields $P^{\frac{1}{2}}(\hat{\theta}-\theta) \overset{A}{\sim} N(0, V), V \equiv (\mathrm{E}\partial g_t/\partial\theta)^{-1} S(\mathrm{E}\partial g_t/\partial\theta)^{-1'}$; see Hansen (1982) for a formal argument in the stationary case, Gallant and White (1988) for the parallel argument, and more complicated formulas, under conditions that allow for the possibility that g_t is not stationary.

In our applications of this result $\partial g_t/\partial\theta$ does not depend on θ and so $\mathrm{E}\partial g_t/\partial\theta$ is a matrix of known constants. The estimator of S that we used was that suggested by Newey and West (1987):

$$\hat{S} \equiv \hat{\Gamma}_0 + \sum_{j=1}^{k}\left[1 - \frac{j}{k+1}\right](\hat{\Gamma}_j + \hat{\Gamma}_j'), \tag{3}$$

Where $\hat{\Gamma}_j$ is the jth sample autocovariance of $\hat{g}, \hat{\Gamma}_0 \equiv P^{-1}\sum_{t=j+1}^{p} \hat{g}_t \hat{g}_{t-j}'$. The value of k in (eq. 3) was determined by a data-dependent automatic rule that has certain asymptotic optimality properties (Newey and West, 1993): Let n be the integer part of $4(P/100)^{2/9}$, so that $n = 6$ for estimates based on the 863 observations in the whole sample (e.g. Table 4.1), $n = 5$ for estimates based on 408 observations in the forecasting sample (e.g. Table 4.4). Also, let w be a vector of ones of the same dimension as $g_t, \hat{\sigma}_j \equiv w' \hat{\Gamma}_j w, \hat{s}^{(0)} \equiv \hat{\sigma}_0 + 2\sum_{j=1}^{n} \hat{\sigma}_j, \hat{s}^{(1)} \equiv 2\sum_{j=1}^{n} j\hat{\sigma}_j$. Then k was set to each integer part of $1.1447 \{\hat{S}^{(1)}/ \hat{S}^{(0)}\}^{2/3} \times \{sample\ size\}^{1/3}$. The resulting values for k in Table 4.1, for example, were Canada –4, France –1, Germany –6, Japan –7, and the UK –11. The values for the remaining tables are available on request.

Some details may be helpful in understanding how we used this framework. In Table 4.1, lines (1)–(4), (13) and (14), begin by defining the (4×1) vector $X_t \equiv (e_t, e_t^2, e_t^3, e_t^4)'$. Let $\theta \equiv (\mathrm{E}e_t, \mathrm{E}e_t^2, \mathrm{E}e_t^3, \mathrm{E}e_t^4)', \hat{\theta} \equiv (P^{-1}\sum_{t=1}^{p} e_t, P^{-1}\sum_{t=1}^{p} e_t^2, P^{-1}\sum_{t=1}^{p} e_t^3, P^{-1}\sum_{t=1}^{p} e_t^4)', g_t \equiv X_t - \theta$, and $\hat{g}_t \equiv X_t - \hat{\theta}$. Then $P^{\frac{1}{2}}(\hat{\theta}-\theta) \overset{A}{\sim} N(0,S)$, $S \equiv \sum_{j=-\infty}^{\infty}\Gamma_j, \Gamma_j \equiv \mathrm{E}g_t g_{t-j}'$. Given an estimate of S (see below), standard errors on the relevant entries in Table 4.1 can be computed using the delta method. A similar method was used in panel A of Table 4.6 below.

In the modified Ljung-Box statistic, Table 4.1, lines (5)–(7), $\theta \equiv (\mathrm{E}e_t e_{t-1}, \ldots, \mathrm{E}e_t e_{t-r})', r = 10, 50, 90, \hat{\theta}$ the corresponding sample moments, $X_t \equiv (e_t e_{t-1}, \ldots, e_t e_{t-r})', g_t \equiv X_t - \theta, \hat{g}_t \equiv X_t - \hat{\theta}$. We assume that conditional first moments of e_t is zero, which implies that g_t is serially uncorrelated, and that $\mathrm{E}e_t^2 e_{t-i}, e_{t-j} = 0$ for $i \neq j$, which implies that $\mathrm{E}X_t X_t'$ is diagonal. With a little algebra, this validates the following: For $j = 0, \ldots, r$, let $\hat{\sigma}_j$ be the jth element of $\hat{\theta}, \hat{\sigma}_j \equiv P^{-1}\sum_{t=j+1}^{p} e_t e_{t-j}$, and let $\hat{K}_j \equiv P^{-1}\sum_{t=j+1}^{p} e_t^2 e_{t-j}^2, \hat{\rho}_j \equiv \hat{\sigma}_j/\hat{\sigma}_0$. Then for any fixed r,

$$P(P+2)\hat{\sigma}_0^2 \sum_{j=1}^{r}(P - j)^{-1}(\hat{\rho}_j^2/\hat{k}_j) \overset{A}{\sim} \chi^2(r). \tag{4}$$

If the data are conditionally homoskedastic, so that $Ee_t^2 e_{t-j}^2 = Ee_t^2 e_{t-j}^2 \equiv \sigma_0^2$, $\hat{k}_j \xrightarrow{P} \sigma_0^2$ and this statistic is asymptotically equivalent to the standard Ljung-Box statistic.[6]

In Tables 4.4 and 4.5 below, which report inference about forecasts or forecast errors, the conceptual experiment that underlies our asymptotic approximation is one in which both the number of observations used in estimation (R, in the notation of (2-2)) and the number used for forecasting ($T - R + 1 \equiv P$) go to infinity, with $(T - R + 1)/R$ approaching a finite constant (possibly zero).

Consider, for example, the one-period ahead *MSPE*. For notational simplicity, assume stationarity (rather than, say, just mixing). Let h_{mt} be model m's population prediction of e_{t+1}^2 at time t (i.e., the prediction it would make if an infinite sized sample had been used in estimation). Let δ be the vector of the entire set of regression parameters, across all models (the constant for the homoskedastic model, the constant and coefficients on e_t^2 and h_{t-1} for the GARCH(1,1) model, ...). Let $u_{mt+1} = e_{t+1}^2 - h_{mt}$, $\sigma_m^2 = Eu_{mt+1}^2 = E(e_{t+1}^2 - h_{mt})^2$, $\hat{u}_{mt+1} = e_{t+1}^2 - \hat{h}_{mt}$:

$$\hat{\sigma}_m^2 = (T - R + 1)^{-1}\sum_{t=R}^{T}(e_{t+1}^2 - \hat{h}_{mt})^2, \ \hat{\theta} \equiv (\hat{\sigma}_1^2, \ldots, \hat{\sigma}_M^2)', \ \theta \equiv (\sigma_1^2, \ldots, \sigma_M^2)', \ g_{t+1}$$

$$(\theta - \delta) = (u_{1t+1}^2 - \sigma_1^2, \ldots, u_{Mt+1}^2 - \sigma_m^2)', \ g_{t+1}(\hat{\theta}, \hat{\delta}) = \hat{u}_{1t+1}^2 - \hat{\sigma}_1^2, \ldots, \hat{u}_{Mt+1}^2 - \hat{\sigma}_M^2)'.$$

It may be shown that under suitable conditions, sampling error in $\hat{\delta}$ is irrelevant for asymptotic inference on θ (West (1993)), and we apply the logic above to $(T - R + 1)^{-1}\sum_{t=R}^{T} g_{t+1}(\hat{\theta}, \hat{\delta}) \equiv P^{-1}\sum_{t=R}^{T}\hat{g}_{t+1}$. The implication is the $P^{1/2}(\hat{\theta} - \theta) \overset{A}{\sim} N(0,S)$, where the (i,q) element of the $M \times M$ matrix S is $\sum_{j=-\infty}^{\infty} E(u_{1t}^2 - \sigma_i^2)$ $(u_{qt-j}^2 - \sigma_q^2)$. A test statistic for the equality of the *MSPE*s across all M models is constructed as follows. Let B be the $(M - 1) \times M$ matrix whose first column is $(-1, -1, \ldots, -1)'$ and whose $(M - 1)$ other columns contain the identity matrix; the null is that $B\theta = 0$. Then for $\hat{S}$ constructed as in (3),

$$(T - R + 1)[\hat{\theta}'B'(B\hat{S}B')^{-1}B\hat{\theta}] \equiv P[\hat{\theta}'B'(B\hat{S}B')^{-1}B\hat{\theta}] \overset{A}{\sim} X^2(M - 1),$$

$$\hat{S} \equiv \hat{\Gamma}_0 + \sum_{j=1}^{k}[1 - j/(k+1)](\hat{\Gamma}_j + \hat{\Gamma}_j'), \ \hat{\Gamma}_j \equiv P^{-1}\sum_{t=R+j}^{T}\hat{g}_1\hat{g}_{t+j}'. \tag{5}$$

Note that since we select k as described and do not constrain k to be zero, we allow the forecast errors to be serially correlated. Similar formulas apply for the 12- and 24-period-ahead predictions, with, e.g., $u_{m,t+12} \equiv e_{t+12}^2 - h_{m,t+12}$ and $\sigma_{m,12}^2 \equiv E(e_{t+12}^2 - h_{m,t+12})^2$.

3.   Basic empirical results

To frame our discussion, Table 4.3A presents estimates of the GARCH(1,1) model for the first of our rolling samples. The Appendix available on request has parallel estimates for the other models; we present GARCH(1,1) here because of its simplicity and because, as we shall see, it worked relatively well in forecasting.

For the benefit of those familiar with GARCH, we briefly note that the estimates suggest, as usual, considerable persistence, since $\alpha + \beta$ is estimated to be above 0.80 in all five countries, above 0.90 in France, Germany and Japan; the null that $\alpha + \beta = 1$ could not be rejected at the 5 percent level for France and Japan (not reported in the table).

What is of particular interest to us is how such parameters translate into for *RMSPEs* at various horizons. Suppose e_t^2 is stationary, ($\alpha + \beta < 1$, under a GARCH(1,1) parameterization). With the exception of IGARCH, all our estimators will then yield the essentially the same predictions in population for a sufficiently long horizon, since all will predict that the e_t^2 will be near its unconditional mean. Accordingly, the *RMSPEs* will also be essentially the same. We use the GARCH(1,1) estimates in Table 4.3A to get an idea of how long a horizon is needed for this to occur.

Table 4.3B reports the ratio of the population *RMSPEs* of a homoskedastic model to that of a GARCH(1,1) model, for each of our three horizons, and for each of the five sets of estimates of α and β reported in Table 4.3A.[7] According to columns (1) and (5) in Table 4.3B, the Table 4.3A estimates for Canada and the UK suggest sufficiently rapid mean reversion that our proposed comparisons of 12- and 24-week horizons are probably not of interest. On the other hand, columns (2) to (4) indicate that other Table 4.3A estimates imply as sharp a difference in *RMSPEs* at one or both of these longer horizons as occurs at a one-period horizon for the UK parameters in column (5).

We will *not* attempt to squeeze an interpretation of the results of our out-of-sample comparison into the Table 4.3 figures. Even under a GARCH(1,1) null, Table 4.3's figures will be misleading insofar as sampling error has affected the point estimates of α and β. Rather, we interpret Table 4.3 as presenting in-sample evidence that it may be possible to distinguish different estimators at horizons of as long as 24 weeks.

Table 4.4 presents our attempts to do so, for forecasts of 1 and 12 weeks as well as 24 weeks ahead, in panels A, B and C, respectively. In each panel, under each country are two columns. The second, labelled "*RMSPE*" gives the root mean squared prediction error, computed according to equation (eq. 2). The other column, labelled "Rank," indicates the relative size of that model's *RMSPE*, 1 indicating the best (smallest) *RMSPE*, 6 the worst (largest). The rows labelled H_A, H_B, and H_C (at the bottom of each panel) will be discussed in the following.

We begin with two general comments, before beginning a comparison of the models. First, as one would expect, given the noisiness of exchange rate data, these out-of-sample *RMSEs* generally are larger than the in-sample *RMSEs* reported in line (14) of Table 4.1. That is, the out-of-sample predictions using the estimated conditional variances are usually less accurate than an in-sample prediction using the in-sample unconditional variance. Second, and somewhat surprisingly, there does not appear to be a tendency for *RMSPEs* to increase at longer horizons; the median Table 4.1 values for the 1-, 12- and 24-week horizons are 4.746, 4.791 and 4.503, for example. In the context of GARCH(1,1)

Table 4.3A GARCH (1,1) estimates, sample = 3/14/73 to 6/17/81

	ω $(\times 10^5)$	α	β
1. Canada	0.5	0.26	0.54
	(0.1)	(0.02)	(0.06)
2. France	1.3	0.35	0.61
	(0.2)	(0.05)	(0.04)
3. Germany	2.0	0.30	0.61
	(0.4)	(0.05)	(0.04)
4. Japan	0.07	0.05	0.94
	(0.03)	(0.01)	(0.01)
5. U.K.	1.9	0.11	0.73
	(0.7)	(0.05)	(0.10)

Table 4.3B Population root mean square prediction errors, homoskedastic relative to GARCH (1,1)

Horizon	Column (1) $\alpha = 0.26$ $\beta = 0.54$	Column (2) $\alpha = 0.35$ $\beta = 0.61$	Column (3) $\alpha = 0.30$ $\beta = 0.61$	Column (4) $\alpha = 005$ $\beta = 0.94$	Column (5) $\alpha = 0.11$ $\beta = 0.73$
1	1.09	1.60	1.23	1.06	1.02
12	1.00	1.15	1.02	1.05	1.00
24	1.00	1.05	1.00	1.04	1.00

Notes:
1. The numbers in parentheses in panel A are asymptotic standard errors.
2. Panel B presents the ratio of *RMSPE*s for the indicated horizons, computed assuming that the data are driven by a GARCH(1,1) model with the indicated parameters, and abstracting from sampling error in estimation of the model parameters. The ratio is invariant to ω. The *RMSPE* for the homoskedastic model is constant for all horizons. The ratio asymptotes to 1 as the horizon approaches infinity, for each pair of α and β.

models, the implication is that mean reversion occurs as rapidly as in, say, column (5) of Table 4.3B. The figures in columns (2) to (4) of that table suggest otherwise, so there is a clear conflict between the out-of-sample and in-sample evidence.

We turn now to comparing the models. At the 1-week horizon, panel A indicates that one of the two GARCH models had the smallest *RMSPE* for all five countries. The IGARCH model was probably the most consistent performer overall, being best in three countries (France, Germany and UK), second and third best in the other two (Japan and Canada). At the 12-week horizon (panel B),

Table 4.4 Root mean squared prediction errors

	Canada		France		Germany		Japan		UK	
	Rank	RMSPE	Rank	RMSPE	Rank	RMSPE	Rank	RMSPE	Rank	RMSPE
A. One-week horizon										
homo	5	0.714	2	5.167	2	4.704	3	4.380	4	5.745
(1,1)	1	0.702	6	5.351	5	4.783	1	4.323	2	5.632
ig	3	0.706	1	5.161	1	4.695	2	4.343	1	5.563
e2AR	4	0.712	5	5.273	6	4.925	5	4.411	5	6.033
$\|e\|$AR	2	0.704	3	5.200	4	4.767	4	4.388	3	5.726
nonp	6	0.737	4	5.201	3	4.724	6	4.442	6	6.537
H_A	9.70 [0.084]		8.91 [0.113]		8.23 [0.144]		6.42 [0.268]		3.76 [0.584]	
H_B	1.24 [0.265]		0.01 [0.918]		0.01 [0.912]		0.77 [0.380]		1.52 [0.217]	
H_C	4.24 [0.237]		8.99 [0.029]		4.13 [0.247]		2.86 [0.413]		3.59 [0.310]	
B. Twelve-week horizon										
homo	1	0.695	1	5.219	1	4.754	3	4.435	5	5.794
(1,1)	2	0.697	6	5.696	6	4.831	5	4.451	4	5.756
ig	6	0.731	5	5.268	5	4.817	6	4.454	2	5.692
e2AR	3	0.700	3	5.251	4	4.796	2	4.433	3	5.726
$\|e\|$AR	4	0.701	4	5.267	3	4.785	1	4.430	1	5.674
Nonp	5	0.704	2	5.250	2	4.762	4	4.447	6	5.841
H_A	16.71 [0.005]		15.06 [0.010]		7.32 [0.198]		1.08 [0.956]		8.49 [0.131]	
H_B	n.a.		n.a.		n.a.		0.01 [0.921]		1.29 [0.256]	
H_C	5.96 [0.114]		13.60 [0.004]		5.83 [0.120]		0.39 [0.943]		5.66 [0.129]	
C. Twenty-four-week horizon										
Homo	1	0.695	3	5.094	3	4.500	2	4.424	4	5.770
(1,1)	5	0.703	6	5.694	1	4.490	6	4.498	1	5.708
ig	6	0.743	1	5.060	5	4.509	5	4.483	5	5.834
e2AR	2	0.695	2	5.087	2	4.498	1	4.422	2	5.721
$\|e\|$AR	3	0.697	4	5.109	4	4.505	4	4.441	3	5.729
nonp	4	0.702	5	5.131	6	4.535	3	4.436	6	5.943
H_A	18.95 [0.002]		18.08 [0.003]		3.80 [0.578]		6.05 [0.301]		5.82 [0.324]	
H_B	n.a.		0.25 [0.619]		0.11 [0.741]		0.12 [0.728]		0.07 [0.789]	
H_C	3.35 [0.340]		17.64 [0.001]		1.07 [0.785]		5.82 [0.121]		1.95 [0.583]	

Notes:

1. The RMSPE columns present the out-of-sample root mean squared error in predicting e^2_{t+j} for horizon j ($j = 1, 12$ or 24) and the indicated country and model. The Rank columns index the relative size of the RMSPEs for a given country and horizon, 1 indicating the smallest RMSPE, 6 the largest.
2. The H_A, H_B and H_C rows present χ^2 statistics (asymptotic p-values in brackets) for the following hypothesis: A: equality of MSPEs of all 6 models ($\chi^2(5)$); B: equality of MSPEs of best and homo models ($\chi^2(1)$); C: equality of MSPEs from homo, (1,1), e2AR and $\|e\|$AR models ($\chi^2(3)$).

the best model was either the homoskedastic (Canada, France and Germany) or autoregression in absolute values (Japan, UK). At the 24-week horizon (panel C), depending on the country, one of four different models had the lowest *RMSPE*, GARCH(1,1) being the only model that was best in two countries (Germany, UK). But the most consistent performer at 24 weeks was probably the autoregression in exchange rate squares, which was second in four countries and first in one (Japan).

Which model performs best, then, varies from country to country and horizon to horizon; if there is an underlying pattern, it is difficult for us to discern, and, at least superficially, Table 4.1 suggests that it might be largely a matter of chance which model produces the smallest *RMSPE*.[8] That performance is quite similar across models is also suggested by casual inspection of the point estimates of the *RMSPE*s; even at a one- period horizon, in only one case is the worst model's *RMSPE* more than five percent larger than the best model's (UK); once again, such point estimates are surprising in light of Table 4.3B.

For an additional measure of similarity of *RMSPE*s, we turn to formal statistical testing of the hypothesis that these are the same across various models, for a given horizon. In Table 4.4, the H_A, H_B, and H_C rows at the bottom of each panel give statistics and, in brackets, *p*-values assuming an asymptotic chi-squared distribution, for the following three hypotheses:

H_A: *MSPE*s for all six models are equal (x^2 (5)).
H_B: *MSPE*s for the best model and the homoskedastic model
    are equal (x^2 (1)).   (6)
H_C: *MSPE*s for the homoskedastic, GARCH(1,1), and two
    autoregressive models are the same ((x^2 (3)).

Hypothesis A is an obvious one.[9] Tests of hypothesis B were performed because the homoskedastic model is the simplest one and, therefore, probably the model of most appeal if, in fact, performance is similar across models. Tests of hypothesis C were performed because the formal asymptotic theory that underlies the test makes assumptions that rule out our nonparametric estimator and possibly the IGARCH estimator as well.

Table 4.4 indicates that the H_A test of the null of equal *RMSPE*s across all models is rejected at the 0.05 level in four of our fifteen experiments (Canada and France, 12- and 24-week horizons) and once at the 0.10 but not 0.05 level (Canada, 1-week horizon). This suggests that the seeming similarity of point estimates of *RMSPE*s might be misleading, at least for Canada and France. In no case, however, can one reject at conventional significance levels the null that the homoskedastic model's *RMSPE* is the same as that of the best model: the lowest of *p*-value for H_B s 0.217 (UK, one-week horizon). The H_C test of equal *RMSPE*s for the homoskedastic, GARCH(1,1), and two AR models rejects at the 0.05 level for France for all three horizons, again suggesting that the seeming similarity of point estimates of *RMSPE*s might be misleading for France.

These asymptotic tests may well be deceptive in finite samples, even if the asymptotic theory eventually yields a good approximation. One indication that this may be the case is that of the four rejections at the 0.05 level of equality of all six models, three occur in experiments in which the homoskedastic model is the best (Canada, 12- and 24-week; France, 24-week). If, indeed, a homoskedastic model were generating the data, at least four of the other five models would produce exactly the homoskedastic forecast in an infinitely large sample (the possible exception is IGARCH, whose asymptotic behavior under these conditions is unclear to us). But this suggests a tendency to reject too much, not too little, a result that we have found in related Monte Carlo studies using data generated by GARCH processes (Newey and West, 1993).

But to double check the possibility that our asymptotic tests are instead rejecting too infrequently, we undertook two exercises. First, we examined a seventh model, which set $\hat{h}_t = e_t^2$ — the conditional variance in week t is equal to the realized square of the exchange rate. (Reminder to readers familiar with the GARCH literature: what we call h_t here is usually called h_{t-1}). To our knowledge, this has not been seriously proposed as a model for exchange rate volatility, for the good reason that it is not an appealing one: the *RMSPEs* for the one-week horizon, for example, are: Canada 0.933; France 7.119; Germany 6.574; Japan 5.593; and UK 7.466. These are a good 25 percent above the Table 4.4A figures for the other models. We use it here to see if our asymptotic tests have enough power to recognize the substantial difference between this model and the others. And they do, as is indicated by the following summary of test results. Of 15 x^2 (6) tests of the equality of *RMSPEs* across all seven models, 11 reject at the 0.05 level, 13 reject at the 0.10 level. Of 15 x^2 (1) tests of the equality of the *RMSPE* from this additional model and that of the worst of the six models reported in Table 4.4, 13 reject at the 0.05 level, fourteen at the 0.10 level (the exception was UK, one-week horizon, which rejects at the 0.15 level). It seems, then, that whatever the problems with our asymptotic tests, these tests do have enough power to reject an egregiously poor model at conventional significance levels.

The second exercise we undertook to check the validity of our asymptotic tests was a small Monte Carlo experiment. Because of space constraints, we limit ourselves to the succinct statement that the experiment suggested that if our asymptotic procedures have a small sample bias, that bias is towards rejecting too much, not too little. A detailed discussion of the experiment is available in the Appendix that is available on request.

4. Additional empirical results

It seems that to a first approximation all our models are equally good as predictors of exchange rates squares. To compare them from a slightly different perspective, we conducted a standard efficiency test (e.g. Pagan and Schwert, 1990a), estimating by OLS the regression

$$e_{t+1}^2 = b_0 + b_1 \hat{h}_{mt} + \varepsilon_{t+1}. \tag{7}$$

If, indeed, $E_t e_{t+1}^2 = \hat{h}_{mt}$, one should get $b_0 = 0$, $b_1 = 1$. One should also find that ε_{t+1} is serially uncorrelated. But a quick look at the autocorrelations of the residuals suggested that this was rarely if ever the case. So we do not formally test for the absence of serial correlation and instead correct the variance-covariance matrix of the estimated parameter vector for conditional heteroskedasticity as well as serial correlation, using the techniques described previously.

Results are in Table 4.5. Asymptotic standard errors for b_0 and b_1 are given in parentheses beneath the point estimates. For all five countries, the x^2 (2) column gives the point estimate and asymptotic p-value for H_0: $b_0 = 0$, $b_1 = 1$. The "**" and "*" after the estimates of $\hat{b}_1$ indicate significant differences from zero, not one.

We note first that the rankings by R^2 are quite similar to those by *RMSPE*. This indicates that models with relatively low *RMSPE*s also have *RMSPE*s whose variance component is relatively low, since R^2 reflects the variance but not bias-squared component of MSPE. Some new information is yielded by the other estimates. Of the 30 x^2 (2) tests of H_0: $b_0 = 0$, $b_1 = 1$, 27 reject at the .10 level (the exceptions are GARCH(1,1) for Japan, IGARCH for Japan and UK), 25 at the 0.05 level (the additional exceptions are the two autoregressions for Canada). The standard errors on 0 and 1 yield compatible conclusions.

Perhaps unsurprisingly, then, none of the models pass this efficiency test: the Monte Carlo simulation indicates that this test has good power, being very likely to reject the null (not reported in the table). More encouraging is that seven of the estimates of b_1 are significantly different from zero at the 0.05 level, five of these being for GARCH models (see the ** entries). This shows that there is some predictive power in the estimated conditional variances. For future reference, note the marked tendency of the models to have predictive power for Canadian data.

We also performed the efficiency test in Table 4.5 for the 12- and 24-week horizons. For these horizons, the results did not help discriminate between models, and we therefore limit ourselves to a summary of the results. Of the 60 x^2 (2) tests, 58 reject at the 0.10 level (the exceptions are GARCH(1,1) for Canada 12-week and UK 24- week), 56 at the 0.05 level (the additional exceptions are homoskedastic for Canada 12 and 24 week). More troubling is that while $\hat{b}_1$ was different from zero at the 0.05 level seven times, only two of those estimates were positive (GARCH(1,1) and IGARCH for UK, 12-week).

Overall, then, it seems that at the one period horizon there is some evidence favoring GARCH models: while Table 4.4 cannot reject the null that the *RMSPE*s are the same for all models, GARCH models do tend to produce lower *RMSPE*s, and Table 4.5 suggests that they have markedly more predictive power for next period's e_{t+1}^2. On the other hand, at longer horizons, we find little grounds for preferring one model over another.

This is a disappointing, and surprising, result. It seems that mean reversion in the conditional variance occurs rapidly enough that no model dominates the others at 12-week or longer horizons. This suggests that the in-sample fits overstate the conditional predictability of exchange rate squares. Lamoureux and Lastrapes (1990) have shown that occasional discrete shifts in the mean level of volatility

Table 4.5 Regression tests of efficiency, one-week horizon

	b_0	b_1	R^2	$\chi^2(2)$	b_0	b_1	R^2	$\chi^2(2)$
	Canada				**France**			
homo	1.34	−2.99*	0.018	8.07	3.92	−0.71	0.004	12.15
	(0.53)	(1.62)		[0.018]	(1.13)	(0.50)		[0.002]
(1,1)	0.15	0.60**	0.044	6.98	2.26	0.09	0.0009	45.45
	(0.06)	(0.17)		[0.031]	(0.40)	(0.14)		[0.000]
ig	0.17	0.55**	0.037	10.04	2.23	0.10	0.0004	13.53
	(0.05)	(0.17)		[0.007]	(0.67)	(0.24)		[0.001]
e2AR	0.20	0.48*	0.019	4.90	2.86	−0.15	0.001	82.32
	(0.09)	(0.28)		[0.086]	(0.41)	(0.13)		[0.000]
|e|AR	0.16	0.66**	0.031	5.44	2.38	0.05	0.0001	25.05
	(0.09)	(0.29)		[0.066]	(0.48)	(0.22)		[0.000]
nonp	0.28	0.27**	0.012	31.66	2.86	−0.16	0.0008	27.63
	(0.05)	(0.13)		[0.000]	(0.57)	(0.22)		[0.000]
	Germany				**Japan**			
homo	2.65	−0.06	0.00003	14.52	3.40	−0.59	0.001	7.46
	(0.74)	(0.35)		[0.001]	(1.37)	(0.70)		[0.024]
(1,1)	1.95	0.23	0.005	19.85	0.89	0.60	0.023	1.25
	(0.44)	(0.21)		[0.000]	(0.79)	(0.37)		[0.537]
ig	1.56	0.37	0.008	7.93	1.02	0.60**	0.011	2.66
	(0.58)	(0.27)		[0.019]	(0.63)	(0.28)		[0.264]
e2AR	2.45	0.03	0.0001	92.85	1.56	0.32	0.008	11.09
	(0.28)	(0.11)		[0.000]	(0.47)	(0.22)		[0.004]
|e|AR	2.18	0.15	0.001	19.73	1.43	0.40*	0.012	11.39
	(0.54)	(0.27)		[0.000]	(0.42)	(0.21)		[0.003]
nonp	2.48	0.02	0.00001	17.94	2.51	−0.14	0.0006	12.44
	(0.59)	(0.25)		[0.000]	(0.73)	(0.32)		[0.002]
	UK							
homo	3.55	−0.42	0.002	19.18				
	(0.81)	(0.36)		[0.000]				
(1,1)	1.25	0.53**	0.045	7.20				
	(0.48)	(0.22		[0.027]				
ig	0.95	0.69**	0.042	3.90				
	(0.61)	(0.30)		[0.142]				
e2AR	2.40	0.12	0.003	45.07				
	(0.44)	(0.13)		[0.000]				
|e|AR	1.84	0.36	0.010	13.08				
	(0.51)	(0.23)		[0.001]				
nonp	2.78	−0.03	0.0003	943.63				
	(0.32)	(0.04)		[0.000]				

Notes:
1. This reports results of the regression $e^2_{t+1} = b_0 + b_1 \hat{h}_{mt} + \varepsilon_t$. For b_0 and b_1, heteroskedasticity and autocorrelation consistent standard errors are in parentheses; for the UK, 95 percent confidence intervals from a Monte Carlo simulation are also given for b_1 and R². The $\chi^2(2)$ tests H_0: $b_0 = 0$, $b_1 = 1$, with asymptotic p-value in brackets.
2. For b_1, "**" denotes significance at the 5 percent level, "*" at the 10% level.

cause substantial upward bias in estimates of the persistence of volatility. We close this section with some evidence that such shifts may have occurred here and thus may help account for our inability to sharply distinguish one model from another.

Panel A of Table 4.6 reports split sample estimates of the standard deviation of e_t. As one can see, the point estimate is markedly higher in the second half of the sample for all countries except, perhaps, Canada.[10] In addition, line (3) of the table indicates that the null of equality is rejected at the 0.05 level for France, Japan and the UK and at the 0.10 level for Germany.

Given that we began forecasting at the sample midpoint, the choice of the midpoint as a date to test for a shift is natural but nonetheless still arbitrary. In panel B, we report a Pagan and Schwert (1990b) test for the constancy of the unconditional variance of e_t that does not require *a priori* specification of a date.

Table 4.6 Subsample statistics on e_t

	Canada	France	Germany	Japan	UK
Panel A. Standard deviation					
(1) Standard Deviation,	0.499	1.185	1.309	1.174	1.093
3/14/73–6/17/81	(0.049)	(0.097)	(0.117)	(0.102)	(0.076)
(2) Standard Deviation,	0.600	1.603	1.609	1.526	1.663
6/24/81–9/20/89	(0.050)	(0.153)	(0.149)	(0.146)	(0.159)
(3) Row 2–row 1	0.101	0.418	0.299	0.352	0.570
	(0.070)	(0.181)	(0.190)	(0.178)	(0.177)
Panel B. Modified range scale tests for constancy of unconditional variance					
(1) 3/14/73–9/20/89	1.428	2.238**	1.901**	1.874**	1.753**
No. of obs. = 863					
(2) 3/14/73–6/17/81	1.413	1.659*	1.540	1.892**	1.046
No. of obs. = 432					
(3) 4/24/77–7/31/85	1.242	1.725*	1.365	1.852**	1.317
No. of obs. = 432					
(4) 6/24/81–9/20/89	1.260	1.226	1.326	1.561	1.667
No. of obs. = 431					

Notes:
1. In panel A, heteroskedasticity and autocorrelation consistent asymptotic standard errors are in parentheses.
2. In panel B, let $x_t = (e_t - \bar{e})^2$ where e is the mean of e_t in the sample in question, and let $\bar{x}$ be the corresponding mean of x_t. Let $\psi(r) \equiv \left[\sum_{t=1}^{r}(x_t - \bar{x})\right]/(T\hat{s})^{1/2}$, where $1 \leq r \leq T$, $T = 431, 432$ or 863 is the sample size and $\hat{S}$ is an estimate of the asymptotic variance of $T^{-1/2}\sum_{t=1}^{T}\left[(e_t - Ee_t)^2 - E(e_t - Ee_t)^2\right]$. The table reports the difference between the maximum and minimum of $\psi(r)$.
3. "**" means significant at the .05 level, "*" at the .10 level, according to Table 1a in Haubrich and Lo (1989).

The details of the test are described in the notes to the table. As indicated in the table, the null of constancy is rejected at the 0.05 level for all countries but Canada, for which it is not rejected at even the 0.20 level. See row (1) of panel B.

Rows 2 to 4 of Table 4.6 report the results of applying this test on three sub-samples for each country: the first half of our total sample (March 14, 1973, to June 17, 1981), the middle two-fourths (April 24, 1977, to July 31, 1985), and the last half (June 24, 1981, to September 20, 1989). Of the 15 tests for constant variances (15 = 3 subsamples times 5 countries), only two tests rejected at the .05 level (Japan, beginning and middle subsamples).

Now, if the data were driven by a stationary model that allows time varying conditional variances, it would not be surprising if tests such as those in Table 4.6 found evidence of shifts in variance at short but not long horizons. We, however, find the converse. And, as briefly noted in Section 2, forecast quality was no better for expanding than for rolling samples, which also seems to suggest a failure of the stationarity assumption.

In this study, we followed many others (e.g. Engle et al., 1990) and implicitly allowed for a failure of stationarity by using rolling samples. We conjecture that it will be productive to explore models that explicitly allow for seeming or actual movement in the unconditional variance of e_t. The sort of movement that one wants to capture appears to be slow enough that it might not be detectable in samples that are eight years long, but rapid enough that it is marked in samples sixteen years long.

Canadian data were unusual in that Table 4.4's tests of equality of *RMSPEs* tended to find differences across models, and Table 4.5's efficiency tests were unusually likely to be able to find predictive power in the estimated conditional variances. Perhaps the distinctive results for Canada are no accident but instead are linked to the stationary behavior of its exchange rates.

5. Conclusions

The in-sample evidence summarized in Tables 4.1 and 4.3 strongly suggests that a homoskedastic model should be dominated by the other models that we studied. This did not turn out to be the case. We speculate that models that allow for seeming or actual drift in unconditional moments may result in superior performance. Possibilities include processes that allow occasional discrete jumps (Jorion, 1988) and models with time varying parameters (Chou et al., 1991).

Notes

* This chapter is reprinted from the *Journal of Econometrics*, pp. 367–391, 1995, which was co-authored with Kenneth D. West.
1 We find this to also be a message, perhaps implicit, in the studies using stock price data by Pagan and Schwert (1990a, 1990b) and Chou et al. (1991), as well in Loretan and Phillips (1992).
2 We also obtained Italian data. But in-sample statistics such as those reported in Table 4.1 suggest a nonzero unconditional mean. Fitted GARCH models tended to be explosive, with $\hat{\alpha} + \hat{\beta} > 1$ in the notation of Table 4.2; apparently this

resulted in part from the nonzero sample mean since removing this mean lessened the tendency to get explosive estimates. We dropped Italy rather than fit means as well as variances.

3   In related work (West, Edison and Cho, 1993) we consider an alternative measure of model quality, which also tends to favor GARCH.

4   We also used these models in another paper (West, Edison and Cho, 1993) and some of the prose in the remainder of this subsection also appears in that paper.

5   For efficiency reasons, one might nonetheless prefer to assume, say, a conditional t distribution, if the conditional density is in fact t. Our reading of the in-sample evidence is that this is not essential (e.g. Baillie and Bollerslev, 1989, found little support for the use of a t in weekly exchange rate data).

6   Diebold and Mariano (1991) have independently suggested conducting inference on forecast errors using similar techniques, and Diebold (1988) suggested our modification of the Ljung-Box statistic in the specific case of a GARCH data generating process.

7   These population figures ignore the effects of sampling error in the estimation of model parameters. Reinsel (1980) and Ericcson and Marquez (1989), among others, have suggested a refinement to the computation of the *RMSPE* that accounts for sampling error in such estimation. But inspection of their formulae and simulation results indicates that the refinement has a noticeable effect only when the following ratio is much larger than in our application: (number of regressors)/(sample size). While neither of these papers considers data that are conditionally heteroskedastic, we take the message to be that such a refinement is unlikely to much affect the Table 4.3B figures.

8   Consistent with this statement, and with the literature surveyed in Clemen (1989), a prediction formed by averaging the six forecasts typically performs better than any of the individual forecasts, at least at the longer horizons. Of the 15 comparisons, the ranking of the average forecast was: 1–7 times (2 of the 7 occur for a one period horizon; IGARCH performs roughly comparably here); 2–6 times, 3-once; 4-once. Details are in the Appendix that is available upon request.

9   For computational convenience, we computed tests for equality of the *MSPEs* rather than the asymptotically equivalent tests for the *RMSPEs*; for expositional convenience, in all discussion apart from the statement of the tests in the preceding paragraph in the text, we refer to these as tests on the *RMSPEs*.

10 This raises the question of whether our exercise would produce different results if applied to split samples, a question also raised by a referee who noted that in the mid-1980s, central banks attempted to drive down the dollar. We computed one-week ahead *RMSPEs* for samples running from (1)6/17/81 to 9/18/85 (number of predictions = 223), and (2)9/18/85-4/5/89 (number of predictions = 185); the split date was chosen because the Plaza Accord was announced on 9/22/85. The *RMSPEs* were generally higher in the later sample. But GARCH or IGARCH still fared relatively well: one or the other was best in all five comparisons in the early sample, in three of the five comparisons in the later sample. Details are in the Appendix.

References

Akgiray, Vedat, 1989. "Conditional Heteroskedasticity in Time Series of Stock Returns: Evidence and Forecasts," *Journal of Business,* 62, pp. 55–80.

Baillie, Richard T., and Bollerslev, Tim, 1989. "The Message in Daily Exchange Rates: A Conditional Variance Tale," *Journal of Business and Economic Statistics,* 7, pp. 297–305.

Bollerslev, Tim, 1986. "Generalized Autoregressive Conditional Heteroskedasticity," *Journal of Econometrics,* 31, pp. 307–327.

Bollerslev, Tim, Chou, Ray Y., and Kenneth F. Kroner, 1992. "ARCH Modelling in Finance: A Review of the Theory and Empirical Evidence," *Journal of Econometrics,* 52, pp. 5–59.

Chou, Ray, Engle, Robert F., and Alex Kane, 1991. "Measuring Risk Aversion from Excess Returns on a Stock Index," NBER Working Paper no. 3643, Cambridge, MA.

Clemen, Robert T., 1989. "Combining Forecasts: A Review and Annotated Bibliography," *International Journal of Forecasting,* 5, pp. 559–583.

Davidian, M. and R.J. Carroll, 1987. "Variance Function Estimation," *Journal of the American Statistical Association,* 82, pp. 1079–1091.

Diebold, Francis X., 1988. *Empirical Modeling of Exchange Rate Dynamics.* Berlin: Springer-Verlag.

Diebold, Francis X., and Roberto S. Mariano, 1991. "Comparing Predictive Accuracy I: An Asymptotic Test," manuscript, University of Pennsylvania.

Diebold, Francis X., and James Nason, 1990. "Nonparametric Exchange Rate Prediction?", *Journal of International Economics,* 28, pp. 315–332.

Diebold, Francis X., and Marc Nerlove, 1989. "The Dynamics of Exchange Rate Volatility: A Multivariate Latent Factor ARCH Model," *Journal of Applied Econometrics,* 4, pp. 1–21.

Engle, Robert F., 1982. "Autoregressive Conditional Heteroskedasticity, with Estimates of the Variance of United Kingdom Inflation," *Econometrica,* 50, pp. 987–1007.

Engle, Robert F. and Tim Bollerslev, 1986. "Modelling the Persistence of Conditional Variances," *Econometric Reviews,* 5, pp. 1–50.

Engle, Robert F., Che-Hsiung Hong, and Alex Kane, 1990. "Valuation of Variance Forecasts with Simulated Options Markets," manuscript, University of California-San Diego.

Ericcson, Neil R. and Jamie R. Marquez, 1989. "Exact and Approximate Multi-Period Mean-Square Forecast Errors for Dynamic Econometric Models," Federal Reserve Board of Governors International Finance Discussion Paper No. 348., Washington, DC.

Gallant, A. Ronald and Halbert White, 1988. *A Unified Theory of Estimation and Inference for Nonlinear Dynamic Models.* New York: Basil Blackwell.

Hannan, Edward J., 1973. "Central Limit Theorems for Time Series Regressions," *Z. Wahrscheinlichkeitstheorie verw. Geb.* 26, pp. 157–170.

Hansen, Lars Peter, 1982. "Asymptotic Properties of Generalized Method of Moments Estimators," *Econometrica,* 50, pp. 1029–1054.

Haubrich, Joseph G. and Andrew W. Lo., 1989. "The Sources and Nature of Long-Term Memory in the Business Cycle," NBER Working Paper no. 2951, Cambridge, MA.

Jorion, Philippe, 1988. "On Jump Processes in the Foreign Exchange and Stock Markets," *Review of Financial Studies,* 1, pp. 427–445.

Lamoureux, Christopher G. and William D. Lastrapes, 1990. "Persistence in Variance, Structural Change and the GARCH Model," *Journal of Business and Economic Statistics,* 8, pp. 225–234.

Lee, Sang-Won and Bruce E. Hansen, 1991. "Asymptotic Properties of the Maximum Likelihood Estimator and Test of the Stability of Parameters of the GARCH and IGARCH Models," manuscript.

Loretan, Mico S. and Peter C.B. Phillips, 1992. "Testing the Covariance Stationarity of Heavy-Tailed Time Series: An Overview of the Theory with Applications to Several Financial Datasets," Journal of Empirical Finance, January, pp. 211–248.

Lumsdaine, Robin L., 1989. "Asymptotic Properties of the Maximum Likelihood Estimator in GARCH(1,1) and IGARCH(1,1) Models," manuscript, Harvard University.

Meese, Richard A. and Kenneth S. Rogoff, 1983. "Empirical Exchange Rate Models of the Seventies: Do They Fit Out of Sample?", *Journal of International Economics*, 14, pp. 3–24.

Meese, Richard A. and Andrew K. Rose, 1991. "An Empirical Assessment of Non-Linearities in Models of Exchange Rate Determination," *Review of Economic Studies*, 58, pp. 603–618.

Newey, Whitney K., and Kenneth D. West, 1987. "A Simple, Positive Semidefinite, Hetroskedasticity and Autocorrelation Consistent Covariance Matrix," *Econometrica*, 55, pp. 703–708.

———, 1993. "Automatic Lag Selection in Covariance Matrix Estimation," NBER Technical Working Paper no. 144, Cambridge, MA.

Pagan, Adrian R., and G. William Schwert, 1990a. "Alternative Models for Conditional Stock Volatility," *Journal of Econometrics*, 45, pp. 267–290.

———, 1990b. "Testing for Covariance Stationarity in Stock Market Data," *Economics Letters*, 33, pp. 165–170.

Pagan, Adrian R., and Aman Ullah, 1990a. "Chapter 3: Methods of Density Estimation," manuscript, University of Rochester.

———, 1990b. "Chapter 4: Non-Parametric Estimation of Conditional Moments," manuscript, University of Rochester.

Reinsel, Greg, 1980. "Asymptotic Properties of Prediction Errors for the Multivariate Autoregressive Model Using Estimated Parameters," *Journal of the Royal Statistical Society*, B, pp. 328–333.

Schwert, G. William, 1989a. "Business Cycles, Financial Crises and Stock Volatilit," in *IMF Policy Advice, Market Volatility, Commodity Price Rules and Other Essays* edited by K. Brunner and A. H. Meltzer, pp. 83–126. Carnegie Rochester Series on Public Policy No. 31, Rochester, NY.

Schwert, G. William, 1989b, "Why Does Stock Market Volatility Change over Time?", *Journal of Finance*, 44, pp. 1115–1154.

West, Kenneth D., 1993, "Asymptotic Inference About Predictive Ability," manuscript, University of Wisconsin.

West, Kenneth D., Edison, Hali J., and Dongchul Cho, 1993. "A Utility Based Comparison of Some Models of Exchange Rate Volatility," *Journal of International Economics*, 35, pp. 23–45.

White, Halbert, 1984. *Asymptotic Theory for Econometricians*, New York: Academic Press.

5   Liberalization of capital flows in Korea

Big-bang or gradualism?*

1.   Introduction

Economic liberalizations and deregulation have become general trends in the era of globalization. The Korean economy is no exception to this trend. Despite the miraculous performance under the government-led growth strategy, Korea began to terminate some regulatory policies in the 1980s and accelerated the liberalization process in the 1990s. With respect to external sectors of the economy, the Korean government introduced a market-based exchange rate system in 1990 and began to open the official capital markets in 1992 by partially allowing foreigners to invest directly in Korean stock markets. Since then, the process of capital market deregulation has become an irreversible trend. The only remaining matter seems to be how fast the liberalization process will, or should, be carried out.

With the current level of interest rate differentials between Korea and developed economies, drastic full-scale liberalization would certainly induce a large amount of capital inflows and appreciate the Korean won. This would affect the price competitiveness of Korean products in international markets, which could bring about significant macro-instability in an economy like Korea which relies heavily upon external transactions. An urgent question among Korean policymakers is whether there exists any policy combination that could minimize the macro-instability associated with the unavoidable trend of capital market liberalization.

This chapter attempts to provide some quantitative, though very crude, assessments of several alternative policy choices. In order to perform simulation exercises, we set up a structural macro-model based on the neoclassical long-run convergence and the Keynesian short-run dynamics. Since the economic environments of the future, particularly in relation to the external capital transactions and the exchange rate determination, will be completely different from those of the past, there are undoubtedly limitations to what we can learn from past data.[1] For this reason, we employ theoretical relationships rather than only utilizing regression results for some parts of the model.

Section 2 reviews recent developments of the exchange rate system and capital market liberalization in Korea, as well as the movements of some relevant macro-variables. Section 3 briefly explains the econometric macro-model used in this chapter and Section 4 presents the simulation results. Section 5 provides concluding remarks.

2.   Capital flows and related macro-variables in Korea

2.1   *Exchange rate system*

With the abandonment of the fixed exchange rate system in 1980, the exchange rate began to float by being pegged to a basket of multiple foreign exchange rates. Nevertheless, the government continued to exercise great discretionary power under the name of "policy considerations", the most important of which seemed to be the maintenance of the current account balance.[2]

It was recognized, however, that the operation with the exchange rate as an independent policy tool would not be possible since Korea's capital markets would no longer be insulated from the gigantic world capital market. To prepare for the forthcoming capital account liberalization process, the "Multiple Basket Peg System" was finally replaced in March, 1990, with the "Market Average Exchange Rate System". Under the new system, the exchange rate is determined by demands for and supplies of the Korean won vis-a-vis foreign exchanges, and the government can affect the exchange rate only indirectly through the market. Although the Korean government still appears to be a major player in the exchange market for the Korean won, its relative market power will certainly diminish as the capital markets of Korea become integrated with the world market.

2.2   Capital market liberalization to date

In Korea, capital market liberalization proceeded gradually, taking into account such factors as the current account balance, money supply, and exchange rate. For example, when the current account showed large deficits in the first half of the 1980s (see Figure 5.1), capital outflows were strictly restricted to slow down the pace of foreign debt accumulation. This situation was completely reversed in the latter half of the 1980s. A large amount of current account surplus, reaching 7.8 percent of GDP in 1988, forced the Korean government to decontrol capital outflows. As a result, the net level of foreign debt plunged from 37.7 percent of GDP in 1985 to 1.4 percent in 1989. But the increased capital outflows were insufficient in containing the growth of reserve money (see Figure 5.2). Hence, private credits were restricted and massive sterilization was conducted through monetary stabilization bonds.[3]

However, controls on capital flows became increasingly difficult as the Korean economy got more integrated into the global economy. Foreign investors, as well as domestic companies, constantly demanded a wider opening of Korean markets to exploit the big interest differential with overseas markets. To meet their demands to a certain degree, a capital account liberalization plan was finally announced in 1993.[4]

Korean residents now have a great deal of freedom as far as capital outflows are concerned.[5] But considerable restrictions still remain on capital inflows.[6] These restrictions on capital inflows are not expected to be removed in the near future unless the interest rate differential substantially narrows.

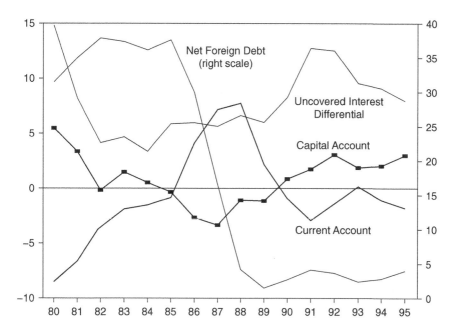

Figure 5.1 External balances as percentage of GDP

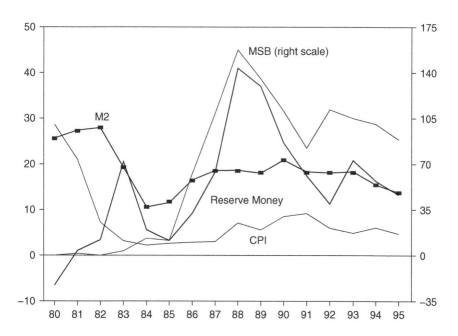

Figure 5.2 Annual monetary and CPI growth rates in percent

2.3   Capital flows and interest rate differential

Since external capital flows were tightly controlled in Korea, the capital account balance was extremely insensitive to the uncovered interest differential.[7] Using the actual rate of the won/dollar exchange rate depreciation as a proxy variable for the expected rate, $\log (e_{t+1}/e_t)$, Table 5.1 shows the results of the regressions of the capital account balance (normalized by potential GDP), k_t, on $i_t - i_t^f - \log (e_{t+1}/e_t)$, where i_t and i_t^f denote the domestic and foreign interest rates at time t, respectively. If capital were perfectly mobile across national borders and there were no uncertainty, this coefficient would in principle approach infinity so that only the exchange rate can, and should, adjust to restore the equilibrium.[8] While the short-term capital account (skb_t) shows a small but significant positive correlation, the long-term capital account (lkb_t) yields a negative correlation.

Although the correlations between the capital account and the uncovered interest rate differential are not strong, it seems clear that the capital account has become more responsive to the interest differential. As a piece of evidence, Table 5.1 reports the results of the regressions in which a linear time trend is included in the regression coefficient: the time trend appears significant in both skb_t and lkb_t regressions.[9] In particular, the estimates for the kb_t regression imply that the coefficient turned to a positive number in 1991, approximately the same time that the stock market began to open to foreign investors.

Table 5.1 Capital flow and uncovered interest rate differential

		$i_t - i_t^* - \log (e_{t+1}/e_t)$		
	constant *(×10⁻²)*	*no time-trend*	*t-1995*	R^2
skb_t	−0.03 (0.13)	0.04 (1.81)		0.06
lkb_t	1.26 (2.83)	−0.11 (2.63)		0.12
lkb_t	1.23 (2.38)	−0.07 (1.47)		0.04
lkb_t	−0.13 (0.54)	0.09 (2.45)	0.01 (1.69)	0.11
lkb_t	0.88 (2.15)	0.09 (1.33)	0.04 (3.76)	0.32
lkb_t	0.76 (1.63)	0.18 (2.39)	0.04 (4.14)	0.29

Notes: skb_t, lkb_t and kb_t denote short-term, long-term, and total capital account balance (normalized by potential GDP), and i_t, i_t^f, and e_t denote domestic interest rate (yield rate of 3-year corporate bond), foreign interest rate (3-month euro-dollar rate), and won/dollar exchange rate, respectively. The sample period is 1983:I to 1995:IV, and numbers in parentheses are t-statistics. The linear time trend, t-1995, is normalized so that t = 1995 yields 0. For further details, see the text.

2.4 Secular trend of the interest rate

The annual yield rate of three-year corporate bonds in Korea is still around 12 percent, which implies approximately 7 percent of real interest rate, given the approximately 5 percent of annual inflation rate. Under this circumstance, it is clear that, for foreign investors, Korea is an attractive market that has not yet been sufficiently explored. Then the most relevant question to our analysis in this chapter is what maintains the high (real) interest rate in Korea and how it will evolve over time.

Figure 5.3 plots three series of interest rates: the official bank loan rate, the yield rate of three-year corporate bonds, and the curb market rate, all of which are converted into real terms by subtracting the actual inflation rates. It is well known that the official interest rates on bank loans as well as corporate bonds were maintained at levels far below the market rate by severe government controls in Korea until the first half of the 1980s. Although the gap between the official rates and the curb market rate substantially narrowed down as a result of the continuous financial deregulations in the 1980s, the curb market rate seemed to be a better measure for the market rate at least until the first half of the 1980s. From Figure 5.3, it appears clear that the curb market rate has been in a downward secular trend from more than 20 percent in the early 1970s to around 7 percent in 1995. Using the corporate bond rate, which is widely used as the representative market rate in the 1990s, we can also find a similar downward trend if the sample period is restricted to a recent period, say, 1983–1995.

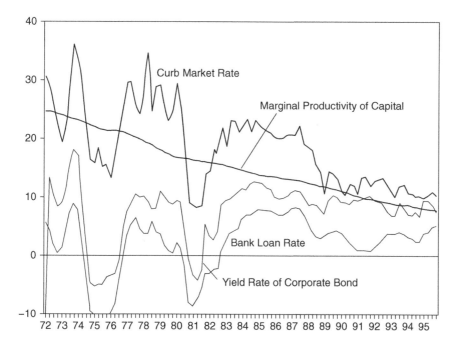

Figure 5.3 Trend of real interest rate (%)

We interpret this downward trend of the real interest rate as evidence for the transitional dynamics of the neoclassical growth model. In a stylized neoclassical growth model, employing the Cobb-Douglas production function, $Y_t = A_t K_t^{\alpha} L_t^{1-\alpha}$, where Y denotes potential output, A the level of technology, K capital stock, and L the labor supply, the interest rate is equated to the marginal productivity of capital, $\alpha Y_t/K_t$, subtracted by the depreciation rate, δ. In an economy with the initial level of K/L lower than the steady state level, the marginal productivity of capital (hence interest rate) declines over time to converge to the steady state level (say, the world level of the interest rate).

In order to be convinced that the transitional dynamics was a plausible description for the secular trend of the Korean interest rate, we also plotted in Figure 5.3 rough estimates of $\alpha Y_t/K_t - \delta$ using $\alpha = 1/3$ and $\delta = 0.066$ per year,[10] which appear to aptly describe the trend of the curb rate. It may be worthwhile to note here that the average growth rate of investment has been far greater than the average growth rate of GDP in Korea since the 1960s.[11] This was the main cause of the declining trend of Y_t/K_t, and it seems unlikely that the trend will suddenly reverse its direction. In order to reflect the downward trend in the long run, therefore, we include $\alpha Yt/Kt - \delta$ in the interest rate specification along with other commonly used variables, such as money supply (see the Appendix for details).

3.   A brief description of the empirical model

The model we used for the simulations is basically neoclassical in the long run, but Keynesian in the short run (details are in the Appendix). That is, all the real variables are determined by the supply side in the long run, which follows the transitional dynamics explained in Subsection 2.4.[12] In the short run, however, demand shocks do matter as in a typical Keynesian model.[13]

Technically, the way we distinguish the long-run from the short-run phenomena is by employing error correction types of specifications in which only the long-run determinants are included in the error correcting terms. That way, the effects of all the other short-run (say, stationary) disturbances eventually disappear, leaving only the effects of long-run determinants. For example, the interest rate is affected by many factors like money supply in the short run, but it will eventually converge to the sum of the inflation rate and capital productivity. What then becomes important for the short-run effects is the speed of convergence toward the long-run equilibrium levels, which we let the data determine from the regressions.[14]

We used quarterly data from 1983.I through 1995.IV for the regressions,[15] although the simulation results will be presented in annual terms. For the future projection, we took the simplest case of the exogenous variables that are presented in Table 5.2. Particularly important is the foreign interest rate in real terms that we assumed to be 4 percent throughout the simulation period.[16]

We are aware of many limitations of our empirical model in particular as well as the simulation experiments in general. After all, the shortcomings of policy simulations using econometric models in general have well been recognized since Lucas (1976). Our model is also far from flawless. Perhaps the most important

Table 5.2 Assumptions about the growth rates of the exogenous variables (unit: %)

	Big-Bang (e)	Gradualism (e)	Gradualism (M)
Y_t^f	3.0	3.0	3.0
P_t^f	2.5	2.5	2.5
i_t^f	7.5	7.5	7.5
L_t^*	2.2	2.2	2.2
e_t	–	–	800
$\bar{M}_t$	14.0 (1996–2000)	14.0 (1996–2000)	–
	13.0 (2001–2005)	13.0 (2001–2005)	–
$\bar{B}_t$	14.0 (1996–2000)	14.0 (1996–2000)	–
	13.0 (2001–2005)	13.0 (2001–2005)	–

Note: See the Appendix for the definitions of the variables.

flaw is that the model is basically backward-looking. For example, the "expected" rate of inflation is simply computed from the past series of the inflation rate, rather than going through the rational expectations of the monetary policy reactions. Our application for forward-looking behavior to determine the exchange rate may then be considered inconsistent with the other parts of the model. Nevertheless, we hope that the following experiments can provide useful, though rough, quantitative assessment about the effects of capital market liberalization in Korea.

4. Simulation results

4.1 A benchmark case: no capital flows

As shown in Figure 5.1, Korea has been maintaining net capital inflows by about 2 percent of GDP since 1992. Therefore, an abrupt shut-down of external capital markets may be interpreted as a regressive big-bang case. We experimented with this case to see how the model works and to obtain the benchmark values of the relevant variables that will be compared with their dynamic paths under different regimes.

In this benchmark case, capital cannot flow to freely seek for higher returns and thus the interest parity does not hold. Specifically, we let the exchange rate adjust to restore the current account balance by $e_{t+1} = e_t \, EXP(-\beta \, cb_t)$, where cb_t is the current account balance normalized by the potential GDP and the parameter for the adjustment speed, β, was estimated from the data. That is, we assume that capital account transactions are just passively adjusted to support current account transactions. This specification of the exchange rate may be interpreted as a policy reaction function that aims at the current account balance using the current account performance as a measure of the exchange rate misalignment, which appears to fit Korean data in the 1980s.[17]

Although we will not report the results for this case, we could get a rough idea of the real exchange rate that would be consistent with the current account balance (called PPP rate, hereafter). Given the assumptions about all the exogenous variables, this value appears to be around 800 won per dollar in the beginning of 1996. In addition, we could confirm that the real interest rate gradually declines to 4.3 percent in 2005, which is mainly generated by the projection of the secular downward trend in the model (see the Appendix for details). It is also confirmed that the rate of CPI inflation converged to around 3 percent under the assumption of the money supply and the labor growth rate.

In the following, the discussion will focus on the results of three cases that differ in the speed of capital market liberalization and the exchange rate policy. Table 5.3 summarizes the exchange rate dynamics and associated money supply mechanisms for each of the three cases, and Figures 5.4A–4L report the simulation results.

Table 5.3 Exchange rate and money supply determination mechanism

	Exchange Rate (e_t)	Money Supply (M_t)
Big-Bang (e)	$e_{t+1} = e_t \, EXP(i_t - i_t^f)$	$M_t = \bar{M}_t$ (exogenous)
Gradualism (e)	$e_{t+1} = e_t \, EXP\{i_t - i_t^f - kb_t/(7.5/(2010 - t)))\}$	$M_t = \bar{M}_t$ (exogenous)
Gradualism (M)	$e_t = 800$	$M_t = \bar{M}_t + 5 \, (KB_t + CB_t)$

Note: We used 5 as the money multiplier in the *Mt* specification of the Gradualism.

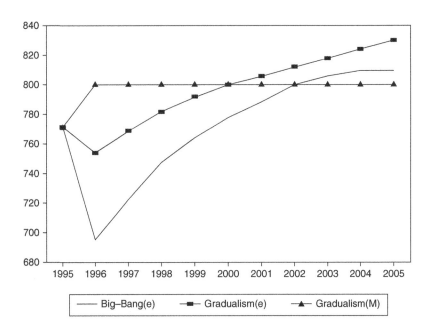

Figure 5.4A Exchange rate (won/dollar)

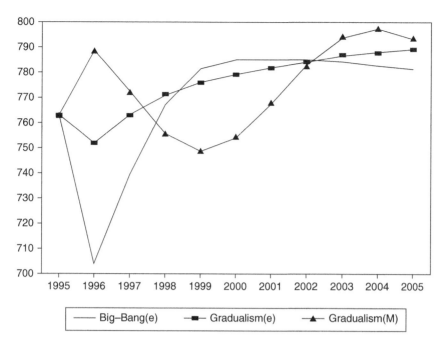

Figure 5.4B Real exchange rate (won/dollar in 1990 prices)

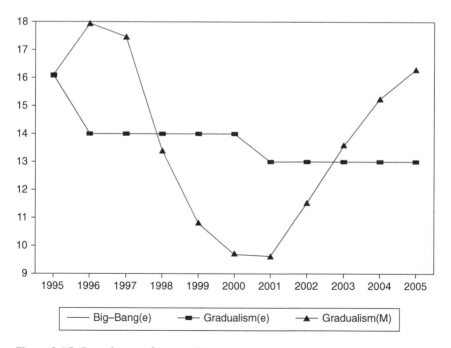

Figure 5.4C Growth rate of money (%)

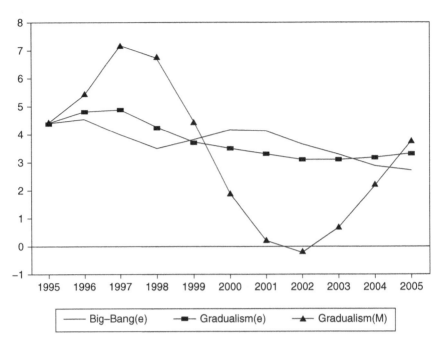

Figure 5.4D Rate of CPI inflation (%)

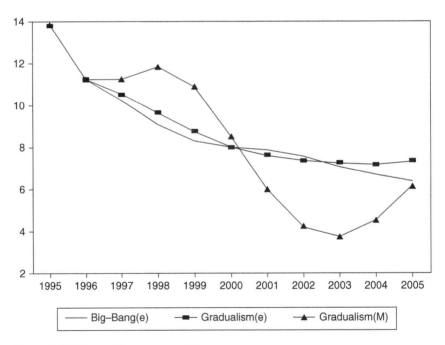

Figure 5.4E Nominal interest rate (%)

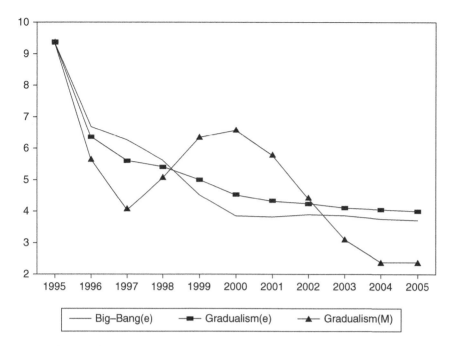

Figure 5.4F Real interest rate (%)

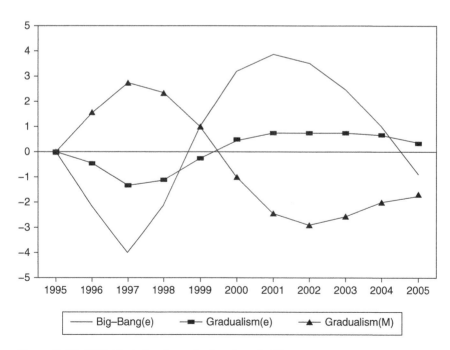

Figure 5.4G GDP (deviation from the benchmark, %)

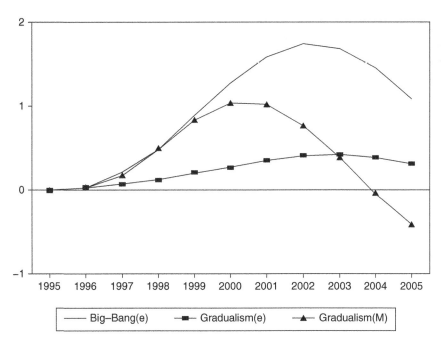

Figure 5.4H Potential output (deviation from the benchmark, %)

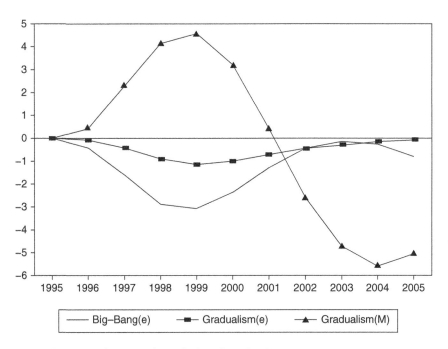

Figure 5.4I CPI (deviation from the benchmark, %)

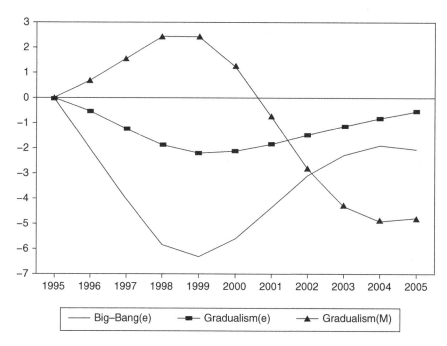

Figure 5.4J PPI (deviation from the benchmark, %)

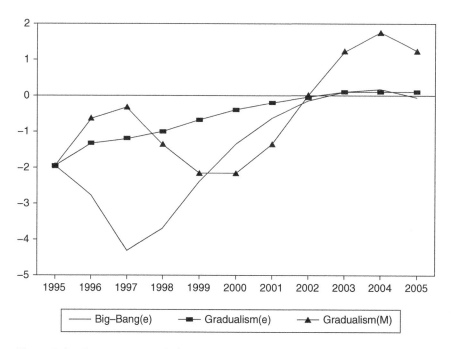

Figure 5.4K Current account balance to GDP ratio (%)

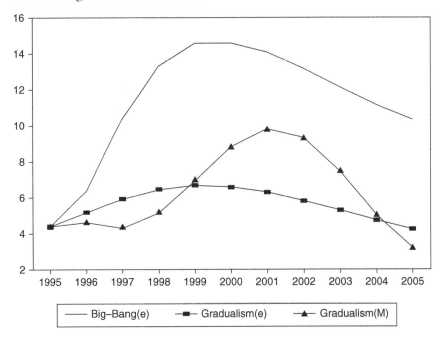

Figure 5.4L Net foreign debt to GDP ratio (%)

4.2   Big-bang

We envision that "perfect capital mobility" is the case in which the uncovered interest parity holds (or the elasticity of kb_t with respect to $i_t - i_t^f - \log(e_{t+1}/e_t)$ is infinity in Table 5.1). In this case, the most active role is assigned to capital account transactions concerning the exchange rate determination, and the current account simply responds to the exchange rate movements. We assume that this new regime of the exchange rate dynamics suddenly replaced the old one at the beginning of 1996. As will be explained below, the only sustainable policy in this case is to let the exchange rate adjust.

4.2.1   Exchange rate adjustment

If the government let the exchange rate absorb the interest rate differential in the case of "big-bang", the exchange rate dynamics can be specified by,

$$e_{t+1} = et\ EXP(i_t - i_t^f),$$

while the money supply is controlled by the government. In order to pin e_t down in the simulation, a terminal condition is needed as in other forward-looking dynamic models. We tried several values for the initial e_t and picked the associated dynamic path of e_t that yielded the most consistent results with the path of i_t at the terminal year, 2005. Since i_t almost converges to $i_t{}^f$ by 2005 (6.5 percent = 4 percent of real rate + 2.5 percent of inflation rate in this case), the real exchange rate should also converge to the PPP rate that was roughly calculated in the benchmark case.

A typical sticky-price monetary-model (Dornbusch,1976), for example) would predict the results for this case. The exchange rate initially jumps to appreciate by approximately 15 percent[18] and then gradually depreciates by the interest differential until it converges to the PPP rate around 2005 (Figure 5.4A). The interest rate declines faster than the benchmark case because of the more active investment[19] and the resulting capital accumulation (Figure 5.4E). The potential output also increases rapidly (Figure 5.4H), but the economy goes through a short-run recession for the first 2–3 years (Figure 5.4G) due to the contraction of foreign demand that is caused by the exchange rate appreciation. Prices, particularly PPI, which is far more affected by import prices, become very stable (Figures 5.4I and 5.4J). But the current account deficit reaches almost 5 percent of GDP in 1997 (Figure 5.4K) and then approaches the balance, rapidly accumulating (net) foreign debt to 15 percent by 1999 (Figure 5.4L).[20]

4.2.2 Exchange rate targeting

Policymakers often fear the rapid accumulation of foreign debt, thereby seeking for exchange rate stability. To see the effects of this policy, therefore, we set the nominal exchange rate at 800 won/dollar, which appears to be approximately consistent with the current account balance at the beginning of 1996. Since the interest parity should hold in this big-bang case, the only way to support the nominal exchange rate stability ($e_{t+1} = e_t$ for all t) is to equate the domestic interest rate to the foreign rate $i_t - i_t{}^f$ for all t.[21]

For the expansionary monetary policy to lower i_t to the level of $i_t{}^f$, we could easily confirm unsustainability: the model exploded no later than 1998 with more than 100 percent of inflation.[22] The initial monetary expansion to set $i_t - i_t{}^f$ brings about inflation, hence i_t begins to rise, which requires the accelerating monetary expansion to keep $i_t - i_t{}^f$. If the interest rate gap is not so wide and the gap is expected to narrow down soon by a third factor, then a temporary expansion of the money supply may be a reasonable choice. But Korea's current situation does not seem to be such a case. As a means of saving space, we did not report the results of this experiment.

Another, though arguable, way to lower i_t may be to run an extremely large budget surplus.[23] From many regressions of the interest rate on the public bonds, however, we only found an extremely small and statistically insignificant elasticity. The interest rate equation in the Appendix is the one that yielded the largest elasticity with respect to the public bonds. Even with this largest elasticity, a simple calculation shows that the required amount of the outstanding bond reduction to equate i_t to $i_t{}^f$ would be 30 to 50 percent of GDP, or two times larger than the current level of total government expenditure, which would be impossible to achieve.

4.3 Gradual liberalization

A general consensus of the empirical literature seems that, while the covered interest parity holds, the uncovered interest parity does not exactly hold even among the countries maintaining the most liberalized capital markets.[24] Considering this empirical finding, it may be rather reasonable to assume that the elasticity of kb_t with respect to $i_t - i_t^f - \log(e_{t+1}/e_t)$ is finite. Particularly for the case of Korea, in which the capital markets are expected to open gradually, we assume that this elasticity (denoted $f(t)$ below) will be increasing at a gradual pace over time:

$$kb_t = f(t)\{i_t - i_t^f - \log(e_{t+1}/e_t)\},$$

where $f(t) > 0$ for all t, $f'(t) > 0$ One can regard the big-bang case as the limiting case in which $f(t)$ goes to infinity from the beginning. We have experimented many specifications of $f(t)$ As can be easily reasoned, the general rule of thumb is that the more rapidly $f(t)$ increases, the closer the results are to the big-bang case: the initial appreciation of the exchange rate is larger, or the model is more likely to explode with the exchange rate targeting.

In this chapter, we only present the results for $f(t) = 7.5/(2010 - t)$, which is one of the most gradual processes we have tried; so gradual that the exchange rate targeting does not explode. The rationale of this specification is that (a) the Korean government will completely open capital markets by the year 2010, when the Korean interest rate is expected to be sufficiently close to the world rate ($f(t)$ goes to infinity for $t = 2010$); and (b) f(1995) = 0.5 is close to the actual elasticity in 1995.[25]

While this specification is tractable, the most critical question behind this gradual process is how sustainable the gradualism itself would be under the potential threat of speculative attacks. The assumption that capital flows are only partially responsive to the interest rate differential hinges on the presumption that potential speculators are limited with the amount of foreign currency transactions. That is, the big proviso of a successful gradualism appears to be the controllability of the quantity of foreign currency inflows until the interest rate differential narrows down, say, by the year 2000.

4.3.1 Exchange rate adjustment

This case is basically the same as the case of big-bang with exchange rate overshooting, except for the magnitudes. The exchange rate determined by $e_{t+1} = e_t \ EXP\{i_t - i_t^f - kb_t/(7.5/(2010 - t)))\}$ initially jumps to appreciate to a relatively mild extent and then depreciates over time until it reaches the PPP rate (Gadualism(e) in Figures 5.4A and 5.4B). The directions of all the other results are the same as the big-bang case, but the magnitudes are smaller.

4.3.2 Exchange rate targeting

Perhaps a more interesting case for the gradual liberalization is the one in which the government policy to fix the nominal exchange rate is sustainable. Since kb_t is not only finite but rather insensitive to the interest rate differential, the government is given much larger room for policymaking.

We fixed the exchange rate at 800 won/dollar as in subsection 4.2.2 and let the central bank accommodate additional money demand to the same extent as the overall balance surplus. Since the level of the exchange rate initially yields approximately the current account balance (Gradualism(M) in Figure 5.4K), the money supply expands almost as much as the capital account surplus, which will inevitably generate faster inflation.

This inflation yields opposite effects on the subsequent money supply. On the one hand, it raises the nominal interest rate and thus more capital inflows, which increases the money supply. On the other hand, however, the inflation appreciates the real exchange rate and the current account turns into deficit, which decreases the money supply. The relative size of the two effects depends on the specification of $f(t)$, but under the case of the very gradual liberalization, $f(t) = 7.5/(2010 - t)$, the latter effect dominates and the money supply declines (Figure 5.4C).[26] The monetary contraction then pushes the economy further into a deep recession, which is about to enter into recession in 1999 after the boom generated by the initial monetary expansion (Figure 5.4G). The deep recession further decreases the rate of inflation (Figure 5.4D), and the nominal interest rate finally drops below the world rate in 2001 (Figure 5.4E), which brings about capital flight out of the country, along with current account surplus from 2002 (Figure 5.4K). While the foreign debt accumulates less than the big-bang case (Figure 5.4L), the potential level of output is smaller (Figure 5.4H), and the economy goes through a similar magnitude of macro-instability in the opposite direction (Figure 5.4G).

Under this gradual liberalization plan and the expected downward trend of the interest rate, the sterilized intervention for the exchange rate stability appears to be sustainable as well as sensible for macro-stability.[27] In order to avoid the initial recession and current account deficit, however, the government should bear the burden of public debt. In other words, the external debt that would otherwise accumulate is replaced by the internal debt of the government (incurring higher interest rates). The benefit is gaining macro-stability, while the cost is foregoing opportunity to exploit foreign savings to enhance the potential capacity of the economy.

5. Conclusion

We have presented rough estimates of the dynamic paths for important macro-variables under several different liberalization scenarios. Fully admitting the limitations of our experiments, we believe that the experiments can provide more concrete ideas of where the economy will be heading for each case.

Among the very many possible combinations of the policies, including the speed of market opening, we are not able to pick the "optimal" one that totally depends on the objective function of policymakers. If the objective is simply to maximize the potential capacity of the economy with price stability, the big-bang in conjunction with the exchange rate overshooting should be recommended. But in this case, policymakers have to convince people that a sweet boom will arrive after the painful recession for the initial couple of years, and that the current account will turn into surplus after, say, ten years.

Perhaps the time horizon here is too long for policymakers, and even when based on economics criteria, it is not clear whether maximizing the potential level at the expense of a recession is the best choice. If it is not, a gradual liberalization process can be recommended. A critical justification for gradualism is then the secular downward trend of the interest rate, and the key to a successful gradualism seems to be the controllability over the quantity of foreign currency inflows. In any case, however, we completely leave unanswered the question of: how gradual is "optimal"?

APPENDIX: THE MODEL

Variable	Content
A	technical level
B	public bond
C^G	government consumption expenditure
C^P	private consumption expenditure
e	exchange rate
I	gross fixed capital formation
KB	capital balance
K	capital stock
L	total labor employed
M	money supply (M2)
MG	imports
MPK	marginal productivity of capital
MPL	marginal productivity of labor
P^c	consumer price index
P^P	producer price index
P^x	unit value index of exports
P^M	unit value index of imports
P^f	foreign wholesale price Index
P^o	unit import price of oil
i	interest rate
i^f	foreign interest rate
t	time trend (quarterly period)
W	wage
XG	exports
Y	gross domestic product
Y^f	foreign GDP
π	CPI inflation rate
τ	tax rate

Notes:
1) * denotes potential level.

2) Δ denotes first difference.

Identities

Definition of Capital Stock (Annual Depreciation Rate of 0.066):

$$K_t = (1 - 0.066/4) \ K_{t-1} + (1/4)(I_t + I_{t-1} + I_{t-2} + I_{t-3})$$

Trend of Labor Force (Annual Increase Rate of 0.028):

$$L_t = EXP(0.02837 \cdot t/4 - 46.6687)$$

Aggregate Production Function (Capital Income Share of 1/3):

$$Y_t^* = A_t \cdot K_t^{1/3} \cdot L_t^{2/3}$$

Technology Progress Rate (Annual Increase Rate of 0.022):

$$A_t = EXP(0.02254 \cdot t/4 - 44.9738)$$

Productivity of Labor:

$$MPL_t = (2/3) Y_t^* / L_t$$

Productivity of Capital (4 to be annualized):

$$MPK_t = (4/3) Y_t^* / K_t$$

Trend of Capital Productivity[1]:

$$MPK_t^* = 0.10 + (4/3) \ EXP(-0.06447 \cdot t/4 + 125.355)$$

Trend of Capital Stock[2]:

$$K_t^* = \left[(3/4) \ A_t / MPK_t^*\right]^{3/2} \cdot L_t$$

Trend of Consumer Price Level:

$$P_t^* = (M_t / Y_t^*) \ EXP(-0.03157 \cdot t/4 + 67.0944)$$

Definition of the Inflation Rate:

$$\pi_t = \log(P_t^C / P_{t-4}^C)$$

Definition of GDP:

$$Y_t = C_t^P + C_t^G + I_t + XG_t + MG_t$$

Notes:
1) This is obtained by regressing $\log(MPK_t - 0.10)$ on t so that MPK_t and the real interest rate converge to 10 percent and 3.4 (= 10.0 − 6.6) percent, respectively.
2) K_t^* is determined by the exogenous time trend alone.

Regression equations[1]

$$\Delta \log\left(C_t^p\right) = 0.26 \cdot \Delta \log\left((1-\tau_t)\,\Upsilon_t\right) + 0.17 \cdot \Delta \log\left(M_t/P_t^C\right)$$
$$\quad(8.09)\qquad\qquad\qquad\qquad(1.70)$$

$$-0.09 \cdot \left[\,\log(C_{t-1}^p/\Upsilon_{t-1})\right] - 0.06$$
$$\quad(2.23)\qquad\qquad\qquad\quad(2.27)$$

$$\Delta \log\left(I_t\right) = -0.31 \cdot \Delta \log\left(I_{t-1}\right) + 0.26 \cdot \Delta \log\left(XG_t\right) + 0.29 \cdot kb_t$$
$$\quad(2.65)\qquad\qquad\quad(1.98)\qquad\qquad\qquad(1.10)$$

$$-0.53 \cdot \left(i_t - \pi_t - MPK_t\right) - 0.30 \cdot \left[\log(K_{t-1}/K_{t-1})\right] - 0.28$$
$$\quad(1.44)\qquad\qquad\qquad\qquad(1.34)\qquad\qquad\qquad(7.04)$$

$$\Delta \log\left(XG_t\right) = 0.30 \cdot \Delta \log(P_{t-2}^f/P_{t-2}^x) - 0.16 \cdot \left[\log\left(XG_{t-1}\right) - 3.04 \cdot \log\left(\Upsilon_{t-1}^f\right)\right]$$
$$\quad(2.33)\qquad\qquad\qquad\qquad(2.11)\qquad\qquad\qquad(36.75)$$

$$-0.12$$
$$\quad(9.75)$$

$$\Delta \log\left(MG_t\right) = 0.21 \cdot \Delta \log(I_t) + 0.27 \cdot \Delta \log\left(I_{t-1}\right) + 0.64 \cdot \Delta \log(C_t^p + C_t^G)$$
$$\quad(1.72)\qquad\qquad\quad(2.32)\qquad\qquad\qquad(0.83)$$

$$+0.17 \cdot \Delta \log\left(XG_t\right) - 0.24 \cdot \Delta \log(e_t \cdot P_t^M/P_t^p)$$
$$\quad(1.19)\qquad\qquad\qquad(1.83)$$

$$-0.15 \cdot \left[\log(MG_{t-1}/XG_{t-1})\right] + 1.67$$
$$\quad(2.03)\qquad\qquad\qquad\qquad(1.92)$$

$$i_t = 0.79 \cdot i_{t+1} + 0.02 \cdot \Delta \log\left(I_t\right) - 0.12 \cdot \Delta \log(M_{t-1}/P_{t-1}^c)$$
$$\quad(11.51)\qquad(1.51)\qquad\qquad(1.98)$$

$$-0.01 \cdot \log\left(M_{t-1}/B_{t-1}\right) + 0.21 \cdot \left[(\pi_{t-1} + MPK_{t-1} - 0.066)\right] + 0.0002$$
$$\quad(1.31)\qquad\qquad\qquad\qquad(3.03)\qquad\qquad\qquad\qquad(0.04)$$

$$\Delta \log\left(W_t\right) = -0.34 \cdot \Delta \log(W_{t-1}) + 0.35 \cdot \log(\Upsilon_t/\Upsilon_t{}^*)$$
$$\quad(2.43)\qquad\qquad\qquad(3.34)$$

$$-0.05 \cdot \left[\log\left(W_{t-1}/P_{t-1}^c\right) - \log(MPL_{t-1})\right] + 0.36$$
$$\quad(1.42)\qquad\qquad\qquad\qquad\qquad(1.31)$$

$$\Delta\log\left(P_t^c\right) = 0.19 \cdot \Delta\log\left(P_{t-1}^p\right) + 0.09 \cdot \log\left(\Upsilon_t / \Upsilon_t *\right)$$
$$(1.54) \qquad\qquad (3.39)$$

$$-0.07 \cdot \left[\log(P_{t-1}^c / P_{t-1}^*)\right] + 0.02$$
$$(1.97) \qquad\qquad (11.07)$$

$$\Delta\log\left(P_t^c\right) = 0.04 \cdot \Delta\log\left(W_{t-1} / MPL_{t-1}\right) + 0.39 \cdot \Delta\log(P_t^c)$$
$$(1.82) \qquad\qquad (4.01)$$

$$+0.12 \cdot \Delta\log(e_t \cdot P_t^M)$$
$$(4.23)$$

$$-0.09 \cdot \left[\log\left(P_{t-1}^c\right) - 0.26 \cdot \log\left(P_{t-1}^c\right) - 0.74 \cdot \log(e_{t-1} \cdot P_{t-1}^M)\right] - 0.004$$
$$(2.49) \qquad\qquad (3.53) \qquad\qquad (13.53) \qquad\qquad (2.14)$$

$$\Delta\log\left(P_t^x\right) = 0.05 \cdot \Delta\log\left(XG_t\right) + 0.60 \cdot \Delta\log(P_t^p / e_t)$$
$$(2.26) \qquad\qquad (3.56)$$

$$-0.11 \cdot \left[\log\left(P_{t-1}^x\right) - 0.85 \cdot \log(P_{t-1}^p / e_{t-1})\right] + 0.002$$
$$(1.37) \qquad\qquad (17.61) \qquad\qquad (0.73)$$

$$\Delta\log\left(P_t^M\right) = 0.46 \cdot \Delta\log\left(P_t^f\right) + 0.08 \cdot \Delta\log\left(P_t^o\right) + 0.40 \cdot \Delta\log(P_{t-1}^p / e_{t-1})$$
$$(3.02) \qquad\qquad (3.43) \qquad\qquad (2.50)$$

$$-0.17 \cdot \left[\log\left(P_{t-1}^M\right) - 0.82 \cdot \Delta\log\left(P_{t-1}^f\right) - 0.18 \cdot \log(P_{t-1}^o)\right]$$
$$(2.18) \qquad\qquad (49.51) \qquad\qquad (10.74)$$

$$-0.001$$
$$(0.27)$$

Notes:
1) Seasonal Dummies were included, but not reported. Numbers in parentheses are t-statistics and the variables in brackets are error correcting terms.

Notes

* This article is reprinted from *Changes in Exchange Rates in Rapidly Developing Countries*, edited by Takatoshi Ito and Anne Krueger, Chicago Press, pp. 285–308, 1999, which was co-authored with Young-Sun Koh.
1 As a leading example, one can think of Lucas' critique (1976).

2 For details of Korea's exchange rate movements, see Oum and Cho (1995).
3 The outstanding monetary stabilization bonds amounted to 88 percent of the reserve money at the end of 1995.
4 This plan was superseded by the Foreign Exchange Reform Plan in 1994, which in turn was revised in late 1995. Further liberalization was recently announced in April, 1996. For a survey of Korea's liberalization process, see Park (1992).
5 Individuals, as well as institutional investors, can make unlimited investments in overseas securities. Institutional investors can hold deposits in foreign banks up to 100 million dollars, while lower limits apply to legal entities and individuals. Outward foreign direct investment (FDI) is going to be completely liberalized by next year.
6 The regulations are as follows: non-residents as a whole can hold up to 20 percent of the outstanding shares of each company, and each non-resident up to 5 percent; bond-holding by non-residents is allowed indirectly through the Korea Trust and Country Fund; direct holding is allowed only for convertible bonds issued by small and medium enterprises; domestic companies can use foreign commercial loan within certain limits only for the import of capital goods and commercial loans within certain limits only for the import of capital goods and for FDIs; delayed payment for imports is currently permitted for up to 120 days.
7 Since futures or forward markets are not yet established in Korea, we could not test covered interest parity.
8 Considering the forecast error about e_{t+1} at time t, there must be measurement errors in the expected appreciation rate, hence a downward bias in the regression coefficient. Nevertheless, there seems no reason to expect that this bias would change the sign of the coefficient estimate, and the increase in the coefficient estimate over time seems to indicate that the capital flows are getting more sensitive to the uncovered interest differential.
9 We also tried several other specifications for the coefficient to test if there is any convexity over time, but the results were not very different from the linear time trend.
10 The estimates of labor income share, $1 - \alpha$, in Korea range from 60 to 70 percent (see Table 2 in Hong, 1994) and the depreciation rate of capital, δ, is estimated to be 6.6 percent per year by Park (1992).
11 For example, the average annual growth rate of investment during the period of 1970–1995 in Korea is approximately 12 percent, while that of GDP is around 8 percent.
12 See Blanchard and Fischer (1989) for the discussion of dynamic responses of a flexible-price model in relation to the capital market opening of an economy with higher interest rates than the world rate. We take this case only as a long-run phenomenon because we assume in our model that prices are sticky in the short run.
13 While the long-run neutrality of money holds in the model, the super-neutrality does not.
14 In a sense, our model can be viewed as a large vector autoregression system with error-correcting terms. To identify the shocks, we tried to minimize the number of two-way causal relations among contemporary variables. Nevertheless, a few contemporaneous variables remain to cause each other (e.g. consumption and GDP). We did not attempt to correct possible simultaneity bias, hoping that the size of the bias is of negligible magnitudes.

15 The major reason that we restricted the sample period to 1983–1995 is to take the longest period in which the corporate bond rate can be used as the representative interest rate.

16 Barro and Sala-i-Martin (1990), for example, report 3 to 4 percent per year as the acceptable range of the "world real interest rate". We took 4 percent to allow a slight margin for the country risk, so that the capital market will be in balance when the real interest rate in Korea reaches 4 percent.

17 In fact, the Korean government appeared to manage the exchange rate, aiming at the current account balance in the 1980s, See Oum and Cho (1995) for details.

18 This estimate of 15 percent is roughly consistent with the result of a simple algebra using the interest parity and the long-run trend of real interest rate without considering feedback effects of all the other variables of the macro-model. From the observation that the real interest rate declines by approximately 0.3 percent point per year, the cumulative sum of interest differential can be roughly computed by
$$\sum_{t=0}^{10}(r_t - r_t^f) = 15 \text{, for } r_t = 7.0 - 0.3t \text{ and } r_t^f = 4.0.$$

19 More active investment is mostly induced by the relatively low interest rate.

20 Net foreign debt is simply computed as the accumulation of the current account deficit.

21 The reason that i_t should be equal to i_t^f is that we assumed perfect foresight of investors.

22 The model exploded no matter where the target level of the exchange rate is set.

23 How sensible this statement is depends on whether the Ricardian equivalence holds.

24 This may be due to either the risk-averse behavior of the investors and/or the "irrational" formulation of the agent's expectations, or something else. See Taylor (1995) for a recent survey.

25 In 1995, kb_t was about 3 percent and the interest differential was about 6 percent.

26 If $f(t)$ is less gradual, the model explodes as in the case of big-bang with exchange rate targeting.

27 As mentioned earlier, the effect of the government bonds on the interest rate is negligible.

References

Barro, Robert and Xavier Sala-i-Martin, 1990. "World Real Interest Rates," in NBER *Macroeconomics Annual*, edited by O.J. Blanchard and S. Fischer, pp. 15–74. Cambridge, MA: MIT Press.

Blanchard, Olivier, and Stanley Fischer, 1989. Lectures on Macroeconomics. Cambridge, MA: MIT Press.

Dornbusch, Rudiger, 1976. "Expectations and Exchange Rate Dynamics," *Journal of Political Economy*, 84, December, pp. 1161–1176.

Hong, Sung-Duk, 1994. "An analysis of the Factors for the Korean Growth: 1963–1992," *Korea Development Review*, Fall, pp. 147–178 (in Korean).

Lucas, Robert E., 1976. "Econometric Policy Evaluation: A Critique", in Carnegie-Rochester Conference Series on Public Policy, edited by Karl Brunner and Allan

Meltzer, Vol. 1, pp. 19–46, Rochester, NY: Carnegie-Rochester Conference Series.

Oum, Bong-Sung and Dong-Chul Cho, 1995. "Korea's Exchange Rate Movements in the 1990s: Evaluations and Policy Implications," Presented at the KDI Symposium on Prospects of Yen-Dollar Exchange Rates and Korea's Exchange Rate Policy, Korea Development Institute, Seoul.

Park, Woo-Kyu, 1992. "A Research on Macro-Policy in Korea," KDI Research Chapter Series 92-01, Korea Development Institute, Seoul (in Korean).

Taylor, Mark P., 1995. "The Economics of Exchange Rate," *Journal of Economic Literature*, March, pp. 13–47.

6   Currency crisis of Korea

Internal weakness or external interdependence?*

1.   Introduction

During the 1997 to 1998 period, the international capital market experienced arguably the most severe turmoil since the Great Depression. Many economists as well as international investors were greatly surprised by the magnitude and abruptness of capital flow reversals from the emerging markets.

Perhaps this surprise was amplified by the fact that the crisis took place in East Asia, which has long been regarded as a model economy in the sense of rapid growth along with macro-stability. Especially to the economists and policymakers who have sought the causes and elements of the remarkable achievements in this region (e.g. World Bank, 1993), the Asian crisis came as a shock. Even to those who were skeptic about the "Asian Miracle," the abrupt collapse of the region may not be a natural implication that can be derived from their skepticism. The main implication of the "input-driven growth" (e.g. Krugman, 1994; and Young, 1995) is the erosion of efficiency, and thus the natural prediction would be a long-term slow-down of growth rather than an immediate collapse. For this reason, many have been led to pay more attention to the effects of contagion (e.g. Agenor and Aizenman, 1997; and Perry and Lederman, 1998).

This chapter examines the currency crisis of Korea – a key country of the Asian crisis as well as the Asian Miracle – in the context of this swirl of the international capital market. In particular, this chapter attempts to provide some clues to the question of whether Korea was a poor victim of or a major contributor to the crisis in the global capital market. As expected from this sort of formidable question, the answer will be indefinite.

Nevertheless, this chapter tries to quantitatively distinguish the effects of weaknesses in domestic fundamentals from the effects of external interdependence (called "contagion" effects in this chapter). We found that the magnitudes of contagion effects were huge, but the Korean crisis could not be completely attributable to these effects alone. Weak domestic fundamentals and poor management of the government appeared to play significant roles as well, particularly at the triggering moment of the crisis.

More specifically, the following three conclusions summarize this chapter's analyses. First, the outbreak of the Korean crisis may not be completely attributable to the contagion effects alone, although the crises of other countries substantially worsened the situation. Second, Korea's fundamentals prior to the crisis were not so strong that economists must have been astonished with the outbreak of the crisis of Korea, although they were not distinctively weak for investors to be able to anticipate the forthcoming crisis. Third, if one considered the structural vulnerability of Korea's financial market in addition to the conventional macro-fundamentals, and if one could have foreseen the stubborn policies of the government to cope with financial turmoil, the Korean crisis might have been easier to anticipate.

This chapter is organized as follows. Employing the conventional probit model methodology for data from approximately 100 developing countries, Section 2 evaluates the position of Korea's fundamentals, which are usually considered important in explaining currency crises in developing countries. Among those fundamental factors, Korea's domestic macroeconomic fundamentals were strong (high growth, low inflation, and mild current account deficits), while its external finance structure was fragile (low reserve-to-short-term debt ratios and low FDI-to-GDP ratios). Overall, Korea's fundamentals were not particularly strong but not particularly weak either. It is true that Korea's fundamentals sharply deteriorated in 1996 (and thus raised the probability of a crisis in 1997) compared to the 1994 to 1995 period, but the overall condition in 1996 was not extremely bad relative to its historical average except for the contagion effects. In this section, we also examine the effect of neighbor countries (or "contagion" effect) using our own index of geographical proximity as well as the trade linkage index developed by Glick and Rose (1998). An important finding is that our geographical proximity index dominates the trade linkage index, which may suggest that investors' psychology really matters in transmitting currency crises.

Section 3 takes a further look at the contagion issue, using daily-frequency data of the exchange rates and sovereign spreads on the US dollar denominated debts for selected countries. We use standard time-series methodologies and similar analyses can be found in Baig and Goldfajn (1998). Unlike Baig and Goldfajn, however, we extend the sample to non-Asian countries such as Latin American countries, Russia, China and Japan, while focusing on the case of Korea. By doing so, we are able to provide a more complete picture and explicitly decompose the contribution of the contagion effects from other parts. We also relate the chronology of daily news on Korea's financial market with the shocks identified by the time-series analyses so that we can have some sense about what sort of news operated negatively to the financial market at the triggering moment of the crisis. Overall, we found that the news about the series of *chaebol* bankruptcies and the government's continued bail-out policies for these *chaebols* and financial institutions appeared to operate negatively in preventing foreign investors from fleeing.

Section 4 notes some additional weaknesses in Korea's financial market structure that we think need to be mentioned. In this section, we do not provide a formal analysis to the degree in Sections 2 and 3. Instead, we briefly summarize several points made by other researchers in Korea, so that readers do not miss important aspects of the Korean crisis simply because the effects of those aspects cannot be easily quantified. In particular, we note the facts that the corporate sector of Korea had long suffered from low profitability and high leverage ratios, while a small number of *chaebols* had extraordinarily high influence in the financial system. Section 5 offers some concluding remarks.

2. Domestic fundamentals vs. contagion: cross-country analysis

In this section, we examine Korea's economic fundamentals during the pre-crisis period in comparison with other developing countries and the role of the contagion effect in the outbreak of Korea's currency crisis. To this end, we employ a probit model using a data set of roughly 100 developing countries.

2.1 Theory

Existing theories on currency crises are often classified into two generations of models.[1] While the first-generation model stresses economic fundamentals such as domestic credit expansion and liquidity (Krugman, 1979), the second-generation model puts more emphasis on investors' expectations and inherent instability in the international capital market (Obstfeld, 1994). In empirical investigation of a currency crisis, however, it is hard to distinguish between the two classes of models. Although the second-generation model emphasizes the role of expectations, expectations are likely to be systematically related to economic fundamentals. Thus, in practice, both classes of models commonly predict that the possibility of a currency crisis increases with deterioration of economic fundamentals. The only way to distinguish between the two classes of models is to prove that some crisis episodes are actually generated by "self-fulfilling" expectations. Clearly, this is a difficult task. Referring to this difficulty, Flood et al. (1996) has concluded that the two classes of models are observationally equivalent.

Similar argument applies to the so-called contagion effect. Contagion effect refers to the phenomenon that a currency crisis spreads contagiously from one country to another, for whatever reasons.[2] Since contagion can take place either because of cross-country correlation in economic fundamentals or because of pure investor psychology, the existence of contagion itself cannot be used as evidence for self-fulfilling expectations. For more concrete evidence, one needs to prove existence of contagion after controlling for all relevant economic fundamentals. In practice, however, it is implausible to control for every relevant variable.[3]

For this reason, this section does not intend to test the relevance of a particular model. The goal of this section is simply to estimate a probit equation that relates crisis episodes to standard macroeconomic fundamentals along with contagion measures and to evaluate how well Korea's currency crisis episode fits the model.

2.2 Dependent variable

The dependent variable for our probit estimation is a crisis index, which has a value of 1 if a currency crisis occurs and 0 otherwise. Specifically, following Frankel and Schmukler (1996), we define a currency crisis as depreciation of the nominal exchange rate (with respect to the US dollar) of at least 25 percent that is also at least a 10 percent increase in the rate of depreciation.[4]

2.3 Explanatory variables

For possible causes of a currency crisis, we consider the following three sets of variables:

- Macroeconomic indicators: GDP growth rate, real domestic credit growth, inflation rate, fiscal deficit/GDP ratio.
- External variables: current account/GDP ratio, changes in the terms of trade, changes in the real exchange rate, foreign reserves/short-term debt ratio, FDI/ GDP ratio, total foreign debt/GDP ratio, short-term debt/total foreign debt.
- Foreign conditions: GDP growth rate and interest rate in developed countries, crisis incidents of foreign countries.

Slowdown in the GDP growth rate increases the possibility of a crisis by weakening general solvency of the country or by engendering expansionary monetary policy. Also, rapid expansion of domestic credit or fiscal deficit increases the possibility of a crisis by generating inflationary pressures in the goods market and depreciation pressures in the foreign exchange market. Factors such as deterioration in the terms of trade, appreciation of the real exchange rate, and current account deficit can produce a crisis by reducing both profitability of the exporting sector and net foreign assets of the economy. Lastly, while a high foreign debt/ GDP ratio increases the probability of a crisis by making the country vulnerable to a negative shock, high foreign reserves/short-term debt or FDI/GDP ratios reduce the probability of a crisis through providing greater liquidity.

In addition to domestic fundamentals, foreign conditions can also play a key role in the outbreak of a currency crisis. Since developed countries are the net creditors in the international capital market, an economic boom in developed countries can lead to a reduction in capital supply for developing countries. Among developing countries, a currency crisis in one country may increase the possibility of crisis in another country. As mentioned earlier, this contagion effect may reflect either cross-country correlation in economic fundamentals or merely investors' psychology. In this section, we simply define the contagion index for each country as a weighted average of the crisis index of all other countries, with the weights given by either the inverse of geographical distance between the country in question and other countries or the trade linkage used in Glick and Rose (1998).[5] Since currency crises appear to be regionally concentrated, we suspect that geographical distance is perhaps the most important determinant of the contagion effect. Glick and Rose, on the other hand, argue that contagion takes place mainly through trade channels. This section considers both our own contagion index and the trade contagion index. Detailed definitions of explanatory variables are provided in the Appendix.

2.4 Data

Our data set covers 103 developing countries, including the crisis-hit Asian and Latin American countries, mostly for the years 1980 through 1996. The nominal exchange rate, however, covers the period 1980 through 1997. As will be seen, this enables us to relate the dependent variable to one-year-lagged values of explanatory variables. Using lags of explanatory variables better serves our goal of identifying "causes" of a currency crisis. Unlike other explanatory variables, however, we let the contagion index take contemporaneous values with the dependent variable, since the contagion effect is expected to be coincident with currency crises. According to our definition of currency crisis, about 10 percent of the total country years are classified as crisis episodes.

2.5 Probit estimation results

Probit estimation results using the aforementioned variables are reported in Table 6.1. Since coefficients from probit estimation are hard to interpret, we calculate the marginal contribution of each regressor to the probability of a crisis, using historical means of the variables. We first report in columns (1) and (2) of the table the estimation results without the contagion effect. For most variables, the estimated coefficients are significant and of the right signs. This suggests that incidence of a currency crisis is not randomly distributed across countries but systematically related to economic fundamentals. Variables such as government deficit, current account, and total foreign debt, however, are insignificant or of the wrong signs. Frankel and Rose (1996) have reported similar findings. As column (2) shows, when these insignificant variables are excluded from the regression, coefficients on the remaining regressors change only slightly.

In columns (3) and (4), we add a contagion index to the equation. We find that the trade contagion index and our contagion index each has significantly positive effect.[6] As mentioned earlier, however, it is not clear what the correlation between the crisis index and the contagion index truly implies. Although we have included standard macroeconomic variables in the regression, the possibility of missing variables still remains. In addition, using one index without the other may produce biased estimates, because the two indexes are likely to be correlated.[7] Only by considering both indexes at the same time, one will be able to properly evaluate the independent contribution of each index to the probability of a currency crisis.

We report the results from this experiment in column (5) of Table 6.1. Note that when the two indexes are included in one regression, our index dominates the trade contagion index and the latter turns insignificant. This result suggests that the trade contagion index works only as a proxy for our contagion index and thus the trade linkage is probably not the main channel of regional contagion of crises.[8] For this reason, we will use column (3) as our benchmark estimates for the rest of this section. Under the benchmark estimates, the average of the fitted probability for the whole actual crisis episodes is 0.18.

2.6 Korea's currency crisis and contagion

In this subsection, we focus on Korea's currency crisis on the basis of the results from previous subsections. First, we report the fitted values for Korea and other crisis-hit countries like Mexico, Thailand, Malaysia, and Indonesia. As row (1) of Table 6.2 shows, when only economic fundamentals in 1996 are considered, the fitted value was 0.127 for Korea and below 0.1 for the other Asian countries. Considering the fact that the unconditional probability of a currency crisis

Table 6.1 Cross-country probit analyses: causes of currency crises

	(1)	(2)	(3)	(4)	(5)
Per capita GDP growth	-0.346 (-2.05)	-0.282 (-2.11)	-0.195 (-1.36)	-0.205 (-1.61)	-0.254 (-1.23)
Fiscal deficit/GDP	-0.001 (-0.61)				
Inflation rate	0.043 (2.02)	0.039 (2.10)	0.040 (2.08)	0.036 (2.12)	0.059 (2.14)
Real domestic credit growth	0.110 (2.32)	0.055 (1.40)	0.068 (1.64)	0.063 (1.74)	0.105 (1.80)
Current account/GDP	-0.002 (-0.93)				
Terms of trade changes	-0.160 (-1.89)	-0.136 (-1.97)	-0.145 (-1.98)	-0.123 (1.90)	-0.210 (-2.02)
Real exchange rate depreciation	-0.216 (-3.19)	-0.175 (-2.92)	-0.189 (-2.96)	-0.195 (-3.34)	-0.295 (-3.16)
Reserves/short-term debt	-0.015 (-2.24)	-0.008 (-2.27)	-0.009 (-2.05)	-0.008 (-2.47)	-0.015 (-2.34)
FDI/GDP	-0.017 (-2.51)	-0.015 (-2.66)	-0.014 (-2.17)	-0.011 (-2.01)	-0.017 (-1.86)
Total foreign debt/GDP	-0.058 (-2.82)				
Short-term debt/total foreign debt	0.001 (0.86)				
Foreign GDP growth	0.021 (2.52)				
Foreign interest rate	-0.001 (-0.37)				
Trade contagion index			0.043 (3.07)		
Our contagion index				0.069 (4.98)	0.095 (3.70)
Memorandum					
Sample size	675	1028	999	1028	999
Unconditional Probability of Crisis	0.114	0.117	0.118	0.117	0.118
Average estimated probability of crisis countries	0.198	0.157	0.165	0.184	0.181
Average estimated probability of no-crisis countries	0.103	0.111	0.111	0.107	0.109

Note: z-statistics are in parentheses.

is 0.1 in our sample1, the Asian crisis as a whole was rather unanticipated. The only exception is Korea, whose economic fundamentals in 1996 appear to have been weak enough to imply a possible crisis in the following year.[9] The finding that the crisis probability of Korea in 1996 was relatively high may be surprising, since many people have argued that Korea's economic fundamentals before the crisis were sound. Row (1) of Table 6.2 does not support this popular claim.[10]

The crisis potential of Asia in 1997 was small not only by international standards but also by its own historical trends. As shown in row (2) of Table 6.2, the fitted probability for the Asian countries was not substantially greater in 1997 than in the earlier years. For example, Korea's crisis potential was about 0.1 even before 1996. Although we find that the Korean economy in 1996 was in fact much weaker than it was during the economic boom of 1994 and 1995, 1996 was not the worst year of the decade.

In rows (3) to (6) of Table 6.2, we examine whether the crisis probability increases for Asian countries when the contagion effect is included as an

Table 6.2 Cross-country probit analyses: probability of a currency crisis

Without contagion index (from eq. (2) in Table 6.1)

	Mexico (1994)	Thailand (1997)	Malaysia (1997)	Indonesia (1997)	Korea (1997)
(1)	0.132	0.084	0.081	0.070	0.127
	Mexico (1987–1993)	Thailand (1987–1996)	Malaysia (1987–1996)	Indonesia (1987–1996)	Korea (1987–1996)
(2)	0.133	0.088	0.041	0.111	0.112

With Contagion Index (From Eq. (3) in Table 1.1A)

	Mexico (1994)	Thailand (1997)	Malaysia (1997)	Indonesia (1997)	Korea (1997)
(3)	0.115	0.106	0.075	0.101	0.148
	Mexico (1987–1993)	Thailand (1987–1996)	Malaysia (1987–1996)	Indonesia (1987–1996)	Korea (1987–1996)
(4)	0.100	0.093	0.043	0.114	0.100

With Contagion Index (From Eq. (4) in Table 1.1A)

	Mexico (1994)	Thailand (1997)	Malaysia (1997)	Indonesia (1997)	Korea (1997)
(5)	0.168	0.182	0.138	0.171	0.208
	Mexico (1987–1993)	Thailand (1987–1996)	Malaysia (1987–1996)	Indonesia (1987–1996)	Korea (1987–1996)
(6)	0.140	0.082	0.040	0.102	0.102

additional regressor. The results vary substantially, depending upon which contagion index is used. When the trade linkage index is used, the estimated probabilities of the Asian countries change only slightly. However, our geographical linkage index substantially increases the estimated probability for the Asian countries from the range of 0.08–0.13 to the average level of ex-post crisis countries, 0.19! According to this result, one could naturally have predicted the Korean crisis after the outbreak of the Southeast Asian turmoil.

Next, we examine which variables have been particularly important in Korea's currency crisis compared with other crisis episodes. To this end, we calculate the contribution of each explanatory variable to the incidence of each crisis by multiplying the benchmark coefficient estimates in column (4) of Table 6.1 with the corresponding values of explanatory variables. Deviation of each crisis from a reference group mean in thus constructed contribution measure can be used to illustrate distinguishing features of each crisis episode. Before examining individual country's episode in detail, however, we first compare the average values of the crisis countries with those of the whole sample in panel A of Table 6.3. This table clearly shows that the crisis countries exhibit weaknesses in all of the considered fundamentals on average. Apart from the contagion, in particular, the reserves-to-short-term debt ratio make the greatest contribution to the crisis probability.

Panel B of Table 6.3 reports the results from the same experiment for each individual country's episode, using the entire crisis countries (column (b) in Panel A) as our reference group to be compared with. A negative number in the table implies that contribution of the corresponding variable to the corresponding crisis episode is smaller than to the whole crisis group in our data set. In Korea's crisis, for example, external factors (such as the terms-of-trade shock, low reserves, and low FDI) have been particularly important, while domestic macro conditions (such as GDP growth and inflation) had limited effects. Also, in most Asian countries, the growth rate of real domestic credit has had positive contribution, supporting the popular view that over-lending and over-investment were critical factors in the Asian crisis.

Panel B of Table 6.3 also indicates that the role of the contagion effect has been more important in the Asian crisis than in other crisis episodes. Even for Korea, which was least affected by contagion among the Asian countries, the contagion effect appears to have played a key role. Figure 6.1 plots the contagion index of Korea along with the world average of the index.

We have so far examined Korea's currency crisis on the basis of a general probit model. In short, the results suggest that the role of the contagion effect in Korea's crisis was significant, but economic fundamentals of Korea (particularly external factors) were not sound prior to the crisis, relative to the other Asian countries in particular. Although the above exercises produce many interesting results, one should acknowledge many limitations as well. Perhaps the most important limitation is that our exercise was performed for virtually a single observation out of more than 2,000 sample points, and thus the related error margin is potentially very large.

Table 6.3 Cross-country probit analyses
Contribution of each explanatory variable to crisis
A. Deviations from average values of the whole sample

	Sample Mean		
	Whole Sample (a)	*Crisis Countries (b)*	*Marginal Contribution*[1]
Per capita GDP growth	0.00477	−0.01056	0.00314
Inflation	0.18787	0.30629	0.00429
Real domestic credit growth	0.01930	0.03707	0.00113
Terms of trade changes	−0.00804	−0.03552	0.00337
Real exchange rate depreciation	−0.01699	−0.05357	0.00715
Reserves/short-term debt	3.39132	1.27950	0.01752
FDI/GDP	1.25291	0.71543	0.00600
Our contagion index	−2.39022	−2.10817	0.01946
Sum of Deviations			0.06206

Contribution of each explanatory variable to the Asian crisis
B. Deviations from average values of crisis countries

	Mexico (1994)	*Thailand (1997)*	*Malaysia (1997)*	*Indonesia (1997)*	*Korea (1997)*
Per capita GDP growth	−0.00106	−0.00987	−0.01049	−0.01150	−0.01154
Inflation	−0.00772	−0.00904	−0.00985	−0.00831	−0.00935
Real domestic credit growth	−0.00046	−0.01887	0.00525	0.00575	0.00561
Terms of trade changes	−0.00398	−0.00484	−0.00710	−0.00879	0.00549
Real exchange rate depreciation	0.00641	−0.00275	−0.00466	−0.00346	−0.00930
Reserves/short-term debt	0.00492	0.00241	−0.00898	0.00602	0.00609
FDI/GDP	−0.00416	−0.00610	−0.04260	−0.03133	0.00263
Our contagion index	0.00724	0.05687	0.05392	0.04985	0.03376
Sum of deviations	0.00118	0.00781	−0.02452	−0.00176	0.02339

Note:
1) Marginal contribution to crisis probability = ×[(b) − (a)].

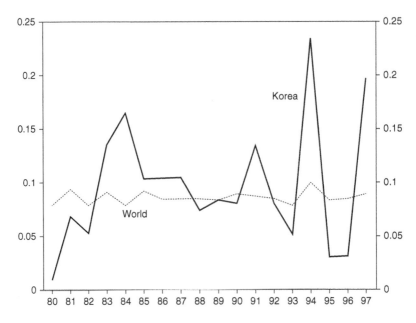

Figure 6.1 Distance contagion index of Korea (1980–1997)

3.   Country shock vs. contagion: further analysis with daily data

The previous section of cross-country analyses suggests that the contagion effect may have been a major cause of the Korea's crisis as well as the Asian crises in general. However, the cross-country analyses cannot examine dynamic diffusion processes of shocks across countries. In relation with the analysis of contagion effects, this seems to be an important limitation. For example, when many countries fall into crises in the same year, it is impossible to investigate whether one country's crisis causes another's or if they together generate a vicious circle of crises through mutual interactions. With the binary definition of "crisis", it becomes even harder to examine to what extent the crises of other countries worsened the situation of one country. In addition, it seems also persuasive to argue that shocks in financial markets are transmitted so rapidly that analyses with annual data can hardly capture the complete picture.

In this section, therefore, we analyze the high-frequency data of the relevant variables, namely, daily data of the exchange rates (against the US dollar) and the spreads (over the T-bill rate) of the US dollar-denominated sovereign debts. When the high-frequency data are used, an obvious disadvantage is the limitation of data coverage across countries as well as the relevant macro-variables that can help identify the sources of contagion. For this reason, we will not seriously question the ultimate sources of the contagion effects in this section. Instead, we will attribute the whole magnitudes "explained" by the shocks of other countries in the regressions to "contagion effects" and the remaining parts to effects from "domestic shocks."[11]

Considering data availability and its importance in the recent crisis, we selected 10 countries: Brazil, Argentina, Mexico, Russia, China, Korea, Malaysia, Thailand, Indonesia, and Japan. Japan is included in order to check whether we can find any systematic evidence for the popular argument that the weakness of the Japanese economy played a significant role in triggering the Asian crisis. The sample period was chosen from 6/19/1997 to 12/31/1998 so that we can cover the situation right before the crisis of Thailand. The sample size is approximately 400 for each country. The recent paper by Baig and Goldfajn (1998) presents similar analyses with this section, but we examine similar data largely from Korea's viewpoint using a wider set of countries. Details of the data sources can be found in the Appendix.

3.1   Exchange rates

A serious difficulty with handling the exchange rate data is that the government, implicitly or explicitly, controls this variable in many countries. For example, the exchange rates of the three Latin American countries, Russia and China are virtu-ally uncorrelated with the exchange rates of other countries (not reported) because the governments of these countries managed their exchange rates. We dropped these five countries from our sample for this reason and analyzed the five Asian countries, even though it is known that the governments in these countries also intervened in the foreign exchange markets from time to time. Probably a more accurate reading of the pure market responses can be found from the sov-ereign spread data in secondary markets, the results for which we will discuss in the next subsection.

Cross-country correlation

Having confirmed that the null hypotheses of unit roots in the log of the exchange rates are not rejected (see Panel A), Panel B of Table 6.4 reports the pair-wise correlation coefficients of the log differences for the five Asian countries. This table shows that the daily fluctuations are closely correlated with one another.[12] However, the correlation coefficients of Korea with other countries are far smaller than those among the three Association of South East Asian Nations (ASEAN) countries. This result may be regarded to be consistent with the finding from the cross-country data that the contagion effect was small for Korea relative to the ASEAN countries.

In addition, Japan's exchange rate does not appear to be significantly correlated with that of Korea's; it is more correlated with the exchange rates of the ASEAN countries. At least from the daily variations for the sample period used in this chapter, it appears difficult to justify the casual argument that the weakness of the Japanese yen was a major cause of the Asian crisis, particularly the crisis of Korea.

A slightly different picture is found from the relatively low-frequency data or the level data. For example, the correlation coefficients of Korea with the other countries are significant for the first differences of the weekly averages (not reported) and for the levels in Panel C of Table 6.4, although the degrees are still smaller than other coefficients. This may indicate that there exist sizable lagged

Table 6.4 Analyses for the exchange rate

A. ADF test for unit root (daily data, lag = 2, including intercept)

	Korea	*Malaysia*	*Thailand*	*Indonesia*	*Japan*
Test Statistic	–2.24	–2.31	–2.62	–1.71	–1.52

Note: 1% critical value –3.45, 5% critical value –2.87, 10% critical value –2.57

B. Pair-wise correlation coefficients (daily data, log-difference)

	Korea	*Malaysia*	*Thailand*	*Indonesia*	*Japan*
Korea	1.00				
Malaysia	0.10	1.00			
Thailand	0.09	0.41	1.00		
Indonesia	0.22	0.49	0.27	1.00	
Japan	0.08	0.12	0.20	0.11	1.00

Note: Asymptotic standard error 0.05.

C. Pair-wise correlation coefficients (daily data, log-level)

	Korea	*Malaysia*	*Thailand*	*Indonesia*	*Japan*
Korea	1.00				
Malaysia	0.81	1.00			
Thailand	0.82	0.82	1.00		
Indonesia	0.67	0.83	0.56	1.00	
Japan	0.51	0.68	0.56	0.77	1.00

Note: Asymptotic standard error 0.05.

D. p-value for the Granger causality test (daily data, log-difference)

		Granger Cause				
		Korea	*Malaysia*	*Thailand*	*Indonesia*	*Japan*
Granger Caused	Korea		0.07	0.40	0.25	0.13
	Malaysia	0.01		0.00	0.48	0.01
	Thailand	0.00	0.02		0.01	0.77
	Indonesia	0.00	0.00	0.00		0.16
	Japan	0.82	0.26	0.65	0.87	

Note: Numbers are p-values of the tests for the nulls of no-Granger causality.

effects in transmitting one country's shock to another country, and, if so, the Granger-causality test exercise can be meaningful.

Granger causality test

Panel D of Table 6.4 reports the p-values of the test statistic under the null of no- Granger causality for each pair of countries, using two days of time lags. It may not be surprising that many countries Granger-cause many other countries. What is impressive, however, is that Korea Granger-caused devaluations of the ASEAN countries far more significantly than the other way around. In addition, it is hard to find any causality connections between Japan and Korea, which is consistent with the result from the contemporaneous correlation coefficients.

Value-at-risk simulation

Then how much of Korea's devaluation can be attributed to the contagion and how much to the country's own shock? In order to provide a mechanical answer to this question, we applied the value-at-risk (VAR) technique for the five countries' data, using two lagged variables and no drift terms.[13] As for the ordering of the countries, we referred the Granger causality results of Panel D of Table 6.4: Korea → Malaysia → Thailand → Indonesia → Japan. Since the VAR results are usually sensitive to the ordering, however, we tried the other extreme case for Korea: Malaysia → Thailand → Indonesia → Japan → Korea. Figure 6.1 plots the actual exchange rate of Korea, along with the two simulated paths by the respective VAR estimations that would have been realized if the shocks to other countries had not occurred. That is, the two dotted lines depict the exchange rate variations that can be attributed to the domestic shocks of Korea and its repercussions through the other four countries in the VAR models.

From these experiments, one can sense that the contagion effects on Korea's exchange rate were large throughout the whole sample period, which is consistent with the results from the cross-country analyses. According to the lower dotted line that attributes Korea's variation to the contagion effects up to maximum, the exchange rate would have returned to the pre-crisis level at the second half of 1999 if there had been no foreign shocks. Also, the decomposition of the variation between domestic shocks and foreign shocks is rather insensitive to the ordering of the equations: that is, the two dotted lines are close to each other. This robustness of the results for Korea may have been expected from the preceding results for the correlation coefficients and the Granger causality tests.

Perhaps a more important message of Figure 6.2 is, however, that the domestic shock must have played a critical role at least in triggering the explosion during the period of November and December 1998. Of course, this experiment has many limitations. As noted previously, for example, the exchange rate data are contaminated by the government intervention, and thus the analysis of the contagion effects was performed for only a limited number of countries. In particular, the

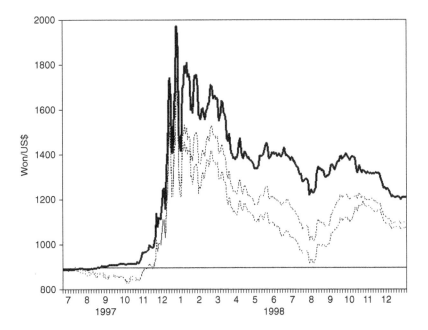

Figure 6.2 Decomposition of Korea's exchange rate: domestic vs. foreign shock-
     driven components

Note: The solid line is the actual won/dollar exchange rate, and the dotted lines are generated
using the VAR estimation results with the foreign shocks set to be zeros. The upper dotted line
is from the VAR with Korea at the highest in the ordering, while the lower dotted line is with
Korea at the lowest. See the text for details.

re-devaluation of the Asian exchange rates in the second half of 1998 was often
attributed to the crises of Russia and Brazil, but the above analysis could not give
any idea to this conjecture. In the next subsection, therefore, we present the results
for the sovereign spread data in the secondary market for a wider set of countries.

3.2   Sovereign spreads

The general methodology employed here is virtually identical to the previous
subsection except for the coverage of the sample countries: for the sovereign
spread data, we can include three Latin American countries (Brazil, Argentina,
Mexico), Russia and China, in addition to the previous Asian five. In parallel to
the previous subsection, we focus on the results for the first differences. This is
different from Baig and Goldfajn (1998), which analyzed the results for the levels
of the sovereign spreads. It is not clear to us which one of the two is a superior
concept in the context of contagion effects. Our choice of the first difference is
based on the test results that do not reject the nulls of the unit roots in the data
(see Panel A of Table 6.5). However, we also report some of the results for the
level data as well since the correlation of the first differences only shows the

Table 6.5 Analyses for the sovereign spreads

A. ADF Test for unit root (daily data, lag = 2, including intercept)

	Brazil	Argentina	Mexico	Russia	China	Korea	Malaysia	Thailand	Indonesia	Japan
Test Statistic	-1.65	-1.53	-1.74	-0.16	-1.47	-1.70	-0.99	-1.72	-1.59	-3.01

Note: 1% critical value* -3.45, 5% critical value -2.87, 10% critical value -2.57.

B. Pair-wise correlation coefficients (daily data, first difference)

	Brazil	Argentina	Mexico	Russia	China	Korea	Malaysia	Thailand	Indonesia	Japan
Brazil	1.00									
Argentina	0.71	1.00								
Mexico	0.76	0.79	1.00							
Russia	0.35	0.45	0.49	1.00						
China	0.08	0.08	-0.02	0.05	1.00					
Korea	0.30	0.36	0.24	0.18	0.17	1.00				
Malaysia	-0.09	0.09	-0.02	0.03	0.09	0.22	1.00			
Thailand	-0.03	0.07	-0.02	0.06	0.03	0.05	0.12	1.00		
Indonesia	0.20	0.14	0.16	0.07	-0.06	0.01	0.04	0.01	1.00	
Japan	-0.10	-0.12	-0.18	-0.16	0.07	0.09	0.12	-0.01	-0.03	1.00

Note: Asymptotic standard error 0.05.

Table 6.5 Analyses for the sovereign spreads (continued)

C. Pair-wise correlation coefficients (daily data, level)

	Brazil	Argentina	Mexico	Russia	China	Korea	Malaysia	Thailand	Indonesia	Japan
Brazil	1.00									
Argentina	0.93	1.00								
Mexico	0.95	0.97	1.00							
Russia	0.80	0.86	0.80	1.00						
China	0.81	0.90	0.85	0.87	1.00					
Korea	0.81	0.88	0.83	0.74	0.89	1.00				
Malaysia	0.86	0.90	0.84	0.93	0.93	0.88	1.00			
Thailand	0.85	0.88	0.84	0.67	0.81	0.92	0.83	1.00		
Indonesia	0.66	0.70	0.62	0.80	0.80	0.81	0.89	0.72	1.00	
Japan	0.01	0.08	0.05	-0.26	-0.03	0.19	-0.15	0.22	-0.18	1.00

Note: Asymptotic standard error 0.05.

Table 6.5 Analyses for the sovereign spreads (continued)

D. p-value for the Granger causality test (daily data, first difference)

	Granger Cause									
Granger Caused	Brazil	Argentina	Mexico	Russia	China	Korea	Malaysia	Thailand	Indonesia	Japan
Brazil		0.00	0.03	0.08	0.00	0.01	0.00	0.02	0.39	0.42
Argentina	0.00		0.79	0.12	0.09	0.00	0.00	0.01	0.39	0.34
Mexico	0.00	0.06		0.16	0.00	0.00	0.01	0.00	0.16	0.92
Russia	0.00	0.00	0.00		0.00	0.92	0.00	0.00	0.61	0.36
China	0.00	0.00	0.00	0.00		0.02	0.70	0.63	0.99	0.81
Korea	0.00	0.00	0.00	0.00	0.33		0.03	0.98	0.23	0.07
Malaysia	0.00	0.12	0.01	0.01	0.06	0.00		0.00	0.48	0.19
Thailand	0.00	0.00	0.00	0.01	0.08	0.00	0.01		0.02	0.16
Indonesia	0.00	0.12	0.04	0.30	0.65	0.42	0.89	0.55		0.45
Japan	0.00	0.00	0.00	0.01	0.00	0.06	0.01	0.02	0.28	

Note: Numbers are p-values of the tests for the nulls of no-Granger causality.

contemporaneous daily contagion while the correlation of the levels may indicate that the contagion cumulated over time with time lags.

Cross-country correlation

Panel B of Table 6.5 reports the pair-wise correlation coefficients of the first differences of the sovereign spreads for the 10 countries. First, the correlation coefficients among the three Latin American countries are extremely high: they are more than 0.7! One may be able to argue that the three countries are taken to be virtually a single market in the international capital market.

In contrast, the correlation coefficients among the three ASEAN countries are far smaller: the correlation coefficient between Malaysia and Thailand is barely significant at the 5 percent significance level, while the coefficients between Indonesia and the other two countries are not significant at all. In fact, Indonesia appears to be more correlated with the Latin American countries than with the other Asian countries. Russia is also more correlated with the Latin American countries rather than with the Asian countries, while China is not significantly correlated with any other countries. It is interesting that Japan shows negative correlation with the Latin American countries, which seems to indicate that the international capital market perceives the crises in Latin America as positive shocks to Japan (or negative shocks to the US: recall that we use the spreads over the US T-bill rate).

Finally, it is surprising that Korea shows stronger correlation with the Latin American countries than with the Asian countries. As in the exchange rate analyses, however, the cross-country correlation appears to be far more significant when the first differences of the weekly average or the levels of the daily data are used.[14] For the first differences of the weekly average data (not reported) or for the levels in Panel C of Table 6.5, for example, Korea turns out to be significantly correlated with all the other countries except for Indonesia. Again, this divergence of the results with respect to the data frequency seems to suggest that there exist substantial time lags in the contagion effects, which cannot be captured by the contemporaneous daily correlation.

Granger causality test

This argument is confirmed by the Granger causality test results reported in Panel D of Table 6.5. Allowing for just two days of time lags, the nulls of no causality were rejected in many pairs for which the contemporaneous daily correlation did not appear to be significant. For example, Thailand appeared to be significantly correlated only with Malaysia in the daily difference correlation, but it appeared to Granger-cause, as well as to be Granger-caused, by many other countries. The passive role of Japan is confirmed again: it was Granger-caused by most of the sample countries, while it did not Granger-cause the crisis countries. As in the previous section, the role of Japan in triggering the crises appeared to be minimal.

Finally, Korea was Granger-caused by the Latin American countries as well as Granger-caused them, but it only Granger-caused the other Asian countries rather than the other way around. All of these results may be out of accordance with the casual assertion that the ASEAN or Japanese financial crises triggered the Korean crisis. Instead, these results seem to support the hypothesis that the Korean crisis was largely triggered by domestic weaknesses and that it was deepened by the crises of Russia and Brazil later on.

VAR simulation

Using similar methodology as described in the previous subsection, Figure 6.3 plots the actual sovereign spread of Korea, along with the simulated paths by the VAR estimations (two lagged variables and no drift terms) that would have been realized if the shocks to other countries had not occurred.[15] As for the ordering of the countries, again, we referred to the Granger causality test results (Brazil → Argentina → Mexico → Russia → China → Korea → Malaysia → Thailand → Indonesia → Japan). In order to check the sensitivity of the result, we also report an additional simulation result that placed Korea at the bottom in the ordering of the countries.

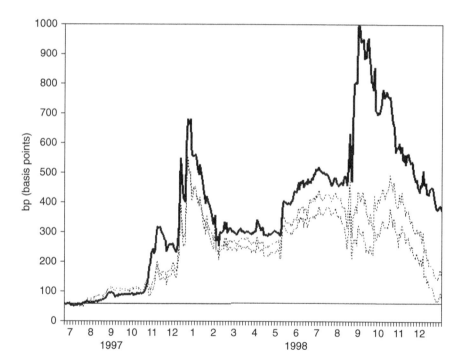

Figure 6.3 Decomposition of Korea's sovereign spread: domestic vs. foreign shock-driven components

Note: The solid line is the actual spread of Korean Development Bank bonds over the US T-bill rate, and the dotted lines are generated using the VAR estimation results with the foreign shocks set to be zeros. The upper dotted line is from the VAR with Korea at sixth in the ordering, while the lower dotted line is with Korea at the lowest. See the text for details.

A literal interpretation of this graph is that the spike in Korea's spread in mid-1998 would not have occurred if there had been no crises in other countries (Brazil in particular): the simulated spread does not exceed 400 basis points, while the actual spread peaked at 1,000 basis points. This is somewhat different from the result for the exchange rate in Figure 6.2, in which Russia and Latin American countries were not considered. That is, this difference indicates that Korea's crisis was significantly affected by the contagion effects from the Russia and Latin American crises in the second half of 1998. Nevertheless, the rise of Korea's spread in 1997 cannot be fully attributed to contagion effects, which is the same conclusion as in the analyses with the exchange rates.

3.3 News

An important result from the analyses of both the exchange rates and sovereign spreads is that the outbreak of the Korean crisis at the end of 1997 is hardly attributable to contagion effects. In this subsection, therefore, we examine more closely what happened inside Korea during this critical period from October to December 1997. For this purpose, we collect major news on the financial market and examine how the market reacted to the news.

Figure 6.4 reports Korea's residuals that were identified from the VAR estimation of the exchange rate and sovereign spreads (with Korea at the fifth position

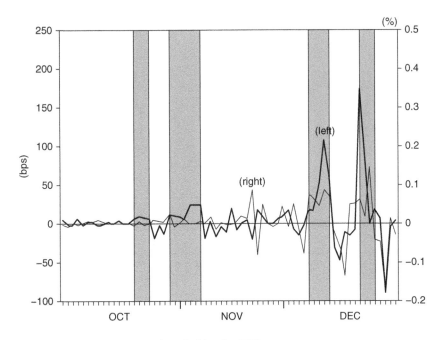

Figure 6.4 Domestic shocks identified by the VAR

Note: The thick line is the shock on the sovereign spread, and the thin line is the shock on the exchange rate.

from the bottom in the ordering). From this figure, one may find the four sub-periods that experienced serious negative shocks (or the positive residuals), which we highlighted with the shaded areas: 10/21–10/25, 10/30–11/8, 12/8–12/13, and 12/22–12/24.

Table 6.6 reports the relevant news that we collected from several Korean newspapers (*Maeil Economic Daily, Hankuk Economic Daily,* and so forth) and Bloomberg. In order to reduce possible selection bias, we tried to collect only the headline news of the financial sections of domestic newspapers and simply skipped the dates on which the headline news was mere descriptions of the financial market situation. From Bloomberg, in contrast, we included the comments on Korea's situation and government policies.

Table 6.6 News on the Korean financial market

Date	Korean Newspapers	Bloomberg
10/3	S&P downgraded commercial banks.	
10/4	Euromoney downgraded Korea.	
10/14	Bank of Korea (BOK) made special loans of 1 trillion won to merchant banks.	
10/20	Gov't led commercial banks to syndicated loans to ailing *chaebols.*	
10/23	Gov't decided to undertake Kia Motors as a public enterprise through Korean Development Bank's debt-equity swap.	
10/24		S&P downgraded Korea because the gov't rescued Korea First Bank and "nationalized" the near-bankrupt Kia.
10/25	S&P downgraded Korea.	
10/27		Free-fall of currency raises concern Korea will follow other Asian nations in seeking IMF assistance, although gov't denies it.
10/29	Moody's downgraded Korea.	
10/29	Bond market will be opened from 1998.	Korea accelerates opening bond market, but it is too late to allure foreign investors.
10/30		Gov't ordered banks and companies to stop hoarding dollars, and investors suspect that the BOK's official reserve of $30 billion does not include dollars borrowed through forward transactions.

(Continued)

Table 6.6 (Continued)

Date	Korean Newspapers	Bloomberg
11/3	Haitai Group applied for composition.	
11/4	NewCore Group applied for composition.	
11/5		A costly – and probably futile – attempt to stabilize the currency value increases systemic risks. Many estimate actual reserves could be as low as $15 billion. The focus of Korean banks' lending to a handful of customers, or chaebols, could make matters even worse.
11/8	Gov't requested foreign press to stop spreading "groundless" bad rumors about Korea.	
11/10		Foreign investors dismiss government optimism in coping with the turmoil.
11/11	Gov't will support 1.3 trillion won for Kia group.	
11/12	Financial Reform Amendment was rejected by the National Assembly.	
11/18	BOK made $1 billion of emergency loans to the 5 major commercial banks that were on the brink of bankruptcy.	Korea may need IMF assistance, although IMF and gov't denied it.
11/19		Finance minister was replaced to clear the way for the gov't to seek $40 billion from the IMF.
11/20	Gov't guaranteed all deposits and interest for 3 years.	
11/20	Exchange rate band is widened from 2.5 to 10 percent per day.	
11/21	Gov't asks for IMF support.	
11/26	Foreign exchange treatments of 8 merchant banks were suspended.	
11/28	International Bank for Reconstruction and Development and Asian Development Bank decided to support Korea.	
12/2		Gov't ordered 9 crippled finance companies to suspend business.
12/3	Halla group asked for syndicated loan.	

12/3	9 merchant banks were closed.	Korea agreed to a $55 billion international bailout.
12/4	IMF and gov't agreed upon a $55 billion rescue package.	
12/6	Korea Securities Co. went bankrupt.	
12/8	Daewoo group acquired Ssangyong Motors with syndicated loans.	
12/8	BOK injected 1.2 trillion won to ailing merchant banks and will make more special loans if necessary.	
12/9	Gov't invested 1.8 trillion won in Seoul Bank and Korea First Bank.	
12/11	5 more merchant banks were closed.	
12/11	BOK made 5 trillion won of special loans to commercial banks.	
12/11	Dongseo Securities Co. was closed.	
12/13	BOK will inject 11 trillion won to nonbank financial institutions.	
12/15	Gov't will allow for redundant layoffs.	
12/16	Exchange rate band was abolished.	Gov't ended limits on foreign exchange trading.
12/16		Gov't will cancel plans to inject capital into 6 banks because of objections from IMF officials.
12/17		Gov't delayed plans to bolster banks and offered aid to brokerages, resisting the reform package of the IMF.
12/18	Dae-Jung Kim was elected as the new president.	Finance and Economy Ministry said financial institutions have "less than $10 billion" in short-term foreign currency debt maturing in January, but independent economists say the gov't figure is optimistic.
12/23	Moody's downgraded Korea to a junk- bond level.	Korea was pushed closer to the economic brink as Moody's cut the country's credit rating to junk status.

(Continued)

Table 6.6 (Continued)

Date	Korean Newspapers	Bloomberg
12/23	IMF is discontented with the gov't treatment of the ailing financial institutions.	
12/23	Vice minister of Finance Department acknowledged that there existed more than $100 billion of offshore borrowings	US officials denied a report that the Clinton administration had offered $5 billion in "emergency credits."
12/24		BOK asks Japan banks to roll-over debts.
12/25	IMF and G7 promised to support $10 billion early.	
12/25	Financial market will be completely opened.	
12/26		Korea will allow bank layoffs.
12/26		Korea's courts rejected applications from Koryo and Dongsuh Securities Co. for court receivership, making it likely the brokerages will be sold or shut down.
12/27	Cheongku Group applied for composition.	
12/30		Korea's external debt totaled $156.9 billion at the end of November, according to the standards used by IMF.
12/30		National Assembly passed a package of economic reform bills.

One can notice that the news for the IMF's rescue plan was not a big shock to the market: it may have been anticipated earlier. Rather, the news that stirred the financial market was the bankruptcy of several *chaebols* and financial institutions and the bailout policies of the government. Readers can also refer Table 6.11 in the following to see how many conglomerates of Korea had gone bankrupt right before the crisis and how large they were in the Korean financial market. The first period matches the news about the bailout policy for Kia, while the second period coincides with the bankruptcy news of Haitai and NewCore. The third period matches the news on the acquisition of Ssangyong Autos by Daewoo and the unconditional rescues for many distressed financial institutions, including two major bankrupt banks (First Korea Bank and Seoul Bank) by the government (and the Bank of Korea). Finally, the last period was driven by the news that Moody's downgraded Korea's sovereign debt to a junk-bond level and the acknowledgement of the Finance Department's vice minister that Korea's foreign debt may exceed $250 billion instead of the official $100 billion.

In short, the news that the Korean government still tried to stick to the old-fashioned bailout policies appear to have operated as bad shocks. At least at the triggering moment of the Korean crisis, the market's reaction appeared to be most negative to the series of *chaebol* bankruptcies and the government's bailout policies.

4.   Further discussion on Korea's crisis

The previous section suggests that the Korean crisis was triggered more by domestic shocks than by contagion effects, although the contagion effects substantially deepened the crisis. This is basically in accordance with the result from the probit analyses, with more emphasis on domestic weaknesses. Yet, the probit analyses indicate that the domestic fundamentals were not extremely bad. This section, therefore, adds some discussion about some important weaknesses of Korea's financial market structure that we could not systematically analyze due to the limitations of comparable cross-country data availability. Instead of providing formal analysis results, we will briefly sketch the crucial points that have been made by other researchers.

4.1   Bank run rather than currency speculation

Table 6.7 shows Korea's balance-of-payment situation during the 1997 to 1998 period. From this table, one can be astonished at how abrupt the capital flow reversal was during the fourth quarter in 1997. The usable foreign reserve, which had been fluctuating around $30 billion until the third quarter, abruptly decreased by $15 billion during just one month, November 1997. In fact, the foreign reserve would have been completely depleted by the end of December if there had not been the emergency loan of $16 billion through the public sector, such as the International Monetary Fund (IMF) and the World Bank.

An important point of this table, however, is that the major component of this abrupt capital flow reversal was the withdrawal of foreign debt rather than the shift of portfolio investment. Private external debt decreased by $6.5 billion in November and by $11.3 billion in December, while the magnitude of equity securities outflow was rather small. If one includes the emergency loan of the Bank of Korea to the overseas branches of the Korean banks that were on the brink of bankruptcy, the decrease of private foreign debt in November was more than $15 billion!

Based on this inspection, Shin (1999) argues that the triggering mechanism of the currency crisis in Korea fits the bank-run theories (e.g. Cole and Kehoe, 1996; Goldfajn and Valdes, 1997; and Chang and Velasco, 1998) better than the speculative attack hypotheses (e.g. Krugman, 1979; and Obstfeld, 1995). Somewhat arbitrarily, Table 6.8 decomposes the demand for foreign reserves into two parts: the component that was not affected by the exchange rate movement from the creditor's point of view and the other component that was subject to the capital

Table 6.7 Trends of the balance-of-payment components

(Unit: billion US$)

	1997				Oct	Nov	Dec	1998			
	1st Q.	2nd Q.	3rd Q.	4th Q.	Oct	Nov	Dec	1st Q.	2nd Q.	3rd Q.	4th Q.
Foreign reserve decrease[1]	8.28	-4.17	2.89	13.55	0.12	**15.04**	-1.61	-15.28	-12.89	-6.33	-5.14
Private foreign asset decrease[1]	-1.88	-1.44	-1.76	-10.00	-1.14	2.37	-11.23	-5.87	-0.80	2.84	3.83
Total	6.40	-5.61	1.13	3.55	-1.02	17.41	-12.84	-21.15	-13.69	-3.49	-1.31
Decrease in external debt[2]	-5.59	-6.47	-2.94	-1.10	-2.95	6.55	-4.70	4.26	-0.83	3.23	2.06
(public)	0.07	0.17	0.06	-15.92	0.04	0.05	-16.01	-6.69	-5.67	-1.42	-0.47
(private)	-5.66	-6.64	-3.00	14.82	-2.99	**6.50**	**11.31**	10.95	4.83	4.64	2.53
Increase in deposit at overseas branches[2]	4.20	0.00	0.00	3.33	0.00	**8.91**	-5.58	-5.93	-1.74	-0.26	-0.07
Net direct investment outflow[1]	0.51	0.23	0.66	0.21	0.10	-0.05	0.16	0.34	-0.34	-0.47	0.08
Net equity securities outflow[1]	-0.54	-2.54	-0.50	1.38	0.76	1.07	-0.46	-2.99	-0.01	0.22	-1.31
Errors and omissions	0.02	-0.15	1.17	4.03	0.50	2.35	1.18	0.50	1.25	1.16	2.16
Current account deficit[1]	7.35	2.72	2.05	-3.96	0.49	-0.86	-3.59	-10.83	-10.91	-9.62	-8.69

Sources: *The Balance of Payments*, The Bank of Korea (various issues) and the data for external debt are from the Ministry of Finance and Economy.

Notes:
1) '-' denotes increase, inflows or surplus.
2) External debt is reckoned based on International Bank for Reconstruction and Development standards and deposit at overseas branches denotes the deposit of the Bank of Korea at the overseas branches of the domestic banks.

Table 6.8 Demand factors of the foreign reserves

	1997							1998			
	1stQ.	2nd Q.	3rd Q.	4th Q.	Oct	Nov	Dec	1stQ.	2nd Q.	3rd Q.	4th Q.
Outflow of foreign currency denominated assets[1]	-1.30[4]	-6.47	-2.93	2.24	-2.95	15.46	-10.28	-1.68	-2.57	2.97	1.99
Outflow of domestic currency denominated assets 1[2]	-0.51	-2.69	0.66	5.41	1.27	3.42	0.72	-2.49	1.24	1.38	0.85
Outflow of domestic currency denominated assets 2[3]	6.84	0.03	2.71	1.45	1.75	2.56	-2.87	-13.32	-9.66	-8.24	-7.83

Sources: All numbers are from Table 6.5.

Notes:
1) Sum of the decrease in external debt and the increase in the deposit at the overseas branches of the domestic banks.
2) Sum of net equity securities outflow and errors and omissions.
3) Sum of the net equity securities outflow, errors and omissions and current account deficit.
4) '-' denotes capital inflow.

loss from currency depreciation. According to this decomposition, one may confirm that the first component outweighs the second in magnitude. This finding seems to support the hypothesis that the abrupt reversal of the capital flow in Korea was triggered by the bankruptcy risks of the major Korean banks, rather than the hypothesis that currency speculation in pursuit of capital gain itself triggered massive capital outflow.

This argument appears to be reinforced by the external liability roll-over rate of the seven major Korean banks in Table 6.9, re-cited from Shin (1999) again. That is, the roll-over rate of the major Korean banks, which already remained below 100 percent before November, sharply declined in November and further in December.

In relation to the contagion issue, the contagious effects from the weak financial system of Japan in particular, Table 6.10, shows that Japan's role was not particularly prominent. That is, the absolute amount of credit withdrawal by Japan was large because of its high exposure to the Korean market, but the flight from Korean banks was a general phenomenon regardless of the creditors' region. This information is also consistent with the result of the previous section that Japan's role appears to be minimal in triggering the Korean crisis.

Table 6.9 Weekly roll-over rate of foreign loans: seven major commercial banks

	July	*Aug.*	*Sept.*	*Oct.*	*Nov.*	*Dec.*
1st Week	157.3	64.1	82.2	83.7	70.0	23.7
2nd Week	95.5	84.9	82.8	83.9	67.2	26.8
3rd Week	83.6	86.9	84.1	80.5	55.9	26.2
4th Week	76.1	76.2	89.8	84.9	48.7	31.9
5th Week	87.5		127.3			53.3
Average	89.1	79.2	85.5	86.5	58.8	32.2

Table 6.10 Trend of regional composition of foreign loans: 13 major banks[1]

	96.12	*97.3*	*97.6*	*97.9*	*97.12*
Japan	259.7 (50.2)	212.8 (42.0)	220.9 (44.8)	206.3 (45.8)	139.5 (47.6)
US	70.1 (13.5)	88.3 (17.4)	86.4 (17.5)	70.5 (15.7)	46.3 (15.8)
Europe	187.6 (36.3)	205.4 (40.6)	185.8 (37.7)	173.0 (38.5)	107.1 (36.6)
Total[2]	517.4 (100.0)	506.4 (100.0)	493.1 (100.0)	449.8 (100.0)	292.9 (100.0)

Notes:
1) seven commercial banks and six specialized banks.
2) This figure excludes foreign loans extended by creditor banks in regions other than Japan, US and Europe.

4.2 Fragile financial market structure that was not considered above

We argued that the Korean crisis appeared to be triggered by bank-runs rather than speculative currency attacks. We also argued that the critical news triggering the crisis seemed to be the *chaebol* bankruptcies and the bail-out policies of the government. In relation to these arguments, this subsection briefly mentions the fragile aspects of Korea's financial system that were not considered in the probit model analyses.

Perhaps the most important weaknesses in Korea's financial structure that were overlooked in the probit analyses were the low profitability and the high leverage ratio of the corporate sector. Figure 6.5, quoted from Nam et al. (1999), shows that the corporate sector of Korea had the lowest profitability and the highest debt/equity ratio among the eight Asian countries. This financial structure of the corporate sector must have been a big potential threat to the banking sector of Korea.

In addition, the high concentration of financial assets in a small number of *chaebols* was perceived to be another factor causing vulnerability in the financial system. Table 6.11 shows that the top 30 *chaebols* governed almost 50 percent of the total assets in Korea. Under this high concentration ratio, a small negative shock to the *chaebols* could develop into systemic risk of the whole banking sector. In this regard, the severe deterioration in the profitability of the top six to

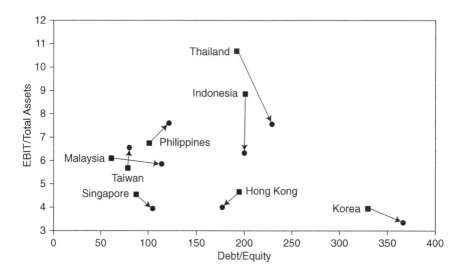

Figure 6.5 Debt equity ratio and earnings before interest and taxes/total assets for east Asian countries: 1991–1996

Unit: (%)

Source: Nam et al. (1999).

Note: ■ denotes average for 1991–1992, • denotes average for 1995–1996.

Table 6.11 Largest *chaebols*: April 1996 (Unit: trillion won)

	Total Assets	Leverage (Debt/Equity)	Number of Subsidiaries	Date of Bankruptcy
1. Hyundai	43.7 (6.94%)	440%	46	
2. Samsung	40.8 (6.48%)	279%	55	
3. LG	31.4 (4.99%)	345%	48	
4. Daewoo	31.3 (4.97%)	391%	25	
5. SK	14.6 (2.32%)	352%	32	
6. Ssangyong	13.9 (2.21%)	310%	23	
7. Hanjin	12.2 (1.94%)	559%	24	
8. Kia	11.4 (1.81%)	522%	16	07/16/97*
9. Hanhwa	9.2 (1.46%)	712%	31	12/17/97***
10. Lotte	7.1 (1.13%)	191%	28	
11. Kumho	6.4 (1.02%)	480%	27	
12. Doosan	5.8 (0.92%)	907%	26	
13. Daelim	5.4 (0.86%)	424%	18	
14. Hanbo	5.1 (0.81%)	648%	21	01/18/97*
15. Dongah	5.1 (0.81%)	362%	16	01/10/98***
16. Halla	4.8 (0.76%)	2457%	17	12/03/97***
17. Hyosung	3.6 (0.57%)	362%	16	
18. Dongkuk	3.4 (0.54%)	223%	16	
19. Jinro	3.3 (0.52%)	4836%	14	09/09/97**
20. Kolon	3.1 (0.49%)	340%	19	
21. Tongyang	3.0 (0.48%)	305%	22	
22. Hansol	3.0 (0.48%)	291%	19	
23. Dongbu	2.9 (0.46%)	219%	24	
24. Kohap	2.9 (0.46%)	603%	11	01/30/98***
25. Haitai	2.9 (0.46%)	669%	14	08/26/97*
26. Sammi	2.5 (0.40%)	3333%	8	03/20/97*
27. Hanil	2.2 (0.35%)	581%	8	12/31/97***
28. Keukdong	2.2 (0.35%)	516%	11	
29. NewCore	2.0 (0.32%)	1253%	18	05/23/97**
30. Byucksan	1.9 (0.30%)	473%	16	
Total	286.9 (45.6%)		669	

Note: Figures in parentheses are the share of total assets of the corporate sector in Korea (629.8 trillion won as of the end of 1996). *, **, *** denote bankruptcy, standstill agreement, syndicated loan, respectively. Data from *Fair Trade Commission*.

70 *chaebols* since 1995 as shown in Figure 6.6 was a growing threat to the whole banking system of Korea. In Table 6.11, we also report the bankruptcy dates to show how many *chaebols* went bankrupt during 1997. Recognizing this structure of Korea's financial system may help readers to better understand why the financial market reacted so drastically to the news of *chaebol* bankruptcies.

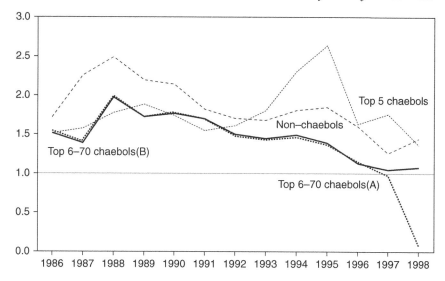

Figure 6.6 Interest payment coverage ratios for listed firms

Data Source: National Information and Credit Evaluation Inc.

Note:
1) Figures for 1998 are those for the first half of 1998.
2) (A) includes all subsidiaries of the top 6–70 *chaebols*.
   (B) excludes Kia and Asia automobile companies among the top 6–70 *chaebols*.

5. Concluding Remarks

This chapter examines the Korean currency crisis, focusing on the weaknesses in domestic fundamentals as opposed to the external contagious effects. The results of this chapter appear to suggest that the contagion effects were large but not sufficient enough to explain Korea's crisis. In particular, the triggering moment of the crisis did not appear to be attributable to the contagion effects.

As for the conventional factors that are considered to be important in explaining the currency crisis, Korea's fundamentals were weak but not extremely so as to generate such a deep crisis. While external transactions were loosely managed, domestic macro- fundamentals appeared to be sound. Nevertheless, the Korean currency crisis seems to have been triggered by runs on the major banks, with the triggering moment associated with the bankruptcies of *chaebols* and the non-transparent bail-out policies of the government. This observation seems to suggest that additional fragile aspects of the financial system may need to draw more attention in explaining Korea's crisis. Examples of such aspects are the low profitability and high leverage ratio of the corporate sector, the high concentration ratio of financial assets in a small number of *chaebols*, and so forth.

A crucial question that arises here is why the bank-runs were triggered by foreign investors while domestic investors were less trembled. A possible explanation is the divergence of expectations about conventional practices of the government's policies. That is, the implicit expectation about bail-out policies for *chaebol* and financial institutions was widely spread out among Korean investors, while it was not among foreign investors. If this proposition is the case, Korea's crisis was a more fundamental crisis for the whole financial system of Korea rather than a simple liquidity crisis for foreign exchanges. In other words, the crisis may have been an inevitable outcome when the implicit bail-out expectation among Korean investors (or the "crony capitalism" of Krugman, 1998) was broken by foreign investors. This is a complex issue that should be further investigated in the future.

APPENDIX: DATA SOURCES

1. Cross-country data

Most of the data used in Section 2 are extracted from the *World Development Indicators on CD-ROM 1998* by the World Bank (hereafter WDI98), unless indicated otherwise.

Crisis index

The crisis index takes value 1 for a currency crisis and value 0 otherwise. A crisis is defined as annual depreciation of the nominal exchange rate (with respect to US dollar) of at least 25 percent that is also at least a 10 percent increase in the rate of depreciation.

Growth rate of per capita GDP

The per capita GDP growth rate is constructed by taking the log difference of per capita GDP.

Growth rate of real domestic credit

Real domestic credit denotes domestic credit extended to the private sector by the banking sector divided by the consumer price index (CPI). The banking sector comprises monetary authorities, depository banks, and other financial institutions (for instance, mutual credit unions and housing financial cooperatives)

Ratio of foreign exchange reserve to short-term foreign debt

The data for foreign exchange reserves are from the *International Finance Statistics CD-ROM March 1999* (hereafter IFS), and short-term foreign debt is obtained by multiplying total foreign debt by the share of short-term foreign debt in total foreign debt. Total foreign debt includes foreign borrowings by the government sector, government-guaranteed foreign borrowings, non-government-guaranteed private borrowings, and credit and short-term debt provided by the International Monetary Fund.

Depreciation of the real exchange rate

The real exchange rate depreciation is the log difference of the nominal exchange rate over CPI. The nominal exchange rate is the year-end market exchange rate from IFS, while CPI is from WDI98.

Changes in the terms of trade

Changes in the terms of trade are constructed by taking the log difference of the ratio of export price to import price. The export and import prices are export and import values (in current US dollars) divided by export and import volumes (in constant local currency), respectively.

FDI/GDP

FDI denotes net foreign direct investment inflow.

Growth rate of foreign GDP

The foreign GDP growth rate is the log difference of the total sum of GDPs of OECD economies.

Foreign interest Rates

Foreign interest rates are the weighted average of lending rates in the US, Japan, UK, Germany, and France. The weights are given by the currency composition of the long-term debt in each country. The currency composition ratios are from the *Global Development Finance* (World Bank, 1997 and 1998) and the *World Debt Tables* (World Bank, various issues).

Regional contagion index

The regional contagion index is a weighted average of the crisis indexes of other countries. The weights are given by the inverse of the geographical distance between the country in question and other countries. For the geographical distance between two countries, latitude and longitude of the corresponding capital cities are used.

Trade linkage index

The trade linkage index in Section 2 is the same with the one used by Glick and Rose (1998). The trade linkage between two countries 0 and i are given by the following:

$$Trade_i \equiv \sum_k \left[\left| \frac{(X_{0k} + X_{ik})}{(X_0 + X_i)} \right| \cdot \left| \frac{1 - |(X_{ik} - X_{0k})|}{(X_{ik} + X_{0k})} \right| \right],$$

where X_{ik} denotes aggregate bilateral exports from country i to k ($k \neq i$, 0) and X_i denotes aggregate exports from country i.

2. Daily data

Sovereign spreads

The spread is defined by subtracting the yield rate on the US treasury bill from the yield rate on each sovereign bond in the secondary market. We collected the yield rate of each country's sovereign bond from Bloomberg Online. The following are the cusip numbers of the sovereign bonds, along with the specific name of the bond and due date.

> Argentina: 040114AN0, ARGENT 11 10/06, GOVT, USD.
> Brazil: 105756AG5, BRAZIL9 3/8, 04/08, USD, GOVT.
> Mexico: 593048bf7, MEX8 5/8. 03/12/08, GOVT.
> Malaysia: PETRONAS 7 1/8, 10/06, USD, PETRONAS.
> China: 712219AE4, CHINA 7 3/4 07/06, USD, GOVT.
> Indonesia: 455780AB2, INDO 7 3/4 08/06, USD, GOVT.
> Thailand: 88322kac5, Thailand Kingdom, Thai, 3/4 04/07.
> Korea: Korea Development Bank due to 2003, 10 years , Global.
> Japan: TOKYO MISTZUBISHI, BOT7 3/4 11/02/02.
> Russia: XS0077745163, RUSSIA 10 06/07, USD, GOVT.
> Treasury Bill: T 5 1/4, 02/15/29, 30 years.

Notes

* This chapter is reprinted from *Regional and Global Capital Flows: Macroeconomic Causes and Consequences*, NBER, edited by Anne Krueger and Takatoshi Ito, Chicago Press, pp. 337–373, 2001, which was co-authored with Ki-Seok Hong.
1 See Eichengreen, Rose and Wyplosz (1995) for a detailed survey on the literature.
2 For discussion on various channels of contagion effects, see Calvo and Reinhart (1996) and Valdes (1996).
3 Nevertheless, there exists pioneering research that attempts to identify fundamental channels of contagion effects. For example, see Doukas (1989) for the channel through co-movements of major macro-variables, Glick and Rose (1998) for the channel through trade, and Frankel and Schmulker (1996) for the channel through the New York investor fund community. For more micro-data analyses that particularly stress the role of incomplete information, see Aharony and Swary (1983, 1996), Park (1991), Karafiath, Mynatt and Smith (1991), Calomiris and Mason (1994).
4 Ideally, the definition of a currency crisis should be comprehensive enough to fully incorporate various events such as violent depreciation of the exchange rate, sharp reduction in foreign exchange reserves and rapid increase in interest rates. For developing countries, however, it is hard to find an interest rate measure that is consistent across countries and free from direct government control. Also, developing countries with weak fundamentals tend to eventually develop a currency

crisis regardless of their efforts to defend their currencies using foreign exchange reserves. Thus, we use only the nominal exchange rate in constructing our crisis index.

5 Since distributions of thus constructed indexes are close to lognormal, we prevent influence of potential outliers by taking logarithms of the indexes. Main results remain unaffected by the use of the original indexes.

6 According to the estimates, a one unit increase in the trade contagion index and our contagion index (100 percent increase in the original contagion indexes) increases the probability of a currency crisis by four and six percentage points, respectively.

7 It is obvious that trade is more active among countries in geographical proximity. In fact, correlation of the two indexes in our pooled data set is 0.7.

8 One problem is that, due to data availability, we used only the 1997 international trade matrix assuming that the trade linkage is constant over time. For more rigorous results, we need to construct the trade linkage for every year. When the sample period is restricted to 1992 through 1997, however, our index still dominates the trade linkage.

9 Rigorously speaking, the estimated probability is not ex-ante, since the contagion index takes contemporaneous values. For countries like Korea where a crisis took place at the end of the year, however, the probability may well be considered as ex-ante.

10 Table 6.2C is not a true out-of-sample exercise, since observations in 1997 are used in the estimation. An out-of-sample exercise, however, changes the results only slightly.

11 Put more precisely, "domestic shock" is defined as the component that is orthogonal to shocks to other countries in the sample. Therefore, it is likely that more variations are attributed to domestic shocks when a smaller number of countries are included in the sample.

12 All of the exchange rates are against the US dollar, and correlation across countries may be spurious in that it may reflect the common fluctuation of the US dollar. In this sense, an interpretation about the absolute degree of the correlation coefficient should be made with caution. However, comparison of the coefficient with other countries is largely immune from this problem.

13 Experiments with more than two lagged variables did not greatly change the simulation results, and the null of no drift term was accepted for all of the regressions.

14 For example, Valdes (1996) used the average of weekly data for the sovereign spreads for Latin American countries.

15 Experiments with more than two lagged variables did not greatly change the simulation results, and the constant terms appeared to be insignificant for most countries.

References

Agenor, Pierre-Richard and Joshua Aizenman, 1997. "Contagion and Volatility with Imperfect Credit Markets," International Monetary Fund, Washington, DC.

Aharony, Joseph and Itzhak Swary, 1983. "Contagion Effects of Bank Failures: Evidence from Capital Markets," *Journal of Business*, 56, pp. 305–322.

———, 1986. "Additional evidence on the information-based contagion effects of bank failures," *Journal of Banking & Finance*, 20, pp. 57–69.

Baig, Taimur and Ilan Goldfajn, 1998. "Financial Market Contagion in the Asian Crisis", IMF Working Paper No. 98/155, November.

Calomiris, Charles W., and Joseph R. Mason, 1994. "Contagion and Bank Failures during the Great Depression: The June 1932 Chicago Banking Panic," NBER Working Paper no. 4934, Cambridge, MA.

Calvo, Sara, and Carmen Reinhart, 1996. "Capital Flows to Latin America: Is there Evidence of Contagion Effects?", Institute for International Economics, Policy Research Working Paper no. 1619, Washington, DC.

Chnag, Roberto and Andres Velasco, 1998. "Financial Crises in Emerging Markets: A Canonical Model", NBER Working Paper No. 6606, June.

Cole, Harold L. and Timothy J. Kehoe, 1996. "A Self-Fulfilling Model of Mexico's 1994-1995 Debt Crisis", *Journal of International Economics*, 41(Nov.), pp. 309–330.

Doukas, John, 1989. "Contagion Effect on Sovereign Interest Rate Spreads," *Economics Letters*, 29, pp. 237–241.

Eichengreen, Barry, Andrew K. Rose, and Charles Wyplosz, 1995. "Exchange Market Mayhem: The Antecedents and Aftermath of Speculative Attacks," *Economic Policy*, 21(Oct.), pp. 251–312.

Flood, Robert, Garber, Peter M. and Charles Kramer, 1996. "Collapsing Exchange Rate Regimes: Another Linear Example", *Journal of International Economics*, 41(Nov.), pp. 223–234.

Frankel, Jeffrey A. and Sergio L. Schmukler, 1996. "Crisis, Contagion, and Country Funds: Effects on East Asia and Latin America," Center for Pacific Basin Monetary and Economic Studies Working Paper no. PB96–04, San Francisco, CA.

Glick, Reuven, and Andrew K. Rose, 1998. "Contagion and Trade: Why Are Currency Crises Regional?", Unpublished Manuscript, UC Berkeley, August 12, (available at http://haas.berkeley.edu/~arose).

Goldfajn, Ilan, and Rodrigo O. Valdes, 1997. "Capital Flows and the Twin Crises: The Role of Liquidity," IMF Working Paper, July, Washington, DC.

Karafiath, Imre, Ross Mynatt, and Kenneth, L. Smith, 1991. "The Brazilian Default Announcement and the Contagion Effect Hypothesis," *Journal of Banking and Finance*, 15, pp. 699–716.

Krugman, Paul, 1979. "A Model of Balance of Payment Crisis," *Journal of Money, Credit, and Banking*, 11, pp. 311–325.

———, 1994. "The Myth of Asia's Miracle," *Foreign Affairs*, 73, pp. 62–78.

———, 1998. "What happened to Asia?", Unpublished manuscript (available at http://web.mit.edu/krugman/www/DISINTER.html).

Nam, Il-Chong, Yeongjae Kang, and Joon-Kyung Kim, 1999. "Comparative Corporate Governance Trends in Asia," Working paper submitted to the Conference on Corporate Governance in Asia: A Comparative Perspective sponsored by OECD and KDI, March 1999.

Obstfeld, Maurice, 1995. "Models of Currency Crisis with Self-Fulfilling Features," NBER Working Paper no. 5285, Cambridge, MA.

Park, Sangkyun, 1991. "Bank failure contagion in historical perspective," *Journal of Monetary Economics*, 28, pp. 271–286.

Perry, Guillermo E. and Daniel Lederman, 1998. "Financial Vulnerability, Spillover Effects, and Contagion: Lessons from the Asian Crises for Latin America," World Bank Latin American and Caribbean Studies, Washington, DC.

Shin, In-seok, 1998. "Currency Crisis of Korea: A Thought on the Triggering Mechanism," Unpublished working paper, Korea Development Institute, Seoul (in Korean).

Valdes, Rodrigo O., 1996. "Essays on Capital Flows and Exchange Rates," Ph.D. Dissertation, MIT, Cambridge, MA.

World Bank, 1993. *The East Asian Miracle: Economic Growth and Public Policy.* New York: Oxford University Press.

Young, Alwyn, 1995. "The Tyranny of Numbers: Confronting the Statistical Realities of the East Asian Growth Experience," *Quarterly Journal of Economics*, 110, pp. 641–680.

7 Interest rates and exchange rates in the Korean, Philippine and Thai exchange rate crises*

1. Introduction

The outbreak of the currency crisis in Asia raised many questions to economists. A main question was, naturally, what was the major cause of the crisis and whether it was predictable?

An equally important question, which we consider here, is whether the policy response was effective: once the stabilization programs were executed and the economic crisis deepened, the macro-policy stance became an important subject for debate. In conformity with the recommendation of the IMF, tight monetary and fiscal policies were followed. Many economists criticized this traditional approach because most Asian countries, unlike Latin American countries, had maintained sound macro-stability in terms of inflation and government budget deficits. Sachs was a forerunner in this line of criticism:

> The region does not need wanton budget cutting, credit tightening and emergency bank closures. It needs stable or even slightly expansionary monetary and fiscal policies to counterbalance the decline in foreign loans. Interest rates will drift higher as foreign investors withdraw their money, but those rates do not need to be artificially jacked up by a squeeze of domestic credit.
>
> (1997, p. 2)

In spite of this criticism, the IMF prevailed upon the crisis countries to sharply raise call rates, largely with the goal of slowing or stopping exchange rate depreciation. Stressing the intention that the high interest rate policy would be maintained only temporarily, Fischer expresses the IMF's view as follows:

> By the time these countries approached the IMF, the value of their currencies was plummeting, and in the case of Thailand and Korea, reserves were perilously low. . . . To reverse this process, countries have to make it more attractive to hold domestic currency, and that means temporarily raising interest rates, even if this complicates the situation of weak banks and corporations. . . . Once confidence is restored, interest rates should return to more normal levels.
>
> (1998, p. 4)

Yet, the criticism did not subside, and some economists even cast doubt on the basic presumption that a high interest rate policy helps stabilize the exchange rate. For example, Furman and Stiglitz (1998) argue that a temporary increase in interest rates can, at best, stabilize the exchange rate temporarily only under stable environments. In countries with unstable financial environments, they further argue, the temporary increase in interest rates could possibly endanger the currency values not only temporarily but also long term by increasing default probability and uncertainty about the future.

The debate gradually subsided after interest rates were lowered and the economies began to recover. To our knowledge, however, there have been few attempts to systematically assess whether the high interest rate policy was indeed effective in stabilizing the exchange rate in the Asian countries. A rare example is Park and Choi (1999). Using offshore forward rates as proxies for the market's expected future exchange rates, they tested the effects of the interest rate policy through a covered interest parity. Their finding is that the high interest rate policy was associated with exchange rate appreciation except for Malaysia but that the sizes of effects were small.

This chapter explicitly considers risk factors, the key variables of the Furman-Stiglitz argument. For reduced form relationships of the variables, we use the daily data on call rate, the won/dollar exchange rate and other variables in the floating period, December 17, 1997–June 30, 1999. Similar to the result of Park and Choi (1999), we find that increases in interest rates are associated with exchange rate appreciation. But the estimated daily elasticity is about 1, a sizable effect. This result holds both in single equation regressions that control for risk variables such as the bankruptcy rate and in vector autoregressions. We also find that the major variable driving the stabilization of the financial market in general was the ratio of short-term external debt to reserves, a measure of foreign currency liquidity. Decreases in this ratio seem to account for most of the appreciation of the exchange rate as well as the fall in the call rate that occurred in our sample.

The chapter is organized as follows. Section 2 briefly explains the trends of the relevant financial variables right before and after the crisis. Section 3 provides an analytic framework to understand the essence of the debate on the relationship between the interest rate and the exchange rate. Section 4 presents various regressions whose specifications are motivated by Section 3's framework. Section 5 adds discussion on broader issues regarding the interest rate policy after the crisis in Korea. Section 6 concludes.

2. Trends of financial variables

Rapid growth of the Korean economy had long hidden vulnerable financial structures. Financial leverage was high and the corporate sector's profit margin low (see Nam et al., 1999 for example). As the economy entered a recession in 1996, many large conglomerates with fragile financial structures began to go bankrupt and financial markets were trembling.

In July 1997, the currency crisis broke out in Thailand, and its adverse effects rapidly reached the Korean economy. The Korean exchange rate was depreciating (see Figure 7.1) and interest rates were rising (see Figure 7.2). As the credit market was tightened, the bankruptcy rate was increasing (see Figure 7.3) and non-performing loans were accumulating at explosive rates. Credit ratings of major banks were downgraded, and foreign investors were losing their confidence about the Korean economy. As an indicator of the diminishing confidence of foreign investors, Figure 7.4 shows that the risk premium of the dollar denominated Korean Development Bank (KDB) bond over the US Treasury bond rose above 1 percent. As foreign investors squeezed credit lines to the Korean market, the exchange rate faced further depreciation pressures. Under the policy goal of "gradual" depreciation, however, the Korean government often intervened in the foreign exchange market, losing foreign reserves (see Figure 7.5).

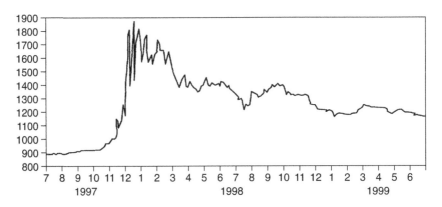

Figure 7.1 Exchange rate (won per US dollar)

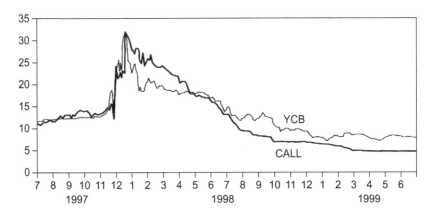

Figure 7.2 Domestic interest rate (%)

Note: CALL is the one-day inter-bank call rate and YCB is the yield rate on three-year corporate bond.

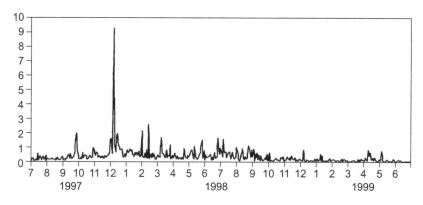

Figure 7.3 Bankruptcy rate (%)

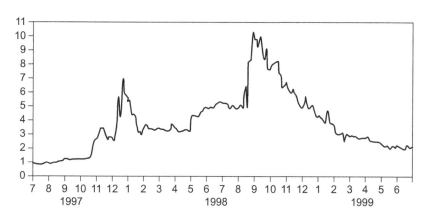

Figure 7.4 Risk premium on the KDB bond (%)

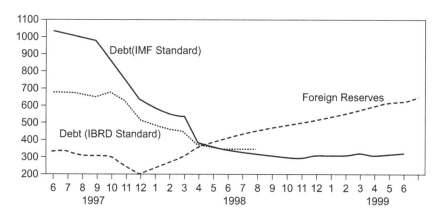

Figure 7.5 Foreign reserves and short-term external debt (hundred million dollars)

In October 1997, currency speculators attacked Hong Kong, and Asian financial markets became even more unstable. As the Korean government kept attempting to defend the currency value, it was widely expected that foreign reserves
would be depleted soon. At the same time, the suspicion was rapidly growing that
if the debt of offshore branches were included, the size of short-term external
liabilities would be far larger than the official statistics (following the International
Bank for Reconstruction and Development [IBRD] standard) of around
$68 billion.

The daily bandwidth on the exchange rate was widened from 2.5 to 10 percent on November 20, 1997. The next day, November 21, 1997, the Korean
government finally asked for IMF support. The daily band on the exchange rate
fluctuation was completely abolished and the exchange rate system moved into
a free-floating system from December 17, 1997. After the IMF program started,
the Korean government confirmed the suspicion that external liabilities were
understated and changed the official statistics to include offshore liabilities of
Korean financial institution's branches. Figure 7.5 shows two series of short-
term external liabilities, one following the IBRD standard and the other following the IMF standard. According to the new statistics, short-term debt amounted
to around $100 billion before the crisis, as depicted in Figure 7.6; this was
approximately three times as large as the foreign reserves at that time. The
exchange rate kept rising up to 1,860 won/dollar on December 24, 1997, and
the monetary authority raised the call rate to more than 30 percent from around
20–23 percent. The exchange rate stopped depreciating further, although volatility was still huge.

In February 1998, the Korean government started to bargain with foreign
creditors to restructure about $20 billion of short-term private debts into long-
term debts with government guarantees. This restructuring was completed successfully, and the Korean economy obtained some breathing space in the foreign
exchange market. As domestic demand collapsed by almost 20 percent, the

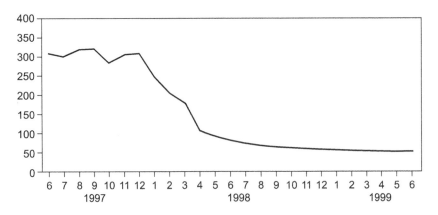

Figure 7.6 Short-term external debt as a percentage of foreign reserves (%)

current account was running huge surplus (more than 12 percent of GDP in 1998) and foreign reserves kept growing. As a result, the exchange rate was stabilized in terms of the level as well as volatility. As the exchange rate was stabilized down to 1,200–1,250 won/dollar in July 1999, monetary policy continued to be eased and the call rate was lowered to 10 percent by the end of July.

In August 1998, the Russian moratorium and subsequent currency crisis of Brazil hit the international capital market, and the risk premium of the KDB bond surged to around 10 percent. The exchange rate depreciated to more than 1,300 won/dollar again, but this time the call rate continued to be lowered. As the turmoil in the international capital market gradually subsided, both the risk premium and the exchange rate were stabilized. In mid-1999, the call rate went below 5 percent, the lowest level in the Korean history, and the exchange rate fluctuated around 1,200 won/dollar.

3. Debate on theoretical justification of high interest rate policy

In accordance with the views of the IMF, the sharp rise of the call rate in December 1997 was intended in large part to slow or stop the depreciation of the won. One simple way to express this view analytically is with *uncovered interest parity*. Let i_t and i_t^* be the net nominal interest rates on Korean and foreign, say US, bonds. Let e_t be the logarithm of the won/dollar rate; as in Figure 7.1, a higher value of e_t means a depreciated currency. Then the net return from converting 1 won into dollars, getting return $1 + i_t^*$, and converting back into won is approximately $i_t^* + e_{t+1} - e_t$. If exchange rate speculators are risk neutral and the bonds are default-free, speculators should expect to make the same return whether they invest in the Korean or US bond. This means

$$i_t^* + E_t e_{t+1} - e_t = i_t,$$ (3.1)

where E_t denotes expectations. Rearranging, we have

$$e_t = i_t^* + E_t e_{t+1} - i_t.$$ (3.2)

If we hold i_t^* and $E_t e_{t+1}$ fixed, increases in the domestic interest rate i_t quite evidently are associated with declines, that is appreciation, of e_t. The foreign interest rate i_t^* arguably does not vary with the Korean interest rate i_t. The same cannot be said of the expected exchange rate $E_t e_{t+1}$. But if increases in i_t increase confidence that the exchange rate will stabilize (see Fischer's statement in the introduction), then increases i_t will cause $E_t e_{t+1}$ to fall, thus reinforcing the effects that result when $E_t e_{t+1}$ is held fixed.

Uncovered interest parity is simple and appealing, but it may not suitably capture the movement in exchange rates. One well-known problem is that speculators apparently are *not* risk neutral; there is a risk premium, call it v_t, associated with attempting to arbitrage differences in expected returns in Korean and US debt. A second problem, applicable to Korea though probably not developed countries, is that even government debt might not have been perceived as nominally riskless. If the probability of complete default is thought to be say δ_t, then the expected return on a Korean bond is $(1 - \delta_t)(1 + i_t) \cong 1 + i_t - \delta_t$, i.e. the net expected return is about $i_t - \delta_t$. After accounting for both a risk premium and possible default, (3.2) becomes

$$e_t = i_t^* + E_t e_{t+1} - i_t + \delta_t + v_t. \tag{3.3}$$

Of course, complete default may seem extreme. But delaying payment of principal or interest was surely a reasonable possibility and such considerations also lead to an expression like (3.3).

Furman and Stiglitz (1998, p. 75) argue that in countries with currency crises, such as Korea, both the default probability δ_t and the risk premium v_t are increasing functions of the domestic interest rate i_t. A direct reason for this is the presence of unhedged foreign debt. As well, since increases in i_t lead to increases in corporate borrowing cost, businesses will find it difficult to finance operations and some may even go bankrupt. If this is expected to cause strains on the economy as a whole, speculators may doubt the government's ability to repay and hence δ_t and v_t will rise. This possibility may have been large particularly in Korea because the government guaranteed most bank deposits right after the outbreak of the crisis and the accumulated burden of non-performing loans in the banking sector was almost entirely transferred to the government.

We see from (3.3) that if δ_t and v_t are increasing in i_t, the effect of increases in i_t are ambiguous, even if we accept the view that $E_t e_{t+1}$ is a decreasing function of i_t. Panel data studies yield mixed evidence on whether increases in interest rates stabilize an exchange rate during a currency crisis. For example, Goldfajn and Gupta (1999) consider currency crises in 80 countries, 1980–1998. They find that, on average, and consistent with the IMF's view, dramatic increases in real interest rates have been associated with currency appreciations. But when they focus on a subsample that endured a banking crisis along with a currency crises, the evidence is mixed. Since Korea is exactly such a country, it is an open question whether the interest rate policy stabilized the exchange rate.

4. Empirical results

4.1 Overview

The first three subsections below present single equation regression results for the log of the exchange rate (LEXCH), the level of which is plotted in Figure 7.1; the difference in yields between dollar denominated KDB bonds and US Treasury bonds (SPREAD), which is plotted in Figure 7.4; and the call rate (CALL), which is plotted in Figure 7.2. Subsection 4.5 presents results for a four variable system that includes these variables as well as the ratio of short-term debt to reserves (ILLIQ), the variable plotted in Figure 7.6.

All variables are daily (five days per week) and are entered in percentage terms. We used daily data because decisions about interest rate policy were made on a day-to-day basis right after the crisis. When the policy depends on the variations of endogenous variables, the use of high-frequency data may help reduce the simultaneity bias. We do, of course, pay the usual price of not having daily observations on many important variables (for example, reserves and debt: we construct daily values of ILLIQ by linearly interpolating the numerator and denominator).

We began by checking stationarity of the variables and found that it seems advisable to take all the variables except the bankruptcy rate (BNKRP) as series with unit autoregressive roots (details available on request). Therefore, our regressions were performed with first-differenced data. We also checked whether there is a structural break in the regressions at 12/17/97 (the date when the complete floating exchange rate system began) and found strong evidence for a break (details available on request). Hence, we report the regression results for the sample period from 12/17/97 to 6/30/99. In fact, the interest rate policy was not used to stabilize the exchange rate before 12/17/97, and thus analyses for the post-floating data seem to be more relevant to the purpose of this chapter.

Throughout this chapter's empirical analyses, we also modeled the contemporaneous daily correlation among variables under an assumption of a recursive causal ordering. First, variables determined outside Korea, such as the LIBOR and the yen/dollar exchange rate, are predetermined relative to Korean variables. As predetermined variables, their contemporaneous values are entered on the right hand side of the regressions below. Second, the sizes of the short-term external debt and foreign currency reserves (and hence ILLIQ, the ratio of debt to reserves) are considered predetermined. Third, the monetary authority determines the call rate day-by-day, taking as given the current values of the predetermined variables and, of course, lags of all variables. Fourth, risk factors such as Korea's risk premium are determined in light of the call rate and all the predetermined variables (and, of course, lagged variables). Finally, the exchange rate is determined, responding to the contemporaneous values of all these variables (and their lags).

4.2 Determinants of the exchange rate: single regression equation

Some single equation regression results for the exchange rate are reported in Table 7.1. The effect of the call rate (CALL) is statistically significant and robust across various specifications. This result is rather surprising, given that the levels of the two variables are positively correlated with high significance. Probably, changes in a third factor contributed to the stabilization of both the call rate and the exchange rate, while the negative correlation between the two variables was maintained. Such a possibility is suggested by the estimate of the constant drift, 0.1 percent per day (37 percent during the sample period), although this estimate is not statistically significant.

Table 7.1 Regressions of the exchange rate

	(1)	(2)	(3)	(4)	(5)	(6)	(7)
CONST	-0.100 (0.101)	-0.092 (0.100)	-0.183 (0.141)	0.000 (0.116)	0.050 (0.120)	-0.090 (0.146)	-0.098 (0.146)
ΔCALL	-1.180** (0.166)	-1.158** (0.164)	-1.172** (0.164)	-1.196** (0.165)	-1.202** (0.164)	-1.214** (0.169)	-1.210** (0.170)
ΔSPREAD		1.085** (0.343)	1.036** (0.348)	1.050** (0.343)	1.072** (0.342)	1.021** (0.351)	1.036** (0.352)
BNKRP			0.270 (0.295)			0.503 (0.307)	0.518 (0.308)
ΔILLIQ				0.141 (0.893)			
$\Delta_{(-20)}$ILLIQ					0.011** (0.005)	0.013** (0.005)	0.013** (0.005)
ΔLEXCH(-1)						-0.030 (0.041)	-0.032 (0.416)
ΔLIBOR							-0.024 (0.022)
ΔLYEN							0.090 (0.086)
R^2	0.120	0.143	0.146	0.149	0.153	0.160	0.166
DW	1.830	1.861	1.874	1.865	1.883	1.886	1.892

Notes:
1. The dependent variable is the log difference of the won/dollar exchange rate, ΔLEXCH.
2. Δ denotes first difference and the definitions of variables are as follows: CALL the call rate; SPREAD the risk premium on the dollar denominated KDB bond over the US Treasury bond rate; BNKRP the domestic bankruptcy rate; ILLIQ the ratio of short-term debt to reserves; $\Delta_{(-20)}$ILLIQ the difference of ILLIQ at time t and ILLIQ at time t-20; LIBOR the 1-month LIBOR rate; LYEN the log of the yen/dollar exchange rate.
3. All variables are expressed in percent.
4. ** denotes an estimate significant at the 1 percent level, * an estimate significant at the 5 percent level.

In fact, country risk can be a good candidate for such a third factor. When a country's risk is lowered, either the exchange rate or the interest rate, or both, can be lowered according to equation (3.3). We considered three variables that can measure the risk of Korea: (1) the risk premium on the dollar denominated KDB bond over the US Treasury bond rate (SPREAD), (2) the domestic bankruptcy rate (BNKRP), and (3) the ratio of short-term debt to reserves (ILLIQ). While SPREAD is expected to measure the perception of international investors about long-term risk in Korea, both BNKRP and ILLIQ are expected to capture short-term default risks. In particular, BNKRP is supposed to proxy the default risk in domestic currency, while ILLIQ measures the risk associated with the currency convertibility. For ILLIQ, the actual values were announced only once (short-term debt) or twice (reserves, after the IMF agreement), and we linearly interpolated to obtain a daily series.

First, the effect of SPREAD appears to be significant and robust. In addition, the coefficient estimate is positive, as predicted by the theory. In contrast, BNKRP and ILLIQ appear to be insignificant. Regarding ILLIQ, however, because we obtained the daily series by interpolation, the first difference of this variable is almost constant for each month. For this reason, we also tried the difference between ILLIQ today and ILLIQ a month ago, so that this variable contains at least one change in the actual information. In our data set, the average number of sample points a month is 20. Using this 20-day difference variable, ILLIQ is statistically significant. The size of the coefficient estimate appears to be slightly larger than $1/20$ of the estimate for the one-day difference variable. These results seem to suggest that ILLIQ affects the exchange rate at a lower frequency than the daily frequency (this argument will be elaborated in subsection 4.5). In relation to the aforementioned constant term that is estimated to be almost zero, this variable appears to capture the secular decline of the exchange rate during the sample period.

In order to check impacts of omitted variables, we also experimented with two variables, the short-term LIBOR and the yen/dollar exchange rate. Both variables are statistically insignificant. We also included one-day lagged variables, one by one, for all of the explanatory variables (details available on request). Only the lagged variable of CALL is significant with another negative sign, and the yen/dollar exchange rate is significant at a 10 percent significance level.

Let us gauge the magnitude of the coefficient estimates in the context of the Korea's crisis, under the admittedly debatable assumption that we can take the estimates in Table 7.1 as structural. Recall that Korea's exchange rate depreciated by about 80 percent (from about 1,000 to about 1,800 won/dollar) during December 1997. The interest rate elasticity of 1.2 in Table 7.2 implies that call rates would have to be raised by more than 60 percent (that is, from about 12 to more than 70 percent) to pull the exchange rate to the pre-crisis level. A more serious problem with this policy is that the call rate would have to have been permanently maintained at that level to sustain the exchange rate stability, unless other factors change in the direction to stabilize the exchange rate in the meantime.

Table 7.2 Regressions of the risk premium

	(1)	(2)	(3)	(4)	(5)	(6)	(7)
CONST	-0.007	-0.004	-0.048*	-0.035	-0.040	-0.035	-0.034
	(0.151)	(0.015)	(0.021)	(0.021)	(0.021)	(0.021)	(0.021)
ΔCALL	-0.020		-0.043	-0.055*	-0.048	-0.057*	-0.057*
	(0.025)		(0.025)	(0.025)	(0.025)	(0.025)	(0.025)
ΔLEXCH(-1)		0.019**	0.020**	0.021**	0.020**	0.019**	0.018**
		(0.006)	(0.006)	(0.006)	(0.006)	(0.006)	(0.006)
BNKRP			0.125**	0.159**	0.142**	0.155**	0.157**
			(0.043)	(0.045)	(0.045)	(0.045)	(0.045)
ΔILLIQ				0.035*		0.034*	0.034*
				(0.014)		(0.014)	(0.014)
Δ(-20)ILLIQ					0.001		
					(0.0008)		
ΔSPREAD(-1)						0.074	0.072
						(0.051)	(0.051)
ΔLIBOR							0.373
							(0.326)
ΔLYEN							0.008
							(0.013)
R²	0.002	0.026	0.053	0.070	0.058	0.075	0.080
DW	1.773	1.859	1.870	1.906	1.879	2.023	2.029

Notes:
1. The dependent variable is the difference between the yields on dollar denominated Korean bonds (KDB) and US Treasury bonds, ΔSPREAD.
2. See note 2 to Table 7.1 for data definitions.
3. All variables are expressed in percent.
4. ** denotes an estimate significant at the 1 percent level, * an estimate significant at the 5 percent level.

In practice, the monetary authority raised the call rate by around 20 percent (30 percent minus the pre-crisis level of 12 percent); this partially offset the 80 percent depreciation leaving a net depreciation of approximately 50 percent (say, to around 1,500 won/dollar from the pre-crisis level of 1,000). While the interest rate was maintained at a high level, the Korean government hurried to announce comprehensive economic restructuring plans to recover investor confidence (in order to lower SPREAD). At the same time, the government tried to rapidly recover foreign reserves and restructure short-term foreign debts into long-term debts (in order to lower ILLIQ).

As for the magnitudes of the effects from the risk factors, most of the exchange rate stabilization can be attributed to the foreign currency liquidity recovery. Taking the daily exchange rate elasticity with respect to ILLIQ to be 0.14, the decline of ILLIQ approximately from 300 to 50 percent during the sample period "explains" 35 percent of appreciation of the exchange rate, say from 1,800 to 1,200 won/dollar. In particular, this variable declined rapidly in the initial period of the crisis, contributing to the early stabilization of the exchange rate.

SPREAD (fluctuating between 2 to 10 percent) accounts for less than 10 percent of the exchange rate movement. However, the fluctuation of the exchange rate right after the Russian moratorium, say from August to November 1998, appears to be mostly attributable to this variable. The direct effect of BNKRP (fluctuating below 3 percent for the most period of time) on the exchange rate appears insignificant both statistically and economically.

4.3 Determinants of the risk premium: possibility of perverse effects

Although the high interest rate policy appears to have appreciated the contemporaneous exchange rate, it may have generated perverse effects by increasing the risk factors as Furman and Stiglitz (1998) argue. We explore this possibility in this subsection. The proxies for risk factors are SPREAD, BNKRP and ILLIQ. We present regression results for SPREAD. We briefly summarize results for BNKRP, omitting details because this variable does not appear to be significant in explaining the exchange rate. Finally, we do not analyze ILLIQ at all, not only because its actual data frequency is monthly (or bi-monthly), but also because this variable was determined by independent policy efforts.

Table 7.2 shows some regression results of SPREAD, with the choice of what variables to include contemporaneously once again consistent with the causal ordering described in section 4.1 and our VAR specification given below. A key result is that the estimated coefficient on the call rate is small, suggesting that the high interest rate policy did not have a substantial direct effect on SPREAD. In fact, the coefficient estimate is negative in all specifications, significantly so in some. This result is rather consistent with the signaling argument that the high interest rate policy signals a serious commitment of the Korean government about painful reforms in the future. In any case, the size of the effect does not appear to be large: the coefficient estimate of about −.05 implies that an increase in the call rate of 20 percent can account for only a 1 percent decline of SPREAD.

Other variables appear to affect SPREAD more importantly. First, the positive and significant estimate of the coefficient on the lagged exchange rate means that depreciation of the exchange rate is associated with increases in SPREAD. This is consistent with investors perceiving that exchange rate depreciation increases the potential risk of the Korean market, perhaps because that market is exposed to large unhedged external debts.[1] Although the size of this effect is not so large (only 1 percent decline of SPREAD, again, can be attributed to an appreciation of the exchange rate by 50 percent), the fact that the estimate is positive has an important implication regarding the interest rate policy effect on the exchange rate. In addition to the direct stabilization effect discussed in section 4.2, we see now that the high interest rate policy has an indirect effect: high interest rates cause exchange rate appreciation (the direct effect seen in Table 7.1), which lowers SPREAD (Table 7.2), which in turn further appreciates the exchange rate (Table 7.1).

Note here that we used a lagged variable of the exchange rate because we attributed (in Table 7.1) the contemporaneous correlation between the two variables to the effect of SPREAD on the exchange rate, not the other way around. Of course, this is an untested assumption. If the contemporaneous positive correlation is attributed to the reversed causality, however, the possibility of the perverse effects diminishes even further and the danger of the exchange rate depreciation increases.

Next, we see in Table 7.2 that the bankruptcy rate also affects SPREAD with statistical significance. Although BNKRP does not appear to directly affect the exchange rate in Table 7.1, it may indirectly affect the exchange rate through the channel of SPREAD. In addition, if the high interest rate policy leads to the high bankruptcy rate, this indirect effect may then provide a channel that supports the Furman and Stiglitz (1988) argument.

To investigate this possibility, we estimated equations similar to those in Tables 7.1 and 7.2 with BNKRP as the dependent variable. We do not report the results in detail here because they indicated that the magnitude of this indirect effect on the exchange rate is too small to merit serious attention. Specifically, the effect of the first difference of CALL on BNKRP appears to be less than 0.1, with the statistical significance sensitive to the specification (details available upon request). In fact, this estimate of 0.1 is a large number in explaining the fluctuation of BNKRP itself: an increase of CALL by 20 percent can raise BNKRP by 2 percent, while BNKRP fluctuated only between 0 and 3 percent for the most of the sample period. However, the increase of BNKRP by 2 percent only raises SPREAD by 0.3 (= 2 × 0.15) percent and hence depreciates the exchange rate by a similar magnitude (the coefficient estimate of SPREAD in Table 7.1 is approximately equal to one). That is, the indirect effect through these many steps can hardly be large.

To return to Table 7.2: in terms of the magnitude of effect on SPREAD, ILLIQ appears to be the most important single determinant, although this variable does not appear as significant as the exchange rate or bankruptcy rate in terms of statistical significance. The coefficient estimate of 0.035 in conjunction with the decline of ILLIQ from 300 to 50 percent implies the decline of SPREAD by almost 9 percent.

Other variables such as the LIBOR, the yen/dollar exchange rate and lagged variables appear to be relatively insignificant. Nevertheless, it seems worthwhile to mention that the hike of SPREAD around September 1998 (see Figure 7.4 in Section 2) cannot be explained by any variables considered in this chapter. In fact, Cho and Hong (1999) argue that most of this hike can be attributable to "contagion effects" of the Russian moratorium and subsequent currency crisis of Latin America, rather than domestic factors. Therefore, there still exists a possibility of omitted variable biases, which we hope are not substantial.

In short, the regression results presented in this subsection suggest that the perverse effect of the high interest rate policy on the exchange rate was either nonexistent or negligible in magnitude.

4.4   Determinants of the call rate: endogenous policy reaction function

We have so far taken the behavior of the call rate as given. As explained in the introduction, however, the IMF recommended that the call rate be raised only temporarily until the foreign exchange market is stabilized. In this subsection, therefore, we examine whether exchange rate stabilization indeed changed the policy stance and more broadly which variables have the strongest effects on the call rate. Table 7.3 reports some regression results. Once again, the choice of what variables to include contemporaneously is consistent with the causal ordering described in subsection 4.1 and the other parts of this section: the monetary authority is assumed to set CALL based on contemporaneous information about ILLIQ but not SPREAD, BNKRP, or LEXCH.

First, the positive estimate of the coefficient on the previous day's exchange rate means that appreciation on one day tends to be followed by lower call rates the next day. This result is interesting, given that the two variables show a significantly negative correlation contemporaneously (see Table 7.1). That is, today's high interest rate tends to appreciate the exchange rate today (Table 7.1), which in turn tends to lower the interest rate next day (Table 7.3). Because the Table 7.3 estimate is only about .05, however, the magnitude of this effect is small: the exchange rate appreciation by 60 percent during the sample period can rationalize a 3 percent fall in the call rate. We shall see in the next subsection that the robust result is not the sign of the response but the fact that the elasticity is small in absolute value.

The most important determinant in magnitude appears to be ILLIQ again. The decline of ILLIQ by 250 percent can account for 20 percent of the decline in the call rate (with an elasticity of 0.08, see Table 7.3).

In contrast with these two variables, other variables do not appear to substantially affect the monetary authority's decision making. It seems clear that, as the IMF urged, the first priority of the interest rate policy was the restoration of stability in the foreign exchange market.

Table 7.3 Regressions of the call rate

	(1)	(2)	(3)	(4)	(5)	(6)	(7)
CONST	-0.039 (0.031)	-0.038 (0.031)	-0.069 (0.043)	0.018 (0.036)	0.014 (0.037)	0.017 (0.036)	-0.034 (0.044)
ΔLEXCH(-1)	0.050** (0.012)	0.045** (0.013)	0.050** (0.012)	0.052** (0.012)	0.050** (0.012)	0.048** (0.013)	0.045** (0.013)
ΔSPREAD(-1)		0.151 (0.107)					0.101 (0.108)
BNKRP(-1)			0.091 (0.090)				0.183 (0.094)
ΔILLIQ				0.082** (0.027)		0.087** (0.027)	0.102** (0.029)
$\Delta_{(-20)}$ILLIQ					0.004* (0.002)		
ΔCALL(-1)						-0.069 (0.051)	-0.081 (0.051)
ΔLIBOR							0.221 (0.684)
ΔLYEN							-0.0003 (0.027)
R^2	0.041	0.046	0.044	0.064	0.057	0.069	0.083
DW	2.068	2.107	2.090	2.113	2.104	1.992	2.059

Notes:
1. The dependent variable is the difference of the call rate, ΔCALL.
2. See note 2 to Table 7.1 for data definitions.
3. All variables are expressed in percent.
4. ** denotes an estimate significant at the 1 percent level, * an estimate significant at the 5 percent level.

4.5 Vector error correction approach: dynamic responses

In this subsection we report results of estimation of a vector error correction in CALL, SPREAD, LEXCH and ILLIQ. Our aim is to trace out the dynamics implied by a system that combines equations such as the ones presented in Tables 7.1 to 7.3. Our conclusion is that this vector system gives answers congruent with those of the single equation estimates.

We began by testing for cointegration. Using Johansen's procedure, we rejected the null of no cointegration at the 1 percent level. With the coefficient on LEXCH normalized to unity, the estimated cointegrating vector was:

LEXCH	ILLIQ	CALL	SPREAD	(4.1)
1.00	–0.48	1.49	–1.67	
	(–0.19)	(1.11)	(–0.67)	

where numbers in parentheses are standard errors. Since the cointegrating combination is stationary, the error correction term

$$LEXCH - .48*ILLIQ + 1.49*CALL - 1.67*SPREAD$$

should be expected to converge to zero over time. Recall that the levels of all four variables declined during our December 1997–June 1999 sample (see Figures 7.1, 7.2, 7.4 and 7.6). In a mechanical sense, stationarity of the combination is then maintained by movements in ILLIQ and SPREAD (which have negative coefficients) offsetting movements in LEXCH and CALL (which have positive coefficients). Focusing on the secular movement of the exchange rate, the long-run appreciation is accounted for by the long-run declines in the risk factors (or ILLIQ and SPREAD), while the steady relaxation of the monetary policy (or long-run decline in CALL) partially offset these appreciation pressures. This result is consistent with the modified version of the interest parity in Section 3 (see Eq. (3.3)) as well as the result of the single equation estimation in subsection 4.2 (see Table 7.1). Compared with the short-run elasticity estimates in Table 7.1, the coefficient estimates in this long-run relationship are slightly larger.

In the dynamic system, we used the Schwartz criterion to select a lag length of five. All regressions also included the error correction term (4.2). We summarize the results by presenting selected impulse response functions of the levels (not the differences) of the variables. To compute these responses, we used a Choleski decomposition, with the variable ordering described at the beginning of this section: ILLIQ, CALL, SPREAD, LEXCH. We focus on the impulse responses of the variables with respect to 1 percent positive shocks to CALL (Figure 7.7) and ILLIQ (Figure 7.8). Period "0" is the contemporaneous (same day) response. Since we measure time in business days, with five days per week, the "50" indicates a response 10 weeks out. Note that the vertical scale on each graph is

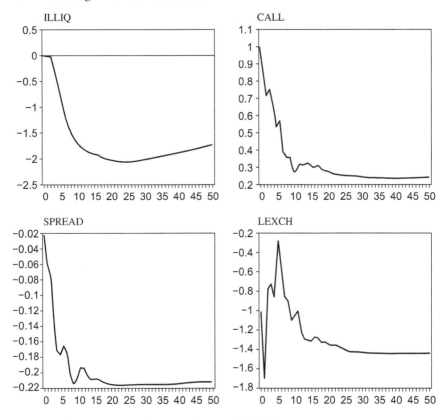

Figure 7.7 Responses to a 1 percent increase in CALL

different. By construction, the responses are such that in the long run, the response of the error correction term converges to zero. As it turns out, this response effectively hits zero only after about 50 days; thus there still is considerable persistence in this system.

Let us work through Figure 7.7 in detail, which describes the responses of the variables to a shock to the interest rate. This figure says that on a day when there is a 1 percent surprise increase in CALL, the exchange rate falls (appreciates) by about 1 percent as in Table 7.1. It then rises (depreciates) for the next several days due to the endogenous decline in CALL in response to the stabilized exchange rate (as in Table 7.3) as well as the mean reversion forces of LEXCH itself (not documented before). After six to seven days, however, the effects of induced decline in both ILLIQ and SPREAD tend to outweigh the offsetting effect of the decline in CALL.[2] Eventually exchange rate appreciation levels off at around 1.5 percent.

Figure 7.8 describes the responses of the system to a 1 percent increase in ILLIQ. Since the daily data of ILLIQ was constructed through interpolation,

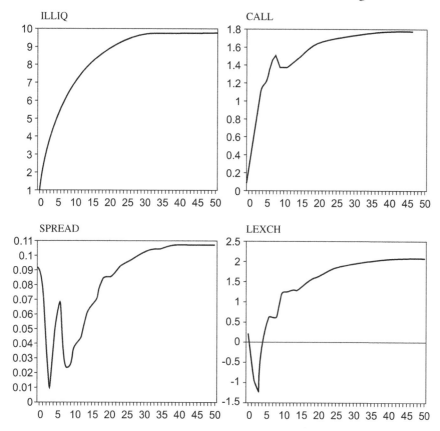

Figure 7.8 Responses to a 1 percent increase in ILLIQ

the slow adjustment of ILLIQ is understandable. It is also consistent with the above single equation results that both CALL and LEXCH rise in response to the increase of ILLIQ in the long run. A rather surprising result is that SPREAD is almost insensitive to ILLIQ (even the long-run response is limited to around 0.1 percent).

All in all, we conclude that this multivariate dynamic system and the single equation estimates tell a consistent story.[3] Increases in interest rates tend to be followed by exchange rate appreciation, and the restoration of the foreign currency liquidity position contributes to the stabilization of both the interest rate and the exchange rate. Thus our results are consistent with the view that increases in interest rates are part of the policy objective of stabilizing exchange rates.

Nevertheless, issues regarding the high interest rate policy still remain. These include the question of whether the exchange rate stability ought to be the foremost objective of the monetary policy and the related question of whether the IMF's advice for the interest rate policy was then appropriate. These issues will be briefly discussed in Section 5.

5. Assessment of the interest rate policy in a broader context

So far in this chapter, we have focused on the effect of the high interest rate policy on the exchange rate after the crisis. However, the goal of interest rate (or monetary) policy in general cannot be just the maintenance of exchange rate stability. An assessment of whether the policy reaction was appropriate or too contractionary should be based on analyses about broader aspects. Although a rigorous and comprehensive analysis is beyond the scope of this chapter, we can present some informal and incomplete evidence that suggests to us that tight monetary policy initially was appropriate but may have been maintained for too long.

First, there is a question about what the goal of monetary policy should be. A large literature in this field recommends the maintenance of general price stability as the long-run goal of monetary policy. In fact, the law for the Bank of Korea explicitly states that the goal of monetary policy is the maintenance of general price stability.

Under this criterion, a high interest rate policy seems necessary right after the crisis. As shown in Figure 7.9, domestic prices were rapidly rising mainly due to the imported inflation through the depreciated exchange rate. That is, the goal of domestic price stability could not be achieved without exchange rate stability.

Perhaps after April 1998, however, there was room for the monetary authority to relax the policy stance more rapidly. Consumer prices stopped rising, and producer prices started to decline as the exchange rate continued to appreciate. In fact, the GDP deflator declined to a large extent in the second quarter 1998 and stayed there since then (see Figure 7.9).

In addition, if one believes that in the short run monetary policy should consider the real side of the economy, the situation of the real side also suggests that a more relaxed stance may have been advisable. Along with the collapse of domestic demand, the current account surplus was exceeding 10 percent of GDP (not shown). GDP fell by more than 7 percent in the second and third quarters

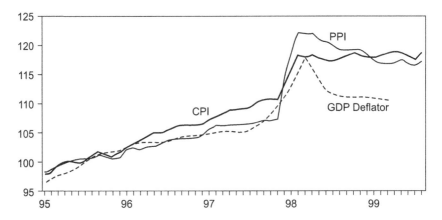

Figure 7.9 Trends of price indices

of 1998, compared with the levels of the same quarters in the previous year (see Figure 7.10). The rate of unemployment kept rising rapidly (see Figure 7.10), and wages continued to decline (not shown). In short, there was virtually no indicator that suggested the possibility of inflation in the medium-run. If anything, the macro-indicators suggested a possibility of deflation.

An analytical approach to this issue is to estimate the aggregate demand gap from potential output. To this end, we applied the methodology of Blanchard and Quah (1989) to the Korean data. In this approach, the supply-side shock is assumed to have a unit root while the demand-side shock is stationary. Following Kim (1996), we used the seasonally adjusted series of GDP and GDP deflator from 1974. Figure 7.11 shows the estimated aggregate-demand-gap series, the

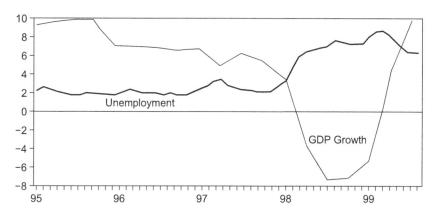

Figure 7.10 Trends of growth and unemployment (%)

Note: GDP growth is the growth rate of GDP relative to the same quarter of the previous year.

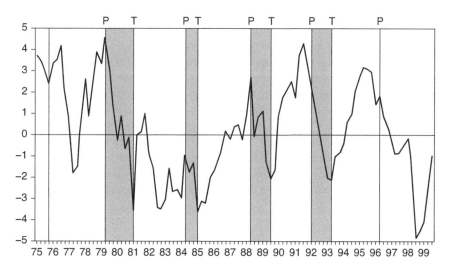

Figure 7.11 Aggregate demand gap (%)

GDP component that is driven by demand shocks alone. We also put peaks and troughs as officially defined by the Bureau of Statistics. According to this estimate, there was a large deflation gap (the largest in the series) in the second and third quarters of 1998, which has been rapidly diminishing since then.[4] Of course, this methodology does not tell us whether the deflation gap should be attributed to the high interest rate policy or some other factors. Nevertheless, this result seems to indicate that there was room for monetary policy relaxation without endangering price stability.

Even ex post, not to mention ex ante, it is a formidable task to precisely assess the appropriateness of monetary policy. It certainly is possible, for example, that earlier loosening of monetary policy would have proved counterproductive in the long run: no matter what the short- and long-run goals of monetary policy, persuasive analysis of the appropriateness of the policy requires understanding the process by which monetary policy affects the economy. Such an analysis is beyond the scope of this chapter. But our partial and informal evidence does suggest that the initial increase in interest rates was broadly appropriate but that downward adjustment could have been faster.

6.   Conclusion

This chapter asks whether the high interest rate policy of the IMF was effective in stabilizing the exchange rate. Our reduced form regression results indicate that the answer is generally affirmative. Although the major driving force of the exchange rate stabilization seems to be the recovery of the foreign currency liquidity position, the high interest rate appears to have contributed to stabilizing the exchange rate until the liquidity position was recovered. According to the expression of Furman and Stiglitz (1998), the temporarily high interest rate policy seems to have "bought time" until economic fundamentals recovered. Our reduced form approach does not, however, allow us to distinguish between expectational and other effects of the high interest rate policy.

In addition, we only provide some comments, rather than rigorous empirical results, regarding a more important and broader question, whether the high interest rate policy was appropriate or too contractionary. Even supposing that the goal of the interest rate (or monetary) policy is domestic price stability instead of exchange rate stability, it seems that the high interest rate policy was inevitable right after the crisis. Perhaps after April 1999, however, there was room to relax the policy stance more rapidly. Of course, more comprehensive and rigorous analyses on this issue need to be accumulated before any conclusion is drawn. We hope that this chapter has made a contribution to the literature on this issue.

Notes

*   This chapter is reprinted from *Management of Currency Crises*, edited by Jeffrey Frenkel and Michael Dooley, NBER, Chicago Press, pp. 11–35, 2003, which was co-authored with Kenneth D. West.

1 This result appears to be consistent with the recent finding of Hahm and Ryoo (1999) that the exchange rate depreciation had adverse effects on Korean stock prices.
2 A natural question that arises here is the extent to which ILLIQ was affected by (the lagged values of) other variables such as CALL or determined by completely independent policy efforts. It seems impossible to suitably answer this question in the context of this paper. But we did experiment with a system in which the estimated ILLIQ equation was replaced by one in which ILLIQ followed a random walk so that the changes in other variables would not affect ILLIQ. The impulse responses were qualitatively the same, but the magnitudes are reduced by a factor of around two-thirds with shorter adjustment periods.
3 One slight discrepancy between the multivariate and single equation results is that in the multivariate system, the long-run response of CALL to a LEXCH shock is slightly negative (–.05%, not depicted). The short-run response, however, is positive and comparable in magnitude to that presented in Table 7.3.
4 Although the estimate of GDP gap is large from a historical point of view, this may be viewed to be small considering the magnitude of the GDP decline in that period. This implies that the model attributes a substantial part of GDP decline to a negative supply-side shock.

References

Blanchard, Olivier J. and Danny Quah, 1989. "The Dynamic Effects of Aggregate Demand and Supply Disturbances," *American Economic Review*, 79(Sept), pp. 655–673.

Cho, Dongchul and Kiseok Hong, 1999. "Currency Crisis of Korea: Internal Weakness or External Independence?", manuscript, Korea Development Institute (forthcoming in the 10th *Annual East Asia Seminar on Economics*, NBER).

Fischer, Stanley, 1998. "The Asian Crisis: A View from the IMF," IMF, Washington, DC, www.imf.org/external/np/speeches/1998/012298.htm.

Furman, Jason and Joseph E. Stiglitz, 1998. "Economic Crises: Evidence and Insights from East Asia," *Brookings Papers on Economic Activity*, 2, pp. 1–135.

Goldfajn, Ilan and Poonam Gupta, 1999. "Does Monetary Policy Stabilize the Exchange Rate Following a Currency Crisis," International Monetary Fund Working Paper no. 9942, Washington, DC.

Hahm, Joon-ho and Jae-Kyun Ryoo, 1999. "Exchange Rate Risks of Financial Institutions Before the Currency Crisis in Korea," *Journal of Economic Policy*, forthcoming (in Korean).

Kim, Jun-il, 1996. "Business Cycles and GDP Gap," Journal of Economic Policy, Spring, pp. 217–270 (in Korean).

Nam, Il-Chong, Yeongjae Kang, and Joon-Kyung Kim, 1999. "Comparative Corporate Governance Trends in Asia," Working Paper submitted to the Conference on *Corporate Governance in Asia: A Comparative Perspective* sponsored by OECD and KDI, March.

Park, Dae-keun and In Choi, 1999. "Is the High Interest Rate Policy Effective in Stabilizing the Exchange Rate? Focusing on the Asian Crisis," manuscript, Korea Finance Institute, Seoul (in Korean).

Sachs, Jeffrey D., 1997. "The Wrong Medicine for Asia," *New York Times*, November 3.

Part III
Global crisis

8   House prices in ASEAN+3

Recent trends and inter-dependence*

1.   Introduction

Since the second half of 2007, the global financial market has been severely disturbed by the collapse of house prices. Initially triggered by the sub-prime mortgage problems in the US, the current financial crisis is rapidly spreading across global markets, including European countries. By now, many seem to agree that the current financial crisis is the most serious global financial and economic crisis since the Great Depression.

Although the magnitude and severity of the current crisis may not have been anticipated, the concerns regarding the possibility of contagion across sectors and countries have been consistently recognized. For example, IMF Managing Director Strauss-Kahn stated in one of his recent public addresses in February, 2008:

> If we look now at the current financial crisis from this perspective we can see that what began as a problem in a single sector in a single country – the housing market in the United States – has become a global problem. And, what was first manifested as a problem for financial institutions is now becoming a problem for economies. This is obviously the case in the United States. I believe that the effects will be felt increasingly in Europe. And I do not think the emerging economies are immune from this crisis.
>
> (Strauss-Kahn, 2008)

As emphasized in this address, the global economy is now realizing how devastating a real estate price bubble can be. In fact, since the ultimate source of financial instability today is rooted in the house price bubble that accumulated during the past decade, the stability of financial market will depend critically on the prospect of house prices.

Many commentators as well as policymakers argue that unlike the US and Europe, Asia is relatively safe, though not fully immune, from this global turmoil because the financial institutions in this region have not been much exposed to the US housing market. Additional grounds for such optimism are that housing markets in Asia went through a major correction during the crisis period in the late 1990s and that they also differ widely due to the different levels of their economic development and systems.

Is this a legitimate assessment? Are the housing markets of Asian economies relatively segregated from one another and the US? Isn't there a possibility that the real estate markets in Asia might have triggered another round of bubble? Although the house prices in Japan, the biggest economy of the region, have been either stable or even deflated for the past decade, there have been many anecdotes of speculation in housing markets in East Asia such as Seoul and Shanghai.

Monitoring house price developments is always important because housing is generally the single largest investment made by households. The experience during the Asian financial crisis has shown that downward corrections in house prices have caused considerable economic distress and that a sharp fall in housing prices can possibly unleash systemic risks. Even in Asia, this fear is not unfounded in view of the disastrous housing bubbles in the 1990s. For example, Japan's housing price bubble from 1985 to 1990 (157 percent) was followed by a fall in real housing prices by 68 percent throughout 1990 to 2005, and in Singapore the bubble from 1990 to 1996 (282 percent) was followed by a fall in real housing prices by 55 percent over the period 1996–1998.

In this regard, it seems necessary to examine whether house prices in ASEAN+3 countries have indeed been on the rise at rapid enough paces to generate concern for a sharp correction. If so, there are many important questions to be addressed. Are the house prices justifiable by fundamentals or should they be considered as important risk factors to financial markets? In which countries do the problems appear to be more serious? Is there any evidence that house prices are affected by the fluctuations of other (presumably large) countries' real estate prices? Are there appropriate policy measures to maintain financial stability? What are the implications regarding monetary and financial policies?

Motivated by these important issues, this chapter attempts to provide preliminary assessments on house prices of the region. Section 2 briefly explains the data used in this chapter. Section 3 overviews the historical development of the region's house prices, while more detailed trends of each country are documented in the Appendix. Section 4 presents the possibility of contagion across countries, including the US. Section 5 provides further explanations of house price developments in comparison with the macro-economic fundamentals such as income growth, financial conditions (short-term interest rate) and general inflation. Section 6 introduces the recent debate regarding monetary and financial policies in relation to the asset price fluctuations such as house prices, followed by conclusions in Section 7.

2. Data

Unlike stock prices, transactions in real estate markets are so infrequent and heterogeneous that designing a reliable aggregate index is a very difficult task even in advanced countries. Despite inevitable limitations in the quality of data, most advanced countries have published useful indexes on real estate prices. For some ASEAN+3 countries, however, the data on real estate prices appear to be either unavailable or non-existent.

Table 8.1 Data for house prices: definition, period and source

	House price definition	Period	Source
Japan (JPN)	Urban Land Price Index (residential)	1975q1–2008q1	Japan Real Estate Institute (http://www.reinet.or.jp/)
Korea (KOR)	Purchase Price Index	1986q1–2008q2	Kookmin Bank (http://www.kbstar.com/)
China (CHN)	Property Price Index	2004q1–2008q2 (1997–2007)	National Bureau of Statistics, CEIC (http://www.stats.gov.cn/english/)
Hong Kong (HKN)	Private Domestic Unit Price Index	1979q4–2008q2	Rating and Valuation Department (http://www.rvd.gov.hk/en/publications/pro-review.htm)
Singapore (SIN)	Property Price Index: Private Residential	1975q1–2008q2	Urban Redevelopment Authority, CEIC (http://www.ura.gov.sg/)
Malaysia (MAL)	House Price Indicators	1999q1–2007q4 (1988–2007)	Central Bank of Malaysia (http://www.bnm.gov.my/index)
Thailand (THA)	HPI: Single-detached house (including land)	1994q1–2007q3	Bank of Thailand (http://www.bot.or.th/English/Pages/BOTDefault.aspx)
Indonesia (IND)	Residential Property indices	2000q4–2008q2	Bank of Indonesia (http://www.bi.go.id/web/en)

*Note: Time-series data of house price are not produced in Vietnam, Cambodia, and Laos.
House price data are not available for Philippines, Myanmar and Brunei.
Years in parentheses for China and Malaysia are the time periods for annual data.

Table 8.1 summarizes the data collected for this research, mostly through the Internet. As for Japan, long time-series data for the nation as a whole and various areas are available, but the problem is that the data are indexes for land prices, not for house prices. Like other researches on Japan's real estate prices (e.g. Girouard et al., 2006; and Van den Noord, 2006), this study uses the urban land price index as a proxy for house prices.

As for Korea, the time span is shorter than that of Japan's, but a relatively large amount of information is available from a semi-government agency (Kook-Min Bank). Besides, the time span is long enough to cover the "East Asian Bubble Period" of the late 1980s and the Asian Crisis period of 1997–1998, and its dataset also provides the price indexes not only for various regions, but also for different house types (e.g. detached vs. apartment).

As for China, a relatively broad set of information (regional, house types, etc.) is available, but its time span is too short: annual data are available from 1997 on and quarterly data only from 2004 on. This is in fact a serious limitation of this study, given the importance of the Chinese economy in the region.

Hong Kong, though not a member country of ASEAN+3, is included because it appears to be closely linked to the ASEAN+3 region and relevant data are readily available. The time span of the data for Hong Kong goes back to the 1980. And that for Singapore is as long as that for Japan: since 1976. There also exists more information about the prices of different types of houses.

Malaysia provides sufficiently long time-series data since 1988, while Thailand and Indonesia provide relatively short time-series from 1994 and 2000, respectively. There are no available data for other member countries (Vietnam, Brunei, Laos, Myanmar and Cambodia).

3.   Historical trends of house prices

3.1   *Nominal house prices*

Figure 8.1A shows the trends of house prices in each country with the fourth quarter of 2000 as the base year. It is well known that Japanese real estate prices have not co-moved with the global house price boom: after the explosive run-up in the late 1980s, the Japanese real estate prices were corrected by around 30 percent during the 1990s and have continued to further decline by approximately 25 percent since 2000. The current level of the price index is more or less a half of its peak in 1991.

Except for Japan, however, the house prices in the ASEAN+3 countries rose after the Asian crisis. In the case of Korea, the current level is approximately 60 percent higher than that in 2000, while it is approximately 40 percent higher in China. A point to be considered, however, is that the house prices in Korea began to rise after a correction of some 20 percent during the 1990s, but no such information can be obtained from the data for China. In fact, the trend of house prices in Korea was similar to that of Japan until 2000, but it has been diverging from Japan's trend since then.

There is an interesting pair of countries, Hong Kong and Singapore, two financial hub cities in Asia, where house prices appear to co-move, though they are more volatile in Hong Kong. With a huge bubble having accumulated until the outbreak of the Asian crisis in 1997, house prices in the two cities collapsed during the Asian crisis in 1998. In the case of Hong Kong, the house price index skyrocketed by almost 50 percent in 1997 and then collapsed to the level of 1996 in one year, recording a drop of almost 40 percent in 1998. In Singapore as well, the house price index declined by around 30 percent in 1998. After a period of readjustment, house prices began recovering in 2003 and the pace has accelerated since 2007. The current level is up 50 percent in Hong Kong and 33 percent in Singapore, compared to the level in 2000.

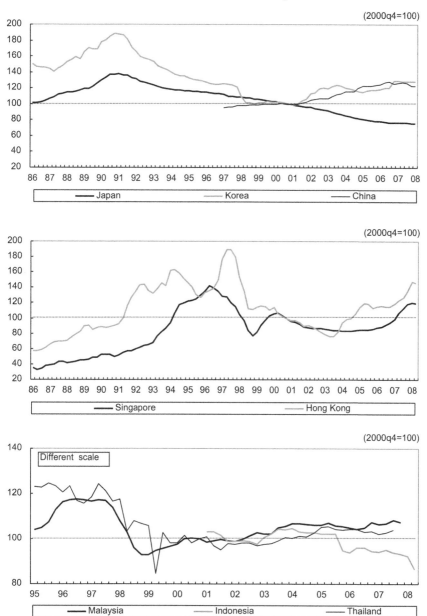

Figure 8.1A House price index (nominal)

Another pair of countries to consider is Malaysia and Thailand. After 15 to 25 percent corrections during the Asian crisis period, their house prices have been steadily appreciating by approximately 25 percent since 2000. The price hike in Indonesia is perhaps most astonishing; its house price index increased by 80 percent since 2000.

3.2   *Real house prices*

However, this rapid increase of house prices in Indonesia is simply a result of
high inflation in general prices. As Figure 8.1B shows, the real house price index

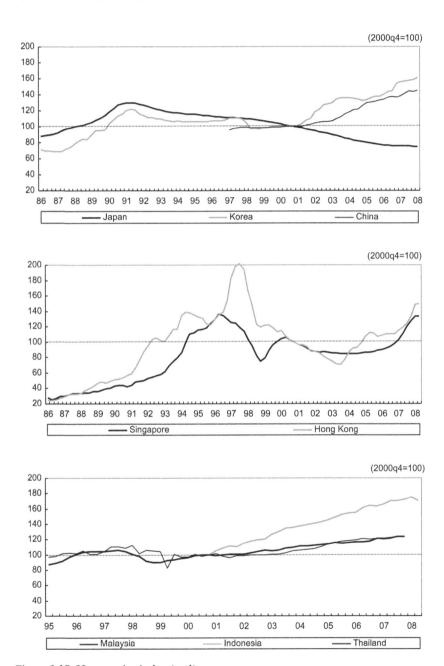

Figure 8.1B House price index (real)

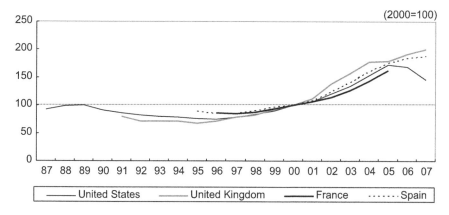

Figure 8.2 House price index (real): US and European countries

in Indonesia has declined by almost 15 percent since 2000. Except for Japan, where both nominal and real prices declined by 25 percent from the 2000 levels, Indonesia is the only country in the sample that has experienced a real loss in house values since 2000.

While Korea has experienced the second largest house price appreciation (next to Indonesia) since 2000, it is Hong Kong that has experienced the largest house price appreciation – almost 50 percent – in real terms since 2000. This magnitude of real price appreciation is not as large as those in advanced countries – ranging from 50 to 100 percent (Figure 8.2) – where house prices finally collapse. Also, the pace of recent price appreciation has been far milder than in 1997 – more than 50 percent within one year – right before the Asian crisis. Nevertheless, both the magnitude of price appreciation and the pace of price hikes for the recent two years appear to be prominent enough to raise concerns. With regard to the recent hike, Singapore is similar to Hong Kong, though its magnitude is far milder – approximately 20 percent since 2000.

In China and Korea, real house prices did not particularly run up in the recent couple of years. However, they have been steadily rising to the level of 25 to 30 percent higher than those in 2000. Nevertheless, there could be an issue with the base year of this assessment. In the case of Korea, for example, the base year happens to be the year when the real house price index hit bottom after a long and significant correction from 187 in 1991 to 100 in 2000, which is more than twice as large as the magnitude of Japan's correction over the same period.

Real house prices also have been steadily rising in Malaysia and Thailand, but their magnitudes are relatively modest, ranging from 5 to 10 percent, compared to those in 2000. In these countries as well, however, house prices have not yet recovered their pre-crisis levels in real terms.

3.3 House price to income ratios

As was discussed, house prices in most Asian countries (except for Indonesia) have been appreciating in real terms since 2000. However, this observation does not mean that houses have become less affordable than in 2000. As the Asians' income (per capita) has grown more rapidly, they can more readily afford to purchase houses now than in 2000.

Figure 8.3 shows a housing affordability index – house price index divided by income per capita. According to this index, houses have become far more affordable

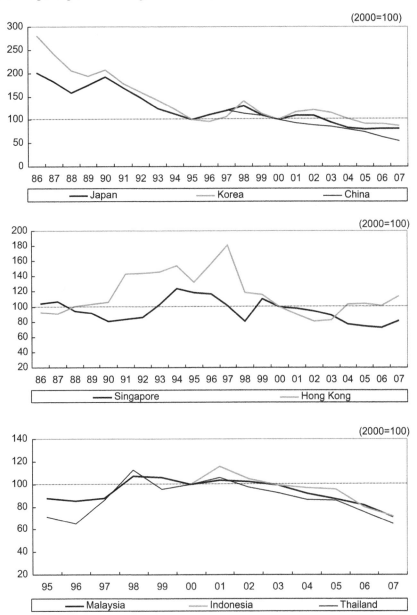

Figure 8.3 Index of house price to income per capita

in most of the Asian countries than in 2000. The only exception is Hong Kong, where houses are less affordable by almost 30 percent than in 2002, though not as unaffordable as in 1996. For the other countries, houses have become more affordable by approximately 10 percent (Korea, Japan and Singapore) to almost 40 percent (China, Malaysia, Thailand and Indonesia) than in 2000.

4. Correlations across countries

In relation to the current financial crisis, another important issue to check is contagion. The world is currently witnessing how fast one country's crisis can be propagated to other countries through integrated financial markets. An obvious piece of evidence for the global contagion is the close co-movement of the respective national stock markets, including Asia even at a daily frequency.

What about the real estate markets? A common conjecture is that real estate markets are far less integrated than stock markets, and thus one country's real estate prices should not be greatly affected by other countries' real estate markets. However, the recent movement patterns of house prices in the US and European countries appear to be closely linked across national borders. In fact, bilateral correlation coefficients of house price appreciation rates between the US and individual European countries are well over 0.5 with statistical significances (see Figures 8.4A and 8.4B).

4.1 Correlations with the US

Are house prices in Asia also closely linked to those in the US? Figures 8.4A and 8.4B indicate that the Asian real estate markets are not greatly influenced by those in the US: the correlation coefficients are negative for a half of the sample countries for both nominal and real house price appreciation rates (as well as for both annual and quarterly frequencies, not reported).

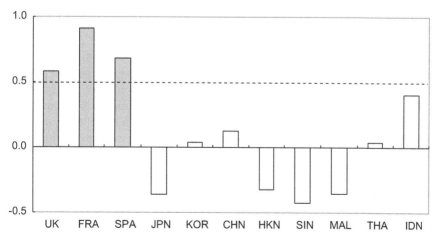

Figure 8.4A Correlation coefficient with the US (nominal)

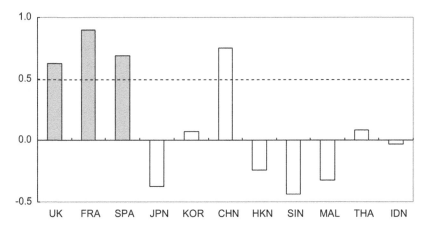

Figure 8.4B Correlation coefficient with the US (real)

However, there is a noteworthy exception: China. The real house prices of China turn out to be closely correlated with those of the US: the correlation coefficient is 0.75. This result is surprising in that Chinese financial markets are not much liberalized. It may be due to an implicit link between China and the US through a deep involvement of the Chinese official foreign reserves in the US financial market. Or, it may be simply due to a small sample problem: China's data are available from 1997, providing only a ten-year data period. In fact, the correlation coefficient for nominal house prices is only 0.13 and statistically insignificant.

Another intriguing result is that house prices, both nominal and real, of Hong Kong and Singapore are negatively correlated with those of the US. In fact, this result is robust for the sample period excluding the Asian crisis (not reported). As far as Hong Kong and Singapore are international financial hubs and maintain either fixed or "stable" exchange rates *vis-à-vis* the US dollar, financial conditions of the two cities are expected to be greatly influenced by the US financial market situation. In this respect, the negative correlations between the two cities and the US may indicate the possibility that the Asian housing market is regarded as a substitute, rather than a complement, for the US (and European countries) in the international capital market. That is, a positive perception for the US market (or a negative perception for the Asian market) tends to move global capital from Asia toward the US, and *vice versa*, generating negative correlations in house prices. Of course, there must be complementary effects as well, such as the global financial crisis or global monetary easing. However, the result for the sample period examined in this study, at least, shows that the substitute effect outweighs the complement effect.

4.2   *Correlations among the ASEAN+3 countries*

Intra-regional correlations indicate that the housing markets of ASEAN+3 countries are not as inter-linked with one another as those in the US and European countries: most of the correlation coefficients among Asian countries in Table 8.2A and 8.2B

Table 8.2A Correlation coefficients among ASEAN+3 countries (nominal)

	JPN	KOR	CHN	HKN	SIN	MAL	THA	IDN
start year	1976 (1976Q1)	1987 (1987Q1)	1998 (1998Q1)	1980 (1980Q4)	1976 (1976Q1)	1989 (1989Q1)	1995 (1995Q1)	2001 (2001Q4)
# of obs.	32 (129)	21 (85)	10 (41)	27 (110)	32 (129)	19 (76)	13 (51)	7 (26)
JPN	1.00	0.51** (0.52**)	-0.54 (-0.51**)	0.15 (0.17*)	0.29 (0.38**)	0.21 (0.23**)	-0.12 (-0.09)	-0.55 (-0.50**)
KOR		1.00	0.24 (0.18)	0.30 (0.05)	0.24 (0.01)	0.33 (0.19*)	0.13 (0.07)	0.35 (0.30)
CHN			1.00	0.71** (0.78**)	0.29 (0.16)	0.37 (0.39**)	0.71** (0.52**)	-0.04 (-0.12)
HKN				1.00	0.54** (0.39**)	0.68** (0.47**)	0.45 (0.42**)	-0.71** (-0.68**)
SIN					1.00	0.77** (0.57**)	0.03 (0.18)	-0.66 (-0.64**)
MAL						1.00	0.26 (0.41**)	-0.14 (-0.01)
THA							1.00	-0.09 (-0.22)
IDN								1.00

Note: Figures in parenthesis are for quarterly data.

Table 8.2B Correlation coefficients among ASEAN+3 countries (real)

	JPN	KOR	CHN	HKN	SIN	MAL	THA	IDN
start year	1976 (1976Q1)	1987 (1987Q1)	1998 (1998Q1)	1981 (1981Q4)	1976 (1976Q1)	1989 (1989Q1)	1995 (1995Q1)	2001 (2001Q4)
# of obs.	32 (129)	21 (85)	10 (41)	27 (106)	32 (129)	19 (76)	13 (51)	7 (26)
JPN	1.00	0.42* (0.40**)	-0.93** (-0.76**)	-0.07 (-0.11)	0.21 (0.25**)	0.21 (0.18)	-0.46 (-0.37**)	-0.35 (-0.37*)
KOR		1.00	0.18 (0.15)	0.27 (-0.004)	0.24 (-0.002)	0.36 (0.18)	0.39 (0.30**)	0.06 (-0.02)
CHN			1.00	0.22 (0.21)	-0.12 (-0.28*)	0.21 (0.13)	0.32 (0.30*)	0.21 (0.31)
HKN				1.00	0.43** (0.27**)	0.65** (0.38***)	0.51** (0.41**)	-0.12 (-0.06)
SIN					1.00	0.76** (0.55**)	0.22 (0.26*)	-0.12 (-0.18)
MAL						1.00	0.46 (0.47***)	0.55 (0.73**)
THA							1.00	0.35 (0.30)
IDN								1.00

Note: Figures in parenthesis are for quarterly data.

are smaller than those between the US and individual European countries. Yet, the house prices do appear to be intra-regionally contagious in that most of the correlation coefficients are positive, ranging from 0.2 to 0.7, except for Indonesia. In addition, there are some blocks of countries within which house prices appear to be closely inter-linked: (1) Japan and Korea, (2) China, Hong Kong and Thailand, and (3) Hong Kong, Singapore and Malaysia

As for the block of Japan and Korea, the correlation coefficients for nominal and real house prices are 0.51 and 0.42, respectively. However, a substantial portion of this correlation seems to be generated from the late 1980s and early 1990s, when the real estate bubbles were formed and busted in both countries. In fact, as the early years of the sample period are excluded from the data, the correlation coefficients decline toward 0–0.2 (not reported).

As for the second block, the correlation coefficients of Hong Kong and Thailand with China are more than 0.7, respectively, for nominal prices. These results indicate that the housing markets of the three countries are very closely linked, although the correlations become weaker for real prices due to a peculiar inflation dynamic of China. In fact, the correlation coefficient for the real prices between Hong Kong and Thailand is more than 0.5.

As for the third block, it was already noted in Section 3 that Hong Kong and Singapore are closely correlated with each other: the correlation coefficient is approximately 0.5. What was not noted in Section 3 is Malaysia, which produces even higher correlations with both Hong Kong and Singapore than the correlation between the two cities, for both nominal and real prices. An interesting observation in relation with the second block is that, unlike Hong Kong, Singapore and Malaysia do not show particularly high correlations with China and Thailand.

Overall, the ASEAN countries (except for Indonesia) are more mutually inter-linked than the +3 countries are. Among +3 countries, China is more linked to the ASEAN countries than to the other +3 countries; the correlation coefficient between Japan and China is even negative. Korea appears to be related to both Japan and China, but the degree of correlations does not appear to be particularly high since the 1990s.

5.   House prices and macro-economic fundamentals

Though not as closely inter-linked as in the US and European countries, house prices in the ASEAN+3 region appear to be correlated across countries. A natural question that should be asked then is why? This co-movement of house prices can be a result of genuine housing market integration in the ASEAN+3 countries or simply a reflection of the co-movement in macro-economic fundamentals that should affect house prices in each country.

5.1   *Cross-country correlations of macro-economic fundamentals*

In this context, it is necessary to examine representative indicators of macro-economic fundamentals: GDP growth, CPI inflation and interest rates. We also tried aggregate money supply indicators but failed to obtain any reliable results (not reported). As for interest rates, both short- and long-term rates were tried. Short-term interest rates (central bank's target interest rates except for China, for which the one-year lending rate was used) were thought to be more relevant to monetary policy effects, while long-term interest rates (10-year government bond yield rates for Japan and Malaysia, 5-year government bond rates for Korea, 12-year government bond rates for Thailand and 5-year lending rates for China) were thought to be more directly relevant to house prices. As will be discussed, however, most of the analysis results are similar regardless of whether short- or long-term interest rates are used. Therefore, this section's discussion will be mainly based on the results with short-term interest rates, which are more readily available than long-term rates for the ASEAN+3 countries.

Tables 8.3A–8.3D present the simple correlation coefficients of the macro-economic fundamentals across countries. A first look at the tables confirms that the macro-economic fundamentals are truly inter-linked across the ASEAN+3 countries except for Indonesia (as for interest rates, China and Hong Kong are also exceptional). In fact, the cross-country correlations of macro-economic fundamentals are higher and more significant than the cross-country correlations of house prices, suggesting the possibility that the house price correlations may be a simple reflection of the co-movement in macro-economic correlations.

5.2   *Regression results of individual countries*

Therefore, we performed regressions of house prices on macro-economic variables in each country, along with another country's house prices as an additional explanatory variable to check whether the contagious effect still remains after controlling for the effects of its own country's macro-economic variables.

The regression results reported in Tables 8.4A–8.4D, where the house price index of the US was used as an additional explanatory variable, are generally in accord with common expectations: house prices rise when growth rates are high and interest rates are low. Also, high inflation rates tend to boost nominal house prices. It is also found that the house prices of the ASEAN+3 region have not been greatly influenced by the US market, with a possible exception of China. These general patterns are observed no matter whether nominal (Tables 8.4A and 8.4B) or real house prices (Tables 8.4C and 8.4D) are regressed and no matter whether short-term (Tables 8.4A and 8.4C) or long-term interest rates (Tables 8.4B and 8.4D) are used as an independent variable.

Notwithstanding these general conclusions, there are some variations in the results across countries. As for Japan, where house prices have ever been declining, the regression results are still encouraging. First, high growth does help boost (or lessening the declining speed of) house prices. A low interest rate also appears to raise house prices in the short run (the same quarter), though not in the long run (negative coefficients for the interest rate were obtained only from the dynamic models with lagged dependent variable). Nevertheless, the most important factor for house prices in Japan seems to be the general price

Table 8.3A Correlation coefficients of GDP growth rates

	JPN	KOR	CHN	HKN	SIN	MAL	THA	IDN
start year	1988 (1988q1)	1991 (1991q1)	1998 (1998q1)	1992 (1992q2)	1991 (1991q1)	1992 (1992q1)	1997 (1997q1)	2001 (2001q4)
# of obs.	20 (82)	17 (70)	10 (42)	16 (65)	17 (70)	16 (66)	11 (46)	7 (28)
JPN	1.00	0.57** (0.47***)	0.65** (0.57***)	0.79** (0.66**)	0.52** (0.45***)	0.68** (0.56***)	0.73** (0.62***)	0.74 (0.37*)
KOR		1.00	0.11 (0.14)	0.62** (0.60**)	0.64** (0.58***)	0.87** (0.83***)	0.80** (0.80***)	0.10 (−0.23)
CHN			1.00	0.61* (0.60**)	0.46 (0.45***)	0.42 (0.40***)	0.47 (0.44***)	0.94** (0.64***)
HKN				1.00	0.79*** (0.74***)	0.77** (0.74***)	0.75** (0.72***)	0.78** (0.54**)
SIN					1.00	0.83** (0.74***)	0.53* (0.49***)	0.84** (0.47***)
MAL						1.00	0.82** (0.78***)	0.74 (0.48**)
THA							1.00	0.32 (0.03**)
IDN								1.00

Note: Figures in parenthesis are for quarterly data; end year (quarter) is 2008 (2008q2).

Source: Bank of Korea, Global Insight, IMF.

Table 8.3B Correlation coefficients of inflation rates

	JPN	KOR	CHN	HKN	SIN	MAL	THA	IDN
start year	1988 (1988q1)	1991 (1991q1)	1998 (1998q1)	1992 (1992q2)	1991 (1991q1)	1992 (1992q1)	1997 (1997q1)	2001 (2001q4)
# of obs.	20 (82)	17 (70)	10 (42)	16 (65)	17 (70)	16 (66)	11 (46)	7 (28)
JPN	1.00							
KOR	0.80** (0.72**)	1.00						
CHN	0.55 (0.44**)	-0.01 (0.06)	1.00					
HKN	0.65** (0.67**)	0.67** (0.66**)	0.80** (0.57**)	1.00				
SIN	0.69** (0.55**)	0.62** (0.40**)	0.85** (0.84**)	0.81** (0.53**)	1.00			
MAL	0.41 (0.53**)	0.55** (0.59**)	-0.31 (-0.11)	0.57** (0.67**)	0.15 (0.18)	1.00		
THA	0.61** (0.64**)	0.68** (0.70**)	0.03 (0.19)	0.57* (0.81**)	0.02 (0.27*)	0.80** (0.76**)	1.00	
IDN	-0.48 (-0.28)	-0.62 (-0.36)	-0.72 (-0.42)	-0.18 (0.05)	-0.56 (-0.15)	0.58 (0.49**)	0.20 (0.31)	1.00

Note: Figures in parenthesis are for quarterly data; end year (quarter) is 2008 (2008q2).

Source: Bank of Korea, Global Insight, IMF

Table 8.3C Correlation coefficients of short-term interest rates

	JPN	KOR	CHN	HKN	SIN	MAL	THA	IDN
start year	1988 (1988q1)	1991 (1991q1)	1998 (1998q1)	1992 (1992q2)	1991 (1991q1)	1992 (1992q1)	1997 (1997q1)	2001 (2001q4)
# of obs.	20 (82)	17 (70)	10 (42)	16 (65)	17 (70)	16 (66)	11 (46)	7 (28)
JPN	1.00	0.53** (0.64***)	0.90** (0.84***)	-0.15 (-0.150)	0.61** (0.50***)	0.57** (0.55***)	0.51 (0.58**)	-0.38 (-0.30)
KOR		1.00	0.66** (0.73***)	0.28 (0.24*)	0.67*** (0.60***)	0.87*** (0.87***)	0.97*** (0.93***)	0.03 (0.13)
CHN			1.00	0.46 (0.43***)	0.62* (0.20)	0.64** (0.76***)	0.50 (0.72**)	-0.24 (-0.24)
HKN				1.00	0.63** (0.59***)	0.19 (0.22*)	0.35 (0.36**)	-0.10 (0.05)
SIN					1.00	0.61** (0.45***)	0.65** (0.57***)	0.16 (0.17)
MAL						1.00	0.93** (0.88***)	-0.18 (-0.03)
THA							1.00	0.15 (0.21)
IDN								1.00

Note: Figures in parenthesis are for quarterly data; end year (quarter) is 2008 (2008q2).

Source: Bank of Korea, Global Insight, IMF

Table 8.3D Correlation coefficients of long-term interest rates

	JPN	KOR	CHN	HKN	SIN	MAL	THA	IDN
start year	1988 (1988q1)	1988 (1988q1)	1998 (1998q1)			1992 (1992q1)	1995 (1995q1)	
# of obs.	20 (82)	20 (82)	10 (42)			16 (64)	13 (54)	
JPN	1.00	0.80** (0.84**)	0.07 (0.35**)			0.50* (0.61**)	0.75** (0.76**)	
KOR		1.00	0.35 (0.70**)			0.90** (0.87**)	0.88** (0.92**)	
CHN			1.00			0.19 (0.52**)	0.43 (0.69**)	
HKN								
SIN								
MAL						1.00	0.83** (0.89**)	
THA							1.00	
IDN								

Note: Figures in parenthesis are for quarterly data; end year (quarter) is 2008 (2008q2).
Source: Bank of Korea, Global Insight, IMF.

inflation/deflation inertia in the sense that the coefficient for the lagged dependent variable is close to 1.

The regression results for Korea's real house prices are just standard: high growth and low interest rates boost the real house prices with a 75 percent of quarterly inertia (the coefficient of the lagged dependent variable). The only noticeable exception is that nominal house price appreciation rates are negatively correlated with general inflation in the short-run (a quarter), though not in the long run. This result seems to suggest the possibility that short-term fluctuations in Korea's inflation have been greatly affected by supply sides such as oil prices that create a negative correlation between inflation and economy's demand conditions.

As for China, the signs of all the coefficients are consistent, though some of them are statistically insignificant due to a small sample size. Most noteworthy for China, however, is the result that the coefficient for the US house price appreciation rate is still significant after controlling for the effects of domestic fundamentals. According to the regression coefficients, a 1 percent fall in US house prices is associated with a 0.20–0.25 percent decline in China's house prices both in nominal and real terms. It is beyond the scope of this study to rigorously examine why China's housing market is influenced by the US market. Nevertheless, considering the recent global trend of house price collapse, this result seems to be worth some concern.

Table 8.4A Regression results of (nominal) house prices (short-term rates)

Sample period (# of obs.)	Lagged Dependent Variable	Growth rate	Short-term interest rate	Inflation rate	Growth rate of US House Price Index	R^2
JPN		**0.872****	**0.806****	**0.866***	−0.029	0.734
1988q1~2008q1		(5.250)	(3.093)	(1.850)	(−0.607)	
(81)	**0.991****	0.100	**−0.244****	0.233	0.007	0.962
	(21.199)	(1.363)	(−2.203)	(1.286)	(0.388)	
KOR		**0.617****	**−0.590****	0.260	−0.066	0.250
1991q1~2008q2		(3.051)	(−2.459)	(0.456)	(−0.637)	
(70)	**0.828****	0.086	−0.045	**−0.805****	−0.058	0.892
	(19.467)	(1.043)	(−0.464)	(−3.568)	(−1.460)	
CHN		**0.664****	−0.177	**0.877****	**0.208****	0.661
1998q1~2008q2		(2.257)	(−0.295)	(4.922)	(3.575)	
(42)	**0.812****	−0.068	**−1.252****	0.197	−0.059	0.870
	(7.097)	(−0.323)	(−2.566)	(1.307)	(−1.145	
HKN		**3.151****	**−2.269****	**1.952****	0.001	0.650
1992q2~2008q2		(7.873)	(−2.297)	(4.387)	(0.003)	
(65)	**0.697****	**1.462****	**−1.427****	−0.166	**−0.316***	0.877
	(10.412)	(5.050)	(−2.390)	(−0.496)	(−1.981)	
SIN		**2.222****	**−2.500***	**2.322***	**−0.741****	0.614
1991q1~2008q2		(6.569)	(−1.940)	(1.807)	(−3.140)	
(70)	**0.816****	**0.837****	**−1.354****	**−1.203***	**−0.358****	0.900
	(13.495)	(4.146)	(−2.028)	(−1.695)	(−2.871)	
MAL		**1.146****	0.019	0.620	−0.062	0.679
1992q1~2007q4		(9.691)	(0.056)	(1.105)	(−0.689)	
(64)	**0.698****	**0.443****	**−0.636****	**0.643****	−0.040	0.910
	(12.204)	(5.182)	(−3.294)	(2.145)	(−0.839)	
THA		**1.055****	0.398	**1.554****	0.189	0.403
1997q1~2007q3		(4.273)	(1.615)	(2.649)	(1.193)	
(43)	0.070	**1.008****	0.389	**1.416****	0.177	0.406
	(0.444)	(3.726)	(1.559)	(2.113)	(1.092)	
IDN		**−0.985***	0.412	−0.232	**0.088****	0.559
2001q4~2008q2		(−2.031)	(1.406)	(−1.329)	(2.135)	
(27)	**0.691****	0.108	0.353	−0.159	**0.072***	0.673
	(2.749)	(0.153)	(1.359)	(−1.010)	(1.914)	

Note: *, ** denote significance at 10% and 5% respectively. Figures in parentheses are t-statistics.

Table 8.4B Regression results of (nominal) house prices (long-term rates)

Sample period (# of obs.)	Lagged Dependent Variable	Growth rate	Long-term interest rate	Inflation rate	Growth rate of US House Price Index	R^2
JPN		0.934**	0.735**	1.344**	−0.015	0.720
1988q1~ 2008q1		(5.445)	(2.270)	(3.230)	(−0.288)	
(81)	0.957**	0.089	−0.115	0.063	0.006	0.960
	(21.207)	(1.162)	(−0.886)	(0.369)	(0.314)	
KOR		1.217**	−1.144**	2.022**	0.100	0.334
1988q1~ 2008q2		(5.889)	(−3.490)	(3.632)	(0.967)	
(82)	0.895**	0.259**	−0.094	−0.255	0.006	0.878
	(18.398)	(2.509)	(−0.615)	(−0.945)	(0.142)	
CHN		0.721**	0.086	0.875**	0.228**	0.660
1998q1~ 2008q2		(2.568)	(0.249)	(4.921)	(4.533)	
(42)	0.845**	−0.007	−0.662**	0.114	−0.037	0.866
	(7.119)	(−0.033)	(−2.311)	(0.727)	(−0.760)	
HKN						
SIN						
MAL		1.146**	0.024	0.616	−0.061	0.679
1992q1~ 2007q4		(9.691)	(0.070)	(1.096)	(−0.685)	
(64)	0.700**	0.441**	−0.646**	0.653**	−0.041	0.911
	(12.255)	(5.179)	(−3.357)	(2.184)	(−0.854)	
THA		0.635**	−0.325	1.672**	0.179	0.324
1995q1~ 2007q3		(3.679)	(−0.718)	(3.881)	(1.290)	
(51)	0.110	0.583**	−0.229	1.415**	0.172	0.325
	(0.666)	(3.040)	(−0.457)	(2.428)	(1.213)	
IDN						

Note: *, ** denote significance at 10% and 5% respectively. Figures in parentheses are t-statistics.

Long-term interest rates are: 10-year government bond yield rate for Japan; 5-year government (National Housing) bond yield rate for Korea; 5-year lending rate for China; 10-year government securities average yield rate for Malaysia; and 12-year government bond yield rate for Thailand.

Table 8.4C Regression results of (real) house prices (short-term rates)

Sample period (# of obs.)	Lagged Dependent Variable	Growth rate	Short-term interest rate	Growth rate of US Real House Price Index	R^2
JPN		0.868**	0.717**	−0.035	0.632
1988q1~2008q1		(5.617)	(4.455)	(−0.751)	
(81)	0.960**	0.053	−0.095	0.003	0.938
	(19.366)	(0.695)	(−1.211)	(0.131)	
KOR		0.664**	−0.761**	−0.030	0.397
1991q1~2008q2		(3.598)	(−4.907)	(−0.305)	
(70)	0.751**	0.241**	−0.371**	−0.022	0.862
	(14.810)	(2.587)	(−4.681)	(−0.465)	
CHN		0.626**	−0.062	0.236**	0.554
1998q1~2008q2		(2.700)	(−0.112)	(4.428)	
(42)	0.634**	0.013	−0.817	0.028	0.707
	(4.030)	(0.052)	(−1.376)	(0.433)	
HKN		3.087**	−2.302**	−0.335*	0.552
1992q2~2008q2		(7.784)	(−2.356)	(−1.737)	
(65)	0.642**	1.446**	−1.384**	−0.128	0.843
	(10.551)	(5.107)	(−2.349)	(−1.098)	
SIN		2.263**	−2.629**	−0.908**	0.579
1991q1~2008q2		(7.245)	(−2.096)	(−5.339)	
(70)	0.783**	0.720**	−1.162*	−0.184*	0.880
	(12.778)	(3.481)	(−1.698)	(−1.710)	
MAL		1.115**	−0.111	−0.048	0.685
1992q1~2007q4		(10.066)	(−0.413)	(−0.557)	
(64)	0.665**	0.444**	−0.497**	−0.052	0.910
	(12.136)	(5.460)	(−3.357)	(−1.110)	
THA		0.893**	0.503**	0.228	0.336
1997q1~2007q3		(4.202)	(2.548)	(1.496)	
(43)	0.132	0.819**	0.438**	0.186	0.351
	(0.915)	(3.592)	(2.082)	(1.161)	
IDN		−1.736**	−1.067**	0.057	0.436
2001q4~2008q2		(−2.338)	(−3.728)	(0.869)	
(27)	0.628**	−0.139	−0.293	0.063	0.560
	(2.429)	(−0.129)	(−0.708)	(0.982)	

Note: *, ** denote significance at 10% and 5% respectively. Figures in parentheses are t-statistics.

Table 8.4D Regression results of (real) house prices (long-term rates)

Sample period (# of obs.)	Lagged Dependent Variable	Growth rate	Long-term interest rate	Growth rate of US Real House Price Index	R^2
JPN		**0.900****	**0.877****	−0.031	0.609
1988q1~2008q1		(5.585)	(3.777)	(−0.619)	
(81)	**0.939****	0.052	−0.053	0.007	0.937
	(19.879)	(0.666)	(−0.509)	(0.332)	
KOR		**1.028****	**−0.668****	0.048	0.318
1988q1~2008q2		(5.363)	(−3.346)	(0.477)	
(82)	**0.817****	**0.333****	**−0.280****	0.018	0.851
	(16.626)	(3.356)	(−2.897)	(0.368)	
CHN		**0.669****	0.109	**0.249****	0.555
1998q1~2008q2		(2.985)	(0.343)	(5.775)	
(42)	**0.645****	0.054	−0.337	0.057	0.700
	(4.012)	(0.225)	(−0.993)	(0.977)	
HKN					
SIN					
MAL		**1.116****	−0.108	−0.047	0.685
1992q1~2007q4		(10.075)	(−0.403)	(−0.551)	
(64)	**0.666****	**0.443****	**−0.501****	−0.053	0.910
	(12.174)	(5.451)	(−3.402)	(−1.132)	
THA		**0.511****	0.062	0.174	0.219
1995q1~2007q3		(3.129)	(0.163)	(1.208)	
(51)	**0.225***	**0.451****	0.080	0.148	0.262
	(1.689)	(2.658)	(0.207)	(1.031)	
IDN					

Note: *, ** denote significance at 10% and 5% respectively. Figures in parentheses are t-statistics.

Long-term interest rates are: 10-year government bond yield rate for Japan; 5-year government (National Housing) bond yield rate for Korea; 5-year lending rate for China; 10-year government securities average yield rate for Malaysia; and 12-year government bond yield rate for Thailand.

In Hong Kong and Singapore, house prices are extremely sensitive to the fluctuations of macro-economic fundamentals of their own countries. For example, a one percentage point increase in the growth rate is associated with a more than 2–3 percent increase in house prices. The results for the dynamic models with lagged dependent variables even imply that a one percentage point increase in the growth rate boosts the house prices by approximately 1.5 percent in Hong Kong and 0.8 percent in Singapore within the same quarter and gradually amply the effects up to 5 percent (= 1.5/(1 − 0.7)) in Hong Kong and 4 percent (= 0.8/(1 − 0.8)) in Singapore over time. Similar arguments also hold for the interest rates and inflation rates. A one percentage point cut in interest rate boosts the house prices by 2 to 3 percent, while a 1 percent increase in the inflation rate is associated with an approximately 2 percent increase in nominal house prices (or 1 percent increase in real house prices).

While house prices in Hong Kong and Singapore are very volatile, their correlations with US house prices still remain negative after controlling for the macroeconomic fundamentals. As discussed in Section 4, this result may imply the possibility that the global capital market regards Hong Kong and Singapore as a substitute market for the US.

The results for Malaysia are very standard and fairly stable. A 1 percent increase in the growth rate boosts the house prices from approximately 0.4 percent in the same quarter to a 1.2 percent in the long run. Although the effect of the interest rate does not appear to be significant in the non-dynamic models, the results for dynamic models are very significant: a 1 percent point cut of the interest rate boosts the house prices by 0.64 percent in nominal terms and by 0.50 percent in real terms.

The regressions for Thailand do not provide the expected sign for the interest rate coefficients: they turn out to be all positive, some of which are even statistically significant. We do not have a good conjecture for why this result is produced for Thailand. Other than the interest rate effect, the coefficients for the growth rate and inflation rate are very stable.

Indonesia is the most extreme outlier as to the general conclusions of the regressions. Considering the small sample size (27 quarters for seven years), however, we are not sure how seriously we have to take the regression results.

5.3 Controlled cross-country correlations within the region

In addition to the regressions reported in Tables 8.4A–8.4D where the US house price index was used as an additional explanatory variable, we also conducted regressions with another ASEAN+3 country's house price index in place of the US. Tables 8.5A and 8.5B report the regression coefficients of another country's house price index (column) for each country (row). For example, the number in row "Japan" and column "Korea" in Table 8.5A, 0.115, reports the coefficient estimate of Korea's house price index in the regression of Japanese house price. In comparison with Tables 8.2A and 8.2B, where unconditional correlation coefficients were reported, the results in Tables 8.5A and 8.5B are the estimates of coefficients after "controlling for" the effects of its own country's macro-economic fundamentals. All the results in Tables 8.5A and 8.5B were obtained from the regressions using short-term interest rates.

Looking at Tables 8.5A and 8.5B, it appears that Japanese house prices are affected by many other ASEAN+3 countries. However, this seems to be a spurious result due to the secular declining trend of Japanese house prices, considering

Table 8.5A Regression coefficients of other countries' house prices (nominal)

Explanatory Dependent	JPN	KOR	CHN	HKN	SIN	MAL	THA	IDN
JPN		0.115**	-0.193**	-0.052**	0.036**	-0.219**	-0.066**	-0.034
		(2.374)	(-5.455)	(-3.514)	(2.979)	(-4.737)	(-2.297)	(-0.430)
Jpn(-1)		-0.013	0.027	0.000	0.006	-0.080**	0.007	-0.095**
		(-0.661)	(1.039)	(0.042)	(1.457)	(-4.402)	(0.979)	(-3.326)
KOR	1.134**		0.277	-0.025	-0.133**	0.339*	0.121	0.969
	(3.339)		(0.827)	(-0.658)	(-2.563)	(1.838)	(0.902)	(2.851)
Kor(-1)	0.174		-0.170	-0.015	-0.032	-0.029	-0.083	0.031
	(1.159)		(-1.139)	(-1.010)	(-1.509)	(-0.379)	(-1.500)	(0.105)
CHN	-2.310**	-0.076		0.123**	-0.071**	-0.125	0.087	-0.100
	(-7.874)	(-1.303)		(3.816)	(-2.919)	(-1.256)	(1.377)	(-0.553)
Chn(-1)	-1.202**	0.020		0.008	-0.013	-0.040	-0.029	0.200
	(-3.265)	(0.537)		(0.282)	(-0.764)	(-0.627)	(-0.682)	(1.151)
HKN	3.193*	-0.138	1.999**		-0.394**	-0.818**	-0.024	-1.861**
	(1.972)	(-0.473)	(2.886)		(-3.437)	(-2.620)	(-0.072)	(-2.141)
Hkn(-1)	3.620**	0.025	1.054		-0.112	-0.331	-0.559**	-0.348
	(3.912)	(0.139)	(1.686)		(-1.351)	(-1.597)	(-2.806)	(-0.509)

(Continued)

Table 8.5A (Continued)

Explanatory Dependent	JPN	KOR	CHN	HKN	SIN	MAL	THA	IDN
SIN	-0.105	0.041	-0.639	-0.025		0.661**	-0.209	-0.401
	(-0.123)	(0.188)	(-1.064)	(-0.288)		(2.673)	(-0.694)	(-0.571)
Sin(-1)	0.593	0.131	-0.410	0.042		0.020	-0.464**	-0.168
	(1.379)	(1.181)	(-1.168)	(0.937)		(0.138)	(-3.294)	(-0.841)
MAL	0.126	0.068	0.166	-0.018	0.064		0.183**	0.031
	(0.353)	(0.648)	(1.489)	(-0.667)	(1.377)		(2.238)	(0.280)
Mal(-1)	0.179	0.043	-0.009	-0.024	0.034		-0.036	0.032
	(0.947)	(0.771)	(-0.147)	(-1.628)	(1.373)		(-0.840)	(0.282)
THA	-0.864	0.030	0.533	0.067	-0.051	0.654**		-0.340*
	(-1.195)	(0.175)	(1.583)	(1.205)	(-0.650)	(2.289)		(-1.895)
Tha(-1)	-0.797	0.012	0.522	0.063	-0.045	0.683**		-0.209
	(-1.049)	(0.068)	(1.473)	(1.123)	(-0.555)	(2.175)		(-1.157)
IDN	-0.408	-0.032	0.030	-0.141**	-0.078	0.322	0.117	
	(-1.693)	(-0.215)	(0.109)	(-4.237)	(-1.574)	(0.966)	(0.607)	
Idn(-1)	-0.209	-0.237	-0.122	-0.109**	-0.041	-0.076	0.145	
	(-0.941)	(-1.626)	(-0.491)	(-2.808)	(-0.867)	(-0.224)	(0.920)	

Table 8.5B Regression coefficients of other countries' house prices (real)

Explanatory Dependent	JPN	KOR	CHN	HKN	SIN	MAL	THA	IDN
JPN		0.110**	-0.287**	-0.059**	0.026*	-0.201**	-0.091**	-0.134**
		(2.301)	(4.954)	(-3.894)	(1.658)	(-4.233)	(-3.100)	(-3.590)
Jpn(-1)		-0.013	-0.031	-0.007	0.009*	-0.079**	-0.021	-0.070**
		(-0.630)	(0.582)	(-1.099)	(1.842)	(-3.873)	(-1.407)	(-2.576)
KOR	0.971**		0.413	-0.024	-0.140**	0.228	0.198	0.384
	(2.779)		(1.153)	(-0.594)	(-2.649)	(1.519)	(1.408)	(1.314)
Kor(-1)	0.187		0.080	-0.031	-0.063**	-0.166**	-0.097	-0.268
	(1.004)		(0.412)	(-1.641)	(-2.387)	(-2.198)	(-1.311)	(-1.216)
CHN	-1.289**	-0.082		0.022	-0.073**	-0.127	0.037	0.027
	(-5.013)	(-1.497)		(0.891)	(-3.059)	(-1.607)	(0.565)	(0.294)
Chn(-1)	-0.628**	-0.007		0.007	-0.030	-0.082	-0.021	0.042
	(-2.289)	(-0.177)		(0.407)	(-1.582)	(-1.352)	(-0.420)	(0.479)
HKN	-0.428	-0.488**	-0.102		-0.180	-0.297	0.109	-0.600
	(-0.294)	(-2.232)	(-0.149)		(-1.568)	(-0.998)	(0.297)	(-1.020)
Hkn(-1)	1.714*	0.035	-0.380		-0.095	-0.224	-0.454	0.797**
	(1.997)	(0.247)	(-0.872)		(-1.389)	(-1.278)	(-2.140)	(2.520)

(Continued)

Table 8.5B (Continued)

Explanatory / Dependent	JPN	KOR	CHN	HKN	SIN	MAL	THA	IDN
SIN	1.302	-0.061	-2.162	0.095		0.899**	0.105	-0.195
	(1.423)	(-0.273)	(-3.277)	(1.039)		(4.158)	(0.337)	(-0.342)
Sin(-1)	0.307	0.115	-0.366	0.020		0.015	-0.410	0.341**
	(0.713)	(1.122)	(-0.826)	(0.474)		(0.114)	(-2.590)	(2.270)
MAL	0.395	-0.002	0.041	-0.033	0.035		0.216	0.355**
	(1.308)	(-0.020)	(0.213)	(-1.166)	(0.854)		(2.365)	(4.620)
Mal(-1)	0.291*	0.001	0.016	-0.034**	0.041		-0.042	0.290**
	(1.789)	(0.030)	(0.182)	(-2.234)	(1.911)		(-0.848)	(2.886)
THA	-1.151*	-0.111	0.465	0.085	-0.056	0.594**		-0.019
	(-1.770)	(-0.694)	(1.176)	(1.457)	(-0.686)	(2.381)		(-0.122)
Tha(-1)	-0.970	-0.103	0.380	0.074	-0.043	0.550*		0.059
	(-1.396)	(-0.648)	(0.944)	(1.238)	(-0.527)	(1.962)		(0.477)
IDN	-0.040	0.410**	0.203	-0.215**	-0.059	0.972**	-0.148	
	(-0.099)	(3.384)	(0.873)	(-4.837)	(-0.656)	(3.439)	(-0.436)	
Idn(-1)	-0.128	0.351**	0.170	-0.194**	-0.056	0.813**	-0.151	
	(-0.332)	(2.688)	(0.736)	(-4.473)	(-0.648)	(2.406)	(-0.489)	

that most of the coefficient estimates are negative and most of these negative coefficients become insignificant in the regressions with the lagged dependent variables.

If there is a meaningful result for Japan, it may be the effect of Korea, 0.115. Literally interpreted, this result indicates that a 1 percent increase of house prices in Korea tends to increase the Japanese house prices by 0.115 percent. However, the reverse effect appears to be approximately 10 times greater than this effect: that is, a 1 percent increase of house prices in Japan tends to increase the house prices in Korea by 1.134 percent. These mutual effects between Japan and Korea are consistent with the close unconditional correlation between the two countries in Tables 8.2A and 8.2B, though the correlations appear to be getting weaker after the Asian crisis.

As for China, an interesting result is the effect of Japan. As seen in the unconditional correlation, the Japanese house price fluctuations appear to have negative impacts on Chinese house prices, in stark contrast with the positive effects of the US house prices. Another country that appears to have positive effects on Chinese house prices is Hong Kong. In the case of Hong Kong, however, it seems that Hong Kong is far more affected by China than the other way around in the sense that the coefficient estimate of Chinese house prices in the regression of Hong Kong's house prices is more than 10 times as high as that of Hong Kong's house prices in the regression of the Chinese house prices.

Hong Kong's (nominal) house prices appear to be greatly affected by the Japanese house prices as well as the Chinese house prices. In fact, Hong Kong is the only country that appears to be significantly affected by both Japan and China, the largest two countries in the region. However, the real house prices of Hong Kong do not appear to be much affected by other countries, reflecting the peculiar inflation dynamics of Hong Kong.

Perhaps the most interesting result in Tables 8.5A and 8.5B is the relationship between Hong Kong and Singapore. Even though their unconditional correlation was very high, they did not have any significant independent effects on the other country (if any, there are negative effects). These results strongly suggest that the high unconditional correlation between the two countries was generated from the co-movements of macro-economic fundamentals rather than an "unfounded contagion."

As for the region of Singapore, Malaysia and Thailand, it appears that Malaysia leads the house prices. For example, Singapore is significantly affected by Malaysia but not by Thailand, while it affects neither Malaysia nor Thailand. Between Malaysia and Thailand, there exist mutual effects, but Thailand appears to be far more sensitively affected by Malaysia than the other way around.

In sum, the unconditional correlations in house prices in the three regional groups of countries do not seem to be completely attributable to the co-movements of the macro-economic fundamentals considered in this study (GDP growth, interest rates and inflation). The only exception is Hong Kong and Singapore, where the high unconditional correlation is completely attributable to the co-movements of macro-economic fundamentals. For the group of Japan and Korea, Japan appears to affect Korea, and for the group of China and Hong Kong, China appears to affect Hong Kong. For the group of Singapore, Malaysia and Thailand, Malaysia leads the house prices.

6. House prices and monetary policy: overview

From a welfare policy perspective, supplying houses at the lowest possible prices may be the policy goal. From a stabilization policy perspective, however, a sharp depreciation of house prices is, at least, as harmful as a sharp appreciation.

In relation to the house price fluctuations, the most arguable is monetary policy response. As was readily confirmed for the ASEAN+3 countries in the previous section, interest rates are probably the most effective policy measure for house price stabilization. Nevertheless, the effectiveness of monetary policy does not warrant the recommendation that it should be used for house price stabilization, or more broadly, asset price stabilization. It is still an ongoing issue in both academia and policy circles whether monetary policy should respond to asset price fluctuations.

The mainstream idea is not to use monetary policy as a direct asset price stabilization tool for the following reasons. First, it is extremely difficult to identify *ex ante* whether asset price fluctuations are due to productivity or bubbles, and thus a systematic response to asset price fluctuations is almost impossible. Second, as far as monetary policy tools are anchored by inflation targeting, this single monetary policy measure cannot be used for another target such as asset price stabilization (see, for example, Bean, 2003). Third, it is believed that asset prices can also be stabilized if monetary policy successfully stabilizes inflation and growth (see, for example, Gilchrist and Leahy, 2002). Therefore, the monetary authority should take asset price into account only to the extent that it conveys meaningful information about the real economy such as growth and inflation.

The monetary authority of the US has repeatedly confirmed this policy stance. Among many others, Alan Greenspan, who served as the chair of the Federal Reserve Board, stated at the American Economic Association's meeting: 'There is little dispute that the prices of stocks, bonds, homes, real estate, and exchange rate affects GDP. But most central banks have chosen, at least to date, to view asset prices not as targets of money, but as economic variables to be considered through the prism of the policy's ultimate objective' (2004, p. 40). Not only the former, but also the current chair of the Federal Reserve Board, Ben Bernanke, presented an almost identical argument, when he was in academia: 'In brief, it is that flexible inflation-targeting provides an effective, unified framework for achieving both general macroeconomic stability and financial stability. Given a strong commitment to stabilizing expected inflation, it is neither necessary nor desirable for monetary policy to respond to changes in asset prices, except to the extent that they help to forecast inflationary or deflationary pressures' (Bernanke and Gertler, 2000, pp. 40–41).

There have been counter-arguments, however, particularly during the period of IT bubbles and global house price run-ups. Perhaps the forerunner of alternative views on monetary policy is Cecchetti (2002) with his colleagues (Cecchetti, Genberg and Wadhwani, 2002, p. 3): 'central banks seeking to smooth output and inflation fluctuations can improve ... macroeconomic outcomes by setting interest rates with an eye toward asset prices in general, and misalignment in particular.' Borio and Lowe (2002) and Helbling (2005), both at the Bank for International Settlement, also emphasized the potential danger of asset price bubbles and called for appropriate policy responses. In particular, Borio and Lowe argued that identifying financial imbalances *ex ante* is not impossible and 'sustained rapid growth combined with large increases in asset prices' are so dangerous for monetary responses to be necessary.

Considering the alternative views, Trichet (2005), president of the European Central Bank (ECB), proposed a monetary policy stance that was a bit more flexible than the Federal Reserve Board regarding asset price bubbles: 'The ECB's primary objective is unambiguously the maintenance of price stability. . . . I mentioned though that boom-bust cycles in asset prices do exist and can potentially harm the entire economy, especially via the effect on the financial system . . . allowing some short-term deviation from price stability in order to better ensure price stability over more extended horizons might – under very restrictive assumptions – be the optimal policy to follow. The principle behind it should not be misunderstood as a systematic reaction to asset price booms, but rather as a selective response based on the careful analysis of all the available information.'

7.   Summary and concluding remarks

This study analyzes house price movements in the ASEAN+3 countries. Though there exist many reservations due to the serious limitations in the data quality and availability, the primary results can be summarized as follows:

(1) Since 2000, house prices in Asia, except for Japan and Indonesia, have been rising in real terms: approximately 50 percent in Hong Kong; 25–30 percent in Korea, China and Singapore; and 5–10 percent in Malaysia and Thailand. These price appreciations are substantial even though they are far less serious than in the US and many European countries, where the real house prices have appreciated by 50–100 percent.

(2) House prices in Asia do not appear greatly affected by those in the US. The only exception may be China, where 20 percent of the price fluctuation in the US appears to be transmitted.

(3) Intra-regionally, house prices in most countries are inter-linked to some extent, except for Indonesia, though not correlated as much as those between the US and European countries.

(4) The blocks of countries with particularly high correlations are: Japan and Korea; China and Hong Kong; Hong Kong and Singapore; and Singapore, Malaysia and Thailand. Within these groups, Japan affects Korea, China affects Hong Kong, and Malaysia leads Singapore and Thailand. The unconditional

correlation between Hong Kong and Singapore appear to be completely attributable to the co-movements in macro-economic fundamentals.

(5) For most of the countries, it is confirmed that house prices are boosted by high growth, low interest rates and high inflation.

From these results, it seems legitimate to claim that the possibility of collapse in the ASEAN+3 region's house prices is smaller than in the US and European countries. The price appreciation in the region was less serious, and the possibility of rapid contagion appears to be smaller.

However, it also seems legitimate to call policymakers' attention to house prices in the ASEAN+3 region. Although relatively less serious than in the US and European countries, the absolute magnitudes of house price appreciation in the region were quite substantial. Also, the result that the region's house prices do not appear to be greatly affected by US house prices should not be over-emphasized as a comforting factor. The current turmoil in housing markets in the US and European countries is very likely to generate a global recession, which will indirectly affect the region's house prices through lowering the growth rates of the member countries. Once house prices begin to decline in one of the countries, house prices in neighbor countries will likely be affected.

If the possibility of house price corrections needs to be reduced, a traditional package of boosting policies – lowering interest rates and increasing government spending – seems to be warranted. Although it is strongly recommended to take expansionary policy stances in a coordinated manner, the degree of boosting policies and the mix of monetary and fiscal policies need to be fine-tuned depending upon each member country's macro-economic situations, such as inflation, fiscal position and exchange rates. In any case, prudent financial supervision cannot be over-emphasized in that the adverse effects of asset price collapses are most likely to be propagated through financial market instability and credit crunches.

Before concluding, it is necessary to re-emphasize that the assessments of this chapter should be taken with many reservations in relation to the data availability. First, many analyses in this study were carried out for relatively short time periods for many countries such as China and Indonesia. Considering the immense magnitude of China's influence on the region in particular, the limited availability of data for China can impair the reliability of the assessment about the whole region. Second, analyses in this study are mostly based on house price *indexes*. This implies that this study could not directly address the issue that the current *levels* of house prices can be justifiable by fundamentals such as rents. Third, this study mostly looks at nationwide data, which may conceal the serious price run-ups of major cities that can be a potential threat to the financial system if real estate lending was focused on those cities.

Note

* This chapter is reprinted from KDI School Working Paper Series 09–12, KDI School of Public Policy and Management, 2009.

References

Bean, Charles, 2003. "Asset Prices, Financial Imbalances and Monetary Policy: Are Inflation Targets Enough?," Bank for International Settlements Working Paper no. 140, Basel Switzerland.

Bernanke, Ben S., and Mark Gertler, 2000. "Monetary Policy and Asset Price Volatility," NBER Working Paper no.W7559, Cambridge, MA.

Borio, Claudio., and Philip Lowe, 2002. "Asset Prices, financial and monetary stability: exploring the nexus?", Bank for International Settlements Working Paper no. 114, Basel, Switzerland.

Cecchetti, Stephen G., 2003. "What the FOMC Says and Does When the Stock Market Booms," *Reserve Bank of Australia*, Sydney.

Cecchetti, Stephen G., Hans Genberg and Sushil Wadwani, 2002. "Asset Prices in a Flexible Inflation Targeting Framework", NBER Working Paper No. 8970, June.

Gilchrist, Simon, and John V. Leahy, 2002. "Monetary policy and asset prices," *Journal of Monetary Economics*, 49, pp. 75–97.

Girouard, Nathalie, Mike Kennedy, Paul van den Noord, and Christophe André, 2006. "Recent House Price Developments: The Role of Fundamentals," Economics Department Working Paper no. 475, OECD, Paris.

Greenspan, Alan, 2004. "Risk and Uncertainty in Monetary Policy," *American Economic Review Papers and Proceedings* 94, pp. 33–40.

Helbling, Thomas, 2005. "Housing Price Bubbles – A Tale Based on Housing Price Bubbles and Busts," 2005. Bank for International Settlements Working Paper no. 21, Basel, Switzerland.

Strauss-Kahn, Dominique, 2008. "Lessons from the Financial Market Crisis: Priorities for the World and for the IMF," Speech to the Indian Council for Research on International Economic Research, New Delhi, India, February 13.

Trichet, Jean-Claude, 2005. "Asset Price bubbles and monetary policy," *Speech and Interview*, Singapore.

van den Noord, Paul, 2006. "Are House Prices Nearing a Peak? A Probit Analysis For 17 OECD Countries." Economics Department Working Paper no. 488, OECD, Paris.

9 Crisis and employment

The case of Korea*

1. Introduction

As an open economy at both financial and export fronts, Korea was one of the countries hit most directly by the global crisis in the fourth quarter of 2008. Immediately after the Lehman Brothers bankruptcy filing in September 2008, both currency and stock values collapsed by more than 30 percent and foreign reserves declined by approximately 20 percent during the three months until the end of the year. Korea's export growth rate (year-on-year) also collapsed at a drastic pace from 27.6 percent in September to –19.5 percent in November 2008.

However, Korea managed to recover at a relatively strong pace from the second quarter of 2009, and its labor market was spared from the recent turmoil. Figure 9.1 shows that Korea, along with Norway, Netherlands and Switzerland, maintained one of the lowest unemployment rates among OECD countries in both 2007 and 2009.

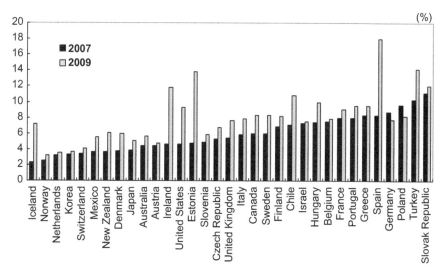

Figure 9.1 Unemployment rates of OECD countries

Source: OECD.Stat Extracts (http://stats.oecd.org).

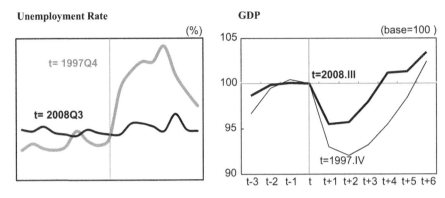

Figure 9.2 Comparison with the Asian crisis period
               Unemployment rate GDP

Source: Korean Statistical Information Service (KOSIS).

Yet, the solid labor market performance of Korea this time was in stark contrast to its own experience during the 1997–1998 Asian crisis. As Figure 9.2 vividly shows, Korea lost more than 6 percent of the total number of jobs, and its unemployment rate soared to almost 9 percent in 1998. How could Korea survive this time in the swirl of the global crisis while it miserably suffered during the Asian crisis period? By identifying the main factors that can answer this question, this chapter draws policy lessons regarding employment protection during a crisis period.

2.   The recent crisis in comparison with the Asian crisis

There must be various factors that can explain the difference in Korea's performance during the two crises. Cho (2011) classifies them into two categories: pre-crisis fundamentals and post-crisis macroeconomic policies.[1]

First, the pre-crisis fundamentals of the Korean economy had been significantly improved as a result of restructuring efforts since the Asian crisis. For example, the ample amount of foreign reserves that had been accumulated since the Asian crisis[2] played a critical role in dampening the adverse impacts of a sudden reversal in capital flows on the domestic banking system.[3] The improved financial positions of firms, particularly large corporations (or *chaebols*), were also crucial in absorbing the impacts that could have transmitted from the banking system to the real economy.[4] In addition, the milder house price hikes in Korea than those in advanced countries during the run-up to the crisis, as shown by Figure 9.3, must have helped keeping them from collapsing, minimizing adverse transmissions of the global crisis to domestic financial markets.

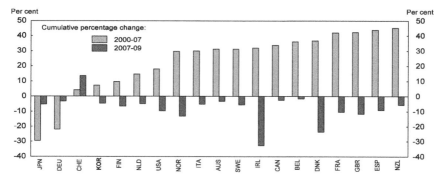

Figure 9.3 Changes in house price to income ratio
Source: OECD (2010).

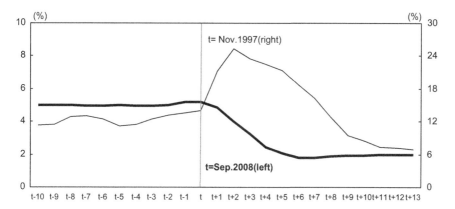

Figure 9.4 Inter-bank overnight call rate
Source: Cho (2011).

Second, the post-crisis macroeconomic policy reactions were also different this time from those during the Asian crisis period. Particularly contrasting was monetary policy: the interest rate target was raised in December 1997 to a level (almost 30 percent) above twice the pre-crisis rate (approximately 12 percent) but it was lowered to the level (2 percent) below half the pre-crisis rate (5.25 percent) in response to the recent crisis (see Figure 9.4).[5] No doubt the monetary easing in 2008 was crucial in guarding the domestic economy from the external storm, whereas the monetary tightening in 1997 aggravated the domestic banking crisis.

Fiscal policy was also more expansionary this time. Although the size of the budget deficit relative to GDP was far larger during the Asian crisis period (see

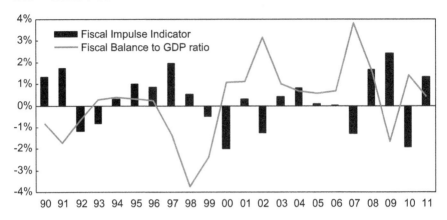

Figure 9.5 Fiscal impulse

Note: Fiscal impulse is the increase in the structural budget deficit to GDP ratio from the previous year.
Source: Consolidated Government Finance Statistics of Korea, various issues.

Figure 9.5), a substantial portion of the deficit was a result of the severe recession rather than discretionary fiscal expansion.[6] In addition, the budget deficit had already increased before the crisis in 1997; the fiscal impulse indicator (essentially measured by the *increase* in the budget deficit net of the portion attributable to cyclical fluctuations) turned out to be near neutral in 1998. This time, however, a relatively conservative fiscal policy until 2007 provided rooms for fiscal stimulus in 2008 and 2009 without incurring huge deficits in absolute sizes. Based on the sound fiscal position, a supplementary budget of 10 trillion won (approximately 1 percent of GDP) was implemented in November 2008, and an additional supplementary budget of 28.4 trillion won (approximately 2.8 percent of GDP) was drawn up by March 2009. Considering time lags common to fiscal policy effects, the prompt execution of fiscal spending must have contributed to stabilizing the economy this time.

With the better pre-crisis fundamentals supported by more appropriate post-crisis policy reactions, Korea could guard the domestic financial system (hence domestic demand) from the external shocks and maintain relatively stable macroeconomic conditions this time. As a matter of fact, Korea was one of the few countries in which the non-performing loan ratio was maintained at low levels.[7] This was a remarkable achievement, considering the magnitudes of external shocks; not only the size of capital outflow was far larger,[8] but also export demand collapsed this time while it kept expanding during the Asian crisis period. Figure 9.6 contrasts the responses of domestic demand and export for the two crisis periods, based on which Cho (2011) refers to the 1997–1998 crisis as the *implosion* triggered by weak internal fundamentals in comparison with the *explosion* of the external financial markets during the recent global crisis.

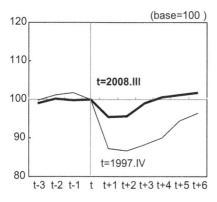 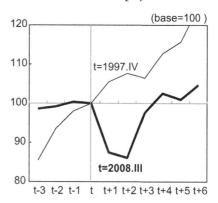

Figure 9.6 Differences of the recent crisis from the Asian crisis period
    Private consumption export

Source: Cho (2011).

3. Factors that mitigated adverse impacts on employment

3.1. Macroeconomic and financial conditions

Korea: time-series analysis

Like other countries, employment in Korea is a function of aggregate demand. Therefore, the lower unemployment rate in 2009 (3.4 percent) than that in 1998 (7 percent) should be explained by the higher growth rate in 2009 (0.2 percent) compared to that in 1998 (–5.9 percent) or equivalently the smaller GDP-gap in 2009 (–2.3 percent) compared to that in 1998 (–7.0 percent).[9] To investigate this point, we ran various specifications of regressions of the unemployment rate on GDP-gap for quarterly data, first quarter of 1990 to fourth quarter of 2010, and found that the coefficient was robustly estimated to be around –0.31.[10] Applying this coefficient estimate, the difference in GDP-gaps between 1998 and 2009, 4.7 percent, can account for a 1.5 percent differential in the unemployment rate between the two years, which is less than a half of the actual differential, 3.6 percent.[11] This result implies that the growth rate alone is not sufficient to explain employment fluctuations during crises periods.

Discussion of the previous section suggests an additional factor that affects employment adjustments – aggregate demand composition. It has been found that most of the short-term employment fluctuations in Korea are driven by domestic demand (particularly private consumption) rather than exports, which makes sense in that export (mostly manufacturing) industries are relatively capital intensive, while domestic demand (mostly service) industries are labor intensive.[12] We explored this relationship by using the ratio of private consumption to GDP as a proxy for the relative importance of domestic demand in short-run fluctuations and found that the coefficient of this variable was significantly esti-mated to be around −0.35 while not much affecting the GDP-gap coefficient. The result implies that the same GDP-gap can have a larger impact on employ-ment when the recession is driven by private consumption, as in 1998, than when driven by export as in 2009. More specifically, the consumption-to-GDP ratio was 1.5 percent *below* its trend in 1998 but 0.8 percent *above* the trend in 2009, which can account for an additional 0.8 percent differential in the unemployment rate between the two years.

Another factor to be considered, particularly in relation to crises, is the degree of financial distress. During the Asian crisis period, many over-leveraged con-glomerates went bankrupt under the tight financial environment and made imme-diate and large-scale lay-offs, whereas most of the major conglomerates and banks remained financially stable during the recent crisis period. As an example, the dishonored bill ratio, an indicator of financial distress, soared to the record-high (0.38 percent) in 1998, while it stayed at a level likely to be seen during a tranquil time (around 0.03 percent) in 2009. We again explored the importance of this factor in a regression framework and found that financial distress (as measured by dishonored bills) can generate a significantly higher unemployment rate, after controlling for the effects of the GDP-gap and demand composition.[13] With a coefficient estimate of around 2.2, an additional 0.8 percent differential in the unemployment rate between 1998 and 2009 can be attributed to the difference in the degree of financial distress.[14]

In short, the contrasting employment performances between the two crisis periods cannot be fully explained by the difference in the growth rate alone. The better maintenance of employment this time was greatly helped by the protection of domestic demand and financial market stability, in addition to a relatively mild decline in growth.

OECD countries: cross-country analysis

We have also explored the importance of these factors using cross-sectional data of 31 OECD countries. In order to control for country-specific effects, we took differences of all the relevant variables between 2007, a pre-crisis year, and 2009, a post-crisis year. Therefore, the dependent variable of regressions measured an increase in the unemployment rate during the crisis period in each country. As for explanatory variables, the growth rate during the same period (subtracted by each country's "potential growth rate") and the increase in the consumption-to-GDP ratio were used.[15] Since dishonored bill ratio data do not exist for OECD coun-tries, we used the rate of change in the house price to income ratio as a proxy for the degree of financial distress for the 19 countries (shown in Figure 9.3) where data were available.

In all of the regression estimates, coefficients for the growth rate and the consump-tion ratio appeared to be statistically significant with correct signs: the more the growth rate collapsed, the more the unemployment rate soared and the more con-sumption-driven the crisis was, the larger the impact on employment was observed.

The regression results for the 19 countries in which the house price-to-income ratio data were available did not appear as reliable as those for 31 countries. Due to the smaller sample size, standard errors became larger and estimates were not robust to specification variations. Yet the results did suggest that the unemployment rate soared more in a country where the house price-to-income ratio collapsed more drastically, though the coefficient estimate was not statistically significant.

All in all, this section's framework is helpful for understanding cross-country variations of the changes in the unemployment rate during the crisis period. For example, approximately 7 percent of GDP was lost (relative to their respective potential) in both Germany and the US for the two years, 2008 and 2009. However, the unemployment rate rather declined in Germany, while it soared in the US. The model explained above suggests that a consumption-driven recession accompanied by a house price collapse (or severe financial crunch) in the US amplified the impacts on employment.

3.2. Labor market structure

The main determinants of aggregate employment during crisis periods seem to be the macroeconomic and financial environment rather than micro-labor market structures. Yet some structural issues deserve to be mentioned. Shin and Cho (2011) argue that there was approximately 2 percent of "over-employment" in the aggregate before the Asian crisis, while no such evidence was found before the recent crisis.[16] We interpret this result as evidence of labor market rigidity before the Asian crisis and contend that even more drastic employment restructuring was triggered upon the introduction of emergency lay-off measures in 1998 than would otherwise have taken place.[17]

Changes in employment structures were also supportive of this view. In 1998, employment restructuring was concentrated mainly on core workers, namely, permanent wage-income workers: more than 85 percent of job losses fell on wage-income workers, out of which two-thirds fell on permanent workers. Even in 1999, when the economy strongly rebounded with 10.7 percent economic growth, firms continued to layoff permanent wage-income workers and responded to the rapid recovery by hiring temporary workers only.[18] In 2009, however, the number of permanent wage-income workers rather increased, while non-wage-income and temporary workers lost jobs. This contrasting performance in 2009, which has benefited from the increased flexibility in the labor market structures since the Asian crisis, contributed to mitigating the impacts of the global crisis by protecting core workers such as household heads.

3.3. Policies directly aiming at employment boosting

In addition to macroeconomic and financial policies, the Korean government implemented various policies to support employment during the crisis period. Among them, the major areas were: (1) increasing short-term public work programs, (2) expanding social services, and (3) subsidizing internship programs for young workers. According to the *2010 White-book on Jobs* (2011), the government supported 1.2 percent of the total employment by these policies. A somewhat smaller, yet comparable, magnitude of an employment increase can also be detected from employment statistics by sectors: the number of workers employed by the public sector was increased by approximately 0.8 percent of the total employment in 2009.

Compared with the Asian crisis period, however, the policy menu was almost the same with similar magnitudes of effects: approximately 1 percent of the total employment was supported by government policies in 1999, too. In this regard, it may be difficult to argue that these policies were great contributors to the solid employment performance this time *relative* to that during the Asian crisis period. Nevertheless, it was a significant size that could relieve the burden of workers at the margin, though the jobs created or maintained by government support were generally low-wage work.

Also interesting was its timing: in both periods, the employment in the public sector began to rise immediately following the second and third quarters after the crisis broke and became normalized as the economy recovered in two years. Considering notorious time-lags in implementing fiscal policies in general, the two- to three-quarter lag does not seem inadequate until the actual employment statistics began to change. It is also appreciable that such policies faded out in one to two years as the economy recovered, not imposing persistent burdens on the fiscal side.[19]

4.   Summary and concluding remarks

This chapter examined Korea's employment dynamics during the crisis periods and analyzed how adverse impacts were mitigated this time in comparison with those during the 1997–1998 Asian crisis period. A clear lesson from Korea's experiences is that unemployment problems during crisis periods cannot be solved by looking at the labor market alone. They are functions of macroeconomic fluctuations, particularly financial market situations that affect firm bankruptcies and large-scale lay-offs. Policies to mitigate adverse impacts on financial markets should, therefore, be given priority to preserving employment. In this regard, expansionary monetary and fiscal policies to keep aggregate demand from collapsing need to be emphasized once a crisis breaks out. However, equally crucial is the maintenance of sound fundamentals during tranquil periods in that it can not only lower the probability of crisis but also help keep negative impacts from proliferating when a crisis happens to be triggered. In addition, sound internal fundamentals can help stabilize domestic demand, which appears to be more important for employment than export demand.

Labor market structures also appear to have affected the sensitivity of employment adjustment in response to a crisis. As witnessed in Korea during the Asian crisis period, for example, rigidly accumulated workers may become vulnerably exposed to drastic restructuring during a crisis period. Finally, temporary policies directly aimed at employment boosting in Korea appear to have been effective in relieving the burden of workers at the margin.

Notes

* This chapter is reprinted from *Journal of Policy Analysis and Management*, pp. 169–177, November 2011, which was co-authored with Sukha Shin.
1 See Cho (2011) for detailed discussions.
2 For example, the ratio of reserve to short-term foreign debt increased from less than a half in 1997 to almost two in 2008.
3 Being an emerging economy with no hard currency, Korea experienced an abrupt and massive capital outflow. The size of financial capital withdrawn on net for just one month of October 2008 was US$25.5 billion (more than 3 percent of annual GDP), which was far larger than US$6.4 billion (1.2 percent of GDP) in December 1997, the worst month during the 1997–1998 crisis.
4 As an example, the average debt-to-equity ratio of the corporate sector fell from more than 400 percent in 1997 to around 100 percent in 2008, and the interest coverage ratio rose from barely more than 100 percent in 1997 to more than 500 percent in 2008.
5 Given foreign reserves were almost depleted in December 1997, the high interest rate policy may have been inevitable, but Korea in 2008 reserved room to maneuver on this front.
6 In 1997, the IMF initially recommended the Korean government maintain a budget balance in December 1997 when fiscal stimulus was most needed. Only after the severe recession was realized, a budget deficit was allowed in 1998 and gradually expanded as the recession deepened. See Chopra et al. (2002) for details.
7 According to IMF's Financial Soundness Indicators (http://fsi.imf.org/), Korea maintained the second lowest non-performing loan ratio in 2009 (next to Switzerland) among the 32 countries for which the data were available. As a reference, the ratios were 0.5 percent in Switzerland, 0.6 percent in Korea, 3.3 percent in Germany, 4 percent in France, 5 percent in the United States and 9.4 percent in Italy.
8 See Footnote 3.
9 GDP-gap was measured by Hodrick-Prescott filtered series.
10 See Shin and Cho (2011) for the detailed regression results.
11 Betcherman and Islam (2001) and Fallon and Lucas (2002) studied employment adjustments of several countries during the Asian crisis period and pointed out that the loss in employment of Korea was the largest among the crisis-hit countries, considering the decline in GDP.
12 Shin and Kim (2008), for example, found that domestic demand is significantly correlated with employment, whereas export is not. In addition, the employment elasticity with respect to production is estimated as approximately twice as large in the manufacturing sector as in the service sector.
13 Shin and Cho (2011) find that the dishonored bill ratio has a particularly large effect on employment during recession periods by estimating an error correction model in which an intersection term of the growth rate and the dishonored bill ratio is included.
14 Again, the inclusion of this variable in the regressions did not greatly alter the coefficient estimates for GDP-gap and the consumption ratio, –0.31 and –0.35.
15 The average growth rate during the 2000–2007 period was used as the proxy for each country's potential growth rate.
16 They measure "over-employment" as the deviation from the co-integrating relationship between employment and GDP.

17 Permanent employment was the norm in Korea for long time, which was regarded as a serious obstacle to prompt restructuring. In order to cope with the crisis, however, the Korean government implemented emergency lay-off measures in 1998.

18 In 1999, the number of temporary wage-income workers increased by 13.3 percent but the number of permanent wage-income workers declined by 6.1 percent.

19 For public work programs, the Korean government deliberately selected small-scale, labor-intensive projects that can be easily terminated, such as remodeling of public facilities, environment preservation projects, and so forth.

References

Betcherman, G. and R. Islam, 2001. "East Asian Labor Markets and the Economic Crisis: An Overview," in *East Asian Labor Markets and the Economic Crisis: Impacts, Responses and Lessons,* edited by G. Betcherman, and R. Islam, pp. 3–37. Washington, DC: World Bank.

Cho, Dongchul, 2011. "Responses of the Korean Economy to the Global Crisis: Another Currency Crisis?" in *Global Economic Crisis: Impacts, Transmission, and Recovery,* edited by Maurice Obstfeld, Dongchul Cho, and Andrew Mason, pp. 57—78. Cheltenham, UK: Edward Elgar Press.

Chopra, Ajai, Kenneth Kang, Meral Karasulu, Hong Liang, Henry Ma, and Anthony Richards, 2002. "From Crisis to Recovery in Korea: Strategy, Achievements, and Lessons," in *Korean Crisis and Recovery,* edited by David T. Coe and Se-jik Kim, pp. 13–104. Washington, DC: International Monetary Fund and Korea Institute for International Economic Policy.

Fallon, Peter and Robert Lucas, 2002. "The Impact of Financial Crises on Labor Markets, Household Incomes, and Poverty: A Review of Evidence," *The World Bank Research Observer,* 17(1), pp. 21–45.

International Monetary Fund. 2014. *Financial Soundness Indicators* (http://fsi.imf.org).

Organisation of Economic Co-operation and Development. 2014. *OECD.Stat Extracts* (http://stats.oecd.org).

Shin, Sukha, and Dongchul Cho, 2011, "Transmission of the Crisis to Employment," in *Korea's Capacity to Cope with Crises in a Globalized Environment,* edited by Dongchul Cho and Hyeon-Wook Kim, pp. 153–177. Seoul: Korea Development Institute.

Shin, Sukha, and Heesam Kim. 2008. "An Analysis on the Recent Slowdown of Employment," *KDI Economic Outlook,* 25(1), pp. 153–164 (in Korean).

Statistics Korea. 2014. *Korean Statistical Information Service,* http://www.kosis.kr.

10 Aggregate demand gap
Based on a simple structural VAR model*

1. Introduction

GDP-gap is a central concept in macroeconomic policymaking, but its estimation remains far from uncontroversial. A vast literature on the Taylor rule, for example, mostly uses Hodrick-Prescott (HP) filtered series as estimates of GDP-gaps.[1] However, this univariate filtering method is likely to cause serious problems in practical policymaking in real time, in particular, mainly concerning the most recent estimates of the sample. As will be shown in Section 3, policymakers using the HP-filtered estimates of GDP-gaps would have perceived that the economy was in recession in 2006 but realized only after the financial crisis that it was actually a boom period.

Seeking an alternative estimation method, this chapter applies a simple two-variable VAR model for GDP and GDP deflator with a standard identifying assumption that, in the long-run, the aggregate supply (AS) curve is vertical and aggregate demand (AD) shocks do not affect GDP.[2] Once AD shocks are identified, a series for "AD-gap" can be constructed as the GDP component generated by historical AD shocks only. To the extent that GDP also fluctuates due to AS shocks, the AD-gap can be considered as a part of GDP-gap. However, this concept may be more appropriate than the entire GDP-gap for macroeconomic policies dealing with AD only.[3] Applying this methodology for data from seven OECD countries, this chapter finds: (1) for all of the sample countries, short-run AD curves are downward-sloped and short-run AS curves are upward, although the magnitudes of the slopes vary across countries; (2) particularly at end-points of the samples, AD-gap estimates appear to be far more robust than HP-filtered series; and (3), the loss in permanent GDP component during the recent financial crisis period is estimated to be sizable.

2. Methodology

Let $Z_t = (\Delta Y_t, \Delta P_t)'$ be a 2-element vector composed of first differences of log(GDP) Y_t and log(GDP deflator) P_t, and $e_t = (e_t^Y, e_t^P)'$ be a reduced-form residual vector. A common representation of VAR, apart from constant and time-trend, is

$$Z_t = A_1 Z_{t-1} + A_2 Z_{t-2} + \cdots + A_k Z_{t-k} + e_t,$$ where A_i is a 2×2 coefficient matrix.

If $e_t = Bu_t$ stipulates the relationship between e_t and $u_t = (u_t^S, u_t^D)'$, the structural innovation vector (composed of AS shock u_t^S and AD shock u_t^D), the elements in the 2×2 matrix B have economic interpretations: b_{11} measures the contemporaneous (or short-run) impact of u_t^S on Y_t (or, $\partial Y_t / \partial u_t^S$), while b_{21} measures the impact of u_t^S on P_t (or, $\partial P_t / \partial u_t^S$). As the impacts of an AS shock on Y_t and P_t move along the AD curve, the slope of the short-run AD curve can be measured by b_{21} / b_{11}. Likewise, the slope of short-run AS curve can be estimated by b_{22} / b_{12}.

In order to identify B, I imposed a standard textbook assumption that a long-run effect of the AD shock on GDP is zero, or $\lim_{s \to \infty} \partial Y_{t+s} / \partial u_t^D = 0$. Once A_i's are estimated and B is identified from this assumption, Z_t can be represented as a moving average of the structural shocks,

$Z_t = Cu_t$, where $C(L) = (I - A_1 L + A_2 L^2 + \cdots + A_k L^k)^{-1} B$ and L is lag-operator.

From this, Y_t (as well as P_t) can be expressed as the sum of two components, AS-gap $= \sum_{b=0}^{\infty} c_{11}(L) u_{t-b}^S$ and AD-gap $= \sum_{b=0}^{\infty} c_{12}(L) u_{t-b}^D$. That is, the AS-gap is defined as the component of Y_t driven by historical AS shocks only, while the AD-gap by AD shocks. The restriction $\lim_{s \to \infty} \partial Y_{t+s} / \partial u_t^D = 0$ makes the AD-gap a stationary variable with mean zero, but the AS-gap is non-stationary. In this regard, the AS-gap has a permanent effect on the level of GDP.[4]

3.   Results

3.1   Data and specification

Quarterly data for GDP and GDP deflator were collected from the OECD (2010), in which full data since 1970 were available for only six countries: Australia, Canada, France, Korea, the UK and the US.[5] I also included Japan in the analysis though its data are available since 1980 and thus had to be extended to 1970 using data from another source.[6] I applied a uniform specification to all countries: eight lags and a time trend were included in the VAR estimation.[7]

3.2   Slopes of short-run AD and AS curves

Table 10.1 reports the estimates of long-run and short-run effects, along with the estimates for the slopes of short-run AD and AS curves. All of the parameters are precisely estimated in that the estimates are statistically significant at 1 percent. Also, the estimates for the slopes are all estimated to have correct signs: AD curves are downward-sloped and AS curves are upward.

However, the magnitudes of slope estimates, particularly those of AS curves, substantially differ across countries: while the slopes of AD curves vary within 1.0 ± 0.4 (except for France), those of AS curves range from 0.16 for the US to 1.56 for Australia. Literally interpreted, a positive AD shock increases GDP by ten times as much in the US as in Australia, at a given sacrifice in the price level. These

Table 10.1 Estimation results

	Long-run Effects			Short-run Effects				Slopes	
	AS→Y	AS→P	AD→P	AS→Y	AD→Y	AS→P	AD→P	AD Curve	AS Curve
Australia	0.60	−0.41	2.29	0.77	0.43	−0.50	0.67	−0.65	1.56
	(0.03)	(0.19)	(0.13)	(0.06)	(0.06)	(0.02)	(0.04)		
Canada	1.08	−0.34	1.77	0.54	0.38	−0.42	0.56	−0.79	1.49
	(0.06)	(0.15)	(0.10)	(0.04)	(0.05)	(0.02)	(0.03)		
France	0.72	−1.23	2.64	0.22	0.42	−0.41	0.13	−1.83	0.30
	(0.04)	(0.23)	(0.15)	(0.04)	(0.03)	(0.02)	(0.01)		
Japan	0.96	−0.94	1.71	0.67	0.68	−0.49	0.30	−0.73	0.44
	(0.06)	(0.15)	(0.10)	(0.07)	(0.04)	(0.04)	(0.02)		
Korea	1.48	−2.34	2.98	1.09	1.22	−1.43	0.72	−1.31	0.59
	(0.09)	(0.28)	(0.17)	(0.12)	(0.10)	(0.07)	(0.04)		
U.K.	1.15	−1.20	1.82	0.75	0.52	−0.78	0.61	−1.04	1.17
	(0.07)	(0.16)	(0.10)	(0.06)	(0.07)	(0.03)	(0.03)		
U.S.	0.97	−1.03	0.96	0.38	0.66	−0.25	0.11	−0.66	0.16
	(0.06)	(0.10)	(0.06)	(0.06)	(0.02)	(0.04)	(0.01)		

Note: Sample periods are first quarter of 1970–fourth quarter of 2009; figures in parentheses are standard errors.

results seem to be consistent with a casual observation that macroeconomic policy appears to be more effective in the US than in other countries.

3.3 AD-gaps

Figure 10.1 shows the estimates of AD-gaps, along with the HP-filtered series. Although there are some discrepancies between the two series (for example, the early 1990s for France), the AD-gaps appear to roughly match with the HP-filtered series in terms of both timing and magnitudes.

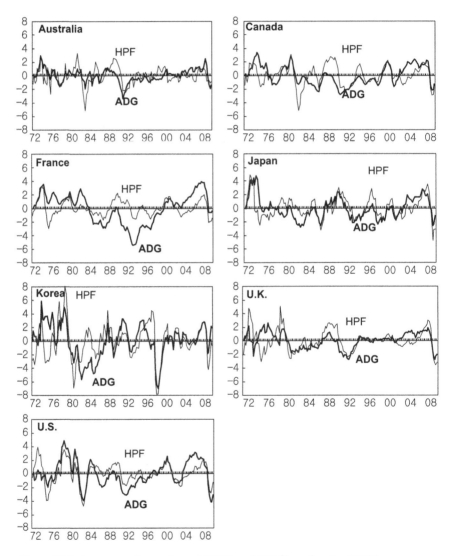

Figure 10.1 Aggregate demand gap (ADG) and HP filtered series (HPF)

However, AD-gaps and HP-filtered series did not even roughly match at end-points of the samples before the crisis broke out in 2008. The left panels of Figure 10.2 show several HP-filtered series for each country, respectively, as the sample periods are extended. In the case of the US, for example, HP-filtering for

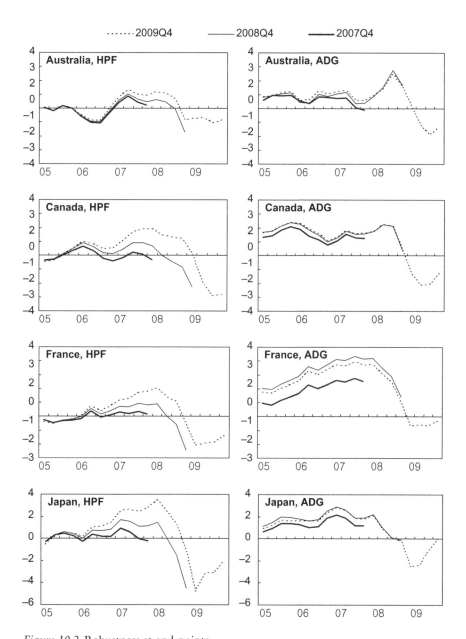

Figure 10.2 Robustness at end-points

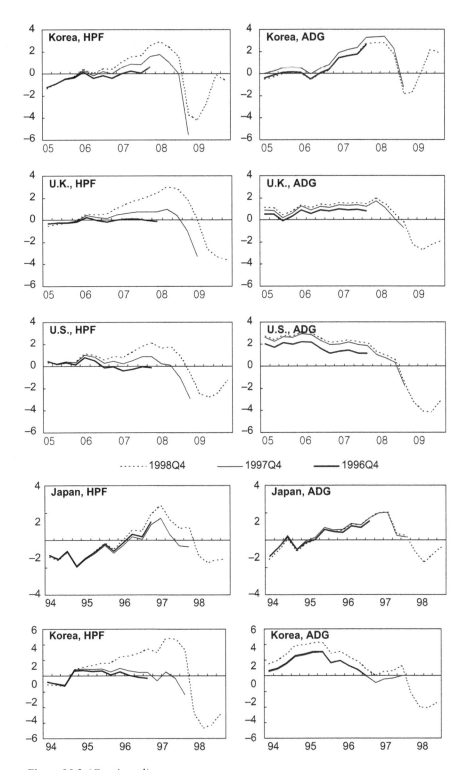

Figure 10.2 (Continued)

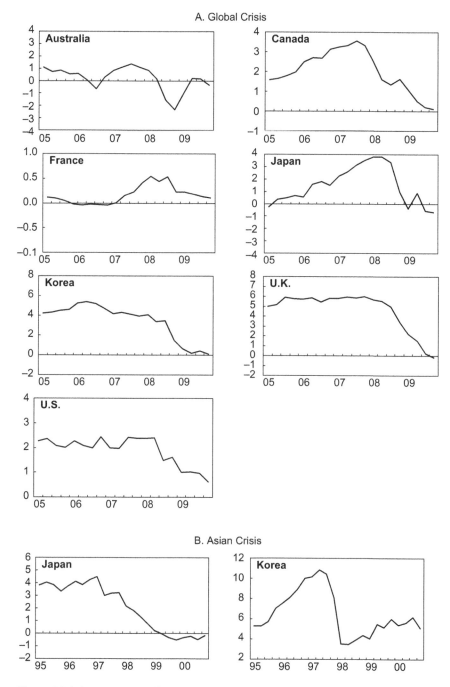

Figure 10.3 Aggregate supply gap

the sample period up to the end of 2007 yields negative GDP-gap estimates for 2007. Had this series been seriously taken as the estimate of GDP-gap, an expansionary policy would have been recommended. However, once the data for 2008 became available, the HP-filtered estimates for 2007 turned into positive values, calling for contractionary rather than expansionary policies. If data were further updated to the end of 2009, the HP-filtered series finally indicate that 2007–2008 was the biggest boom period since 1982. This end-point problem of HP-filtering is apparent in other countries, as well.

The AD-gaps (right panels), in contrast, are fairly robust with respect to data-updating. No matter where the samples are cut-off, the 2006–2007 period is estimated as a period with the biggest AD-gaps since 1982, not only in the US but also in most of the other countries. In addition, the AD-gaps are consistently estimated to be positive until the third quarter of 2008 in most of the seven countries, regardless of the sample period.

The same pattern can also be confirmed for Asian countries during the 1998 crisis (Panel B). The AD-gaps are relatively robust to the data-updating, while the HP-filtered series are extremely sensitive, especially for Korea, which experienced a big swing in GDP.

3.4 *AS-gaps*

Figure 10.3 shows AS-gap estimates for the 2006–2009 period. While the recent financial crisis hit the economy largely by contracting AD, it appears to have shifted AS curves as well. The losses in GDP attributable to AS shocks are estimated to be 2–5 percent for most countries, which have permanent effects on GDP as the AS-gaps are not mean-reverting.[8] This result is comparable to the estimates provided by Cerra and Saxena (2008) who recently established a stylized fact that financial crises, particularly banking crises, caused permanent and sizable output losses. In this regard, it is suggestive that the fall in AS-gap is the largest in the UK, but the smallest in Australia, which did not experience a serious banking crisis.

The Asian crisis is also estimated to have negative impacts on AS-gaps (Panel B). The AS-gap drastically collapsed immediately after the outbreak of the crisis in Korea, but it gradually declined in Japan.

4. Concluding remarks

This chapter examines empirical performances of AD-gaps estimated by a simple structural VAR model. The estimates have clear interpretations consistent with standard macroeconomics textbooks, and the results appear to be sensible and useful in practical policymaking.

Notes

* This chapter is reprinted from *Economics Letters*, pp. 228–234, February 2012.
1 See Taylor (1999), for example.

2 This methodology of long-run restrictions was originally suggested by Blanchard and Quah (1989). Gamber (1996) also used this model for the US data in a different context.

3 This limitation of GDP-gap in this regard has been noted by many economists. See McCallum and Nelson (1999, p. 27), among others.

4 This definition of the AS-gap may not be exactly consistent with a conventional definition of "potential GDP." Apart from the deterministic terms such as constant and time-trend, the AS-gap contains a yet-to-adjust part (dynamic impulse response) while a usual concept for potential GDP does not.

5 Data from the OECD source were only available from 1991 for Germany, 1981 for Italy, and 1995 for Spain, among major countries.

6 For the period from 1970 to 1979, I extended the data using those provided by the Cabinet Office of Japan (http://www.cao.go.jp/index-e.html.).

7 I also tried several other specifications, but the results were similar.

8 The AS-gap is not directly translated into a permanent loss in GDP to the extent that AS shocks have dynamic effects on GDP, as implied by the differences between the estimates in the second column and those in the fifth columns of Table 1. For the cases of France and the US, in particular, where the long-run effects are almost three times as large as the short-run effects, the negative impacts of the crises are not yet fully reflected in the estimates until 2009.

References

Blanchard, Olivier J., and Danny Quah, 1989. "The Dynamic Effects of Aggregate Demand and Supply Disturbances," *American Economic Review*, 79, pp. 655–673.

Cerra, Valerie, and Sweta Chaman Saxena, 2008. "Growth Dynamics: The Myth of Economic Recover," *American Economic Review*, 98(1), pp. 439–457.

Gamber, Edward, N,1996. "Empirical Estimates of the Short-run Aggregate Supply and Demand Curves for the Post-War U.S. economy," *Southern Economic Journal*, 62(4), pp. 856–872.

McCallum, Bennett T., and Edward Nelson, 1999. "Performance of Operational Policy Rules in an Estimated Semiclassical Structural Model," in *Monetary Policy Rules*, edited by John Taylor, pp. 15–45. Chicago: University of Chicago Press.

Organization for Economic Cooperation and Development. 2010. *OECD.StatExtracts*, http://stats.oecd.org/index.aspx.

Taylor, John, 1999. "A Historical Analysis of Monetary Policy Rules," in *Monetary Policy Rules*, edited by John Taylor, pp. 319–347. Chicago: University of Chicago Press.

11 Policy reports for the G20 summit meetings*

1. The framework and exit strategies

March 17, 2010

1.1. The framework

The global community has succeeded in protecting the world from plunging into another Great Depression by taking unprecedentedly bold and coordinated policies. The global economy, having passed the trough in the second half of 2009, is currently recovering, though the pace is bumpy and unequal across countries. The excess demand of the pre-crisis economy has been wiped out, and the global imbalance also corrected halfway in 2009.

It is now time to design strategies to smoothly exit from the crisis-response policies, while envisioning a new landscape of the post-crisis global economy we desire to construct. Clearly, the pre-crisis state is not a candidate for a desirable future. We do not want to go back to the overheated state of demand driven by asset bubbles and over-leveraged financing. We do not want to re-expand the global imbalance over the course of demand recovery. We have to deal with an additional problem of public debts that have resulted from the crisis resolution. At the same time, however, we have to be sufficiently cautious to preserve the hard-earned recovery momentum.

The difficulty in solving this complex problem is reflected in the G20 Framework for Strong, Sustainable, and Balanced Growth. By recognizing the pre-crisis problems of the global economy, the adjectives "sustainable" and "balanced" can be easily substantiated and well communicated with the market. However, the word "strong" might appear at first glance to indicate simply a rapid recovery, which does not go well with "sustainable." In order to avoid any possible miscommunication, it is better to clarify the meaning of the word "strong" and inform the market that its meaning is to close the GDP (or unemployment) gap *over the years to come.*

It may be well agreed as a general principle of the exit strategy that the intensity of demand-boosting policies should be gradually alleviated in line with the diminishing pace of GDP (or unemployment) gap. And this principle, which considers the pre-crisis state of the economy as well, is conceptually superior to that focusing only on growth rates. While it is clear that the global economy is currently running substantially below potential, thereby requiring continued stimulus, the magnitudes of GDP (or unemployment) gaps should differ across countries reflecting different pre-crisis states as well as following dynamics. The gap may be relatively small for a country that had been overheated prior to the crisis in spite of a large fall in GDP (or a large increase in the unemployment rate) after the crisis.

Therefore, in order to better assess and coordinate the exit policies, it is recommendable to include the GDP gap estimate and/or the medium-term target rate of unemployment in the template that is being reviewed by the IMF. Although it may be controversial to set appropriate medium-term targets in each country, the new GDP target should not be set at the level linearly extrapolated from the overheated pre-crisis GDP, and the target unemployment rate should not be set at the exceptionally low pre-crisis level. This caution is particularly relevant to the countries in which current account deficit is expanding and/or public debt is reaching an uncomfortable level. Setting appropriate targets is critical for designing sound exit strategies, and sharing the perceptions on other member countries' targets is important for drawing a constructive consensus at the G20.

1.2. Exit strategies

A one-fits-all exit strategy does not exist. To the extent that economic situations differ across countries, each country should design its own exit strategies. For example, countries in which public debts remain at comfortable levels but inflation rates (and asset prices) are rising should consider monetary normalizations prior to fiscal consolidations. However, considering the overall situation of the global economy, it is necessary that the G20 gives top priority to fiscal consolidations of advanced countries.

Top priority on fiscal consolidation

The current size of public debts in many advanced countries are already immense, still rapidly rising and politically difficult to unwind, whereas monetary expansions lie within relatively manageable ranges. The market already perceives fiscal sustainability as the biggest threat to the global economy, as has been evidenced by the case of Greece. Also, it is generally recommended (with due consideration to country-specific factors) to begin to withdraw fiscal stimulus as the economy recovers, while leaving the monetary policy to flexibly react against the remaining country-specific uncertainties. Monetary policy, rather than inherently rigid fiscal policy, needs to cope with short-term fluctuations of capricious financial markets and control medium-term inflation that will depend on different recovery paces across countries.

There are also several reasons that fiscal consolidation needs to be coordinated and thus discussed at the G20. First, fiscal tightening would directly transmit to other countries its negative effects on demand, unlike monetary tightening, whose negative spill-over effects can be neutralized to an extent by a resulting currency appreciation (if the exchange rate is floated). As far as their effects are directly transmitted to other countries, fiscal consolidations of large countries in particular should be a common concern of member countries. Second, there exists a *collective* danger associated with *simultaneous* increases in the fiscal burdens of advanced countries. If a monetary authority were faced with financial difficulties, a non-inflationary solution could be found as long as the government has maintained fiscal soundness. Even when one of the governments in advanced countries were faced with financial difficulties, the global economy could still find a way out of disastrous outcomes through policy coordination among the other governments. However, *simultaneous* fiscal deterioration implies that the global economy is losing the "safeguard of last resort." Insofar as it has an externality implication on the global economy, fiscal consolidation needs to be coordinated. Third, fiscal consolidation is an unpopular political agenda inside a country. Peer pressure and external reputations can be utilized as leverages to help push through internal fiscal reforms.

In order to reassure the market about fiscal sustainability, it would be necessary to announce concrete and credible consolidation plans with definite timeframes. Among many others, a three-step approach can be considered at the G20: (1) Set the eventual target of the public debt-to-GDP ratio below a specific level (60 percent, for example); (2) ask the countries currently above the threshold for submitting their own consolidation plans to attain the target by 2020 (For countries that are projected to be unable to reach the threshold in the near future, ask for commitments to meet other conditions such as ceasing to increase the debt ratio by 2020 or restoring the budget deficit-to-GDP ratio back to the pre-crisis level by 2015.); and (3) review the feasibility of submitted plans at the G20. While allowing individual countries to be flexible in designing their own consolidation plans, this approach will help increase the commitment levels of member countries to fiscal consolidation and contribute to alleviating the concerns of the market.

The G20 can also take the initiative in enhancing the quality and consistency of public debt statistics. As the concern grows, demand for the relevant statistics will increase. The supply of quality data will become more important for reducing uncertainties in the market and will also help increase peer pressure on fiscal consolidation efforts at the G20. The agenda includes unifying definitions and coverage of the statistics across countries, collecting data for semi-public debts and contingent liabilities of the government, and so forth.

Exit from ad hoc *measures prior to traditional policies*

The crisis has invited many governments to introduce emergency policy measures. The government guarantee on foreign short-term debts of private financial institutions was a typical example. The "quantitative easing" of monetary policy, particularly the extension of central banks' operating instruments to risky assets, also can be regarded as an example of emergency measures.

While these measures have substantially contributed to relieving the pain during the crisis, some of them appear to be *ad hoc* and are likely to distort incentive structures if maintained for too long. Therefore, as the economy normalizes, it is generally advised (with due consideration to compelling country-specific factors again) to withdraw *ad hoc* emergency measures prior to traditional policies that have been tested over several decades. If some emergency measures are considered desirable, it will be better for reducing market uncertainties and moral hazards to explicitly institutionalize them than to indefinitely postpone terminating them.

An example of emergency measures that can be institutionalized are currency swaps among central banks. This measure was introduced at the height of crisis on a rather *ad hoc* basis but greatly contributed to stabilizing foreign exchange markets. A formal institutionalization of such facilities will continue to function as a stabilizing factor for the exchange markets of emerging countries, in particular, that cannot provide internationally convertible liquidities in response to currency crises. Strengthening global liquidity provision mechanisms also has an important implication for global rebalancing. Following the Asian crisis, many emerging economies have run large current account surpluses and accumulated substantial amounts of foreign reserves for better self-insurance. Establishment of a strong international liquidity provision system would alleviate their worry about a liquidity crisis and reduce the incentives to aggressively accumulate foreign reserves through current account surpluses, eventually contributing to global rebalancing.

1.3. *Suggestions*

1   Inform the market that the meaning of "strong" is to close the GDP (or unemployment) gap *over the years to come*.
2   Gradually alleviate the intensity of boosting policies in line with the diminishing pace of GDP (or unemployment) gap, instead of focusing only on growth rates.
    2.1   Include the GDP gap estimate and/or the medium-term target rate of unemployment in the template that is being reviewed by the IMF.
3   Give top priority to coordinating fiscal consolidation efforts.
    3.1   Note that the market already perceives fiscal sustainability as the biggest threat to the global economy and that the *simultaneous* fiscal deterioration can have a negative externality implication on other countries.
    3.2   Prepare a framework that can increase the commitment levels of member countries to fiscal consolidations while allowing individual countries to be flexible in designing their own plans.
    3.3   Take the initiative in enhancing the quality and consistency of public debt statistics.
4   Exit from *ad hoc* emergency measures prior to traditional policies.
    4.1   Explicitly institutionalize emergency measures that are considered desirable. The currency swaps among central banks are such an example, which can also contribute to global rebalancing.

2.   Global economy and framework

September 17, 2010

2.1.   Global crisis and the G-20

The recent crisis that broke out in September 2008 sparked bold policy reactions in the global community. In many countries, interest rates were lowered to near zero and fiscal deficits were greatly expanded. Many emergency measures to rescue financial markets also were taken simultaneously. History will record the past two years as the period of the most active policy coordination across countries and place the G-20 summit meeting at the heart of this critical event.

Thanks to these policy efforts, the global economy turned around from the second half of last year. This was truly a big achievement, considering the panic of the market in 2008, when analysts and commentators pushed out extremely gloomy forecasts and referred to the trauma of the Great Depression. After two years, however, Bordo and Landon-Lane (2010) concluded "the economic impact of the Great Depression dwarfed that of the recent crisis," based on their study on crisis experiences since 1880.

This success was not achieved without cost; it was accompanied with huge costs, particularly in fiscal soundness. Budget deficits in 2009–2010 were expanded to obviously unsustainable levels in many countries, resulting in the explosive increase of public debts to levels that began to concern the market. In fact, the "unprecedented" impact of the recent global crisis was not manifested on GDP or employment but on public debts. Further stimulation by fiscal policy, at least in some countries, could rather destabilize the global financial market, as was evidenced by the case for some South European countries in the first half of this year. Faced with this development, the G20 summits at the Toronto meeting in June announced, "Advanced economies have committed to fiscal plans that will at least halve the deficits by 2013 and stabilize or reduce the government debt-to-GDP ratios by 2016."

This stance of the G-20 for fiscal consolidation has been challenged whenever downside risks emerged and financial markets jittered. As long as macro-policies are based on uncertain forecasts about the future, it is impossible to design an unarguable policy stance *ex ante*. Nevertheless, identifying and checking relevant issues are always proven fruitful in minimizing the probability that we end up with regrets about policy mistakes *ex post*.

2.2.   Global economic prospect and assessment

In order to properly discuss macro-policies at the G-20, the following issues regarding economic prospects need to be examined:

1   Is "double-dip" a likely scenario?
2   Is recovery to the pre-crisis level an appropriate reference?
3   Is there a risk that growth slowdown is structural rather than cyclical?

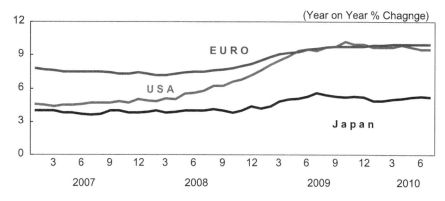

Figure 11.1 Unemployment rates

Source: Eurostat (Euro), Census Bureau (US), Statistics Bureau (Japan).

"Double-dip"?

Despite economic recovery, unemployment rates remain high and non-performing loans have not been significantly reduced in many advanced countries (Figure 11.1). Against this backdrop, if fiscal stimulus is rapidly withdrawn, it may hamper overall recovery momentum – according to the double-dip scenario.

This is a risk scenario, however. The base-case scenario in most forecasts, including the IMF's and OECD's, is a slow but steady recovery over the years to come (at 4–5 percent of annual growth for the world and 2–3 percent for advanced countries). The private sector's recovery momentum is being accumulated and fiscal consolidation is projected to be carried out gradually. The fiscal consolidation plan recommended by the G-20 also provided a reasonable degree of short-term leeway for gradualism. While a Plan B needs to be prepared for a risk scenario, the Plan A should be based on the base-case scenario of the consensus forecast.

A related issue is how deep it would be and what would be its main cause if a double-dip scenario were realized. Since the Lehman Brothers bankruptcy filing, major risk factors in the private sector have been revealed and adjusted to an extent. In particular, the potential risks associated with asset market bubbles have been reduced to the extent that asset prices have been corrected. The US consumers' saving rate, which had long been pointed to as a warning signal, also restored its pre-bubble period level (Figure 11.2). Even for a pessimistic scenario, it seems unlikely that such a panic as the one in September 2008 will resurge.

While the risks of the private sector have been reduced, those associated with public debts have been substantially increased. Although it seems impossible to pin down the threshold level of public debt, it is clear that the financial market is increasingly concerned about public debt problems of advanced countries and that it would be disastrous if the panic were ever triggered. Of course, this is a very unlikely scenario for the near future but it is important to bear in mind that the risks are being transmitted from private to public sectors.

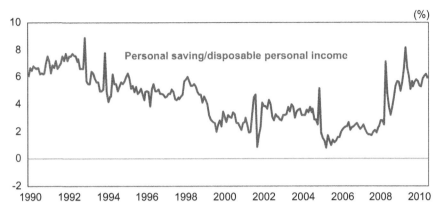

Figure 11.2 US personal saving ratio

Source: U.S. Department of Commerce, Bureau of Economic Analysis.

Recovery to the pre-crisis levels?

Another issue to be considered is how to assess the current economic states. It is widely agreed that demand conditions of major advanced countries are still weak, thereby requiring continued policy stimulus, but the perceptions about magnitudes appear to differ.

Theoretically, it would be ideal to estimate the gaps between the current and potential levels of GDP (or the current and natural rates of unemployment) in order to gauge the required policy stimulus. While such estimates are always controversial in practice, the idea itself provides an insight that the pre-crisis economic states may not be the desirable targets that we wish our economies to recover to in the near future. For example, the unemployment rate below 5 percent in conjunction with around 4 percent of economic growth in the US before the crisis were regarded as signals of unsustainable overheating for several years. The US stock price index has not recovered to the pre-crisis level but the current level does not appear to be particularly low compared to its long-run trend (Figure 11.3). While housing markets are still weak in many advanced countries, house prices in real terms are still higher than historical average levels (Figure 11.4). The current recovery pace can be perceived to be "painfully slow," as US President Barack Obama described it. However, a substantial portion of this pain may be attributable to the excessive enjoyment before the crisis.

Structural vs. cyclical?

Furthermore, there is uncertainty about whether the current economic difficulties are entirely attributable to cyclical factors. Many research results (Figure 11.5 from Cerra and Saxna, 2008, among others) show that crisis-hit countries could not completely restore their pre-crisis paths of GDP as well as pre-crisis levels of

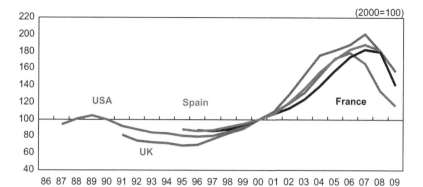

Figure 11.3 Real house prices

Source: Banco de Espana (Spain), INSEE (France), Nationwide (UK), S&P/Case-Shiller Home Price Indices (US).

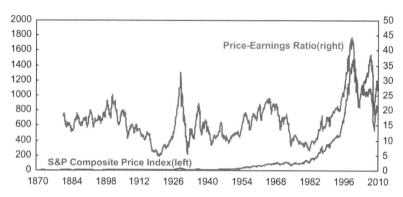

Figure 11.4 US stock price and price-earnings ratio

Source: http://www.econ.yale.edu/~shiller/data.htm.

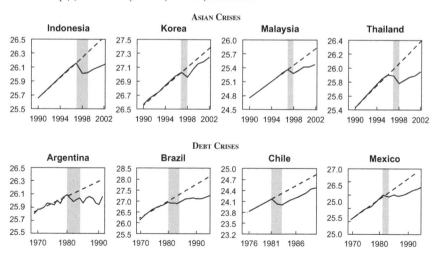

Figure 11.5 Crisis and GDP

Source: Cerra and Saxena (2008).

unemployment rates even after 10 years from the crises, which strongly suggests that a substantial portion of the loss in GDP and/or employment due to the recent financial crisis may be permanent (or structural) rather than temporary (or cyclical).

If this is the case for advanced countries, then the risk to the global economy is not just a short-term double-dip but a structurally sluggish recovery for several years. In this case, continued expansionary policy cannot be the solution; it should be dealt with by structural policies.

2.3.   *Fiscal vs. monetary policy*

Although the baseline scenario for the global economy is a gradual recovery, it is necessary to prepare for a downside risk. The next question then is which one among fiscal and monetary policy measures would be better to cope with risk scenarios. For this question to be properly answered, the following issues need to be considered:

1   Which policy is more flexible?
2   Which policy is more sustainable?
3   Is there room for further monetary stimulation?

Flexibility

It is largely agreed that monetary policy can be more flexibly adjusted than fiscal policy because monetary policy does not have to go through complicated political processes. In addition, spill-over effects on other countries' demand are more pronounced for fiscal policy than for monetary policy, whose effects can be neutralized by a resulting currency value adjustment (if the exchange rate is floated). Therefore, the more uncertain and country-specific the risks are, it would be more efficient, in general, for monetary rather than fiscal policy to react to unexpected high-frequency shocks.

Of course, if a shock is expected to generate a devastating outcome for a prolonged period of time (such as the shock we experienced in the fourth quarter of 2008), it would be justifiable to re-engineer the projected trajectory of fiscal policy. Particularly if the shock paralyzes the financial market as in 2008, so that monetary policy alone cannot cope with the problem, more active pump-priming efforts from the fiscal body would be necessary. In this regard, not only the existence of downside risks but also the expected intensity of the risk scenarios need to be discussed. At the moment, however, the probability that such a major shock will be realized seems slim.

Sustainability

Another dimension to be considered is the sustainability of expansionary policies. As far as fiscal stimulation is defined as an increase of fiscal deficit (in percent of GDP) from the previous period, it cannot be extended indefinitely almost by definition. For many advanced countries, even maintaining the current levels of fiscal deficit (in percent of GDP) does not seem to be sustainable considering their implications on public debt-to-GDP ratios. Although the tolerance level of public debt remains unclear both theoretically and empirically, the recent finding of Reinhart and Rogoff for advanced countries is suggestive: 'median growth rates for countries with public debt over roughly 90 percent of GDP are about one percent lower than otherwise' (2010, p. 573). The implication of this finding is that it is extremely unlikely for debt-ridden countries to simply "grow" their way out of the problem without fiscal consolidation. Currently, public debt-to-GDP ratios are already more than 90 percent for some advanced countries and are projected to reach this level within the years to come for many other countries.

In contrast, monetary expansion has no physical limit: central banks can print money indefinitely. The market cannot cast doubt about its sustainability *per se*. The associated risk of excessive money supply is the loss of paper money's attractiveness, namely inflation of prices for either goods and services or assets. But this is something that policymakers are aiming for under the current economic situation with deflation risks. Compared to the risks associated with public debt overhang, the inflation risk is relatively easy to detect and likely to be short-lived as far as inflation targeting is credibly committed.

Furthermore, if it is unclear whether the downside risk is structural or cyclical, monetary stimulation can be less dangerous than fiscal expansion in the long run. When potential growth rates are lowered, the natural (or "neutral") interest rates are also lowered, thereby reducing the risks associated with low-interest rate policies. In contrast, if fiscal stimulation is continued in response to structural slowdown, it will only worsen the public debt problem to the extent of reduced fiscal revenues due to slow growth in the long run.

Japan's case is illustrative. In response to the recession in the early 1990s, fiscal spending was increased and interest rates were lowered (with hesitation). Since then, these policy stances, notwithstanding some short-term variations, have been largely maintained, while it remained unclear whether the sluggish performance stemmed from structural or cyclical factors. After 20 years, the Japanese government inherited huge debts of almost 200 percent of GDP, which was increased from approximately 70 percent in 1990. This explosive increase in public debts was not because the fiscal stimulation was ineffective in boosting the economy in the short run (see Kuttner and Posen, 2002). It was simply because fiscal policy could not enhance long-term sustainable growth inherently and monetary policy failed to generate a reasonable rate of inflation, both of which were crucial in reducing the growth rate of fiscal revenue (Figure 11.6). In contrast, the damage caused by "excessively" low interest rate policy appears to be nonexistent. A lesson to learn from Japan's monetary policy experiences may be that it needs to be sufficiently aggressive with respect to deflation risks that would be harmful not only for economic vitality but also for fiscal consolidation.

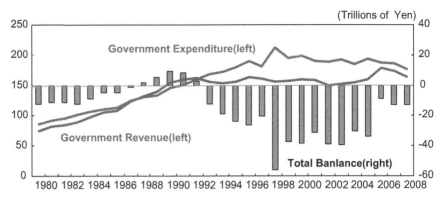

Figure 11.6 Japan's fiscal revenue, expenditure, and balance
Source: OECD (2010).

Feasibility of additional monetary stimulation

As for monetary policy, the current concern is not its flexibility in a conventional context, but its capability to further stimulate the economy under the circumstances of near-zero target interest rates. That is, the question is whether central banks still reserve effective tools for defending their economies from possible deflationary shocks.

To this question, US Federal Reserve Chair Bernanke (2010) recently listed three options that the Fed reserves in his address at Jackson Hole: (1) conducting additional purchases of longer term securities; (2) modifying the committee's communication; and (3) reducing the interest on excess reserves and discussed the pros and cons of each option, respectively,. These options are not completely new now, but they (particularly the first option) proved to be effective in weathering the financial market turmoil of the 4th quarter 2008. Additional and more drastic options for monetary easing can also be innovated if the economic situation deteriorates further. For example, central banks can lower the interest rate below zero for their short-term loans to commercial banks (i.e. providing subsidies for commercial banks' short-term borrowing from central banks) to encourage more aggressive investment of commercial banks.

It is not clear whether the recent economic indicators require that these unorthodox policy options to be exercised. In most countries, inflation rates are getting out of last year's severe deflationary pressures and economic recoveries are progressing (Figure 11.7). Yet, the very recent developments differ across countries, indicating that country-specific rather than common forces are becoming more important, requires a more active role of monetary than fiscal policy. In any case, it is extremely important to keep convincing the market that the central banks are fully committed to price stability and that they do have effective tools as well as strong wills to defend their economies from any possible deflationary shocks.

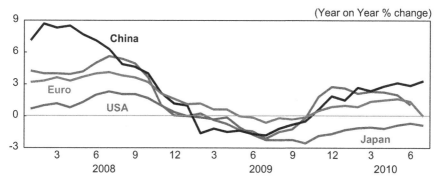

Figure 11.7 Inflation rates

Source: Eurostat (Euro), Census Bureau (US), Statistics Bureau (Japan), National Bureau of Statistics of China (China).

2.4. Summary and recommendations

The global recovery is an ongoing process. Although its pace is bumpy and expected to moderate in the second half of 2010, the baseline scenario is still a steady recovery over the years to come, based on which the G-20 needs to design the main policy recommendations.

Yet it is also necessary to prepare for risk scenarios. Under the current circumstances, the market will want to hear about how the G-20 perceives downside risks and what the contingency plans are. For this purpose, risk factors should be identified from various perspectives, such as: (1) how likely the risk scenario is to be triggered; (2) how severe the impacts would be; and (3) whether the risk factors are structural or cyclical. This chapter argues that, under many uncertainties about the nature of risks, it would be more productive and less dangerous to have monetary than fiscal policy to flexibly respond to possible disturbances.

This background discussion leads to the recommendation that the Toronto G-20's basic stance on fiscal consolidation be carried over to the Seoul meeting. Unless another round of global disruption is triggered, a major revision in the fiscal plan in five months would only damage the credibility of the G-20. As announced, each member country should submit its "growth friendly" fiscal consolidation plan, and the G-20 needs to perform the mutual assessment process. In this process, however, the G-20 can allow member countries to have a limited degree of flexibility, such as the pace of fiscal adjustment to the goal in 2013 being tailored to each member country's different economic situations (Figure 11.8). At the same time, the G-20 can call for strong commitments of central banks to price stability so that any deflationary shocks would be actively coped with.

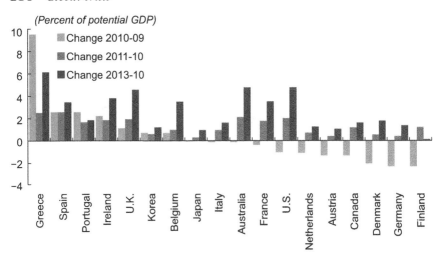

Figure 11.8 Projected changes in cyclically adjusted primary balances
Source: IMF (2010).

3.   Macro-policy normalization and the G20

May 25, 2011

3.1.   Global economy and exit policies

The global economy continues to recover. Though the recovery remains unbalanced between advanced and developing regions, the global economy has been recovering for almost two years since the second half of 2009. The IMF (*World Economic Outlook*, 2011a) expects the world economy will continue to grow at about 4.5 percent in both 2011 and 2012, with 2.5 percent for advanced economies and 6.5 percent for emerging and developing economies. Earlier fears of a double-dip recession have been replaced by fears of commodity price hikes that reflect strong global demand and abundant liquidity.

While the global recovery is gaining strength, macroeconomic policy exits did not virtually begin in many advanced countries. The fiscal deficit of the US, over 10 percent of GDP in both 2009 and 2010, is still perilously high and expected not to be reduced in 2011.[1] In fact, the structural deficit expanded from 6.8 percent in 2009 to 7.5 percent in 2010 and is expected to further expand to 8.1 percent in 2011. As a result, the size of public debt of the US will breach the threshold level of 100 percent of GDP in 2012. Fiscal policies of the Euro area are by and large similar. Fiscal deficits of more than 6 percent (structural deficit of more than 4 percent) continued in 2010, ballooning public debt to nearly 100 percent of GDP. Monetary policies are not much different either.

Quantitative easing at zero interest rates continues in the US and a 25 basis point (bp) hike in April was followed by inaction in the Euro area.

3.2. Output-gap estimation

The easy stances on macro-policies are based on the perception that output-gaps are still large in advanced countries. For example, the IMF estimates that the output-gap of the US and Canada is around –5 percent in 2010 and expects it to remain below –2 percent by 2012. As for Europe as well, the IMF expects that the output-gap will not close by 2012 (Figure 11.9).

Output-gap estimates, however, are extremely sensitive with respect to estimation methodologies. It involves the estimation of unobserved potential GDP (or supply-side GDP), regarding which there is no consensus. For example, the results from an alternative estimation using Blanchard-Quah-type structural vector auto-regressions (SVAR) yield substantially different views on output-gaps (or "aggregate demand gaps").[2] For the US and UK, the two countries most severely hit by the financial crises, the output-gaps are estimated to have recovered from –3 to –4 percent in the first quarter of 2009 to almost zero by the fourth quarter of 2010. The output-gap of France is estimated to be currently turning around into a positive region as the IMF projects.

The first crucial issue regarding the stark differences between the two output-gap estimates is the assessment about pre-crisis states. According to the IMF estimates, there was no overheating in the US (and Canada) before the crisis and a 2–3 percent positive gap in Europe. In contrast, the SVAR-based estimates detect large positive output-gaps throughout advanced countries, including the US, for a substantial period of time before the crisis. In fact, the magnitudes of the sharp decline in the output-gaps immediately after the crisis are similar in both estimates: 4–6 percent. The critical difference is whether to assess

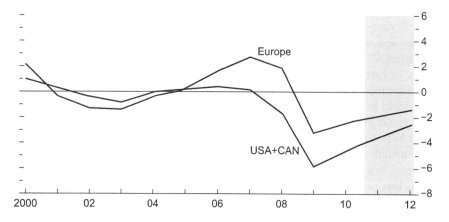

Figure 11.9 Output-gap estimates by IMF

Source: *World Economic Outlook* (IMF, April 2011a).

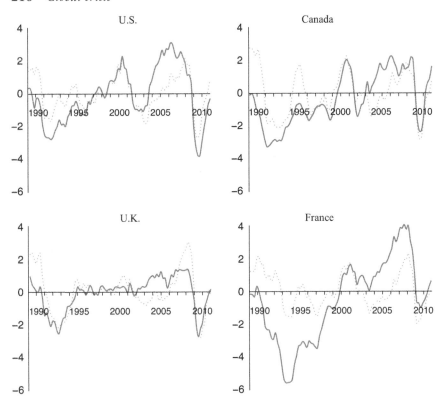

Figure 11.10 Output-gap estimates based on structural VAR

Note: Red solid lines are obtained from SVAR and blue dotted lines from HP filtering.

the pre-crisis period of housing market bubbles and over-leveraged credits as a normal state or not.

The second crucial issue is the possibility that financial crises reduce potential GDP. There exists a growing literature that financial crises (banking crises, in particular) can permanently damage potential GDP. If potential GDP was substantially damaged by financial crises in advanced countries, the output-gaps could be smaller than those estimated as deviations from the linearly extrapolated trend lines. The above-mentioned SVAR estimates identified 2–4 percent losses in potential GDP (or supply-side GDP) after the crisis, which appear to be of comparable magnitudes to those estimated in the literature.[3]

These output-gap estimates may not go well with high unemployment rates, but one should be cautious in reading the implication of unemployment rate on business cycle. First of all, it is a well-known stylized fact that the unemployment rate is a lagging indicator. In addition, the above-mentioned two issues also need to be addressed: (1) whether the pre-crisis level was a long-run equilibrium rate; and (2) whether the financial crisis can permanently alter the

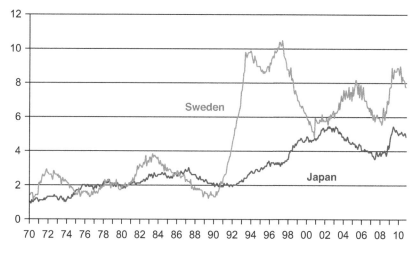

Figure 11.11 Unemployment rates in Sweden and Japan
Data Source: OECD.

unemployment rate. For the first issue, we have to ask, for example, whether to regard the unemployment rate below 5 percent in the US before the crisis as a sustainable long-run equilibrium level. For the second issue, we have to bear in mind many crisis-hit countries in which unemployment rates became permanently higher. The unemployment rate in Sweden was increased from 2–3 percent to 6–8 percent after the abrupt financial crisis in the early 1990s. In Japan, where a prolonged rather than a drastic crisis prevailed, the unemployment rate was increased from 2–3 percent to 4–5 percent.

Though many uncertainties remain regarding output-gap estimation, it seems legitimate to call for more caution on the current macro-policy stances. The gap-estimation business is always very controversial, and no single method can produce a consensus view. Nevertheless, the discussion of this section raises the possibility that current output-gaps may be far smaller than those casually presumed by many policymakers as well as ordinary people. The pre-crisis economic states, with huge excesses in both financial and real markets, may not be the desirable (or even feasible) targets that we wish our economies to recover to in the near future. Considering these, it seems to be the right time to reassess the unprecedented policy stances that have been taken to cope with crisis for the past two years, with upside risks taken into account in balance with downside risks.

3.3. Fiscal consolidation

It has been largely agreed that fiscal consolidation should be addressed in most advanced countries, ahead of monetary exit. First, the risks associated with fiscal expansion appeared more imminent than those associated with monetary expansion. The financial market already sent woeful signals on fiscal sustainability for some countries, while inflation has not been of great concern until recently. Second, given the unbalanced recovery paces across countries, monetary policy was regarded as a better option to cope with country-specific risk factors. While fiscal policy effects are diffused to other countries, monetary policy effects can be more contained within the country as the spill-over effects to other countries are neutralized by a resulting currency value adjustment (if the exchange rate is floated). Therefore, the more uncertain and country-specific the risks are, the more efficient monetary policy is in reacting to unexpected high-frequency shocks than fiscal policy.

However, no significant progress on fiscal consolidation has been achieved in most advanced countries. This year, many advanced countries are trying to reduce their fiscal deficits, but the US and Japan have put necessary adjustments on hold. Public debt ratios are still rising in most advanced countries, and financial needs are at historical highs. Clearly, fiscal sustainability risks are being elevated not only with respect to global financial market stability but also with respect to long-term growth of the global economy.[4]

In this regard, fiscal consolidation needs to be emphasized at the G20. Fiscal policies of large countries generate significant spill-over effects on other countries, and this was the first reason that fiscal policies became the main theme of the G20 immediately after the crisis broke out in 2008. In the same context, the fiscal sustainability problems of large countries should be the concern of other countries, as they are likely to generate adverse spill-over effects on other countries in the long-run.

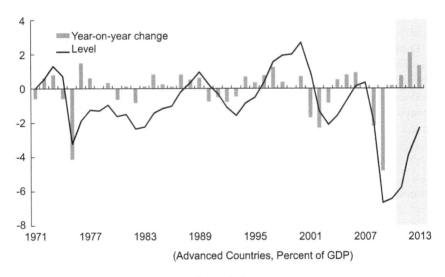

Figure 11.12 General government primary balance

(Advanced Countries, Percent of GDP)

Source: *Fiscal Monitor* (IMF, April 2011b).

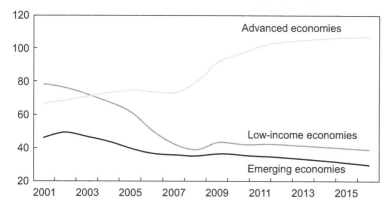

Figure 11.13 General government gross debt ratios
Source: *Fiscal Monitor* (IMF, April 2011b).

3.4. Monetary policy

Though not as urgent as fiscal consolidation, it appears that monetary policy in advanced countries also needs to begin gradual unwinding. Of course, monetary policy tools should be, in principle, reserved to cope with unexpected country-specific shocks. Yet, as the economy continues to normalize, policies taken for crisis resolution need to be normalized. If bold fiscal consolidation is implemented, it may be reasonable to maintain a low interest rate policy for a while to mitigate its adverse impacts on aggregate demand. But, monetary policy should not delay necessary adjustments in response to inflation dynamics under the unrealistic assumption about fiscal consolidation.

An implication of the above-mentioned SVAR-based output-gap estimates is that deflation pressures have almost disappeared. Since the output-gap (or aggregate-demand-gap) is estimated as the location along the supply curve identified by the SVAR, a zero output-gap implies that further demand stimulation begins to trigger inflation. The recent global inflation trend appears to be consistent with this diagnosis, though it is arguable whether the recent oil price hikes are driven by demand or supply factors.

As for post-crisis monetary policy, it may be worth looking back at the experience of Japan in the late 1980s and the experience of the US in the 2000s. After the Plaza Accord, the Bank of Japan aggressively lowered the interest rate in response to the economic downturn in 1985. However, it began meaningful unwinding starting from 1989, two years after the economy gained recovery momentum in 1987. During this period, real estate prices soared, which later collapsed to cause the "Lost Decade". The US in the 2000s were a *déjà vu*. In response to the IT bubble collapse and economic downturn, the Fed aggressively lowered the interest rate. However, it began meaningful unwinding only from 2005, two years after the economy gained recovery momentum in 2003. During this period, house prices soared, which collapsed to cause the "Great Recession".

Figure 11.14 Inflation rates

Data Source: OECD.

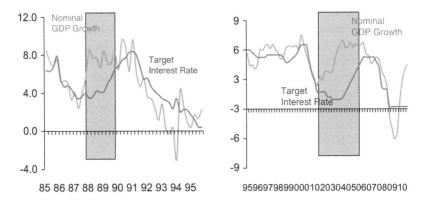

Figure 11.15 Nominal GDP growth and interest rate target

Given the exceptionally low levels of current interest rates, it may be desirable to begin unwinding not too late in order to avoid any abrupt adjustments in the future. There are always risks associated with policy reversals. However, more serious policy risks arise when the policy changes abruptly. In this regard, as soon as deflation possibilities are believed to have vanished, monetary authorities can send signals for policy normalization.

3.5.   *Theme of G20 discussion*

The G20 discussion for macro-framework in 2010 was focused on global imbalance. This was understandable since current account is the most straight-forwardly inter-connected problem across countries and the discussion on global imbalance suits the purpose of G20. In fact, the G20 successfully delivered visible progress by agreeing to the provision of suggestive guidelines for current account imbalances.

However, the global imbalance issue gradually languishes, while concerns on fiscal sustainability are proliferating. The current account deficit of the US was substantially narrowed as a result of the financial crisis and is expected to linger around 3 percent of GDP for the years to come (*World Economic Outlook*). While the China's nominal exchange rate is still rigid, the *real* exchange rate is clearly appreciating as inflation spreads and wages pick up in China; this should help reduce the global imbalance. Of course, China's exchange rate flexibility is still desirable for smoother macroeconomic adjustments of China itself as well as other countries. Likewise, fiscal consolidation of the US should help reduce the current account deficit of the US as well as risks in the global financial market.[5]

It is now the time for the G20 summits to show leadership on fiscal consolidation. The global crisis in 2008 launched the G20, which effectively delivered fiscal policy coordination to rescue the world from economic crises. After two-and-one-half years, as the global economy recovers, the G20 should take initiatives on fiscal policy coordination again – in the opposite direction this time. That way, the G20 will be remembered as having been accountable, not leaving the mess to the global economy.

Notes

* This chapter combines the three reports that were presented in a series of high-level G20 seminars held in 2010 and 2011. Section 1 was delivered at the Canada-Korea G20 Seminar held in Ottawa on March 17, 2010, and Section 2 at the Canada-Korea-France G20 Seminar held in Seoul on September 17, 2010. Section 3 was delivered at the Korea-France-Mexico G20 Seminar held in Paris on May 25, 2011.
1 The World Economic Outlook (IMF, 2011a) projects the US fiscal deficit to expand to 10.8 percent of GDP in 2011.
2 This alternative estimation applies a simple two-variable VAR model for GDP and GDP deflator with a standard identifying assumption that, in the long run, aggregate supply curve is vertical and aggregate demand shocks do not affect GDP. Once aggregate demand shocks are identified, a series for "aggregate demand gap" can be constructed as the GDP component generated by historical aggregate demand shocks only. To the extent that GDP also fluctuates due to aggregate supply shocks, the aggregate demand gap can be considered as a part of output-gap. However, this concept may be more appropriate than the entire output-gap for macroeconomic policies dealing with aggregate demand only. See Cho (2011) for details of estimation methodologies and results for seven OECD countries.
3 See Cerra and Saxna (2008), among others.
4 For the adverse effects of high public debts on growth, see Reinhart and Rogoff (2010) and Kumar and Woo (2010), among others.
5 See Chinn and Ito (2008), among others, for the effects of budget deficit on current account. Despite many control variables considered in the regressions, they consistently find the significantly positive relationship between the two variables for virtually all sample groups. The point estimate is 0.15, implying that a one percent reduction in the budget deficit to GDP ratio reduces current account deficit by 0.15 percent of GDP.

References

Bernanke, Ben S., 2010. "The Economic Outlook and Monetary Policy," Speech at the Federal Reserve Bank of Kansas City Economic Symposium, Jackson Hole, Wyoming, August 27, http://www.federalreserve.gov/newsevents/speech/bernanke 20100827a.htm.

Bordo, Michael D., and John S. Landon-Lane, 2010. "The Global Financial Crisis: Is it Unprecedented?", in *The Global Economic Crisis: Impacts, Transmission and Recovery*, edited by Maurice Obstfeld, Dongchul Cho and Andrew Mason, forthcoming. Cheltenham: Edward Elgar.

Cerra, Valerie, and Sweta Chaman Saxena, 2008. "Growth Dynamics: The Myth of Economic Recovery," *American Economic Review*, 98, pp. 439–457.

Cho, Dongchul, 2011. "Aggregate Demand Gap Based on a Simple Structural VAR Model," KDI School of Public Policy and Management, manuscript.

Chinn, Menzie, and Hiro Ito, 2008. "Global Current Account Imbalances: American Fiscal Policy vs. East Asian Savings," *Review of International Economics*, 16(3), pp. 479–498.

IMF, 2010. "Global Economic Prospect and Policy Challenges," prepared by IMF staff for the Meeting of G-20 Deputies, September 4–5, Gwangju, Korea.

IMF, 2011a. *World Economic Outlook*, April. Washington, DC: IMF.

IMF, 2011b. *Fiscal Monitor*, April. Washington, DC: IMF.

Kumar, Manmohan, and Jaejoon Woo, 2010. "Public Debt and Growth," *IMF Working Paper* no. 10/174, Washington, DC.

Kuttner, Kenneth N., and Adam S. Posen, 2002. "Passive Savers and Fiscal Policy Effectiveness in Japan," *Journal of Japanese and International Economies*, 16, pp. 536–558.

OECD, 2010. *Factbook: Economic, Environmental and Social Statistics*. Paris: OECD.

Reinhart, Carmen M., and Kenneth S. Rogoff, 2010. "Growth in a Time of Debt," *American Economic Review: Papers and Proceedings*, 100, pp. 573–578.

Part IV

Crises and recoveries of the Korean economy

12 Korea's stabilization policies in the 1980s*

1. Introduction

Korea is well known for its rapid economic development since the 1960s. Indeed, the economy took off with a series of five-year development plans led by President Park Chung-hee's regime. Despite a temporary setback due to the First Oil Shock in 1972, the average annual growth rate during the two decades of the 1960s and 1970s was almost 10 percent, which pushed up per capita income from below $100 in 1960 to around $1,700 in 1979. The whole society was truly dynamic and became more and more confident of its own economic success.

However, it is not as well known that Korea suffered greatly from high inflation and its side effects during the same period of the 1960s and 1970s. Nam observed:

> From the 1960s through the early 1980s Korea had one of the highest inflation rates in the world. Among over a hundred countries included in the World Bank, *World Development Report* (1983) for which inflation data for 1960–81 in terms of the GDP deflator are available, Korea stood in eleventh place, behind only the Latin American countries that had suffered from hyperinflation.
>
> (1991, p. 237)

In particular, doubts regarding the sustainability of the government-led development strategy were rapidly growing in the late 1970s. Heavy and chemical industries, the most important strategic industries selected and favored by the government, were suffering from a vast amount of idle facilities due to over-investment. Inflation was soaring to double-digits due to the monetary policy that was abused to support industrial policies and government's deficit financing. Current account was running chronic deficits due to the increased imports of machinery to support ambitious development plans, in addition to the heavy reliance on imported oil whose prices skyrocketed in 1973 and 1979. Korea's macro-economy was becoming more and more fragile, finally plunging into a crisis in 1979 when the Second Oil Shock was triggered and President Park was assassinated.

Against this backdrop, bold stabilization policies were unfolded in the early 1980s. Fiscal expansion was suppressed and monetary policy was liberated from industrial policies and government's budget deficit. It may not be extremely difficult to argue for such a macro-policy shift toward stabilization, but its actual implementation always faces fierce resistance from various groups. Korea's case in the early 1980s was no exception. As a matter of fact, it was more difficult in Korea because such a policy shift had to overhaul the whole economic policy framework that was believed to be indispensible for rapid development until then. There were intense debates among bureaucrats regarding alternative policy frameworks from the mid-1970s, but the camp for stabilization policies could not get over the legacy of the government-led development ideas. Proactive stabilization policies continued to be delayed and the economic situation further deteriorated until 1980. Nevertheless, it was actually after the leadership change from President Park to President Chun Doo Hwan that stabilization policies were finally implemented on a full scale.

Convinced of the new framework, President Chun continued to give a firm support for stabilization policies despite the fact that the desired results could only materialize in several years. After weathering the painful recession and balance-of-payments crisis until 1982, the Korean economy finally began to stabilize from 1983. First of all, the inflation rate was brought down from double digits to around 3 percent, which led nominal wage growth rate and interest rates to also stabilize. Based on this macroeconomic stabilization, exporting companies recovered their competitiveness and overall economic activities became revitalized. By the mid-1980s, the growth rate surged to double digits, while the inflation rate stayed around 3 percent. The government budget deficit continued to decline to zero, decreasing the public debt-to-GDP ratio. A sizable amount of current account surplus was realized, overcoming the balance-of-payments crisis.

All in all, it is clear that the stabilization policy carried out in the early 1980s bore great economic fruits. However, its historical significance was not confined within macroeconomic performance. Perhaps a more important implication of the success of the stabilization policy was to prove that the government-led development strategy was neither the only nor a sustainable policy framework for prosperity and that inflation is not a necessary evil for growth promotion. A better understanding of drawbacks as well as the merits of the "Korean model of development" should greatly help many aspiring policymakers in developing countries to shore up their development strategies.

The purpose of this chapter is to document and assess this historic event that took place in the early 1980s. Section 2 will review the political and economic environment of Korea in the 1970s that gave rise to the ideas on stabilization policies. Section 3 will then document the policy-making processes, focusing on the differences in the perception of economic policies between the two presidents, President Park and President Chun. Section 5 will assess its achievements and Section 6 will conclude with implications of Korea's stabilization policies on developing countries.

2. Political and economic environment in the 1970s

2.1 External environment

The 1970s was a decade of global inflation. The Bretton Woods system, a cornerstone of the international financial order for more than 20 years, collapsed at the beginning of the decade. It was obvious that the abolition of the Bretton Woods system generated a great deal of uncertainty in international transactions, but it also eroded the discipline of monetary policy. Since the ultimate reference of the value of money vis-à-vis gold was lifted, monetary policy was more likely to be accommodative and global inflation surged. By the end of the 1970s, the inflation rates of many advanced countries recorded double-digit figures for the first time in history.

The 1970s was also a decade of resource war. Major oil-producing countries made a strong cartel, the Organization of Petroleum Exporting Countries (OPEC) and quadrupled oil prices to exploit monopoly rents in 1973. For a resource-poor country such as Korea that followed an energy-intensive industrialization strategy, it was a devastating shock. According to Krause and Kim (1991), oil purchases would have required 1.4 percent of Korean GDP (3.7 percent of imports) had the oil price of 1972 prevailed but actual purchases required 8.8 percent of GDP (22.1 percent of imports), implying that the national cost reached more than 7 percent of GDP. The Korean economy barely managed to survive this First Oil Shock by taking several emergency measures but finally plunged into a crisis in 1979 when the Second Oil Shock and the assassination of President Park coincided.

From the perspective of international relations, the 1970s was a decade of hardship for the President Park's regime. Since the US President Richard Nixon declared the Guam Doctrine in 1969 that urged Asian countries to rely more on themselves for their own security, the US reduced by one-third the ground troops that used to be stationed in South Korea. During the US presidential campaign eventually won by Jimmy Carter, the idea was further advocated that the US should make another significant reduction of its ground forces in Korea. Although the US reiterated its commitment to come to the aid of South Korea in the event of an external attack and ultimately did maintain its troop strength, President Park's regime felt unsecured.

The concern about national security was particularly intensified by the rapidly deteriorating Korea–US relations during the Carter administration. President Park, who had been in power for more than 15 years and severely suppressed opposition leaders, could not get along with President Carter, who emphasized peace and democracy in international diplomacy (see Park, 2009, for details). It was alleged that Korea was constantly pressed by the US to advance to a more democratic system, which could not be willingly accepted by President Park. The more the Korea–US relation deteriorated, the more the Park's regime had to cling to self-defense from North Korea, which profoundly affected Korea's economic policy in the 1970s.

2.2 Domestic political environment

During the 1970s, the Park regime solidified its power base. In particular, the amendment of the Constitution in October 1972 declined the basic principle of democracy, namely, the separation of legal, administrative and judicial powers. According to the amended "Yushin Constitution," the president was to be elected by the members of the "National Council for Reunification," instead of people's direct voting, and the term of the presidency was extended from four to six years with no restrictions on multiple re-elections. The National Assembly was deprived of the right of inspecting government offices and one-third of the congressmen were to be elected by the National Council for Reunification. The Yushin Constitution even granted the president the power to dissolve the National Assembly and severely restrained basic rights of the people. Under the new Constitution, it seemed clear that President Park could indefinitely maintain the presidency and exercise more power than ever.

This event triggered resistance from the people as well as the opposition party, but the degree of political suppression was only increased as the opposition movement became violent. Political opponents including Kim Dae Jung (an opposition leader who was later elected as the president of Korea in 1997) were banished abroad, put in jails or under house arrest, and many student leaders of anti-government demonstrations were conscripted into the army.

Nevertheless, people's resistance did not cease and the political legitimacy of the Park's regime was eroded. In May 1979, Kim Yong Sam (who was later elected as the president of Korea in 1992) was elected as the leader of the New Democratic Party, a leading opposition party at the time, and conducted aggressive democratic movements. As a result, he was expelled from the National Assembly, then under the influence of President Park, in October 1979. A fierce demonstration to protest this incident took place centering in Busan and Masan (two cities in the southern region of Korea), which rapidly spread throughout the entire country. Inside the Park's camp, there were intense debates regarding how to cope with the people's resistance. Some argued for a conciliatory stance, whereas others contended for a crackdown by military force. In the midst of this mess, President Park was assassinated by the director of the National Intelligence Service, who was alleged to support the conciliatory position, on October 26, 1979.

2.3 Industrial policy to promote heavy and chemical industries

The most distinctive characteristic of economic policies during the entire Park regime was a strong government leadership, as denoted by a "government-led development strategy." In particular, the government selected "strategic" industries and provided ample support to promote them. For example, exporting manufacturing industries, such as textile, shoes, and so forth, were given preferential tax treatment and policy loans as well as preferential access to import licenses in the 1960s.

Entering the 1970s, the main strategic industries were shifted from light industries to heavy and chemical industries (HCI), such as steel, petrochemicals, ship-building, machinery, nonferrous metals, electronics and so forth. The rationale for light industries in the 1960s was simple and clear: Korea had to earn scarce hard currency through exporting the goods that could be relatively easily manufactured by abundant unskilled labor at the time. However, it was far more controversial to select HCI as strategic industries in the 1970s. The economic justification for this shift was given by the government that Korea had to create a basis for a new comparative advantage in HCI since Korea would lose its competitive position in labor-intensive light industries as the economy developed. Yet, the rationale for this policy shift rested more on political than economic justifications. As US foreign policy changed in the 1970s as explained above, Korea needed more self-sufficiency in national defense, which could not be supported by light industries. From the Third Five-Year Plan that began in 1972, the intention of the government to encourage HCI became clear, and the policy drive to promote HCI was strengthened as Korea–US relations deteriorated in the late 1970s.

The push given by President Park toward HCI was truly unprecedented. Perkins describes the situation as follows:

> The Blue House staff made decisions as to which industries should form the core of the HCI drive. They saw to it that an industrial park (Changwon) was built that could accommodate these new enterprises and they even determined the appropriate scale at which each factory was to be built. . . . Projects were not put out for bids. Instead individual *chaebol* companies were asked to carry out each project. If they agreed, the government saw to it that they got wide ranging support. There was a major diversion of state bank loans to the HCI sector at preferential interest rates. Favorable access to import license were guaranteed. The tax authorities would treat the companies gently using a corporate tax system that was quite "flexible." And the government was prepared to do more if necessary. When Hyundai ships rolled into the water and into a dead market for supertankers, the government took steps to create a market giving advantages to oil imports brought in on Korean made ships. Where positive incentives failed, there was President Park's big stick – the implied threat of the removal of this support system from a company's existing enterprises.
>
> (1997, pp. 81–82)

Whether this HCI promotion policy was successful or not depends on what perspective is adopted (see Lee, 1991, for example). However, its economic cost was huge, as assessed by Krause:

> . . . the economic dislocations were substantial. Light industries were starved for capital which reduced Korea's international competitiveness since these were the principal export industries at that time. Moreover, many bad investments were made by state-owned enterprises (SOEs) and private firms in

heavy industrial facilities that were not fully utilized. These uneconomic investments meant that the firms that borrowed money to create them could not repay their loans, and bad loans accumulated on the books of commercial banks. Also the government's budget was drained to cover losses of SOEs. Furthermore, a shortage of skilled workers, along with rising domestic protection for heavy industrial products and agriculture, led to an acceleration of inflation. Meanwhile the balance of payments deteriorated requiring even more foreign borrowing. Finally the second oil shock hit early in 1979 which combined with perverse macroeconomic policies – real interest rates were negative since 1973 and large tax preferences were provided to selected "strategic" industries – led to serious economic problems.

(1997, p. 113)

2.4   Financial repression to support the HCI drive

In order to promote HCI, every possible policy measure was mobilized. Among many, financial policy tools were very actively utilized. Kim describes the situation as follows:

President Park had to deal with two crucial issues: first, how to facilitate and ensure the allocation and delivery of funds to the targeted destinations; and second, how to prevent the misappropriation of delivered funds. To cope with these issues, the government devised the system of policy loans and firm-level credit controls. The policy loan system was a credit pipeline to serve at the government's needs, and firm-level credit control system was to keep the pipeline from being leaked at the receiving end.

(1997, p. 208)

Naturally, financial markets were severely repressed to serve these government policies and provide cheap credit to the strategic industries. Out of total loans by deposit money banks, the share of policy loans, mainly for heavy and chemical industries, rose to approximately 50 percent by the end of the 1970s. Policy loans to the strategic industries included foreign exchange loans, export loans and loans to development institutions such as the Korea Development Bank and the Korea Export-Import Bank. Bank interest rates were also regulated at low levels in an effort to stimulate investment. The real interest rate on time deposit with one-year maturity was virtually zero during the 1970s, and policy loans in particular carried preferential interest rates that were even lower than those on general bank deposits, so that the average borrowing cost to firms remained below the inflation rate during the 1970s.

In this context, monetary policy was also mobilized as a tool for providing so called growth money. Just like other commercial banks, the Bank of Korea (BOK) was also under the control of the government since the Amendment to the Bank of Korea Act on May 24th, 1962. This amendment downgraded the function of the Monetary Policy Board from policymaking to policy implementation. The

Table 12.1 Policy loans of banks and interest rates (period average)

| | Portion of Loan Amount (Deposit Money Banks) | | | Average Interest Rate | | | |
| | | | | Loan (Manufacturing) | | Bank Deposit (1-Year Time Deposit) | |
	Policy Loan	Loan to Manuf.	Loan to HCI	Nominal	Real[1]	Nominal	Real[2]
1971–1975	44.5	52.9	24.5	11.1	–8.6	15.7	0.1
1976–1980	47.3	55.3	29.2	14.1	–6.7	17.9	0.5
1981–1985	41.4	46.5	27.6	15.2	7.8	11.5	4.2
1986–1990	45.9	43.8	27.5	12.9	7.3	10.0	4.6

Note:
1) Nominal interest rate – GNP deflator inflation rate.
2) Nominal interest rate – CPI inflation rate.

Source: Nam and Kim (1995, p. 133)

power of the Minister of Finance was increased so as to make a request that the board reconsider a resolution that had already passed. If the request was overruled by the board, the final decision was to be made at a cabinet meeting. Under this governance structure, the government attempted to direct the maximum amount of credit to the target industries at low interest rates and the resulting losses of banks were often bailed out by the money-printing power of the BOK. For example, the commercial banks' policy loans were *automatically* rediscounted at the window of the BOK, implying that the costs of policy loans were largely borne by inflation tax.

2.5   Soft budget constraint of the government

In order to support the industrial policies, fiscal resources were also mobilized in addition to financial resources. In particular, the government maintained strong will to construct foundation for HCI and substantially increased its own spending for this purpose. The statement of Kim and Whang indicates how aggressive the government was for the HCI drive:

> . . . total fiscal investment and loans increased from 309.8 billion won in 1972 to 4,560.3 billion won in 1981, which is almost 15 times that of 10 years earlier. In terms of the ratio relative to GNP, the low was down to 5.1 percent in 1973, and the high reached 10.0 percent in 1981.
>
> (1997, p. 262)

From the taxation side, too, the government applied various tax incentives, including preferential depreciation allowances, tax reductions and exemptions for exporters and strategic industries. For example, Kwack (1984) estimated that net benefit from tax incentives for investment in key manufacturing industries reached 36.9 percent of expenditures in 1976, which jumped from 7.8 percent in 1970.

In addition, the government had to forcefully increase its expenditures on national defense, the largest item in government budget at that time, as Vietnam became a Communist country and the reduction of the US army was announced. Of the total central government expenditures, its portion ballooned from 27 percent to 33 percent in 1978.

Despite these policy measures that imposed huge burdens on the budget, the central government managed to maintain surplus in general accounts by squeezing the budget for education, health, welfare and so forth. This was a remarkable achievement, but the picture looked different if the special funds for public projects were also considered. In fact, while the central government's general account recorded surpluses throughout the 1970s, the consolidated budget recorded deficits every year due to the structural deficits in special accounts.

Special funds were established by law when the government needed to have separate accounts from the general account to manage special projects. They were established when needed and abolished when not. However, a more important characteristic of special funds was that they were not directly monitored by the National Assembly, which inevitably caused laxness of fiscal management. Kim and Whang write:

> Meanwhile, many government funds were established during the 1970s. A notable characteristic of government funds was that they were not dependent on the revenue and expenditure budget, and they were not under the direct control of the National Assembly. The first funds were the Public Servant Pension Fund and the Military Personnel Pension Fund, which were both established in 1963. Since then, one or two funds were established each year, totaling eleven government-managed funds by 1972 and nineteen by 1979. The increase in funds made fiscal management convenient for the fiscal authority since the funds were managed off-budget, but this brought laxness to fiscal management.
>
> (1997, p. 269)

As a result, the government continued to run a consolidated budget deficit of 2 to 5 percent of GNP. The absolute size of the deficit was not small, but it might not have been unsustainably large given the rapid economic growth (and inflation) of Korea in the 1970s. Regarding the laxness of fiscal management, however, a more serious problem than its absolute size was the way the government financed the budget deficit. How to finance deficient resources for special funds in particular was almost entirely decided by the government discretion, which always considered borrowing from the BOK as an option. That is, the government could always rely on its money-printing power to finance special projects.

The Grain Management Fund, among others, was the largest fund that heavily relied on borrowings from the BOK. In order to stabilize farmers' income, the

Table 12.2 Consolidated budget balance in the 1970s

	1972	1973	1974	1975	1976	1977	1978	1979	1980
1. Central Government	-103	35	-33	-89	-15	-146	-300	-289	-474
General Account	62	143	243	430	706	137	255	222	24
Special Accounts	-155	-112	-252	-409	-556	-93	-239	-144	-202
Other Funds	-10	4	-59	-110	-165	-190	-316	-367	-296
2. Public Enterprises	-35	-89	-130	-353	-201	-50	-325	86	-440
Special Accounts						-1	-59	-49	-325
Gov't Supply & Grain Management Fund						-149	-267	-135	-114
3. Total	-139	-54	-198	-443	-216	-296	-626	-203	-914
(GNP Ratio, %)	(-3.3)	(-1.0)	(-2.6)	(-4.4)	(-1.7)	(-1.7)	(-2.6)	(-0.7)	(-2.5)
4. Off-Budget	-58	-62	-97	-112	-177	-170	-328	-255	-375
5. IMF Standard (3+4)	-197	-115	-295	-555	-393	-466	-954	-459	-1288
(GNP Ratio, %)	(-4.7)	(-2.1)	(-3.9)	(-5.5)	(-2.8)	(-2.6)	(-4.0)	(-1.5)	(-3.5)

Source: Ministry of Finance, *Government Finance Statistics in Korea*, Kim and Whang (1997).

Note: All units are in billion won, except for the rows for which "GNP Ratio, %" are indicated.

government committed to purchasing rice and rye at pre-set prices. The problem was that the purchase prices were always set at higher levels than the market prices. This "dual prices policy" was designed to subsidize farmers' income with public resources and thus the Grain Management Fund in charge of this project was destined to incur losses, which only increased as the gap between the purchase and resale prices became widened over time. By 1976, the gap between the two prices exceeded more than 50 percent of the purchase price, expanding the fund's deficit to 250 billion won. However, instead of financing the deficits either from tax revenue or by issuing bonds, the government almost entirely relied on borrowings from the BOK. According to the Economic Planning Board (1977), the fund's borrowing from the BOK accumulated for the five years from 1972 to 1976 was 626 billion won, which was almost a half of the base money outstanding at the end of 1976. In fact, the deficit of a single year in 1976 amounted to 250 billion won, which was more than 60 percent of the increment in base money (1,473.7 – 1,077.0 = 398.7 billion won).

Though smaller than the Grain Management Fund in size, many other special funds such as the Fertilizer Account Fund were also run in the same fashion. The

Table 12.3 Grain prices set by the government

		1972	1973	1974	1975	1976
Rice	Purchase Price	9,888	11,377	15,760	19,500	23,200
	Resale Price	9,500	11,264	13,000	16,730	18,400
	Difference	–388	–113	–2,760	–2,770	–4,800
Rye	Purchase Price	6,357	6,993	9,091	11,100	13,000
	Resale Price	4,300	4,800	6,000	6,900	8,320
	Difference	–2,057	–2,193	–3,091	–4,200	–4,680

Source: Economic Planning Board, *Rationalization of the Grain Management Fund*, 1977.

Note: All units are in won per hop ≒ 180ml.

Table 12.4 Finance of the deficit of the grain management fund

	1972	1973	1974	1975	1976	1972–1976
Total	36.0	50.0	160.0	230.0	250.0	726.0
BOK Borrowing	36.0	50.0	160.0	230.0	150.0	626.0
Long-term	36.0	50.0	160.0	230.0	130.0	606.0
Short-term					20.0	20.0
Bond					100.0	100.0
Base Money	427.5	624.1	775.0	1,077.0	1,437.7	

Source: Economic Planning Board, *Rationalization of the Grain Management Fund*, 1977.

Note: All units are in billion won.

special funds were structurally designed to run deficits, most of which were financed by borrowing from the BOK. Of course, the government also tried to reduce the BOK borrowing by running surpluses in the general account. However, as long as the consolidated budget was in deficit due to the deficits of the special funds, the easy option of financing from the BOK continued to be utilized. It appeared that no hard budget constraints existed for the government in the 1970s.

2.6 Monetary expansion and the surge of inflation

In any sense, the HCI drive and its supporting policies were not in accordance with an order one would expect in a market-based economy. It was natural that moral hazard proliferated and resources were inefficiently allocated as the degree of government intervention increased. Perhaps a more serious problem, however, was that the government attempted to achieve multiple goals contradictory to one another. The BOK's monetary policy in the 1970s was a typical example.

As explained above, the financial market was simply regarded as a pipeline to convey the maximum amount of resources to strategic industries under the control of the government. Commercial banks had to provide approximately half of their deposits as policy loans with extremely low interest rates and the remaining half should also be lent at the interest rate set by the BOK. With this structure, commercial banks could not sustain their profits, and thus the BOK had to be involved in supporting them. In addition, the BOK also served as the back pocket of the government to finance structural deficits mainly run by special funds such as the Grain Management Fund. Indeed, there were multiple sources of monetary expansion in this economic policy structure.

Under this environment superimposed by the government, it was a truly formidable task to control aggregate money supply. By directly controlling the amount of bank credits, the BOK tried to achieve two contradictory goals, supplying a sufficient amount of cheap money and suppressing the amount of money under control. Credit allocation of banks was tightly controlled so that consumers could hardly access bank loans. On the one hand, the BOK supplied a massive amount of money to support commercial banks and the government, but on the other hand, it attempted to control the aggregate money supply by directly

Table 12.5 Money growth rates in the 1970s

	1972	1973	1974	1975	1976	1977	1978	1979	1980
Base Money	48.3	46.0	24.2	39.0	33.5	44.1	35.3	23.8	−6.5
M1	39.9	39.7	26.9	25.3	32.7	45.0	38.7	23.1	21.0
M2	33.6	36.1	21.5	25.2	35.1	40.1	35.4	29.7	44.5

Source: The Bank of Korea.

Note: All numbers are annual growth rates in percent.

controlling the amount of bank credits. Obviously, the priority of the government policy was given to the strategic industries and deficit financing rather than inflation control, and the efforts of the BOK only aggravated distortions in credit allocation. Money supply was rapidly increased, with its growth rate hovering around 30 percent per annum.

As a result, the inflation rate that was expanded to more than 20 percent in 1974 due to the First Oil Shock was not stabilized and stayed at a high level. Double digit inflation was taken for granted and economic agents began to reflect inflation in their economic activities such as wage bargaining and financial contracts. A typical pattern of vicious circle of inflation – inflation expectation and actual inflation reinforcing each other – was set off in the second half of the 1970s.

More painful for poor people during this period, however, were probably the skyrocketing real estate prices. Many business firms who could access policy loans with negative real interest rates borrowed as much money as possible from banks and purchased real estate rather than investing in productive businesses, pushing up real estate prices to unimaginable levels. Although there were no official nationwide indexes for house prices in the 1970s, it was frequently observed in many locations that the prices more than doubled within a one- to two-year period. According to Lee (1996) who reports land price indexes of major cities, the prices rose by 25 percent in 1976, continued to rise by 50 percent in 1977, and further rose by 79 percent in 1978.

The rise of inflation brought about another dimension of distortions. Although the root cause of accelerating inflation was the abused monetary policy, the government attempted to control individual prices. An extensive price-monitoring system was run, and a wide range of individual prices could be raised only after approval by the government. However, such a direct price-control system has many implementation problems: trouble in finding the "right" price based on production cost data that would not force the least productive producers to go bankrupt; difficulty of suppressing firms' rent-seeking behavior to collect extra profits by delaying distribution of products whose controlled prices were imposed at the point of production; and the cost of monitoring that was ever increased as

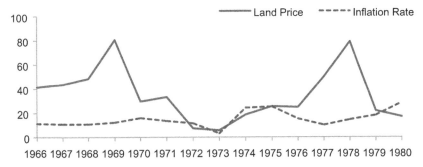

Figure 12.1 Inflation rates of consumer prices and land prices

Source: The Bank of Korea and Lee (1996)

inflation was accelerated and stricter price controls were enforced. More importantly, direct price controls significantly infringed on the market rules and eroded efficiency in various dimensions: malfunctioning of price signals that would provide firms to enhance productivity and improve product qualities; losses in social surpluses due to the difference between market and controlled prices since people would be willing to pay premiums for the goods in shortage; and failure of price adjustment that should flexibly reflect market situations as well as locations.

Such an inefficient and inflexible price control system could not be sustainable. In the second half of the 1970s, a high rate of inflation continued, notwithstanding the full-scale efforts of the government to control prices. Not only the prices of goods and services, but also real estate prices and wages, soared hand-in-hand, eroding export competitiveness and the balance of payments. This unstable macroeconomic situation in the late 1970s is described by Nam as follows:

> The Korean economy during the later years of the 1970s was full of distortions and resource misallocations typical of any high-inflation country. Financial saving, which usually entailed earning a negative real interest rate, was not attractive. Instead, feverish demand for real estate and other real assets caused their prices to shoot up. Many business firms were preoccupied with borrowing as much as possible from banks, only to invest in real estate by expanding unproductive businesses, leading to an increasing fragile corporate financial structure. The government's attempt to repress inflation through price controls led only to inadequate investment, supply shortages, black markets, and deteriorating product quality.
>
> (1988, p. 79)

2.7 Deterioration of the balance of payments

Just like many other underdeveloped countries, Korea relied heavily on foreign aid to balance external payments until the 1960s. While depending almost entirely on imported oil for energy consumption, Korea could not earn as much foreign currency by exports as needed to settle imports. Trade balance was always in deficit, whose size easily exceeded 10 percent of GDP. A substantial portion of this gap between exports and imports were filled by foreign aid, mostly from the US.

However, the size of foreign aid continued to decline since 1957, pressing the balance of payments of Korea. For example, foreign aid could cover trade deficits by $383 million (more than 20 percent of GDP) in 1957, but by only $8 million (less than 0.1 percent of GDP) in 1977. As the amount of foreign aid diminished, it became increasingly difficult to finance the explosive investment demand induced by the HCI drive. Deficit in the trade account was directly translated into a deficit in the current account or external borrowing, making the country vulnerable to foreign debt problems. According to Cho and Kim (1997, p. 59), the amount of total foreign debt was only $89 million (3.8 percent of GNP) in 1962. With the decrease of foreign aid and the continued trade deficit, however, it was

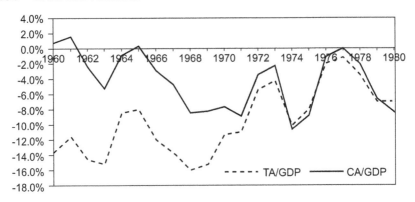

Figure 12.2 Trade account and current account as percent of GDP

Source: Cha Dong-se (1995), *A Half Century of the Korean Economy: Sourcebook.*

Figure 12.3 Won/dollar and real effective exchange rates

Source: Cha Dong-se (1995), *A Half Century of the Korean Economy: Sourcebook.*

rapidly increased to $2,277 million dollars (23.7 percent of GNP) in 1970 and further to $8,457 million (41.8 percent of GNP) in 1975.

In order to cope with the difficulties in the balance of payments, the government continually devalued the exchange rate from 130.0 won per dollar in 1963 to 398.3 until 1973; more than 200 percent during the 10 years. Despite high domestic inflation, this devaluation was large enough to depreciate the Korean won in real effective terms by more than 30 percent. Finally, the trade deficit began to respond and was reduced from approximately 15 percent of GDP in 1968 to 4 percent in 1972.

Since then, Korea's balance of payments has swung wildly depending upon oil price fluctuations. In 1974 and 1975, trade deficits drastically widened to approximately 10 percent of GDP due to the First Oil Shock, seriously destabilizing Korea's external financing since it could not rely on foreign aid any longer. By contrast, as oil prices stabilized and construction demand from the oil-producing

Middle East countries increased at an explosive pace, the deficit size was significantly reduced in 1976 and 1977 to almost zero.

While trade and current accounts were fluctuating along with oil prices, the underlying price competitiveness of Korean exporters was seriously eroded due to chronic inflation. In particular, during the 1975–1979 period, when the HCI drive was at its peak, the nominal exchange rate was not adjusted at the level of 484 won/dollar despite accelerating domestic inflation, which appreciated the real effective exchange rate by approximately 10 percent. This rigid exchange rate policy was maintained essentially to reduce the burden of HCI industries that heavily relied on imports for their raw materials as well as investment facilities. Under this macroeconomic environment, however, it was natural to increase imports from abroad rather than trying to produce domestically and thus to deteriorate balance-of-payments. Yet, the government, again, attempted to overcome this macroeconomic imbalance by strengthening direct controls over imports at micro levels rather than by adjusting macro-variables, such as the exchange rate or inflation. Of course, these kind of micro-policies could not successfully tame the desire to import more, just as the tightened controls over individual prices without monetary policy adjustment could not tame inflation.

Moreover, inflation was naturally accompanied with wage and land price inflation. As the cost of living was increased by inflation, workers demanded higher wages, which could not be refused indefinitely by business firms. Land prices rapidly rose, too, as the cheap credit to support HCI flowed into real estate markets to seek speculative profits. The higher wages and land prices significantly increased the production costs of the firms, which was particularly detrimental to exporters who could not pass the higher costs to customers in the international market. While accelerating inflation under the rigid exchange rate management was weakening exporters' competitiveness, the Second Oil Shock broke out in 1979. The trade deficit was sharply expanded again and the Korean government had to hurry borrowing from abroad to cover the deficit. Foreign loans were rapidly accumulated up to $27,170 million (48.2 percent of GNP) in 1980, driving the Korean economy to the edge of a balance-of-payments crisis.

3. Paradigm shift toward stabilization

3.1 New ideas challenging the government-led development policy

Chronic inflation, among many problems explained in the previous section, became the central concern of leading policymakers as well as general public. Yet, explicitly recognizing its true causes, and thereby designing proper policy reactions, was not easy both politically and practically, since they was closely intertwined with the government-led development strategy that could not be challenged. As a macroeconomic principle, the most orthodox policy measure to cope with high inflation should be the control of the money supply in the market through appropriate monetary policies (higher interest rates) rather than direct price controls. However, the government-led development strategy, the HCI drive in particular, left little choice available. As long as the HCI was supported by policy loans with preferential interest rates, commercial banks had to suffer from negative interest rate margins, and thus the BOK had to subsidize the troubled commercial banks by printing money (by automatically rediscounting policy loans). The only way to control money supply was to transfer this burden of the BOK to the government by retrenching other fiscal spending but that was also almost impossible due to national defense and the dual-pricing of rice and fertilizer to achieve a self-sufficient food supply. Enhancing competition pressures by opening the economy for free trade as a means of price stabilization was unthinkable since infant domestic industries had to be protected.

In short, controlling inflation would require a paradigm shift in economic policies. In particular, the whole system of a controlled economy under the name of the government-led development strategy had to be challenged. The idea about a new economic system was growing among the young generations of government officials, in particular the Economic Planning Board (EPB). They were concerned about the effectiveness of the HCI drive and more fundamentally regarding the government-led economic development strategy in general. They began to believe that the Korean economy could not sustain its economic development with the existing controlled system. They believed, instead, that the Korean economy had to transform into a more market-oriented system in order to stabilize macro-economy and sustain its development.

3.2 Stabilization policies under President Park: passive implementation

Almost a full year of initial consensus-building among the government officials within EPB had not produced any meaningful results, until Shin Hyun-Hwak was appointed to be vice prime minister as the head of the EPB after the December 12 general election in 1978. With the appointment of Vice Prime Minister Shin, the stabilization policy could gain momentum since he was highly favorable to the stabilization policy. Yet, the ultimate decision-maker was President Park. With strong support by Vice Prime Minister Shin, the idea of stabilization policies were presented to President Park at the beginning-of-the-year briefing session on January 11, 1979. However, his initial reaction right after the briefing session was indeed not positive. Although he did not make any comments on the report right away, his disapproval of the policy became apparent through a number of comments he made on other occasions. For example, he said, "Recently some crazy nuts in the government says we should decrease support for the export industry" during his remarks at the beginning-of-the-year briefing session of the Ministry of Foreign Relations, and, "Today I heard the most promising and ambitious plan that hits the nail right on the head" at a similar session of the Ministry of Commerce and Industry on "Fostering 10 Strategic HCI Industries".

Since then, the stabilization policy has had to face opposition from almost every corner. The Economic Cooperation Bureau disagreed with the EPB, and the Ministry of Commerce and Industry was against the idea of liberalizing the imports and reducing the amount of export financing. The Ministry of Finance harshly argued against the idea of financial deregulation in that it was too premature to reduce government control of the financial industry. And there was the Ministry of Agriculture and Fishery opposing the abolishment of the dual-pricing system of rice and fertilizer. In addition, all of the stakeholders that would be worse off by adoption of the stabilization policies tried very hard to lobby against them. Almost all of the business entities that anticipated losing from the stabilization policies opposed the intention of raising the loan interest rates. Export industries were against reducing and gradually abolishing the export finance and subsidies. HCI industries were against the policy of restructuring investments and subsidies. Lifting the price controls (actualization of prices) was not welcomed by the producers. Importing agricultural goods was not welcomed by the farmers as well as the Ministry of Agriculture and Fishery. Kang recalled the situation of the EPB at the time as follows:

> It was as if we (EPB) were alone, surrounded by enemies and there was no way out. And it became so evident that we needed a series of consensus building strategy to adopt and implement the stabilization policy since it would be up to them (government officials in every ministry) to implement the policy once it gets approved by President Park. For this reason, we held numerous conferences on the stabilization policy, and became quite successful initially in gaining the support from the academics and the media.
>
> (1988, pp. 143–144)

A change in President Park's position was finally sensed right after his visit to Changwon Industrial Park, the center of HCI, in February 1979. After witnessing huge idle capacity in HCI, he ordered a thorough re-examination of the current state of the Korean economy. It was to be conducted independently by the BOK and the KDI. In addition, he ordered the Economic-Science Council to conduct an extensive survey from scholars in the field. All of these reports were to be delivered to the president by March 31. He intentionally excluded the EPB and even the Vice Prime Minister Shin while he presided over the forum. However, all of the three sources reported similar findings and conclusions as the EPB previously had. This reconfirmed the need for making a major shift in economic policy, and President Park finally gave his approval of the full implementation of the stabilization policies, consolidating all of these reports into a single comprehensive economic stabilization plan. On April 17, 1979, the Comprehensive Economic Stabilization Policy (CESP) was announced to the public with the official approval by the president.

The CESP emphasized three core catchphrases: stabilization, autonomy and open economy. The first principle, economic and social stabilization, focused upon controlling inflation as the first priority and subsequently improving the well-being of the Korean people as the policy goal. Laying the groundwork for inflation control required actualization of market prices before anything else and, at the same time, very strict fiscal and monetary policy that was highly painful yet unavoidable. The second principle, autonomy, focused upon strengthening the market mechanisms for allocating resources by reducing government interventions in the market and at the same time reforming market institutions to promote fair competition. Making the financial industry more independent from the government, as well as political influences; actualization of market prices; reducing the inefficiency in distribution system; moving from a single to multiple basket currency exchange system; and establishing the Fair Transactions Departments, and so forth marked a series of attempts to reform market institutions. The third principle, open economy, focused upon promoting competition in domestic markets and increasing consumption opportunities based upon comparative advantage theory in international trade. Lifting prohibition of imported goods in stages, simplifying and reducing tariffs, ending the protective industrial and trade policies, and so forth were adopted and implemented. In retrospect, such an increase in competition in domestic goods market contributed greatly to the firms improving the quality of goods they used to produce monopolistically, thereby increasing the overall well-being of Korean people.

3.3   Stabilization policies under President Chun: a full drive

Unfortunately, early 1979 marked the beginning of the Second Oil Shock, and by the time of the implementation of the CESP, the world economy was moving toward recession. The domestic political environment was also rapidly deteriorating, with rising social and political conflicts with a series of events leading to the Pusan-Masan civil riots. These sudden changes in the economic, political, and social environments forced the government to focus more upon reducing policy-induced distortions in the economy and less upon cooling down the overheated economy. It was necessary then to incrementally adjust the CESP while maintaining its basic principles.

What made the situation worse was the assassination of President Park on October 26, 1979. In a dictatorial governance system, a sudden vacuum of political power would create a chaos because people, including the top decision-makers in the cabinet, would not be accustomed to making final calls themselves. Prime Minister Choi Kyu-Ha succeeded the Park regime, assuming the president's office in November 1979, while leading politicians were discussing a new election process by enacting constitutional amendments to signify the end of dictatorship. However, another military coup followed rather quickly on December 12, 1979, led by General Chun and his close followers in the military.

Right after the military coup, the National Security Council (NSC) took over the government by expanding martial law throughout the whole nation on May 17, 1980 (one day before the Kwangju Civil Revolution on May 18) until August 27, when the chair of the NSC, General Chun, finally assumed the president position officially through indirect election. It was also the members of the NSC that made all of the economic policy decisions.

However, the year 1980 marked negative 6.2 percent GNP growth rate for the first time since the government collected statistical data on economic performance.

The economic situation was getting serious and overcoming the economic depression became the main target of the new political elites to secure legitimacy of the military coup. For this reason, the NSC hasted to make reforms. As to economic policy, the basic attitudes of the NSC members with military backgrounds were: 'You policy specialists make the optimal decisions and we will push through the political opposition.'

Sometimes, this attitude of the NSC helped the CESP to be quickly implemented through fierce resistance of interest groups. A good example was the Fair Transaction System Law that was approved by the NSC Legislative Council on December 23, 1980. The agenda had been around since 1960s, and the EPB reinitiated it, but faced severe opposition from the private sector and those within the government that had to give up the regulatory power. However, Chun, then the working official at the Fair Transaction Division in the EPB, had a chance to raise this issue with NSC members over dinner, and the NSC jumped right on the agenda since it served the image of the new military power that the NSC tried to promote. With the passage of the law, the Fair Transaction Department was established inside the EPB, despite many difficulties implementing the law due to lobbying from private sector.

As such, much of the economic policy agenda under the CESP got adopted and implemented with strong-arms tactics between April 17, 1979 and toward the end of the 1980, piggy-backing on the new political power. The survival of the CESP as the official economic policy of the government and the NSC throughout the transitional period was partly due to the fact that there were a number of economists in the NSC who had strong preferences over making institutional reforms. One of those who believed in strengthening market mechanism was the late Kim Jae-ik, *the* economic policy decision-maker during President Chun's regime.

Right after Chun assumed the president position in September 1980, according to Lee (2008), Chun wanted to appoint Kim as the Senior Secretary. At the time, Kim asked Chun that the only condition for his acceptance was 'if you are to implement economic policies as I advise you, you will have to face grave oppositions from almost everyone out there. Would you be willing to accept and implement my words against all others?' Chun's reply was simple and to the point: 'No need to say anything else. You are *the* president when it comes to economic policies.'

It was evident that Kim gained the full trust of President Chun for making economic policy decisions and this meant a lot for the full implementation of the CESP. Kim focused on educating Chun by stressing the limitations of government engagement in market mechanisms, the importance of keeping surpluses that would require patience over pain, the importance of "real" statistics where the real income would decline with a high inflation rate, and eventually the detailed "grand design" of reforming the Korean economic structures and systems: namely the CESP. With the economic education Chun received from Kim, Chun seemed to have developed a strong fixation over controlling inflation, and most of his policy decisions in the early 1980s reflected it. Such tendencies of

Chun's played a major part in maintaining the consistency of economic policies throughout his term during the 1980s.

4. Macroeconomic performance in the 1980s

4.1 Inflation stabilization and macroeconomic policy

The first half of the 1980s was probably the most successful stabilization period in Korean history. The inflation rate in terms of the Consumer Price Index (CPI), which hovered around 20 percent per annum, was stabilized to around 3 percent from 1983. This rapid moderation of CPI inflation could have severely squeezed firms' profitability, had production costs not been stabilized in line with sales prices. However, production costs represented by the Producer Price Index (PPI) virtually stopped rising from 1983, providing firms with room for profit margins. Along with prices of consumers and producers, feverish speculation on real estate began to subside and their prices were also stabilized.

It is true that the 1970s was a decade of global inflation while the 1980s was that of dis-inflation. However, the performance of Korea (15.0 percentage point lowered from the 1977–1981 period to 1982–1986) stands out compared to those of other major countries. During the 1982–1986 period, Korea became a country whose inflation was as stable as in major advanced countries.

Table 12.6 Inflation rates

	1977	1978	1979	1980	1981	1982	1983	1984	1985	1986
CPI	10.1	14.5	18.3	28.7	21.4	7.2	3.4	2.3	2.5	2.8
PPI	9.0	11.7	18.7	39.0	20.4	4.7	0.2	0.7	0.9	−1.5
Land Price										
Nation	33.6	49.0	16.6	11.7	7.5	5.4	18.5	13.2	7.0	7.3
Seoul	31.7	135.7	6.4	13.4	3.6	8.7	57.7	23.3	8.1	3.7

Source: The Bank of Korea.

Note: All numbers are annual growth rates in percent.

Table 12.7 CPI inflation rates of major countries

	Korea	*France*	*Germany*	*Japan*	*U.K.*	*US*
(1) 1977–1981	18.6	11.3	4.5	5.8	13.5	9.9
(2) 1982–1986	3.6	7.5	2.6	1.9	5.5	3.8
(1)–(2)	15.0	3.8	1.9	3.9	8.0	6.1

Source: OECD.

Note: Numbers are average annual inflation rates for the indicated periods in percent.

4.1.1 Stabilization of oil prices

There were many factors that contributed to the successful stabilization in the early 1980s. Among others, fall of raw material prices, including oil, was definitely one of the biggest contributors. International oil prices, which soared from below $15 per barrel to more than $30 in 1979 and further rose to more than $35 dollars in 1980, began to stabilize to $30 from 1981.

Thanks mainly to the oil price fall, the overall import price inflation rate (in dollar terms) was drastically brought down from around 27 percent in 1979 and 1980 to 4 percent in 1981 and –5 percent in 1982. In Korean won terms, the situation was more dramatic. Since the won was devalued against the dollar by more than 20 percent (from 484 to 580 won/dollar) in the beginning of the year, the import prices rose by almost 60 percent in 1980 before brought down to 17 percent in 1981 and 2 percent in 1982.

It is clear that such chance factors operated as the biggest contributors to domestic inflation stabilization in 1982. (See Corbo and Nam, 1986b, for details.) It is also clear, however, that inflation stabilization thanks to good luck could not be sustained. Theoretically, the fluctuations of oil prices as well as the exchange rate (so called "cost shocks") only affect the *level* of prices not its *rate* of change (or inflation), which implies that their impacts on inflation rates should be temporary (though persistent for several years) rather than permanent. Empirically, the evidence for the temporary nature of the impacts of oil prices on inflation can be found from Korea's own experience after the First Oil Shock in 1974. Although the oil prices became stabilized from 1975 at around $12 per barrel after a big jump in 1974, Korea's domestic inflation rate was not significantly lowered and bounced up again. In contrast, the inflation rate was permanently stabilized in the early 1980s even after the effects of oil prices dissipated in years. The key differences between the two periods was in macroeconomic policy stances. (See Kim and Cho, 2001, who disentangled "aggregate demand pressures" from cost- or supply-side pressures, employing a structural vector auto-regression technique and showed how significantly demand contraction contributed to stabilization in the early 1980s.)

4.1.2. Fiscal contraction

One of the most impressive achievements in the early 1980s was fiscal consolidation. Recognizing that the budget deficit was a main source of monetary expansion, the government exerted itself to reduce inefficiencies. For example, by adopting the "zero-base" budgeting system, the government could save a substantial amount of taxpayers' money and reduce the deficit from 1983. Under this system, the government reset its priorities every year by appraising the costs and benefits of the projects from a zero baseline, even for the continuing projects from the previous year. This concept was distinguished from the traditional budgeting system in that the latter appraised the costs based on the previous year's budget.

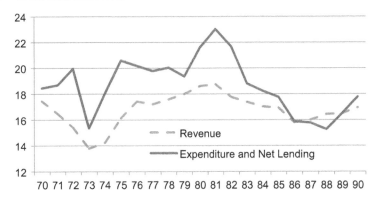

Figure 12.4 Expenditure and net lending, and revenue (% of GDP)

Source: Cha Dong-se (1995), *A Half Century of the Korean Economy: Sourcebook.*

At the same time, the government continued to rationalize operation schemes of the special funds and gradually eliminated their structural deficits. For example, the Grain Management Fund, whose borrowing from the BOK once accounted for more than one-third of the total increase of base money in the 1970s, finally began to run a surplus from 1985. As a result of all these efforts, the consolidated budget deficit was gradually reduced and turned around to a surplus in 1985. Even in IMF standards, including off-budget accounts, the consolidated budget virtually attained the balance in 1986.

This fiscal consolidation was truly remarkable in that it was not achieved by an increase in tax revenue; in fact, the ratio of tax revenue relative to GDP was lowered from 19 percent in 1981 to 16 percent in 1986. In order to achieve the consolidated budget balance, the government reduced its total spending (including net lending) to GDP ratio by 7 percent points during the five years – from 23 percent in 1981 to 16 percent in 1986. Since then, the sound management of government budget became a long-lived tradition in Korea, although both revenue and expenditure have been increasing relative to GDP.

It is also notable that the government attempted to flexibly respond to business fluctuations while maintaining efforts to remove structurally inefficient spending. In particular, the government expanded supportive policies to business sectors in response to the slow recovery in 1980 and 1981. Financial supports for public construction, small- and medium-sized enterprises, residential construction for low-income families and exports of heavy industrial products on a deferred payment basis were augmented. The tax system was also actively utilized with temporary investment tax credits, lower personal and corporate income taxes and selective use of capital gains and excise taxes. These fiscal measures temporarily increased the budget deficit in 1981, which can be regarded as a rational response of fiscal policy to cope with the recession. According to Corbo and Nam (1986a), who analyzed the fiscal policy stance using the measure of fiscal impulse, Korea's fiscal policy was fairly expansionary (by approximately 1.6 percent of GNP) in

1981, while contractionary in 1982 and 1983 (by almost 2 percent of GNP in 1983). That is, the government made efforts to boost the economy while the adverse effects of the Second Oil Shock lingered in 1981 but began to reduce in earnest the overall spending as economic recovery secured momentum from 1983.

4.1.3. Monetary contraction

As the fiscal deficit and policy loans were scaled down, pressures on monetary expansion were gradually reduced and the room for discretionary monetary policy was widened. In 1980 and 1981, the expansion in current account deficit happened to operate as a factor to contract base money supply. (Although the Korean government introduced a "managed floating exchange rate system" in 1980, the exchange rate was still under the government control and thus current account deficit contributed to the contraction in base money supply.) Yet, genuine contraction in monetary policy was delayed until 1983 as in fiscal policy. In terms of the growth rate of M2 (a broader set of monetary assets), the official target of monetary policy at that time was still staying at around 40 percent until 1982. The growth rate of M1 (a narrower set of monetary assets) in 1982 even exceeded 60 percent.

This delay in monetary contraction was intentional, just as in fiscal contraction, in order to mitigate the adverse shocks from the oil price hikes and the resulting recession. Instead of pulling down the already shaky economy by abruptly tightening monetary policy, the BOK maintained the previous pace of M2 growth through weakening credit controls over bank loans until 1982. From 1983, however, the M2 growth rate was substantially lowered to around 20 percent. (See Corbo and Nam, 1986a, who quantitatively assessed how drastic this change in monetary policy was.)

Since this bold adjustment made in 1983, the monetary policy of Korea has been structurally changed. By witnessing the successful outcome of the contractionary monetary policy in stabilizing inflation, ordinary people as well as policymakers could recognize that the chronic inflation in the 1970s was a monetary phenomenon, which was what they had been educated in by the government. This general perception about the relationship between monetary policy and

Table 12.8 Money growth rates in the 1980s

	1977	1978	1979	1980	1981	1982	1983	1984	1985	1986
Base Money	44.1	35.3	23.8	−6.5	−13.6	36.5	7.1	3.7	1.7	16.2
M1	45.0	38.7	23.1	21.0	23.4	62.8	16.3	5.7	22.8	34.3
M2	40.1	35.4	29.7	44.5	36.1	37.0	22.9	19.0	18.1	29.5

Source: The Bank of Korea.

Note: Numbers are annual growth rates in percent.

inflation then served as a social pressure against lax monetary policy. Although the money supply growth rate temporarily rose to around 30 percent due to the huge current account surplus in the late 1980s (which resulted in the blip in the inflation rate up to almost 10 percent in the early 1990s), it was stabilized again in the 1990s with the introduction of a more flexible exchange rate system and the reduction in current account surplus. As the money supply growth rate was permanently lowered, the chronic inflation vanished and never returned to the Korean economy.

4.2   Factor price stabilization and income policy

As inflation subsided, factor prices such as wages and interest rates were also stabilized. Economic agents began to realize that a lower increase rate in *nominal* wages and a lower *nominal* interest rate could secure higher *real* purchasing powers, if inflation rates were sufficiently stabilized.

For example, nominal wage growth rates in the second half of the 1970s, more than 20 percent per annum, were far higher than those in the first half of the 1980s, around 10 percent. However, the real growth rates of wages in terms of purchasing power were even higher in the first half of the 1980s, with around 3 percent inflation rates, than in the second half of the 1970s, with around 20 percent inflation. The same was true for interest rates. Although market interest rates (for example, three-year corporate bonds rates) were lowered to around 15 percent in nominal terms in the first half of the 1980s, they could secure higher real purchasing power than 20 to 30 percent of nominal interest rates during the second half of the 1970s, when a double-digit inflation eroded the real return rate. Realizing this, people began to come back to formal financial markets to deposit their savings even at lower nominal interest rates and the financial market could be deepened and developed.

However, this process was not entirely smooth in the early stage of the stabilization policy period. Agreeing to a lower rate of wage increase prior to actual inflation stabilization could imply a loss in workers' purchasing power if the inflation rate were not lowered as expected. Conversely, inflation stabilization could imply the loss of business profits if wages were not stabilized as much. Government efforts to transform the vicious circle of wage-inflation spiral into a virtuous circle of stabilization evidently entailed sharp conflicts between workers and businesses Apart from the natural adjustments to the changes in macroeconomic environment, therefore, the government made additional efforts to stabilize factor prices. That is, the government urged pain-sharing by imposing informal wage guidelines to moderate wage increases and controlling interest rates and dividends, as well as adjusting its purchase prices for grains.

The government's motivation for the wage restraint was clear: stable wages were essential for export competitiveness as well as price stability. The wage guidelines could also be justified by a well-established macroeconomic theory, such as the wage-contract model. According to this model, recessions in the early stage of disinflation period are caused by wage increases exceeding productivity increases due to the inertia in inflation expectation and, therefore, the magnitude of output loss can be minimized if the inflation expectations are lowered in line with the actual speed of disinflation. Nevertheless, it was an extremely difficult task to enforce the wage guidelines by adjusting workers' expectation on the inflation rate before it was actually lowered. Nam describes how difficult it was to enforce the policy:

> Under government influence, negotiated base salary increases in the private sector in 1982 and 1983, which averaged 9.5 and 6.9 percent, respectively, were very close to those for public servants. However, de facto wage increases in the private sector were much higher than the negotiated rates – 15.8 percent in 1982 and about 12 percent in 1983 – indicating that effective wage guidelines depend on a broad consensus among labor, management, and the government. Otherwise, businesses can easily circumvent guidelines under the existing complicated wage structure.
>
> (1991, p. 232)

4.3 Stabilization of the balance of payments

Inflation stabilization also made a great contribution to resolving the balance of payments crisis that overshadowed the Korean economy. The amount of foreign debts to finance trade deficits was explosively increased in the 1970s as explained in Section 2. By 1980, when trade deficit substantially deteriorated due to the Second Oil Shock, this amount reached $27,170 million or 48.2 percent of GNP.

The first response of the government to cope with the crisis was to devalue the exchange rate from 484 to 580 won/dollar in January 12, 1980. This was the first devaluation since 1974. At the same time, the fixed exchange rate system was replaced by a multiple-currency basket system to continue to depreciate the currency value. As a result, the average exchange rate was raised to 731 won/dollar in 1982, approximately a 50 percent depreciation compared to 484 won/dollar in 1979. Nevertheless, it is estimated that exporters' price competitiveness was not much improved in terms of the real effective exchange rate because of the high inflation during the 1980–1982 period. In fact, it was 1983 when the real effective exchange rate indeed began to depreciate, although the magnitude of the nominal exchange rate depreciation was rather mild. For example, the won/dollar exchange rate was depreciated to 801 won/dollar by 1984, approximately 10 percent from 1982, but the entire 10 percent of nominal depreciation could be translated into the real effective exchange rate depreciation, or the recovery of exporters' price competitiveness, because the domestic inflation rate was stabilized to those of competing countries.

In fact, exporters' price competitiveness represented by the real effective exchange rate reflects many aspects of macroeconomic adjustments. For example, if factor costs such as wages are stabilized along with the general inflation, exporters can secure profit margins although the nominal exchange rate does not depreciate. According to Nam's (1988) estimation, the rate of increase in unit labor cost (= wage divided by labor productivity) substantially declined from 20 percent

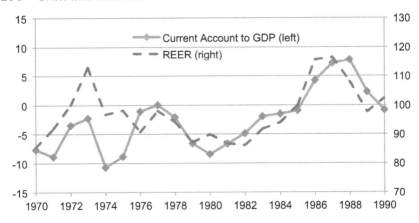

Figure 12.5 Current account-to-GDP ratio and real effective exchange rate
Source: Cha Dong-se (1995), *A Half Century of the Korean Economy: Sourcebook.*

or more per annum in the 1970s to around 7 percent in the early 1980s. Even this 7 percent increase in unit labor cost was fully compensated for Korean exporters by the same 7 percent of currency depreciation per year during the 1981–1984 period. That is, Korean exporters were completely free from the wage cost increase in dollar terms in the early 1980s.

As price competitiveness of exporting firms improved, trade (as well as current) account narrowed its deficit and finally turned around into a surplus of $4.2 billion = (4.0 percent of GNP) in 1986 – the first time in Korea's history. The size of the surplus continued to expand to $11.4 billion (6.4 percent of GNP) in 1988, resolving the balance-of-payments problems. The amount of foreign debts, which had been only accumulating up to $46.7 billion to finance deficit until 1985, began to decline in 1986 with a trade surplus and was reduced to $31.7 billion by 1990. While the absolute size of foreign debts was decreased by approximately one-third during the five-year period, its relative size to GNP substantially dropped from 56 percent in 1985 to 13 percent in 1990 as the economy rapidly expanded. Having seen this performance, no foreign creditors doubted the creditworthiness of the Korean economy.

4.4 Revival of growth

As inflation was stabilized and export competitiveness was secured, the Korean economy regained its growth momentum. Although the growth rate rebounded to around 8 percent in 1981 and 1982, it was largely due to technical effects of low base in 1980. As the economy stabilized, however, the Korean economy could continue to grow at a 10 percent rate per year during the 1983–1985 period and further thrived with almost 12 percent of annual growth during the 1986–1988 period. In fact, the three years from 1986 to 1988 were the most memorable heyday of the Korea economy: it enjoyed fast growth, maintained low and stable inflation and achieved sufficient amounts of trade surplus to resolve the balance of payments problem.

Several facts are noteworthy from the national account data. First, government consumption growth did not slow down in 1980 despite negative GDP growth. Rather, this value was significantly lowered during the 1981 to 1985 period, indicating that the government deliberately delayed fiscal consolidation until the economy began to recover. Second, investment in facilities could not pick up until 1982 even after it was contracted by 20 percent in 1980. This indicates how serious the over-investment problem in the late 1970s was, as evidenced by 35 percent of annual increase for the four years from 1976 to 1979. Third, the growth rate of import was suppressed throughout the early 1980s, which was also the reaction of excessive demand in the late 1970s. As the economy was overheated, the import base was rapidly expanded at an annual rate of more than 20 percent in the late 1970s, with which the trade account could hardly turn into surplus despite rapid export growth. It took more than five years until 1985 to adjust the situation by moderating import growth to the rate far lower than that of export. It was only after 1985 that Korea could sufficiently increase import without deteriorating balance-of-payments.

4.5 Structural changes toward a market-oriented economy

Efforts made in the early 1980s were not confined to macroeconomic adjustments. As a matter of fact, they included an extremely wide range of structural

Table 12.9 Growth rates of main aggregate demand components

	1971–1975	1976–1979	1980	1981–1982	1983–1985	1986–1988
GDP	9.7	11.0	−1.9	7.9	9.9	12.1
Consumption	7.2	7.4	1.2	6.0	7.2	8.4
Private	7.3	7.7	−0.2	6.3	8.0	8.6
Government	6.6	5.9	9.1	4.5	3.4	7.3
Investment	11.7	25.7	−12.0	3.7	11.1	15.2
Construction	9.3	17.8	−4.5	6.3	11.4	11.6
Facilities	16.5	35.3	−20.1	0.9	10.4	19.5
Export	29.3	18.2	8.6	10.6	10.5	19.4
Import	15.5	21.4	−4.0	4.7	6.4	17.2

Source: The Bank of Korea.

Notes:
1. Numbers are average annual growth rates for the indicated periods in percent.
2. All figures are from the most updated national accounts and thus different from the growth rates that policymakers in the 1980s were actually reporting at that time. For example, the GDP growth rate in 1980 was reported −6.2 percent at the time (see Subsection 3.1.1), not −1.9 percent.

policies from import liberalization to financial deregulation. Yet, the whole theme was clear and simple: making the Korean economy more market-oriented. Various regulations and controls imposed under the government-led development era were lifted. More economic freedom was allowed and the market function was established.

These structural reforms, though pursued for the sake of economic efficiency, were also reinforced by macroeconomic stabilization. As inflation was stabilized, the need for the government to resort on administrative measures for individual price controls were reduced to a substantial degree. As factor prices were also stabilized, the government did not have to attempt to keep wages or interest rates under control. As inflation expectation was tamed, the discrepancy between the regulated interest rate in the formal market and the unregulated rate in the black market was substantially reduced, providing a favorable environment for interest rate liberalization. As the fixed exchange rate system was abolished, the discrepancy between the official and black market rates was also reduced, paving the path to foreign exchange market liberalization. Indeed, the macroeconomic stabilization achieved in the early 1980s was an indispensible infrastructure for further development of Korea toward a market-oriented economy.

5. Conclusion and lessons

The comprehensive stabilization policy in the early 1980s was one of the boldest reforms in Korea's economic policy history. It was not just a macroeconomic adjustment. Indeed, it was a paradigm shift that overhauled the economic policy framework from the government-led development strategy to a market-based economic policy.

Of course, the primary goal of the stabilization policy was to control chronic inflation, which was a result of monetary expansion. The monetary expansion, however, stemmed from the accommodative role of the BOK supporting the banking and fiscal sectors that were mobilized for the HCI drive. The stabilization policy, therefore, had to begin with the negation of the heavy involvement of the government in the market system, which had been regarded as the backbone of the "Korean Miracle" for almost two decades. Industrial policies that had been at the heart of the government-led development strategy were weakened and the financial market began to secure its own breathing room from the government's repression. A full-scale restructuring of government spending was carried out to eliminate another source of monetization. Many prices that had been under the government's control were liberalized and the import market was actively opened. Freed from the distorted task of supporting industrial policies, the BOK began to restore its original position that should aim at price stability.

As such, the inflation stabilization policy of Korea in the early 1980s was an extremely complex process far beyond a simple monetary contraction. There was a great deal of opposition not only from interest groups but also from some elites. It may be true that the stabilization policy would not have been politically feasible without the full support and commitment of the dictator, President Chun.

Though born from the same military blood, President Chun was convinced of the importance of the stabilization policy that could not be appreciated by President Park, who designed and implemented the government-led development strategy.

One may say that Korea was lucky to have a new leadership at the critical moment, but it was not entirely a matter of luck. The conviction of President Chun about the stabilization policy did not come by chance; rather it was a precious outcome of unremitting efforts by awakened economic advisors. With clear understanding and logical reasoning on the big picture of the economic system, they kept teaching and persuading President Chun about why the stabilization policy was so crucial for the sustainable development of Korea. Finally convinced himself, President Chun could then push through the reforms that would wait long until bearing fruits.

There must be many important lessons from this experience of Korea that can be learned by developing countries. Yet, some lessons need to be adapted to different global environments and political systems between Korea in the 1980s and developing countries these days. For example, political leaders' sound understanding of economic policies was crucial under the dictatorship in Korea at that time but more broad-based institutional approaches should be considered under democratic systems these days.

Note

* This chapter is a substantially reduced version of the report that was co-authored with Younguck Kang in 2012. The original full-length report can be found at *Korea Knowledge Sharing Program: Modularization of Korea's Development Experience*, KDI School of Public Policy and Management (https://www.kdevelopedia.org/resource).

References

Cha, Dong-se, 1995. *A Half Century of the Korean Economy: Sourcebook*, Korea Development Institute, Seoul (in Korean).

Cho, Yoon je, and Joon Kyung Kim, 1997. *Credit Policies and the Industrialization of Korea*, Korea Development Institute, Seoul.

Corbo, Vittorio, and Sang-Woo Nam, 1986a. "Recent Evolution of the Macroeconomy," in *Structural Adjustment in a Newly Industrialized Economy: The Korean Experience*, edited by Vittorio Corbo and Sang-Mok Suh, pp. 35–67. Baltimore, MD: The Johns Hopkins University Press.

———, 1986b. "Recent Experience in Controlling Inflation," in *Structural Adjustment in a Newly Industrialized Economy: The Korean Experience*, edited by Vittorio Corbo and Sang-Mok Suh, pp. 95–114. Baltimore, MD: The Johns Hopkins University Press.

Economic Planning Board, 1977. *Rationalization of the Grain Management Fund* (in Korean). Sejong City: Economic Planning Board of Korea.

Kang, Kyongshik, 1988. *Days with Economic Development*, Busan, Korea: The Busan Development Systems Research Institute (in Korean).

Kim, Dong Kun, and Seong Hyun Whang, 1997. "The Role of Tax and Fiscal Policy," in *The Korean Economy 1945–1995: Performance and Vision for the 21st Century*, edited by Dong-se Cha, Kwang Suk Kim, and Dwight H. Perkins, pp. 143–185. Seoul: Korea Development Institute.

Kim, June-Il and Dongchul Cho, 2001. "Diagnosis of Business Conditions through Estimation of GDP-Gap," *Analyses of the Korean Economy*, 7, pp. 187–235 (in Korean).

Kim, Pyung-Joo, 1997. "Financial Policies and Institutional Innovation," in *The Korean Economy 1945–1995: Performance and Vision for the 21st Century*, edited by Dong-se Cha, Kwang Suk Kim, and Dwight H. Perkins, pp. 143–185. Seoul: Korea Development Institute,

Krause, Lawrence B., 1997. "The Political Economy of South Korea: Fifty Years of Macroeconomic Management, 1945–1995," in *The Korean Economy 1945–1995: Performance and Vision for the 21st Century*, edited by Dong-se Cha, Kwang Suk Kim, and Dwight H. Perkins, pp. 143–185. Seoul: Korea Development Institute.

Krause, Lawrence B., and Kim, Kihwan (eds.), 1991. *Liberalization in the Process of Economic Development*. Berkeley: University of California Press.

Kwack, Taewon, 1984. "Investment Incentives in Korean Tax System and their Economic Effects," in *Tax Reforms in Korea: Major Issues and New Direction*, edited by Kwang Choi, pp. 65–113. Seoul: Korea Development Institute (in Korean).

Lee, Jang Kyu, 2008. *You're the President When it Comes to Economic Policies*. Seoul, Korea: Ollim (in Korean).

Lee, Jin Soon, 1996. "Alternative Perspective of Land Problems in Korea," in *Land Taxation in Korea: A Critical Review of Current Policies and Suggestions for Future Policy Direction*, edited by Younghoon Ro, pp. 8–24. Seoul: Korea Institute of Public Finance.

Lee, Suk-Chae, 1991. "The Heavy and Chemical Industries Promotion Plan, 1973–1979," in *Economic Development in the Republic of Korea: A Policy Perspective*, edited by Lee-Jay Cho and Yoon Hyung Kim, pp. 431–471. Honolulu: University of Hawaii Press.

Nam, Sang-Woo, 1988. "Alternative Growth and Adjustment Strategies of Newly Industrialized Countries in Southeast Asia," in *Beyond Adjustment: The Asian Experience*, edited by Paul Streeten, pp. 68–105. Washington, DC: International Monetary Fund.

———, 1991. "The Comprehensive Stabilization Program (1979)," in *Economic Development in the Republic of Korea: A Policy Perspective*, edited by Lee-Jay Cho and Yoon Hyung Kim, pp. 207–244. Honolulu: University of Hawaii Press.

Nam, Sang-Woo, and Jun-Il Kim, 1995. "Macroeconomic Policies and Evolution," in *A Half Century of the Korean Economy: Performance and Vision for the 21st Century*, edited by Dong-se Cha and Kwang Suk Kim, pp. 121–178. Seoul: Korea Development Institute (in Korean).

Park, Won-Kon, 2009. "Carter Administration's Policy for Korea: An Application of Ethical Diplomacy around October 26," *Journal of Korea's Political Science*, 43, pp. 215–234 (in Korean).

Perkins, Dwight H., 1997. "Structural Transformation and the Role of the State," in *The Korean Economy 1945–1995: Performance and Vision for the 21st Century*, edited by Dong-se Cha, Kwang Suk Kim, and Dwight H. Perkins, pp. 143–185. Seoul: Korea Development Institute.

13 Overcoming the 1997–1998 crisis

Macroeconomic policy adjustments*

1. The Korean economy before the crisis

1.1 Pre-crisis state of the Korean economy

1.1.1 Sound macroeconomic indicators

Korea had for a long time been a model economy for many developing countries. It had achieved rapid growth under a reasonably stable macroeconomic environment since the 1960s. This trend of high growth and stable inflation continued into the first half of the 1990s. Though it no longer grew at double-digit growth rates, the Korean economy still maintained a fairly rapid growth rate of higher than 7 percent per annum on average. Inflation subsided from 9.1 percent in 1991 to around 5 percent during the 1993–1995 period (see Figure 13.1).

Although the current account ran some deficits due to the investment boom, the size of the deficits – less than 2 percent of GDP until 1995 – did not appear to be a big burden. In addition, a long tradition of budget discipline that began in the early 1980s continued until the early 1990s; the government sought to maintain a balanced budget. A casual glance at major macroeconomic indicators tells us that the Korean economy appeared to cruising very smoothly (see Figure 13.2).

1.1.2 Fragile financial structures

Under the surface of the sound macroeconomic indicators, problems laid hidden in the financial structure of private sector. First of all, the corporate sector was basically run on borrowings rather than its own capital. The average debt-to-equity ratio of Korea's manufacturing firms, which were already at high levels, hovering around 300 percent, soared further to almost 400 percent in 1996.

This debt-ridden financial structure was potentially very dangerous, because it significantly eroded the net profit margins of the corporate sector, hence weakening their financial buffers against unexpected adverse shocks. The average interest coverage ratio (= interest expense/operating profit) of manufacturing firms was barely over 100 percent; the average Korean firm needed to spend almost its entire operating profits simply to cover interest expenses. Obviously, this left shareholders a small margin of net income.

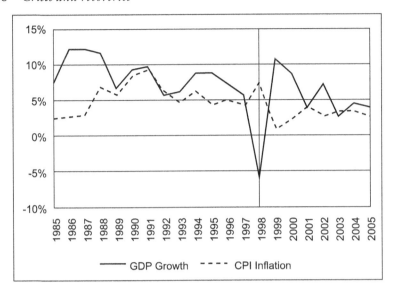

Figure 13.1 Growth and inflation of the Korean economy
Data Sources: Bank of Korea, Statistics Korea, Yearly.

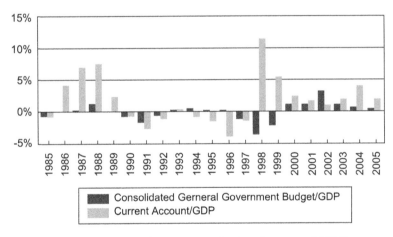

Figure 13.2 Current account and government budget (percent of GDP)
Data Sources: Bank of Korea, Statistics Korea, Yearly.

Particularly important in relation to the subsequent currency crisis was that a substantial portion of this debt was short-term and foreign currency denominated The Korean government began to liberalize capital accounts from the early 1990s, resulting in many financial institutions rushing out and securing cheap funding. The interest rate in the international financial market, far lower than the domestic rate of around 15 percent at the time, was attractive to many of Korea's financial institutions and firms. Further, short-term debt appeared even more attractive in terms of financing cost. Financial institutions lent to Korean firms with cheap money borrowed from abroad, which led to a rapid accumulation of short-term foreign debt in Korea's financial system. As such, the Korean economy became more vulnerable to external shocks (see Figures 13.3–13.5).

Moreover, large corporation groups, also known as *chaebols*, were another important aspect of the Korea's corporate sector. (See Lim, 2003, for further information on *chaebols*). The firms within a *chaebol* were closely linked by mutual credit guarantees to each other. Under this structure, a financial shock had a

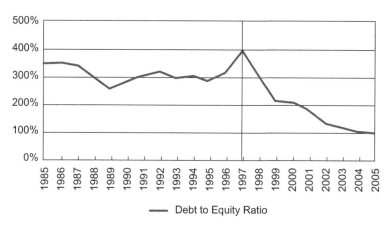

Figure 13.3 Debt-to-equity ratio of the manufacturing sector

Data Sources: Bank of Korea, Yearly.

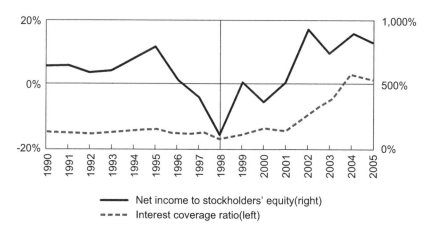

Figure 13.4 Profitability of the manufacturing sector

Data Sources: Bank of Korea, Yearly.

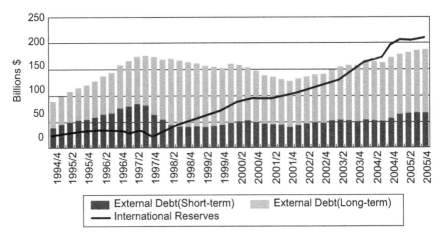

Figure 13.5 Short-term foreign debt in percent of foreign reserve
Data Sources: Bank of Korea, Quarterly.

ripple effect, reverberating throughout the group to other firms in the same *chae-bol*. Therefore, it was widely believed that a failure of a big *chaebol*, like a failure of a major financial institution, could have threatened the financial stability of the whole country. This expectation of "too-big-to-fail" nourished moral hazard in the financial market, the ultimate cause of many financial crises, which in turn provided "cheap capital" to *chaebols*. As a result, the soundness of Korea's entire financial system hinged on the financial state of the big *chaebols*.

1.2   Path to crisis

1.2.1   Collapse of export prices

Under this environment, the price of semi-conductors, Korea's biggest export item, collapsed in the second quarter of 1996. This abruptly swelled the size of Korea's current account deficit, which led to increasing concern about its balance of payments. Foreign investors became reluctant to inject money into the Korean market, weighing down on the value of the Korean won. Yet, the Korean government resisted the depreciation pressures, only allowing a modest depreciation of the won from around 780 won/dollar in the beginning of 1996 to around 840 won/dollar by the end of the year. This exchange rate policy substantially delayed the necessary adjustments of the Korea's macro-economy, including the current account.

However, a greater danger than the deterioration of the current account was the heightening risk of default among the over-leveraged major *chaebols*. The collapse of export prices was a direct revenue hit to Korea's major export companies, most of which were *chaebols*, severely squeezing their already narrow profit margins. In gauging the extent of this shock to the profitability of Korea's corporate sector, Cho wrote:

> The decline of the terms of trade by 20 percent meant the profit loss of approximately 30 trillion won (applying 1,000 won/dollar as the exchange rate and 150 billion dollars per year as the export volume of the Korean economy) of the corporate sector. Using a back of the envelop calculation, one can recognize that this size of the profit loss was big enough to erode the profit margin of the whole corporate sector by half at least. (Remember that the annual GDP is approximately 400 trillion won, out of which about 70 percent is labor income and about 20 percent is the interest rate cost for the outstanding debt, leaving 10 percent of GDP or 40 trillion won as the profit margin).
>
> (1999b, p. 3)

1.2.2 Widespread failures of chaebols

As a result of this shock to the terms-of-trade, the Korean economy slowed down from the second half of 1996; subsequently, *chaebols* began to collapse one after another. Hanbo, the 14th-largest *chaebol* by asset size, was the first *chaebol* to go bankrupt in January 1997. The bankruptcy of an over-leveraged *chaebol* cast a dark shadow over Korea's financial market. Foreign banks began to decline rolling over their loans to Korean banks, and further depreciation pressures to the Korean won mounted. With credit tightening from abroad, a series of *chaebol* failures followed: Sammi (26th largest) in March, NewCore (25th) and Jinro (17th) in May. Afraid of the economic and social repercussions of the massive failures of *chaebols*, the government introduced an ambiguous system called the "Bankruptcy Suspension Agreement" that was entered into between failed firms and creditor banks in April. But this system did not provide a clear way to resolve bankruptcies nor did it inject new capital, which worsened the uncertainties and non-performing loans in the financial market. In July, the 8th largest *chaebol*, which operated a major automobile company, Kia, also collapsed. By then, non-performing loans began to soar, and the financial crisis was becoming a matter of time (see Table 13.1).

1.2.3 Outbreak of the East Asian crisis

While the failures of *chaebols* heightened tensions in the financial market within Korea, a financial crisis had been spreading since July 1997 hitting Thailand, Indonesia, Malaysia, and Philippines. In September, speculators descended on Hong Kong, the financial center of the region. Although Hong Kong succeeded in defending its currency value by significantly raising the inter-bank interest rate, it paid a price in the form of a collapse of the stock market. At the same time, Japan, the biggest creditor to the region, was also suffering from its own financial market troubles, which led to a further depreciation of the Japanese yen against

Table 13.1 Top 30 *chaebols* as of the end of 1996

Order	Chaebol (in the order of asset size)	Total Asset (Billion KRW)	Debt to Equity Ratio(%)	Net Income (Billion KRW)	Bankruptcy (Workout) Date
1	Hyundai	53,597	459	125	
2	Samsung	51,651	459	174	
3	LG	38,376	373	308	
4	Daewoo	35,466	316	350	1999/8 Workout
5	SK	22,927	391	255	
6	Ssangyong	16,457	387	−127	1997–1998 Selling Major Subsidiaries
7	Hanjin	14,309	598	−161	
8	Kia	14,287	518	−129	1997/7 Bankruptcy
9	Hanwha	10,967	789	−212	
10	Lotte	7,774	196	53	
11	Kumho	7,495	552	−40	
12	Halla	6,640	1,986	23	1997/12 Bankruptcy
13	Dong Ah	N/A	659	N/A	1998/6 Workout
14	Doosan	6,370	692	−108	
15	Daelim	6,177	371	−6	
16	Hansol	4,346	433	2	
17	Hyosung	4,131	370	35	
18	Dongkuk Steel	3,956	376	119	
19	Jinro	3,951	3,619	−154	1997/9 Bankruptcy
20	Kolon	3,910	389	8	
21	Kohab	3,690	579	30	1998/7 Workout
22	Dongbu	N/A	464	N/A	
23	Tongyang	3,445	638	−119	
24	Haitai	3,398	658	36	1997/11 Bankruptcy
25	NewCore	2,798	1,224	23	1997/11 Bankruptcy
26	Anam	2,659	486	12	1998/11 Workout
27	Hanil	2,599	578	−122	1998/9 Broken/up
28	Keopyong	2,477	615	20	1998/5 Broken/up
29	Daesang	2,238	412	−30	
30	Shino	2,158	486	−5	1998/10 Workout

Source: Fair Trade Commission (1997), published in 1997 based on the financial statements as of the end of 1996.

the US dollar. Investors lost confidence in the Asian market and rapidly withdrew their money from the region. The Korean won came under huge pressure in the foreign exchange market, forcing the government to defend the currency value. Knowing that the government's effort would be futile, speculators – both domestic and foreign – began to sell off the Korean won. The Korean government finally abandoned its efforts to defend the currency value and widened the one-day fluctuation bandwidth from 2.25 to 10 percent in November, but it was too late. By then, investors appeared to have lost confidence in Korea; its financial market appeared to be very risky and the political situation seemed unstable, especially with the upcoming presidential election in December.

1.2.4 Political uncertainty

History shows that many currency crises coincided with a changing of the political leadership. It might be that the currency crisis brought about a change in the existing political leadership or, conversely, the increasing uncertainties brought about by anticipated changes in the leadership may have triggered a currency crisis. It is unclear which direction of causality worked more strongly in Korea's case, but it seems clear that the political uncertainty at least, contributed to aggravating the crisis.

With the presidential election scheduled on December 18, the Korean government could not exercise strong leadership from the beginning of 1997. Pressed by fierce demonstrations by workers in January, the president, Young-sam Kim, revoked the Labor Market Reform Act that was passed by the National Assembly in December 1996. This action was interpreted by the market as a signal that the Korean government did not have a strong will to enhance labor market flexibilities. As for the *chaebol* failures, the government took a noncommittal stance by introducing the aforementioned Bankruptcy Suspension Agreement. The government's stance on its exchange rate policy was also ambiguous. In the name of "smoothing intervention," the government managed a gradual (and predictable) pace of depreciation, which could only encourage speculation. In October and November, when the financial market was driven to crisis, the government mustered the "Financial Reform Act," which was approved by the National Assembly. However, the political situation at the time was extremely tenuous with the presidential election looming, while the government was left rudderless. The Reform Act was only passed by the National Assembly in December 30 after the IMF intervened and Dae-Jung Kim, the new president elect, took the helm.

During the run up to the elections, the government finally announced on November 21 that Korea had sought financial assistance from the IMF. Yet, the policy uncertainties lingered as the presidential nominations, running in a dead heat, took different positions on the IMF programs. Korea's foreign reserves were almost depleted, while the exchange rate continued to depreciate until the end of December, even after the Korean government and the IMF agreed to a $55 billion rescue package on December 4.

2.   Initial responses: the IMF program

Most of the initial policies to cope with the crisis were designed by the IMF, the main frameworks of which were submitted to the IMF executive board on December 3 and approved on December 4.

2.1   *Stabilization of foreign currency liquidity*

The most imminent policy objective of the IMF program was to redress the foreign currency liquidity. This was quite natural, since the need for foreign liquidity was the reason why the Korean government sought help from the IMF. In fact, Korea's foreign currency liquidity situation was truly critical. Although the official foreign reserve was announced at around $30 billion (approximately 6 percent of GDP) until November, the amount of "usable reserves" fell far below $10 billion during the time the Korean government was negotiating the rescue package with the IMF. The Bank of Korea lent out a substantial portion of the foreign reserves to many Korean commercial banks operating abroad, which could not roll over their short-term debt at the time. Although offshore foreign reserves are considered by the conventional definition as part of the official reserve, these reserves were not readily usable. The amount of usable foreign reserves fell to $6.69 billion as of December 1, spiking to $11.06 billion on December 5 after the IMF's first liquidity injection ($5.5 billion), only to fall again to $6.44 billion on December 15, before falling to $3.94 billion on December 18, the day of presidential election. Literally, the whole country was on the brink of defaulting on its foreign currency denominated debt.

2.1.1   *Charging penalty interest rates and floating the exchange rate*

All of the policy measures aimed at shoring up Korea's foreign currency liquidity. The first policy action to achieve this goal was to charge a penalty interest rate on foreign currency loans lent to commercial banks by the Bank of Korea. In the first agreement on December 4, the penalty interest rate was set at 400 basis points above LIBO, and was raised to 700 basis points on December 18, which was raised again to 1,000 basis points on December 27, as foreign liquidity had not improved by this time.

Another decisive policy action was introducing a free-floating exchange rate system. December 16 marked a historic moment, as the daily exchange rate band was completely abandoned. But the value of the Korean won continued to be in a free fall, pricing extremely frantic as the financial and political uncertainties reached a fever pitch. Yet, some transactions began to be made in the foreign exchange market – a dim signal indicating a recovery of the market function – once the price of the Korean won was sufficiently lowered.

2.1.2   *Securing additional foreign currency liquidity*

The Korean government also continued to make efforts to secure additional foreign currency liquidity through the public sector aside from the IMF, resulting in

$3 billion from the IBRD and $2 billion from the ADB of additional liquidity. Nevertheless, foreign currency liquidity was extremely tight. Kyu-sung Lee, the Minister of the Department of Finance and Economy during the crisis period (March 1998–May 1999) wrote:

> The prospect for complete depletion of the foreign exchange reserves of the central bank became very real, and the most urgent problem was to prevent a national insolvency. By December 11, the reserves stood at US$9.6 billion. But even with the US$5.5 billion in the pipeline from the IMF and the ADB by the year's end, it was doubtful whether they would be enough to cover US$13.0 billion needed by domestic financial companies and US$2 to 3 billion needed by others. The outlook was grim.
>
> (2010, p. 97)

To avoid national default, it appeared that the international community had to send a stronger signal that Korea would be rescued at all costs. In return, the international world had to be convinced that Korea would reform itself into a viable economy; the Korean government needed to carry out very bold structural reform policies. The government gave ultimatums to some banks and pledged to implement the Financial Reform Act. The president elect, Dae-Jung Kim, even committed to resorting to emergency lay-off measures that had been prohibited for a long time in Korea.

Finally, the US government, on behalf of 13 countries that had committed to assisting Korea, announced on December 24 that $10 billion of additional liquidity would be deployed if necessary while major creditor banks would be asked to roll over their loans to Korea. This announcement was taken by the market as a strong signal that the US would not let Korea default, an important factor in checking the depreciation of the Korean won.

2.2 Macroeconomic policies

Under this environment, macroeconomic policies were also implemented to stabilize the foreign currency liquidity condition. The main objective of the macroeconomic policies is identified in the opening paragraph of the IMF program:

> The program is intended to narrow the external current account deficit to below 1 percent of GDP in 1998 and 1999, contain inflation at or below 5 percent, and – hoping for an early return of confidence – limit the deceleration in real GDP growth to about 3 percent in 1998, followed by a recovery toward potential in 1999.
>
> ("Republic of Korea," 1997)

Clearly, policy priority was placed on stabilizing the balance of payments, which required a tightening of macroeconomic policies. To this end, tight monetary and fiscal policies were then implemented.

2.2.1   Monetary policy: controversial high interest rate policy

Right after it signed the agreement with the Korean government, the IMF raised the inter-bank overnight call rate – the monetary policy target rate – from around 13 percent to around 25 percent, raising it further to around 30 percent in late December.

This extremely high interest rate policy triggered a great deal of controversy, not only from within Korea but also from international scholars. For example, Joseph E. Stiglitz, the Senior Vice President and Chief Economist of the World Bank at the time, and a 2001 Nobel Prize Laureate, was very critical of the IMF's overall policies, particularly its high interest rate policy. In many articles and speeches, he argued that the high interest rate policy was not appropriate considering the macroeconomic conditions of Korea, nor an effective tool to stabilize the exchange rate (Furman and Stiglitz, 1998, for example). He even argued that the high interest rate policy could destabilize the currency value even further by raising the risk premiums of crisis-hit countries.

As was emphasized earlier, however, the most urgent policy goal of the initial IMF program was shoring up liquidity in foreign currency, against the usual objective of macroeconomic policies; maintaining the stability of major macroeconomic variables such as growth, employment, and inflation, was of secondary importance. (See Fischer, 1988, and Krueger, 2000, for example) Under this policy priority, it was necessary, or probably inevitable, to impose a high interest rate policy. Especially given that a penalty interest rate was charged on foreign currency loans lent by the Bank of Korea. Otherwise, the commercial banks that were desperate for foreign currency would have borrowed domestic currency from the Bank of Korea at relatively low interest rates and converted it into foreign currency to pay back their foreign currency borrowings with high penalty interest rates from the Bank of Korea. This situation could have further de-stabilized the foreign exchange market that was already in a near-panic state.

Therefore, as long as a penalty interest rate was charged on foreign currency loans, the interest rate on domestic currency had to be raised similarly. This is why the domestic call rate was raised to around 25 percent when a penalty rate of 400 basis points above LIBOR was charged on foreign currency loans. It was further raised later in December when the penalty rate was raised by another 600 basis points. In other words, the domestic monetary policy could not be separated from the foreign currency liquidity policy in the eyes of the IMF; thus, a high interest rate policy with the goal of quickly restoring foreign currency liquidity was implemented. The objectives of the IMF's high interest rate policy were clearly outlined in its program, which combined the monetary and exchange rate policies together under a single heading:

> To demonstrate to markets the authorities' resolve to confront the present crisis, monetary policy will be tightened immediately to restore and sustain calm in the markets and contain the impact of the recent won depreciation

on inflation. In line with this policy, the large liquidity injection in recent days will be reversed, and money market rates, presently 14–16 percent, will be allowed to rise to a level that stabilizes markets. Money growth during 1998 will be limited to a rate consistent with containing inflation at 5 percent or less. A flexible exchange rate policy will be maintained, with intervention limited to smoothing operations.

("Korea Letter of Intent," 1997)

This was consistent with the classic textbook policy recommendation for economies with open capital accounts (the framework often called "Impossible Trinity", which had not been fully appreciated by the Korean government until the currency crisis broke out). In particular, the high interest rate policy appeared to be inevitable under the environment of the international financial market in which a lender-of-last-resort did not exist and a swift and orderly restructuring of foreign debts was not feasible. (See Section 1 of Chapter 3 for the discussion about foreign debt restructuring in late January 1998.) (See Figure 13.6 and 13.7)

2.2.2 Fiscal policy: balanced budget dogma

The initial IMF's fiscal policy recommendation called for a balanced budget. Later, Chopra et al., from the IMF, justified this fiscal policy recommendation by writing:

> When the financial crisis hit, the program called for the policy of fiscal con-servatism to be continued. The reasons were four-fold: First, the depth of the recession that occurred was not anticipated. Second, the authorities believed

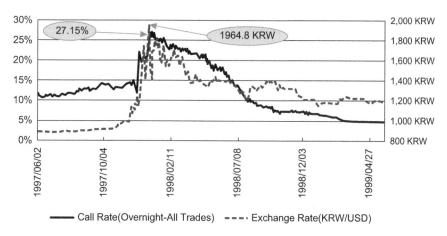

Figure 13.6 Exchange rate and interest rate

Data Sources: Bank of Korea, Daily

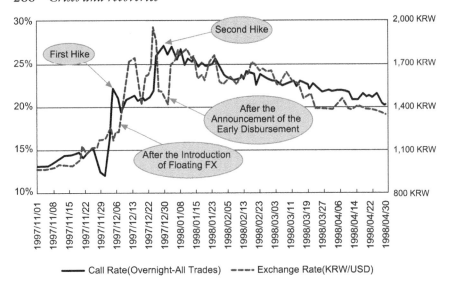

Figure 13.7 Exchange rate and interest rate, highlighted

that a worsening fiscal position would have placed a greater burden on monetary policy in the overall macroeconomic adjustment. Third, the expected contingent liabilities from the costly financial sector restructuring would require an offsetting policy response in other components of the fiscal balance. Fourth, a tight fiscal policy would provide a positive signal to financial markets and foster a return of confidence.

(2000, p. 41)

However, this fiscal policy recommendation attracted fierce criticism from all over the world. The typical recipe of the IMF for the countries facing an external debt crisis had been a policy of fiscal tightening to improve the current account. This policy recommendation had been sensible for many Latin American countries, in which government (external) debt problems were serious. Unlike those countries, however, the Korean government had maintained fairly sound fiscal discipline. The debt problems, both internal and external, were mostly confined within the private sector, not the public sector. If public debt was not a serious problem, the textbook policy response was to allow for budget deficits during recession periods.

The current account also rebounded, and ran a surplus from November 1997, as a result of the sharp depreciation of the currency value and the collapse of domestic demand (particularly facility investment that heavily relied upon imported goods). From this perspective, sticking to the dogma of a balanced budget in Korea's case did not appear to be sensible. In fact, the IMF retracted its initial fiscal policy recommendation, as the economic recession turned out to be far more serious than initially anticipated (see Figure 13.8).

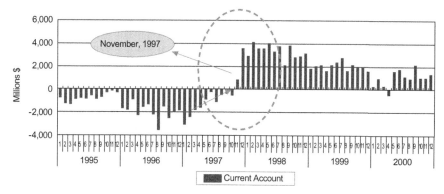

Figure 13.8 Monthly current account, 1995–2000

2.3 Structural policies

Along with tight macroeconomic policies, the IMF program also covered a wide range of reforms. Usually, structural policies are intended to change the fundamental rules of the game and took a long time for its intended effects to materialize. In the wake of the crisis, however, even structural reform policies could not be considered independent of the imminent economic situations. In particular, international investors were criticizing the Korean government for being non-transparent with no strong will to reform, ready to take any announcement as a litmus test for the Korean government's intention. Against this tenuous background, the structural policies also had to be designed to help restore international investors' confidence, and the basic direction of the policies had to align Korea's economic structure with "global standards". Some commentators often interpreted the direction of the policy as an effort of the western world to dismantle the "Asian model"; notwithstanding, the IMF pressed ahead with its reform agenda.

One of the first requests made by the IMF to the Korean government was to re-establish official statistics on foreign currency liquidity. This was critical since the Korean government completely lost its credibility in the international financial market. As explained earlier, the Korean government introduced a new definition of foreign reserves, taking into account "usable foreign reserves". At the same time, the Korean government was asked to come up with a new definition of foreign debt, "external payment burden", which included foreign debt financed and used by Korean firms offshore. These new statistical definitions explicitly revealed Korea's foreign currency liquidity situation. According to the old definition, Korea had maintained approximately $30 billion of foreign reserves until October 1997 and approximately $100 billion of foreign debt at the end of 1996 (the Korean government had not officially released stats on foreign debt since the beginning of 1997), but the new statistics showed that usable foreign reserves were less than $10 billion and the external payment burden was larger than $170 billion. The new statistics painted a far more gloomy picture of Korea's foreign currency situation, but at the same time, it showed the newfound willingness of the Korean government to take a more transparent approach with the international financial market. Since then, Korea has made meaningful progress in enhancing the transparency of its entire economic system. The accounting system was upgraded to levels of advanced economies, where the financial statements of firms were strictly monitored under the newly introduced system.

At the same time, financial market restructuring was initiated and drastically executed under the supervision of the IMF. First, it was announced that troubled major banks would be either sold to or merged into other (possibly foreign) banks and non-viable small banks (merchant bank corporations) would be closed. This was experimental, as something like this had never been implemented in Korea's history. For the longest time, banks were regarded as a policy arm of the government in controlling the corporate sector, including *chaebols*. Therefore, this announcement, particularly the government's commitment to sell one of the major banks to foreign investors within a short period of time, was taken as a strong signal that Korea was truly serious in its efforts to abandon "crony capitalism," which Korea had been harshly criticized for practicing by the international community.

In the wake of the financial crisis, it was natural that the reforms centered on the financial market. But the reform agenda was not confined within the financial market, since Korea had to show that it would expedite corporate and financial restructuring. In relation to rapid restructuring, the reform to enhance labor market flexibility was particularly important since the rigidity in the labor market was regarded as the most serious obstacle to economic restructuring. It was an extremely difficult task for Korea, where the security of lifetime employment was a given for more than 30 years. Indeed, the government had been frustrated with similar efforts to reform the labor market just a year ago. The difference from a year ago was that a sense of crisis had pervaded among Koreans and the political leadership. Right after being elected as the new president, Dae-Jung Kim committed to implementing emergency lay-off measures in a public conference.

2.4   *Negotiations between the Korean government and the IMF*

Clearly, the Korean government did not see eye-to-eye with the IMF regarding the policy package, particularly the degree to which the macroeconomic policies should be tightened, and the pace to which the restructuring policies should be implemented. Kyu-sung Lee (2010), the former minister of the Department of Finance and Economy wrote:

> The Korean government and the IMF in principle shared the basic strategy and thrust of the economic program, but disagreement did come up on such issues as the scope and the severity of the economic measures to be implemented. For its part, the government wanted to avoid drastic drop in growth and skyrocketing hike in interest rates in 1998. The government also wanted to buy some time for the failing merchant banks and commercial banks as it

had hoped when it announced restructuring measures on November 19, 1997. For accelerated trade and capital liberalization, the preferred position for the government was to pace it at the speed it agreed to under WTO and OECD negotiations. But the IMF had far more extensive and strong measures in mind. It demanded high interest rates and wanted to impose a cap on government budget. It also insisted on immediate shut down of the failing merchant banks and full removal of barriers to foreign trade and investment.

(2010, p. 85–86)

However, the Korean government, on the brink of default, was in desperate need of liquidity support from the IMF, leaving it hardly any negotiation power whatsoever. The Korean government also had all but lost its credibility in the eyes of the international financial market following a series of unclear and anti-market policies. Time was surely not on the side of the Korean government. In addition, there was no strong principal agent within the Korean government amidst the swirl of the presidential election. From the beginning, the IMF was destined to get its way, which to a large extent was in line with the position of the US. Kyu-sung Lee describes how Korea had to take the back seat, writing:

It was also during this time that David Lipton, the U.S. Under Secretary of the Treasury for International Affairs, visited Korea and held frequent talks with Hubert Neiss, IMF Director of Asian Affairs, to push for IMF measures. Michel Camdessus, the IMF Managing Director, also visited Korea as the technical details were being hammered out and demanded sharply enlarged response and liberalization packages. The IMF also insisted that the major presidential candidates made a pledge ahead of the presidential election to abide by the terms of the stand-by arrangement. The government did attempt to water down some of the more austere measures being put forth by the IMF, but in the end it had no choice but to accept what the IMF asked for. To urge the nervous government officials, Michel Camdessus emphatically argued that the crisis was a "blessing in disguise" that could help Korea cure its long-overlooked ills and came out of the crisis wholly revitalized and reinvigorated for a confident, bright future.

(2010, pp. 17–18)

It was under this atmosphere that Dae-Jung Kim hastened to commit to using emergency lay-off measures. During the presidential campaign, he pledged to re-negotiate the "stringent" IMF program if elected. His comments were severely criticized by the media, both domestic and international, forcing him to tone down the "re-negotiation" rhetoric just a few days later. On December 18, he was finally elected as the next president of Korea, grabbing the attention of the world. Within the world of Korean politics, President Kim was known as being pro-labor, likely to resist policies that favor labor market flexibility. After discussions with his advisors, however, President Kim decided to take emergency lay-off measures, which was expressed to David Lipton, who had been sent by the US government to find out if the new president indeed had the will to reform. The meeting was thought to have been critical in getting the US to announce on Christmas Eve its intention to provide additional liquidity support and to support the roll-over of loans lent to Korea by major creditor banks.

The National Assembly did not dare to resist the IMF either. The Financial Market Reform Act was passed on December 29, just one day after it was submitted to the National Assembly. This act was almost identical to the one submitted before the crisis and then suspended after a month of discussions only. But the IMF's endorsement of the act made it different this time. In short, the dire state of Korea's economic situation marginalized the Korean government's role to become a meaningful negotiation partner.

3.   Macroeconomic policy adjustments

The liquidity conditions continued to worsen, with little signs of abating despite $57 billion of support from the IMF in line with strong monetary and fiscal adjustments. Despite tight controls on the use of foreign exchange and upfront funding from the IMF, the economy continued to hemorrhage two weeks into the program. Private financing dried up, but worse, Korean banks had severe difficulty in rolling over their short-term debt in the midst of the turmoil and a cascade of credit downgrades by the credit rating agencies.

On top of this, the Korean economy began to contract far more rapidly than the IMF had anticipated. Under the extremely stringent financial conditions, many highly leveraged Korean firms went under, leaving many workers out in the street. For just one month from December 1997 to January 1998, approximately 5.7 percent of all workers lost their jobs. More tragic was that Korea, having never experienced such a massive loss of jobs, did not have a system to cope with the effects of mass unemployment. Clearly, this was a far more serious situation than the IMF had expected. Surprised by these unanticipated economic developments, the initial IMF program was augmented in some areas and revised in other areas.

3.1   *Restructuring short-term foreign debt maturities*

The IMF and the Korean government both clearly understood that the announcement of additional support with no real financial backing was at best a temporary fix for the liquidity problem, although it may offer some breathing room. They had to find a more durable and credible solution for the liquidity problem in order to break the downward spiral brought on by falling reserves and falling market confidence. Given the limitations of the IMF's financial support, a durable solution that addressed the financing need, not its availability, had to be found. A partial solution was already built-in to some extent into the IMF-supported economic program: namely macroeconomic policy tightening intended to suppress absorption in the short run and promote production in the medium run. But the continued liquidity problem demonstrated that the market was not willing to wait for the policies to take effect.

Against this background, a debt exchange program – the conversion of short-term debt into long-term debt – emerged as a durable and affordable solution to manage liquidity. In December 1997, the National Assembly approved a provision to guarantee foreign currency debt of up to $20 billion (plus interest) with a maturity of up to three years that was issued by domestic banks. At the same time, it approved the issuance of sovereign debt up to $10 billion. Various proposals on the specific format of debt exchange were made by international investors. Broadly speaking, the proposals could be classified into two types. The first format took the classic approach, which converts short-term debt into longer-term debt at a price directly negotiated with creditors. The second format took a market-based approach whereby short-term debt liabilities of individual banks were securitized and then auctioned off in the market. Since the underlying debt liabilities were all private, both formats demanded as a prerequisite some form of credit enhancement by the government. Specifically, a government guarantee was needed to consummate the deal under the first format, while government bonds were needed as collateral to back the securitization under the second format. In essence, the debt exchange program was a government bailout of the private debtors.

For good reasons, the government decided on the first format, conducting direct negotiations with the major creditors while restricting the eligibility of the debt exchange program to debt obligations of domestic banks. The market-based approach was perceived to be more risky because pricing could be very sensitive to market sentiments and investor herding behavior, for which the government had no way of controlling the outcome. In contrast, under the first approach, there was *prima facie* considerable room for the government to take advantage of non-price factors to get more favorable pricing, such as the long-term and strategic business interests of creditors in the profitable Korean market. Moreover, the government had little experience in dealing with short-term investors such as investment banks or hedge funds but found banks far more comfortable to deal with since they had a longer-term investment horizon.

The government requested Citibank, a long-time business partner with domestic banks, to coordinate meetings with 13 major creditor banks to conduct debt-exchange negotiations. The negotiations took place in New York in January 21, 1998, and were completed within 10 days. Before negotiations began, the government delegation had met with high-level US officials in Washington, including Treasury Secretary Robert Rubin and the Fed Chair Alan Greenspan, in order to signal Korea's strong resolve to overcome the crisis and garner their support to conclude successful negotiations. The basic message from Washington was that time was of the essence in respect to market confidence while pricing was secondary. Washington's message to Korea was not to waste time in trying to secure marginally better pricing. While there was some truth in Washington's view, pricing was equally, if not more, critical to the success of the negotiations from the perspective of the Korean government, as it had already become a highly politically charged issue in Seoul. The government was concerned about a possible political backlash if the debt exchange came at too high of a cost.

Despite the Korean government's guarantee of eligible debt, creditors demanded a high risk premium to participate in the debt exchange, questioning the financial credibility of the government guarantee. Korea dismissed their demand on the following grounds: (1) creditors should in principle be liable to losses since they would purchase debt that could default at a discount; (2) Korea had never defaulted on its external debt, either private (bank) or public; (3) Korea's strong fiscal austerity with very low public debt should have been taken into account when assessing the credibility of the government guarantee; and (4) any predatory pricing would do more harm than good for both parties by potentially putting solvency at risk at least in the near term. The final outcome of the negotiation resulted in the conversion of eligible (short-term) bank debt falling due in 1998 into government-guaranteed longer-term debt with maturity of up to three years at a premium (over the LIBOR) of 225, 250 and 275 basis points, respectively. The two- and three-year tranches were attached with a call-back option, exercisable six months after the debt exchange.

Compared with other debt restructuring cases in the context of crisis resolution in emerging market countries, Korea's experience stands out in two respects. First, the debt exchange agreement was reached very quickly – within 10 days. Second, no investor haircut was required to consummate the debt exchange. The existing literature on debt restructuring highlights the free-rider problem among investors as the key source of costly delays in debt negotiations. Given that the free-rider problem is more acute when investor haircuts are greater, the absence of a haircut in Korea's debt exchange program seems to have contributed to the quick conclusion of the negotiation.

This view begs the question: Could Korea have done better if it had pushed for a haircut? Albeit speculative (as no counterfactual is known), there are several reasons to believe that the answer is likely to be no. First, the cost of delay would seem to be far larger for Korea than for creditors who had already provisioned the expected loss from their exposure to Korea. Securing adequate external financing was of utmost priority to Korea simply because its economy was heavily dependent on exports; trade credit had almost vanished completely at the onset of the crisis while major exporters – large conglomerates – were already facing the heightened risk of default because of liquidity in both foreign and local currencies had dried up. A delay in the negotiations could thus have resulted in a greater output loss than realized. By contrast, the financial cost of paying a premium to rollover debt was only moderate if not small in terms of net present value because the extension of the debt maturity was expected to be short at less than three years. Second, Korea might have had to pay the price of the haircut later if it had pushed for a haircut. The existing evidence suggests that countries end up paying a higher risk premium on new debt and become less tolerant of debt after taking a haircut when restructuring their debt.

The debt exchange program was a great success. Thanks to the participation of 134 creditor banks in 32 countries, more than 96 percent of the total eligible debt ($21.84 billion out of $22.65 billion) was converted into debt with longer maturities: 17 percent of the debt was converted into debt with a one-year maturity;

45 percent into two-year maturity and 38 percent into three-year maturity. Successful completion of the debt-exchange provided real room for crisis resolution and paved the way for a successful issuance of $4 billion in global sovereign bonds in late 1998, marking the return of Korea to the international capital markets.

While the primary objective was to help mitigate the immediate liquidity shortage, the debt-exchange program yielded other desirable effects in the overall dynamics of the crisis, some of which were realized even before the completion of the debt exchange. First, by resolving the liquidity problem at a moderate cost in relation to the increase in the present value of external debt, the debt exchange program helped Korea avoid the pending risk of inefficient default brought about by a liquidity crunch rather than by unsustainable long-term fundamentals, which subsequently altered the risk calculation of investors and their appetite for Korean assets. Second, it also enabled domestic banks to reduce the risk of default due to the adverse impact of foreign currency liabilities on their balance sheets. In principle, the effect of a currency devaluation on the balance sheet applies to all unhedged foreign currency liabilities. However, the actual cost from this effect on the balance sheet would arise from the debt that is serviced during the period when the exchange rate is at abnormal levels, ceasing once rates returned to normal levels. By converting a large amount of the domestic bank's short-term debt, the debt exchange program effectively reduced the cost of balance sheet effects insofar as the exchange rate is expected to return to more normal levels within a year. In this respect, the moderate premium paid for exchanging debt may not constitute a real economic cost. As discussed below, this benefit of the debt-exchange program has important implications when the monetary policy is eased in the later part of 1998. Third, the debt-exchange program provided enough breathing room to implement macroeconomic policies, allowing Korea to avoid unnecessary and painful tight policy actions intended to close the financing gap.

3.2 Fiscal policy adjustments

Along with the restructuring of external debt, some adjustments were made to Korea's internal macroeconomic policies to match changing economic conditions (see Figure 13.9). The IMF began to ease its restrictive fiscal policy stance. Chopra et al. describes this process from the IMF's perspective:

> By the end of December 1997 the extent of the crisis was becoming more clear, leading the government and the IMF to reconsider the appropriateness of the initial fiscal policy response. Rather than trying to maintain a fiscal balance, the revised December program focused on allowing the automatic stabilizers to operate and tolerating a deficit in the short term . . . By early 1998, at the urging of the Fund the government changed the direction of its fiscal policy and started to put greater emphasis on providing fiscal stimulus and lessening the consequences of the crisis on the poor and the unemployed.
>
> (2000, p. 42)

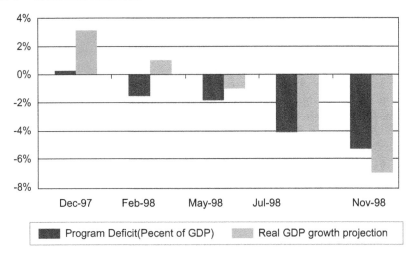

Figure 13.9 Growth forecasts and budget plans
Reproduced from Chopra et al. (2000).

As the perception of Korea's economic conditions changed, the fiscal policy in the fifth agreement between the Korean government and the IMF was officially revised in February 1998. Yet, the first revision was extremely modest and focused on temporary fiscal outlays for the unemployed. Chopra et al. continues:

> In February . . . the government concluded an agreement that increased unemployment-related spending by about 1/2 percent of GDP. This effort, as well as other increases in safety net spending included in the March 1998 supplementary budget, led to an increase in the projected deficit to 1 and 1/2 percent of GDP. . . . By July, following a sharp fall in output and amid increasing social pressures, the authorities dramatically shifted gears with an introduction of supplementary budget.
>
> (2000, pp. 42–43)

Any meaningful change in the fiscal policy, more accommodative to economic expansion, did not come until July 1998. That is, a very restrictive fiscal policy regime reigned during the most painful period of the crisis, the first half of 1998. This was probably due to the inaccurate economic projections, which were a product of the IMF's under-estimation of the severity of the crisis and the destructive effects of a high interest rate policy given the fragile financial structure of the Korean firms. Roughly speaking, the debt size of the corporate sector was 1.8 times as high as Korea's annual GDP, which implies that a 5 percentage increase in the interest rate would squeeze the corporate sector's cash-flow by 9 percent of annual GDP! A profit squeeze of this magnitude could have the potential to wipe out almost the entire corporate sector's profit. At least *ex post*, the adjustment to the fiscal policy, taken in 1998, seems to have lagged.

3.3 Monetary policy adjustments

Unlike the fiscal policy, which was tightened in the very early phase of the program but relaxed relatively soon, monetary tightening lasted, albeit being gradually eased, until the third quarter of 1998. The main underlying rationale for the tight monetary policy was the concern about the exchange rate stability, which the IMF viewed was improving but fragile at least until mid-1998.

The government viewed the situation rather differently from the IMF as the usable foreign reserve recovered and the exchange rate was steadily appreciating in 1998. In due course, the government urged the IMF to change its view on monetary policy several times during IMF program reviews and policy consultations and international meetings. But the IMF remained reluctant to make discrete changes to the monetary policy and opted for a more gradual approach.

3.3.1 Cautious easing until Q3, 1998

By 1998, the foreign currency liquidity situation began to stabilize and foreign reserves began to increase. This was in large part due to the early redemption by the commercial banks, which only eroded public reserves before the penalty interest rates were charged. In addition, the successful conclusion to the restructuring of the foreign debt by extending their maturity substantially relieved liquidity pressures on the foreign currency. The amount of usable foreign reserve rapidly recovered to almost $20 billion by the end of February and continued to increase and recover back to the pre-crisis level of $30 billion by the end of April. The improvement in foreign currency liquidity was critical of itself in avoiding the possibility of a national default. At the same time, its implication of the interest rate policy were validating, as far as the single most important reason for implementing a high interest rate policy was to restore foreign currency liquidity. In particular, the remaining balance of the commercial banks' borrowings from the BOK (roughly measured by the difference between the total and usable foreign reserves) fell sufficiently by the end of April 1998, suggesting that the marginal benefit of imposing high penalty rates on these borrowings was substantially reduced (see Figure 13.10).

In line with steady improvement in the foreign exchange market and foreign currency liquidity condition of domestic banks, the tightening bias in monetary policy was gradually relaxed. The overnight call rate fell from its peak at almost 30 percent at the end of 1997 to below 20 percent in May 1998 and further down to around 15 percent in July. The yield curve, which had remained inverted since the crisis, reflecting the immediate default risk associated with the liquidity crunch, also returned to positive slope in June 1998 (see Figure 13.11).

However, the economy remained depressed in the midst of serial corporate bankruptcies and high unemployment. Domestic credit fell in nominal terms due in part to economic contraction but also due to heightened risk aversion on the side of banks, many of which were desperate to meet the capital adequacy requirements. The government and the BOK instituted various prudential and incentive measures as well as moral suasion to encourage banks to take greater risks in

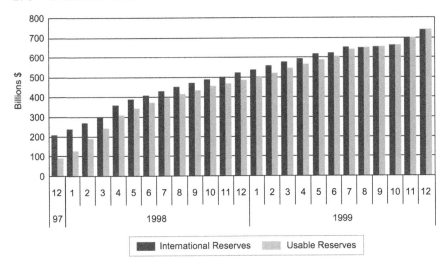

Figure 13.10 Foreign reserves, total and usable

Data Sources: Bank of Korea, Monthly.

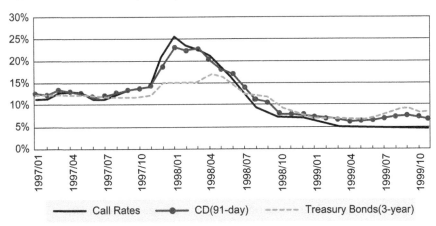

Figure 13.11 Interest rates by maturity

Data Sources: Bank of Korea, Monthly.

lending and help ease funding difficulties and credit crunch faced by firms – particularly small- and medium-sized enterprises (SMEs). Government credit guarantees were issued to loans to SMEs while the BOK increased the credit ceiling for lending to SMEs. In addition, restrictions on equity and corporate bond issues were relaxed in order to help large corporations to fund directly from the market while at the same time government insurance was provided on trade credit.

Notwithstanding various microeconomic policy measures to dampen economic difficulties, major macroeconomic indicators rapidly deteriorated. During the first half of 1998, industrial production collapsed by almost 8 percent, and private consumption and facility investment contracted by more than 14 percent and

40 percent, respectively. The unemployment rate that had skyrocketed to 4.7 percent in January 1998 from 2.1 percent in October 1997 kept rising toward almost 8 percent. The economy was literally in a state of "depression".

Along with the collapse in the real economy, the rate of inflation also soared to almost 10 percent in the first half of 1998. But this year-on-year inflation rate is likely misleading and needs to be interpreted with care. The inflation caused by currency depreciation is usually unsustainable and likely to subside as soon as the exchange rate stabilizes. In fact, the CPI increased at a slower rate from March 1998 as the exchange rate began to stabilize and the month-to-month inflation rate fell down to almost zero. That is, although the year-on-year inflation rate was hovering around 10 percent, there were no sustainable pressures on inflation from domestic economic conditions (see Figures 13.12–13.14).

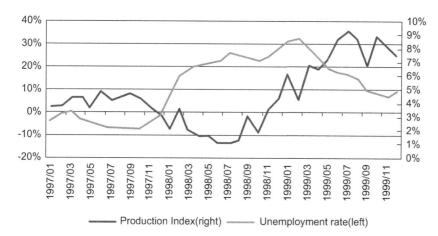

Figure 13.12 Industrial production (year-on-year growth) and unemployment rate
Data Sources: Bank of Korea, Statistics Korea, Monthly.

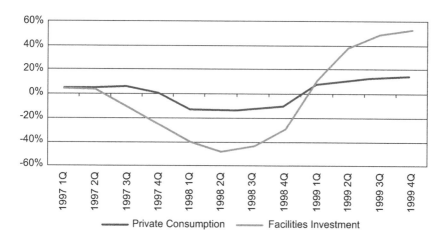

Figure 13.13 Private consumption and facility investment (year-on-year growth)

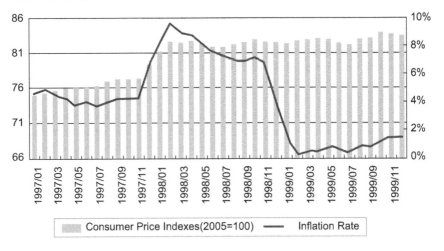

Figure 13.14 CPI and the year-on-year inflation rate
Data Sources: Statistics Korea, Monthly.

Nevertheless, the interest rate policy was eased very cautiously until the third quarter of 1998, as can be seen in the series of agreements between the Korean government and the IMF.

> Money market rates will be allowed to rise sufficiently and will be maintained at that level or higher as needed to stabilize the market.
>
> (Dec. 3, 1997)

> Raise call rates to 30%, or above if needed, to stabilize the exchange rate.
>
> (December 24, 1997)

> Call rates have been at around 30% since Dec. 26 and will be kept high until the foreign exchange situation improves.
>
> (January 1998)

> With the mitigation of the immediate foreign exchange crisis, call rates will be cautiously allowed to ease, in line with continued exchange rate stabilization.
>
> (February 1998)

> Interest rate policy will continue to be conducted in a flexible and symmetric manner. Subject to the objective of maintaining stability in the foreign exchange market, call interest rates will continue to be lowered, in line with market conditions.
>
> (May 1998)

Interest rate policy will continue to be conducted in a flexible manner with upward and downward adjustments as necessary.

(July 1998)

Easy monetary stance will be maintained . . .

(November 1998)

Clearly, the IMF was reluctant to send a message to the market that aggressive monetary policy actions would be taken to boost the economy until the fourth quarter of 1998.

3.3.2   Aggressive easing from Q4, 1998

By the end of the second quarter in 1998, the macroeconomic trends – both external and domestic – were clearly suggesting that the major risks to the recovery lay more on the side of depressed economic activities than on unstable external financing. On the external side, the capital account stabilized noticeably and the usable foreign reserves reached a comfortable level of almost $40 billion with further increases expected, while the current account was projected to record a surplus of over $30 billion by the year's end. By contrast, the economy kept deteriorating further and the unemployment rate hovered at 8 percent. In the forecast published on June 30, 1998, the Korea Development Institute, a public economic think tank, projected the GDP growth rate in 1998 to be –4.2 percent, while expecting the annual current account surplus to reach $35 billion.

The government was keen on persuading the IMF and the BOK to change their views on the appropriate monetary policy. While clearly understanding the risk arising from the credit crunch and corporate failures, the BOK as well as the IMF was nevertheless far less flexible than the government in changing their policy stance, preferring to stay on a course of gradual rather than aggressive easing. The BOK was also concerned about the risk to destabilizing the exchange rate after the hard won victory of stabilizing it, as the Russian debt moratorium in August 1998 and the ensuing long-term capital management (LTCM) crisis created significant jitters in the international financial markets.

The IMF and the BOK were not alone; many opinion leaders in Korea voiced their concern against aggressive easing of the monetary policy. Their basis of reasoning was diverse. Some simply argued that any further interest rate cut was not necessary because (nominal) interest rates were already at pre-crisis levels of around 12 percent by July 1998. Others argued that real interest rates were already very low considering the year-on-year inflation rate was almost 10 percent, although real interest rates should be assessed considering the expected inflation rate rather than the rate realized in the past. Also, there were opinions that monetary easing would not be effective in revitalizing the economy under the prevailing credit crunch. In this vein, the BOK even argued that it was impossible to supply additional liquidity to the market because commercial banks kept returning it back to the BOK. But, this was evidence for a higher-than-normal policy interest rate in that commercial banks found it sufficiently more attractive to put their money in the BOK rather than increasing risk-bearing investments. Another popular argument against monetary easing was that it would derail the corporate restructuring efforts and thus should be carried out after the restructuring process was completed. However, no exact definition was provided on what the "end of the restructuring process" would be or how long it would take.

On the other hand, the KDI had kept arguing for monetary easing since April. In August at last, KDI, backed by supporting analysis and evidence, reported directly to the Finance Minister Kyu-Sung Lee on the urgent need to ease monetary policy to combat deflationary rather than inflationary pressures. The report pointed out why the above-mentioned arguments against monetary easing were groundless and argued that the exchange rate was stable enough to withstand lower interest rates. In fact, economic contraction constituted the most serious risk to the recovery. The report was immediately discussed in a high-level emergency meeting attended by the BOK governor, the finance minister, and the president of KDI. The report was not disclosed to the public but was a breakthrough in shaping a consensus between the BOK and the government on the need for aggressive monetary easing. Against this backdrop, the government was ready to consult with the IMF on monetary policy with strong analytical support. In September, the IMF finally agreed to hand over monetary policymaking discretion to Korea, paving the way for monetary policy aimed at stimulating a recovery over the coming months.

On the last day of September, the BOK made a bold move and cut the overnight call interest rate target by 100 basis points from 8.25 to 7.25 percent, along with a clear announcement that it would continue to lower the interest rate to boost the economy. It was the first time in the Korea's economic history that the target interest rate was lowered by 100 basis points within a day. The interest rate continued to be lowered to unprecedented levels. At the risk of exaggeration, the steep lowering of the policy interest rate since September 30 was almost equally as dramatic as the steep increase that ensued immediately after the crisis a year ago. The overnight call rate fell to below 5 percent by March 1999, falling by nearly half of what it was at the end of September.

As the monetary policy stance swung to stimulus from tightening, the economy began to respond. The most immediate response was observed in the stock market. The stock price index that had collapsed to around 300 points after the crisis began to soar and reached around 1,000 points within just 10 months. Foreign investors rushed into the Korean stock market, pushing the currency value despite lower interest rates. Macroeconomic indicators also began to rebound, showing signs of a recovery. Private consumption began to recover and corporate investment followed. As the overall economic condition improved, firms resumed hiring workers. The perpetual rise in the unemployment rate peaked at 8.8 percent in February 1999 and then began to subside at a rapid pace. The Korean economy in 1999 grew by more than 10 percent of GDP and less than 1 percent of CPI inflation. After labeling Korea as a country torn by economic crisis, the world turned around to acclaim its successful recovery from crisis.

In retrospect, the Russian and LTCM crises were a market test for Korea's resilience to international financial shocks, and Korea passed the test with virtually no signs of major dislocation in economic or financial activities. These two events and Korea's successful navigation through rough waters assured the government and the IMF that the exchange rate stability thus far maintained was indeed sustainable. As discussed earlier, resolving the liquidity shortage early on and in a sustainable manner through the debt-exchange program was essential in building up Korea's resilience to external shocks. Such confidence in the exchange rate stability, together with depressed economic activities driven by a severe credit crunch, formed a strong basis for making major changes in the macroeconomic policy – in particular, reversing the tightening bias in monetary policy that had been maintained since the onset of the crisis. The dramatic turnaround in the course of monetary policy in the last quarter of 1998 was a turning point for Korea in overcoming the crisis.

4. Summary and assessments

The Korean economy was on a rollercoaster ride for the three years from 1997 to 1999. It suffered from the deepest recession since its takeoff in the 1960s and achieved a brisk recovery that surprised the whole world. It successfully altered a flood of criticism into a deluge of complements. Behind this turn-around lay a dramatic swing in macroeconomic policies.

Normally, macroeconomic policies that expand the magnitude of economic fluctuations can hardly be justified: standard textbooks teach us that the goal of macroeconomic policies is to stabilize economic fluctuations. It may be justifiable, however, if the economic situation is exceptional, as was the case of Korea with the onset of the currency crisis. At the brink of national default, it seemed inevitable that policy priority was placed on restoring foreign currency liquidity, while all policy measures were aligned with this objective in mind.

In this regard, the high interest rate policy immediately after the outbreak of the currency crisis was necessary and appeared to have contributed to the early recovery of Korea's foreign reserves. In contrast, however, the basis for a tight fiscal policy was not sound in the case of Korea, in which the government's financial state was sound and, therefore, a short-term fiscal expansion would not have had any negative implications on foreign currency liquidity. Although the stance was reversed afterwards, the fiscal tightening in the initial stage of the crisis can hardly be assessed to be appropriate.

As for the monetary policy, reservations remain, particularly in consideration of the situation after March 1998, when the maturities of the short-term debt had been successfully restructured and foreign currency liquidity stabilized. With the wisdom of hindsight, Cho assessed the monetary policy during this period, writing:

> It is always difficult to determine an appropriate monetary policy, not just ex ante but also ex post. . . . Of course, data on current macroeconomic conditions become available only with a lag, and monetary policy must be

formulated on the basis of uncertain forecasts. In practice, however, it is hard to invoke uncertainty as a justification for the maintenance of high interest rates beyond the first quarter of 1998. Few if any macroeconomic indicators signaled the danger of accelerating future inflation after March; if anything, most variables pointed to the danger of deflation. The exchange rate, which was the leading indicator of short-term price movements during the crisis, began stabilizing in February 1998. Nominal wages, which may be a more informative guide to medium-term inflationary pressures, actually fell in 1998 relative to the preceding calendar year. In short, it is hard to justify the maintenance of the high interest rate policy after the first quarter of 1998, unless one sticks to a possibly deficient indicator like the year-on-year inflation rate.

(2004, p. 109)

However, the root cause of the high interest rate policy stemmed from the past mismanagement of foreign currency liquidity. In this regard, the rigid exchange rate policy in 1996 that delayed the necessary adjustments to the balance-of-payment deserves blame. Had the government taken the market pressures to deflate the Korean won earlier, the balance-of-payments would have turned around earlier and the Korean economy would have had preserved a minimum level of foreign reserve as a buffer, which in turn would not have forced the hand of the monetary authority to take such a painfully high interest rate policy.

More fundamentally, of course, Korea's crisis was caused by the fragile financial structure of the whole economy. Highly leveraged investments that had low returns could not be sustained indefinitely. In particular, when this behavior is heavily geared toward short-term foreign debts – public or private – the economy becomes highly susceptible to a simultaneous crisis in both domestic and foreign currency finances – a twin crisis.

In this regard, the structural reforms led by the IMF greatly helped the Korean economy in the long run, though it added more pain to an already struggling economy in the short run. Most of these reforms were already proposed by Korean experts and some of them were even submitted to the National Assembly before the crisis, but the political environment was not ripe to push through the reforms. Many would agree that, without the crisis and the intervention of the IMF, those reforms would have been delayed for possibly some decades. At least in this sense, the crisis may have been a "blessing in disguise" in the long run, as often dubbed by Michel Camdessus, the managing director of the IMF, during the crisis. Yet, the long-run benefits of the blessing might have been realized more smoothly if more appropriate macroeconomic policies had been taken.

Note

* This chapter is reprinted from the *Korea Knowledge Sharing Program Report*, Ministry of Strategy and Finance of Korea and Korea Development Institute, March 2010.

References

Cho, Dongchul, 1999. "Recovering from the Crisis: Where the Korean Economy Stands?" *KDI Working Paper*, Seoul.

———, 1999b. "A year after the Korean Economic Crisis: What Next?" Korea Development Institute, January.

———, 2004. "The Monetary Policy Response to the Crisis," in *The Korean Economy Beyond the Crisis*, edited by Duk-Koo Chung and Barry Eichengreen, pp. 89–112. Cheltenham: Edward Elgar Publishing Inc.

Chopra, Ajai, Kenneth Kang, Meral Karasulu, Hong Liang, Henry Ma, and Anthony Richards, 2000. "From Crisis to Recovery in Korea: Strategy, Achievements, and Lessons," in *Korean Crisis and Recovery*, edited by David T. Coe and Se-jik Kim, pp. 13–104. Washington, DC: International Monetary Fund and Korea Institute for International Economic Policy.

Fischer, Stanley, 1998. "The Asian Crisis: A View from the IMF," IMF, Washington, DC, www.imf.org/external/np/speeches/1998/012298.htm.

Furman, Jason, and Joseph E. Stiglitz, 1998. "Economic Crises: Evidence and Insights from East Asia," *Brookings Papers on Economic Activity*, pp. 1–114.

Government of Korea, 1997–1998. "Letter of Intent," www.imf.org, various issues.

Korea Development Institute, 1998. "KDI Economic Forecast," Seoul (in Korean).

"Korea Letter of Intent," December 3, 1997, www.imf.org.

Krueger, Anne O., 2000. "Conflicting Demands on the International Monetary Funds," *The American Economic Review*, 90(2), pp. 38–42.

Lee, Kyu-sung, 2010. "Korea's Financial Crisis: Onset, Turnaround and Thereafter," *manuscript* (forthcoming, World Bank).

Lim, Wonhyuk, 2003. "The Emergence of the *Chaebol* and the Origins of the *Chaebol* Problem," in *Economic Crisis and Corporate Restructuring in Korea*, edited by Stephan Haggard, Wonhyuk Lim and Euysung Kim, pp. 35–52. Cambridge: Cambridge University Press.

"Republic of Korea: IMF Stand-By Arrangement, Summary of Economic Program," December 5, 1997, www.imf.org.

14 The monetary policy response to the crisis*

1. Introduction

Korean history will probably record the last three years of the 20th century as a period of dramatic economic policy experiments. Reforms affected virtually the entire economy, from financial and labor markets to the corporate and government sectors.

Macroeconomic policy was no exception. Immediately following the outbreak of the crisis, the fiscal authority decided to mobilize funds totaling more than 12 percent of GDP for purposes of financial sector restructuring. But this was nothing compared to the revolution in monetary policy. In November and December 1997, when the currency crisis was triggered, stabilization of the exchange rate had been the foremost policy objective. The fluctuation of the currency was limited to a narrow range and a variety of restrictions were maintained on capital inflows and outflows. The crisis led to a complete about face: the exchange rate was allowed to float freely and the capital account was liberalized. Inflation targeting was introduced as a legal mandate, and the intermediate target of monetary policy was shifted from the monetary aggregates such as M2 to short-term interest rates.[1]

Perhaps the most dramatic and controversial aspect was interest rate policy. Overnight inter-bank call rates were raised to more than 30 percent from the previous level of 12 to 13 percent in order to attract capital inflows and limit outflows. Partly in response, the GDP growth rate plunged to –8 percent (year-on-year) in the second quarter of 1998, and the unemployment rate skyrocketed to more than 8 percent, from less than 3 percent before the crisis. A large number of firms, unable to bear the now higher costs of servicing their debts, were plunged into bankruptcy, and the volume of non-performing loans in the financial sector rose explosively.

Eventually, the foreign exchange market stabilized, and the call rate was lowered to 8 percent by the end of September 1998. On September 30, the Bank of Korea lowered the call rate target by 100 basis points, signaling that the goal of monetary policy had shifted from stabilizing the currency's value to boosting the economy. The call rate continued to be lowered until it hit historically low levels of 4 to 5 percent, inaugurating the era of "super-low interest rates". The path of interest rates is shown in Figure 14.1, together with the won/dollar exchange rate, and along with the corresponding variables in Thailand and the Philippines.

There has been no shortage of arguments criticizing and defending the interest rate policies adopted in response to the crisis. The relevant literature is already very

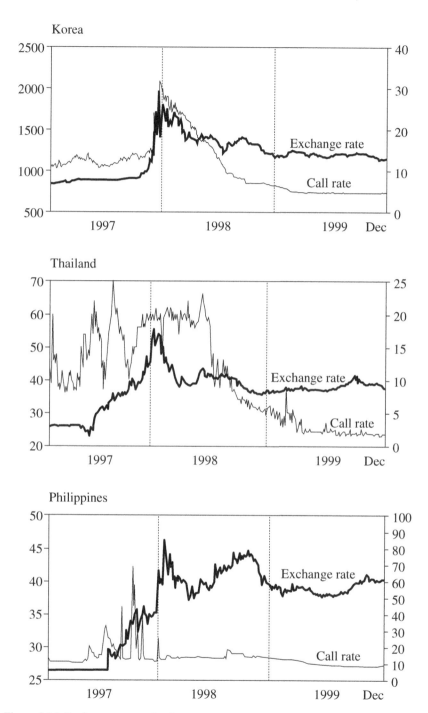

Figure 14.1 Exchange rate and call rate

large. Rather than surveying this terrain again, in this chapter I focus on two issues that require further clarification and that would benefit from additional research. These issues are whether the high interest rate policy was effective in stabilizing the exchange rate and whether post-crisis interest rate policy was too tight or too lose when judged from the vantage point of the literature on optimal interest rate rules.

2.   The high interest rate policy

Interest rate policy was at the center of the crisis program designed by the International Monetary Fund and implemented by the Korean government. The country's agreement with the IMF essentially declared that the immediate goal was to stabilize the exchange rate (not inflation or the level of output) and that the interest rate would be raised substantially to achieve this end.[2]

2.1   *Theoretical underpinnings*

Along with questions about whether this focus on stabilizing the exchange rate was justified as a way of restoring confidence in financial markets and stability to the Korean economy, given that the country had already taken some steps toward making its exchange rate more flexible in the years leading up to the crisis, the presumption that interest rate hikes were the appropriate device for achieving that goal was also challenged in the literature on the Asian crisis countries (see e.g. Furman and Stiglitz, 1998). The conceptual framework laid out by Cho and West (2001) is helpful for addressing this question. That framework starts with the uncovered interest parity condition, which can be written as:

$$i_t = E_t s_{t+1} - s_t + d_t. \tag{1}$$

where i_t is (net) domestic interest rates; s_t is the log of the spot exchange rate (with higher values indicating depreciation); E_t denotes expectations; and d_t is a risk premium that incorporates the fluctuation of foreign interest rates. The orthodox relationship follows directly: if i_t is increased, but $E_t s_{t+1}$ and d_t are unchanged, then s_t must fall (the exchange rate must appreciate).

This channel may be offset, however, insofar as increases in the interest rate are associated with increases in the risk premium. That is, the effect of i_t on s_t depends on the indirect but endogenous movement of d_t, which may be represented by:

$$d_t = di_t + u_{dt}, \tag{2}$$

where d is a parameter and u_{dt} is a disturbance term. The conventional view would be $d < 0$ or $d = 0$. In an alternative view, such as that of Furman and Stiglitz (1998), $d \gg 0$, higher interest rates are associated with higher risk.

It is important to note that while the monetary authority sent consistent signals that the high interest rate policy was temporary, it also indicated that the timing of its abandonment would depend on the movement of the exchange rate. Since investors in the currency market were forward looking, they presumably incorporated this information into their expectations. This idea can be captured by modeling i_t as endogenously determined through the policy reaction function:

$$i_t = aE_{t-1}s_t + u_{mt} \tag{3}$$

where a is a parameter and u_{mt} is a disturbance term. The IMF's preferences can be modeled by assuming $a > 0$; in other words, the monetary authority leans against expected exchange rate depreciation.

Equations (1)–(3) can be used to derive solutions for the three endogenous variables, i_t, s_t, and d_t, under the stability assumption $0 < b \equiv [1 + a(1 - d)]^{-1} < 1$. In order to make the implications more transparent, assume that both u_{dt} and u_{mt} follow AR(1) processes with the AR coefficients $0 < \phi_d < 1$ and $0 < \phi_m < 1$, respectively: $u_{dt} = \phi_d u_{dt-1} + \varepsilon_{dt}$ and $u_{mt} = \phi_m u_{mt-1} + \varepsilon_{mt}$, where ε_{dt} and ε_{mt} are innovations. The Appendix uses these assumptions to derive explicit solutions for the effects of exogenous variables. Figure 14.2 summarizes those solutions intuitively.

Suppose that there was a shock to the risk premium term, ε_{dt}, at time 0. (This can be thought of as capturing the impact of the crisis elsewhere in Asia on Korea.) This unanticipated increase in risk causes the exchange rate to depreciate and the interest rate to rise (i.e. both i_t and s_t rise). In Figure 14.1, this is represented by an upward shift of the interest rate-exchange rate frontier which connects the equilibrium values of s_t and i_t (where the parameter a is still to be determined).[3] If it is assumed that the risk premium is persistent (that is, that $\phi_d > 0$) and that the system is stable ($0 < b \equiv [1 + a(1 - d)]^{-1} < 1$), then the frontier gradually shifts back to the origin following the shock. One may justify this persistence by the fact that the restoration of market confidence or foreign reserves takes time.

Given this frontier, a monetary authority for which the level of the exchange rate appears in the objective function can resort to two tools. First, it can operate on investors' expectations by announcing a monetary policy rule. This can be captured by assuming an increase in the parameter a and by the upward rotation of the diagonal line in Figure 14.1. By announcing their policy rule, the monetary

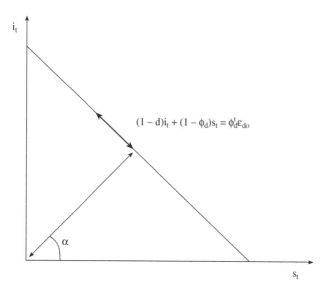

Figure 14.2 Determination of the exchange rate and the interest rate

authority chooses a value of a, which pins down the economy's position (in other words, it pins down a particular equilibrium pair of s_t and i_t along the interest rate-exchange rate frontier). In the extreme case where a approaches infinity, we have the case of a currency board system, as in Hong Kong. At the other extreme, as a approaches zero, only s_t adjusts, while i_t is fixed. By raising a, the case in question, the monetary authority declares that interest rate policy will henceforth more closely target fluctuations in the exchange rate. If credible, this policy announcement can feed into the investors' expectations about the future path of the interest rates, which will be stabilizing immediately. This is the "signaling effect".

The monetary authority's second tool is to adopt a policy stance that is even more contractionary than anticipated by the market. This is represented by a positive value for ε_{mt} and by movement in Figure 14.1 along the interest rate-exchange rate frontier in a northeast direction. As shown in the Appendix, a contractionary monetary shock (under the assumption of stability) causes the interest rate to rise and the exchange rate to appreciate; again, this is the orthodox effect. By this interpretation, the collapse of Korea's exchange rate was caused by an increase in the perceived level of risk, and the exchange rate would have collapsed still more dramatically than was actually the case had the monetary authority not pursued a policy even more contractionary than anticipated by the market.

One important point to note from this discussion is that the goal of the high interest rate policy taken to stabilize the exchange rate was not just to surprise the market with an unusually tight monetary policy but also to impress upon investors the intentions of the monetary authorities. That is, the authorities sought to stabilize the exchange rate by exploiting what is referred to above as the signaling effect. The repeated announcements of the Korean government and the IMF regarding the stance of monetary policy suggest that the policymakers were attempting to utilize this signaling channel.

Unfortunately, this analysis suggesting that high interest rate policy was indeed effective in stabilizing the exchange rate is contingent on the validity of the stability assumption – in other words, that $0 < b \equiv [1 + a(1 - d)]^{-1} < 1$. If the risk premium is sufficiently responsive to the interest rate ($d > 1$), then the model becomes unstable and the preceding logic breaks down. In this case, the appropriate policy for stabilizing the exchange rate is to reduce interest rates ($a < 0$). This may be the case that Furman and Stiglitz (1998) had in mind – that higher interest rates so increased the cost of servicing the heavy debt loans of Korean banks and firms that investors began worrying about the possible bankruptcy of Korean enterprise, leading them to demand a higher risk premium for holding Korean assets. This, then, is the heterodox result. While the preceding model helps by identifying the issues and assumptions on which the controversy turns, that controversy can be resolved only by examining the data.

2.1   Empirical findings

Table 14.1 summarizes empirical research on the impact of interest rates on the exchange rate in the context of the Asian crisis. General conclusions are evidently difficult to draw. Indeed, there may be good reasons why empirical work in this

Table 14.1 Summary of previous empirical research

Authors	Data	Methodology	Conclusion
Goldfajn and Baig (1998)	Various data including daily time-series datafive Asian crisis countries (1997–1998): Indonesia, Korea, Malaysia, Philippines, Thailand Five other crisis countries: Mexico (1982), Chile (1982), Sweden (1992), UK (1992), Mexico (1994)	Estimation of real exchange rates, real interest rates, and real interest parity relation	The evidence is mixed, but on balance favors the view that the higher interest rates were associated with appreciations in crisis-hit Asian countries.
Park and Choi (1999)	Daily time-series data Korea (97/4/1–98/10/30) Indonesia (97/1/3–98/7/24) Malaysia (97/1/3–98/7/24) Thailand (97/1/20–98/7/24)	Single equation regression using forward exchange rates as control variables	High interest rates appear to cause exchange rate appreciation except for Malaysia.
Dekle, Hsiao and Wang (1999)	Weekly time-series data (1997–1998): Korea, Malaysia, Thailand	VAR	Interest rate hikes led to exchange rate appreciation, though with long and variable lags.
Goldfajn and Gupta (1999)	Cross-country data for the countries that have undergone currency crises during the period of 1980–1998.	Panel data regressions with various descriptive measures	Dramatic increases in interest rates have been associated with currency appreciation. But there was no clear association for a subsample of countries that have undergone a banking crisis along with a currency crisis.
Tanner (1999)	Monthly time-series data (1/1990–12/1998): Indonesia, Korea, Thailand, Brazil, Chile, Mexico	VAR, whose variables include exchange market pressures (the sum of exchange rate depreciation and reserve outflows), monetary policy stance, and the differential between domestic and foreign interest rates.	Contractionary monetary policy helps reduce exchange market pressures.

(Continued)

Table 14.1 (Continued)

Authors	Data	Methodology	Conclusion
Gould and Kamin (2000)	Weekly time-series datafive crisis-hit Asian countries (1997–1998): Indonesia, Korea, Malaysia, Philippines, Thailand	Use measures of international credit spreads and of domestic stock prices as proxies for investor concerns about creditworthiness and country risk.	Unable to find a reliable relationship between interest rates and exchange rates.
Cho and West (2000)	Daily time-series dataKorea (12/17/97–6/30/99)	Single equation regressions and Vector Error Correction Model	Although the major driving force of the exchange rate stabilization seems to be the recovery of the foreign currency liquidity position, the high interest rate appears to have contributed to the stabilization of the exchange rate.
Barsurto and Ghosh (2000)	Monthly time-series data (1/1990–12/1998): Indonesia, Korea, Thailand	Identify the risk premium by the difference between the actual exchange rate and the (pure monetary model based) theoretical exchange rate, and relate thus defined risk premium with the interest rate policy.	Tighter monetary policy was associated with an appreciation of the exchange rate, and there is little evidence of higher interest rates contributing to a widening of the risk premium.
Aart Kraay (2000)	Data for speculative attack periods in a sample of 75 developed and developing countries over the period 1960–1997.	Examine the behavior of interest rates around successful and failed speculative attacks.	There is no systematic association between interest rates and the outcome of speculative attacks.
Cho and West (2001)	Weekly time-series data: Korea (12/17/97–12/16/98), Philippines (7/23/97–7/22/98), Thailand (7/23/97–7/22/98)	Estimate structural parameters of the model composed of two equations, a monetary policy reaction function, and an interest parity relationship.	Point estimates indicate that exogenous increases in interest rates led to exchange rate appreciation in Korea and the Philippines, depreciation in Thailand, but the confidence intervals are huge.

area is inconclusive. First, the high interest rate policy was maintained for only a limited time, six months to a year depending on the country concerned. Even if weekly data are available, this still provides only 25 to 50 observations and few degrees of freedom for empirical work. Daily data provide more degrees of freedom but contain substantial amounts of noise.

Second, there is the problem of identification (whether we observing the impact of monetary policy on the variable or variables of interest – the exchange rate, for example – or the effect of those other variables on monetary policy). Although identification problems are pervasive in empirical macroeconomics, identification is likely to be particularly difficult in currency crisis periods, which feature large disturbances and structural shifts.

Nevertheless, there is some evidence of the orthodox effect of high interest rates in Korea. Park and Choi (1999), Dekle, Hsiao and Wang (1999), Tanner (1999), Barsurto and Ghosh (2000), and Cho and West (2000, 2001) all find evidence for the orthodox effect in the Korean data, although their findings for other Asian countries is more mixed. As an experiment, Figure 14.3 shows the impulse responses estimated from bivariate vector autoregressions (VARs) for the exchange rate and the interest rate, country by country.[4] Bearing in mind all the reservations why VARs like these should be regarded cautiously, the left-hand figure for each country can be interpreted as showing the effect of an increase in the interest rate on the exchange rate. These results suggest that Korea was the only country where interest rate hikes led to appreciation of the exchange rate.

Why then was the result different in Korea? There are several potential explanations. The first of these is destructive: it is the possibility of misidentification. Specifically, there is the danger of misattributing to monetary policy the effects of two important country-specific events that may have significantly affected the investors' expectations in the currency market and thereby the exchange rate. The first such event was the announcement by the US government on December 24, 1997, that a second line of emergency loans from G-7 countries would be made available. The second was the successful completion of the negotiation in February 1998 between the Korean government and foreign creditors for converting more than $20 billion in short-term debt into long-term debt. These two events occurred soon after the interest rate was raised, complicating efforts to isolate the effect of the high interest rate policy.

A second possible explanation for the contrast with other countries is that the high interest rate policy was more credible in Korea. In comparison with Thailand and the Philippines, the interest rate in Korea moved far more closely with the exchange rate (Figure 14.1). The simple correlation between the two variables is 0.300 for Korea but only 0.064 for Thailand and −0.135 for the Philippines. The impulse responses estimated in Figure 14.3 show that the interest rate rose (or, more precisely, was raised by the monetary authority) in response to the increase in the shock to the risk premium only in Korea. The variance decompositions in Figure 14.4 also suggest that the interest rate was largely determined by the exchange rate shock in Korea, while it was determined independently in the other

1. Korea

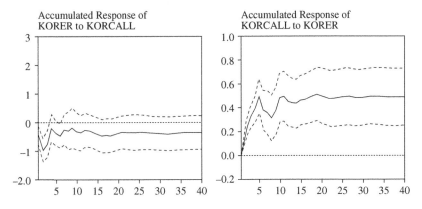

2. Thailand

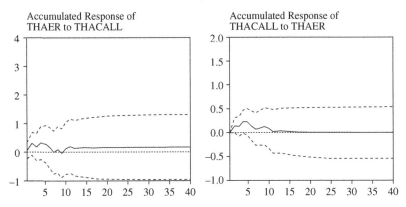

3. Philippines

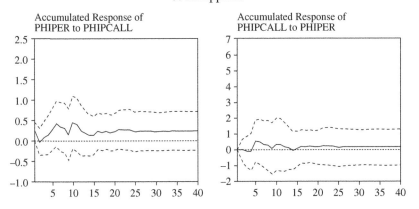

Figure 14.3 Impulse responses from VARs using daily data

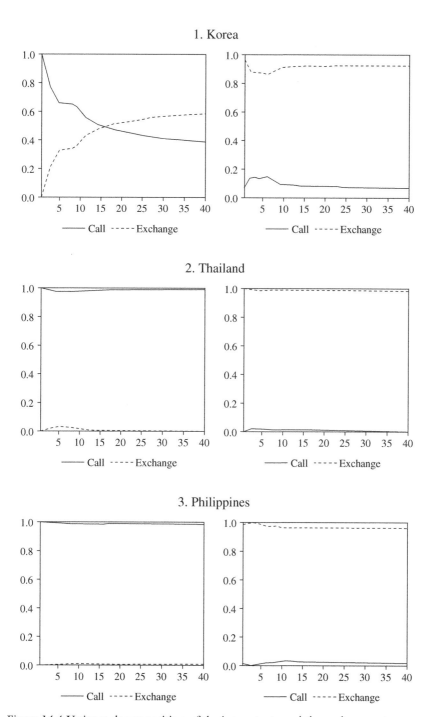

Figure 14.4 Variance decomposition of the interest rate and the exchange rate

countries. That is, the announcement by the government and the IMF that interest rates would be raised and kept at higher levels for as long as needed to stabilize the exchange rate appears to have been more credible in Korea, at least *ex post*. Investors may have come to believe that the Korean monetary authority was very serious about achieving its goal of exchange rate stabilization while continuing to regard skeptically the policy announcements of other countries.[5]

Although this evidence is less than definitive, it is also true that many arguments critical of the high interest rate policy are equally or perhaps even more questionable. For example, there is criticism that high interest rates actually aggravated the problem of capital outflows in December 1997, but this criticism overlooks the fact that an even larger capital outflow (reflecting the actions of domestic as well as foreign investors) might have resulted had interest rates not been raised. In this regard, it may be noteworthy that, while foreign banks drastically reduced their exposures to Korea in December 1997, a substantial amount of foreign currency flowed into Korea seeking high interest rates. For example, net private transfers, which had been slightly negative until October 1997, increased sharply to approximately 2 percent of monthly GDP in December 1997 and then gradually declined to zero as the call rate was lowered.

3. Monetary policy and standard policy objectives

If the high interest rate policy was ineffective or, rather, contributed to further depreciation of the exchange rate after the crisis, it was then a mistake. But even if the policy helped to stabilize the exchange rate, as suggested by the preceding evidence, it still does not follow that the policy was optimal. In other words, the question is whether stabilization of the exchange rate should have been the intermediate target of policy – that is, whether it was an efficient means of achieving the ultimate goals of concern to the authorities.

3.1 *Policy objectives and the optimal policy rule*

The standard way of modeling optimal policy is to assume that the monetary authority minimizes a loss function of the form:

$$\text{Min. } (1 - \alpha)(\pi - \pi^*)^2 + \alpha(y - y^*)^2, \tag{4}$$

where π and y are the inflation rate and the level of output, respectively, *denotes the target levels of these variables, and α is a parameter that reflects the preferences of the authorities (the relative weights they attach to these targets). The standard assumption, then, is that stable output and low inflation are the ultimate goals of policy. Strictly speaking, a central bank with a legal mandate to target inflation, like the Bank of Korea after the crisis, should set $\alpha = 0$.[6] In practice, however, most countries expect the monetary authority to be concerned with the stabilization of business cycles within an "acceptable" range of inflation; that is, the monetary authority is expected to set α such that $0 < \alpha < 1$, since economic activity would experience severe fluctuations otherwise. Thus, while the Bank of Korea announced a medium-term inflation target of 2.5 percent in 1999, annual inflation was allowed to deviate from that target by ±1 percent.

One implication of this formulation is that exchange rate stabilization, in and of itself, is not the ultimate goal of economic policy. For a small, open economy like Korea, Ball (1999) shows that the optimal monetary policy rule relates a linear combination of the interest rate and exchange rate (what is referred to in the literature as the Monetary Conditions Index, or *MCI*) to the two gaps in the preceding objective function:

$$MCI = w(r - r^*) - (1 - w)(e - e^*) = \beta^*(\pi - \pi^*) + \gamma^*(y - y^*),$$

where r and e are the real interest rate and log of the real exchange rate, respectively, and w, β' and γ' are the parameters that depend on the underlying economic structures and the policymaker's preferences.[7] Ignoring the distinction between control and state variables and the distinction between expected and actual inflation, rearranging this equation yields an expression for the nominal interest rate, $i \equiv r + \pi$;

$$i = (\pi + r^*) + \beta (\pi - \pi^*) + \gamma (y - y^*) + \delta (e - e^*), \tag{6}$$

where the parameters β, γ, and δ are appropriately transformed from equation (5).[8]

According to Equation (6), the interest rate should be raised, even if there has been no change in current levels of inflation and output, in response to depreciation of the currency. Currency depreciation boosts aggregate demand, which implies both faster inflation and higher levels of output in the future. Optimal policy today will respond to this information about economic conditions tomorrow – information conveyed by the exchange rate – even though the level of the exchange rate itself is not a policy objective. Ignoring the distinction between nominal and real variables, which is sensible for the very short-term, Equation (3) can be interpreted as a special case of Equation (6), where a = δ and u_{mt} comprise the remaining inflation and output gap terms. Intuitively, the interest rate policy in response to the crisis had to be tied to the fluctuation of the exchange rate fluctuation because the latter was the dominating factor determining macroeconomic fluctuations.

3.2   Calibration

Even if there is some theoretical justification for using high interest rates to defend the exchange rate following the shock of the crisis, there remains the question of whether the authorities' response was too much or too little. Were the interest rate responses optimal, in other words? Or were there alternative interest rate paths that would have resulted in a lower social loss, as measured by Equation (4)?

One way of addressing this question is by calibrating the optimal interest rate rule of Equation (6). Doing so is useful not just for assessing the high interest rate policy adopted in response to the crisis but also for analyzing the "super-low" interest rate environment established once confidence had been restored. (Compared with pre-crisis levels of around 12 percent, call rates were reduced to approximately four percent, depths that had not been experienced in Korea since the 1960s.)

I imposed a value of 5 percent for r^*, reflecting the commonly cited potential growth rate of Korea after the crisis, and 2.5 percent for π^*, the medium-term target declared by the Bank of Korea in 1999. As for π, there are important issues. The first issue is which inflation indicator should be used. An obvious candidate is core CPI, the official inflation target variable used by the Bank of Korea since 1999, which excludes irregular elements such as the prices of agricultural products and petroleum. However, a GDP deflator that covers a wider range of prices than the CPI or core CPI better represents aggregate economic conditions. After the crisis, in particular, there were significant discrepancies between the core CPI and GDP deflator due to the deterioration of the terms of trade (as shown in Figure 14.5). In 1999, for example, the core CPI inflation rate was more than 2 percent, while the GDP deflator inflation rate was negative. Therefore, I used both indexes in the following calibration.

A second issue is whether to use data on *ex ante* expected inflation or *ex post* actual inflation. Expected inflation is conceptually preferable (particularly when calibrating the real interest rate), but it must be estimated. And, in practice, results are likely to differ substantially depending upon the techniques used in estimation. I, therefore, used the *ex post* (year-on-year) inflation rate in the benchmark case and an estimate of expected inflation for comparison.

For the core CPI and GDP deflator, respectively, Figure 14.5 compares the actual with expected inflation rates.[9] According to Figure 14.5, expectations of inflation (in terms of the core CPI) had turned negative by the end of 1998 before gradually returning to 2 to 4 percent rates of expected inflation thereafter. Another feature of this figure is that expected inflation leads actual inflation, especially in the post-crisis period.

An even more dramatic contrast between the actual and expected inflation rates is in Figure 14.5. While the actual inflation rate (in terms of the GDP deflator) exceeded 10 percent in the first quarter of 1998, expected inflation remained at zero, according to these estimates. Expected inflation is far smoother than the actual inflation and remains continually below the target level of 2.5 percent.

It is common in the literature to calibrate $y - y^*$ as the deviation of actual output from the hypothetical level that would have obtained in the absence of demand-side shocks. In order to obtain this output gap, I applied the structural vector autoregression (SVAR) methodology of Blanchard and Quah (1989), using seasonally adjusted real GDP and price index (core CPI or GDP deflator) data from the first quarter of 1980 to the first quarter of 2002, and eight lags of the respective variables.[10] Figure 14.5 shows the estimated output gap series, the GDP component that is driven by the demand shock alone, along with the peaks and troughs officially defined by the Statistics Bureau of Korea. According

A. Actual vs. expected inflation (Core CPI)

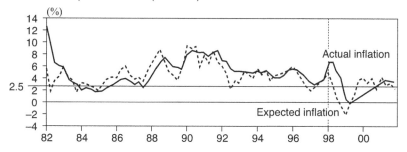

B. Actual vs. expected inflation (GDP deflator)

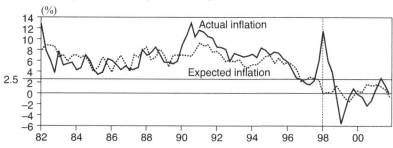

C. Output gap (core CPI and GDP deflator)

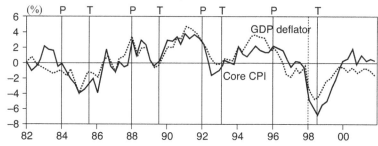

D. Real effective exchange rate (won vs dollar and yen)

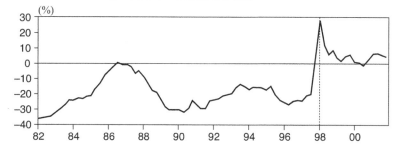

Figure 14.5 Variables for calibration

to these estimates, the output gap plunged to historically unprecedented depths in 1998 but recovered to approximately zero by 2000. After the crisis, the output gap estimated using the GDP deflator appears to be lower than that estimated using core CPI, reflecting differences in the behavior of the two price indexes.

For $e - e^*$, I constructed a simple real effective exchange rate (or REER) index based on two currencies, the US dollar and the Japanese yen, with equal weights of 0.5.[11] Figure 14.5 plots this REER series in percent changes from the base year of 2001. According to this series, the exchange rate in the first quarter of 1998 was approximately 30 percent undervalued.

With these variables in hand, the parameters β, γ and δ still need to be calibrated. Although this calibration should in principle be based on estimates of the relevant parameters derived from the Korean data, this chapter simply borrows values from Ball (1999). For both β and γ, Ball assumes a range from 0.5 to 2.0. (The value of β becomes smaller as the weight on the inflation fluctuation in the loss function becomes smaller.) For δ, Ball (1994) and Gerlach and Smets (2000) all recommend a value of 0.3, although estimation results in Cho (2002) suggest that a value of 0.1 is more plausible in the Korean case.

3.3   Results and discussion

Figure 14.6 shows calibration results using actual inflation rates and $\beta = \gamma = \delta = 0$, along with the actual call rate (measured as a quarterly average). When the

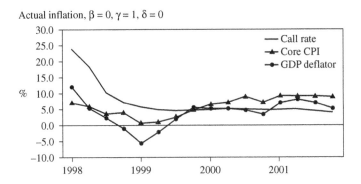

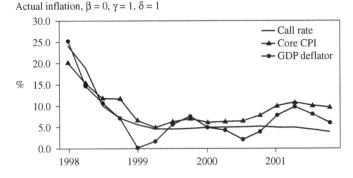

Figure 14.6 Calibration results

Actual inflation, $\beta = 1$, $\gamma = 1$, $\delta = 0.3$

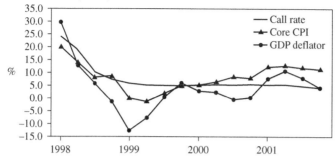

Actual inflation, $\beta = 0$, $\gamma = 0$, $\delta = 0$

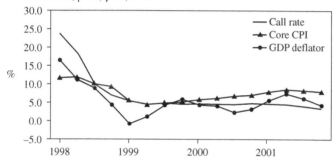

Actual inflation, $\beta = 0$, $\gamma = 0$, $\delta = 0$

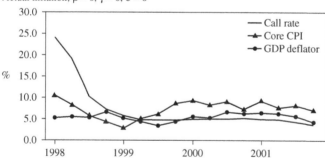

Actual inflation, $\beta = 1$, $\gamma = 0$, $\delta = 0$

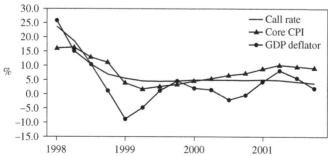

Figure 14.6 (Continued)

core CPI is used to measure inflation outcomes, actual interest rates appear to have been too high in the first two quarters of 1998 but too low in 2000 and 2001. When the GDP deflator is used, in contrast, call rates appear to be too high throughout all four quarters of 1998, before falling to roughly appropriate levels in 2000 and 2001. That is, the "super-low interest rates" since 1999 do not appear to be too low if the GDP deflator accurately captures inflationary conditions.

However, call rates immediately following the outbreak of the crisis are too high no matter which price index is used. This finding is placed in relief in Figure 14.6, where expected inflation (estimated from a VAR) is used in place of actual inflation. Here optimal interest rates do not exceed 10 percent even in 1998, which contrasts with the 30 percent rates actually observed.

In contrast, Figure 14.6 shows that the high interest rate policy in the first half of 1998 may have been justified had the authority actively tried to stabilize the inflation or exchange rates and judge the inflation conditions by the actual GDP deflator. In these cases, however, the optimal interest rate falls below zero in the first quarter of 1999, which raises doubts about this policy response.

In short, the key assumption on which assessments of post-crisis interest rate policy appears to turn to which index of inflation is the appropriate guide to policy outcomes, rather than the particular parameter values that are assigned. The question, in other words, is whether Korean policymakers should care about core CPI inflation or the GDP deflator and whether they can formulate reliable estimates of expected inflation. Using expected inflation rates, no reasonable combination of parameter values can justify an interest rate as high as 15 percent in the first half of 1998. The crucial issue when judging the low interest rate policy put in place in 1999 is whether the core CPI or GDP deflator should be used. Using core CPI, it is again the case that no combination of reasonable parameter values can justify the authorities' decision to cut interest rates to less than 5 percent after 2000.

The question of which index of inflation is more relevant and reliable is not easily answered. However, the actual year-on-year inflation rate used in calibration has a clear shortcoming, despite the fact that the year-on-year changes are commonly used in Korea to calculate baseline inflation rates. For example, while the level of the GDP deflator rose substantially in the first quarter of 1998, it then declined significantly in the second quarter. These wide fluctuations quarter to quarter will not be picked up by the year-on-year inflation rate. Although the volatility of annualized quarter-to-quarter inflation rates (actual, not expected) obtained using the calibrated model raise questions of reliability, taken at face value, they can justify the high level of interest rates actually observed only in the first quarter of 1998, not thereafter (and recall that interest rates were maintained at high through 1998-Q2 and only gradually reduced in the second half of the calendar year).

Of course, data on current macroeconomic conditions becomes available only with a lag, and monetary policy must be formulated on the basis of uncertain forecasts. In practice, however, it is hard to invoke uncertainty as a justification for the maintenance of high interest rates beyond the first quarter of 1998. Few if any macroeconomic indicators signaled the danger of accelerating future inflation after March; if anything, most variables pointed to the danger of deflation. The exchange rate, which was the leading indicator of short-term price movements during the crisis, began stabilizing in February 1998. Nominal wages, which may be a more informative guide of medium-term inflationary pressures, actually fell in 1998 relative to the preceding calendar year. In short, it is hard to justify the maintenance of the high interest rate policy after the first quarter of 1998, unless one sticks to a possibly deficient indicator like the year-on-year inflation rate.

It is always difficult to determine an appropriate monetary policy, not just *ex ante* but also *ex post*. But, in the Korean case, evidence suggests that had the authorities begun lowering interest rates earlier, they would not have been forced to shift monetary policy so dramatically in October 1998. Had they starting reducing interest rates earlier and more gradually, they might have helped to avoid a deflationary recession in 1998 and a bubble-like recovery in 1999. They would have avoided what turned out to be the largest biggest business cycle fluctuation experienced in Korea in nearly four decades.

4. Summary and conclusions

This chapter has discussed Korea's post-crisis monetary policy, focusing on whether the high interest rate policy adopted immediately after the outbreak of the crisis was effective in stabilizing the exchange rate and whether post-crisis interest rate policy can be justified in light of the literature on optimal monetary policy. While it is impossible to determine conclusively whether tight money was effective in stabilizing the exchange rate, if there is any country in Asia for which the policy worked, that country was Korea. As for whether post-crisis monetary policy was too tight, too loose or just about right, the answer hinges on which index of inflation is appropriate for such calculations. The high interest rate policy maintained in the first quarter of 1998 can be justified if the actual (year-on-year) inflation rate as opposed to the expected inflation rate (estimated from vector autoregressions) is used. The low interest rate policy in place since 1999 can be justified if the GDP deflator rather than the core CPI is used. But whatever uncertainty remains about the advisability of raising interest rates to observed heights in the first quarter of 1998, analysis suggests that the authorities should have started moving to reduce them at an earlier date. In fact, there appears to have been considerable latitude for interest rate reductions starting in the second quarter of 1998.

This chapter has also revealed that many important issues related to the conduct of monetary policy in Korea remain unresolved. It will have succeeded even if it only provokes more active discussion of them.

APPENDIX: SOLUTIONS OF THE MODEL IN SECTION 2

The reduced-form solutions to the system in the text are:

$$E_{t-1}s_t = b \sum_j \{ b^j E_{t-1}[u_{dt+j} - (1-d)u_{mt+j}] \},$$
$$i_t = aE_{t-1}s_t + u_{mt},$$
$$s_t = [-(1-d)i_t + E_t s_{t+1} + u_{dt}].$$

An **unanticipated risk shock:** With respect to a unit shock to ε_{dt} at time 0, both the interest rate and the exchange rate jump up initially (s_0 and i_1), but both variables then smoothly decline.

$$i_0 = 0,$$
$$s_0 = 1/(1 - b\phi_d) > 0,$$
$$d_0 = 1 > 0,$$
$$i_t = a\, s_t > 0, \qquad \text{for } t > 0,$$
$$s_t = \phi_d^t\, b/(1 - b\phi_d) > 0, \qquad \text{for } t > 0,$$
$$d_t = \phi_m^t\, adb/\{(1 - b\phi_d) + 1\} > 0, \quad \text{for } t > 0.$$

An **unanticipated monetary shock:** With respect to a unit shock to ε_{mt} at time 0, the interest rate rises and the exchange rate appreciates initially, both gradually approaching zero over time.

$$i_0 = 1 > 0,$$
$$s_0 = -\{(1-d)/(1 - b\phi_m)\} < 0,$$
$$d_0 = d > 0,$$
$$i_t = \phi_m^t\, b\, (1 - \phi_m)/(1 - b\phi_m) > 0, \qquad \text{for } t > 0,$$
$$s_t = -\phi_m^t\, b\, (1 - d)/(1 - b\phi_m) < 0, \qquad \text{for } t > 0,$$
$$d_t = \phi_m^t\, bd(1 - \phi_m)/(1 - b\phi_m) > 0, \qquad \text{for } t > 0.$$

Notes

* This chapter is reprinted from *The Korean Economy Beyond the Crisis*, edited by Duk-Koo Chung and Barry Eichengreen, Edward Elgar Publishing Inc., pp. 89–112, 2004.
1 Detailed explanations about the evolution of monetary policy scheme in Korea after the crisis can be found in Cho (2002).
2 The Letter of Intent (http://www.imf.org/external/country/KOR/index.htm) stated that '[m]oney market rates will be allowed to rise sufficiently and will be maintained at that level or higher as needed to stabilize the market' (12/3/1997); 'Raise call rates to 30%, or above if needed, to stabilize the exchange rate' (12/24/1997); 'Call rates have been at around 30% since Dec. 26 and will be kept high until the foreign exchange situation improves' (1/1998); 'With the mitigation of the immediate foreign exchange crisis, call rates will be cautiously allowed to ease, in line with continued exchange rate stabilization' (2/1998); 'Interest rate policy will continue to be conducted in a flexible and symmetric manner. Subject to the objective of maintaining stability in the foreign exchange

market, call interest rates will continue to be lowered, in line with market conditions' (5/1998); 'Interest rate policy will continue to be conducted in a flexible manner with upward and downward adjustments as necessary' (7/1998); 'Easy monetary stance will be maintained. . . . (11/1998).

3 This frontier, $(1 - d) i_t + (1 - \phi_d) s_t = \phi_d^t \varepsilon_{a0}$, is derived by eliminating a from the solutions for i_t and s_t, for $\varepsilon_{mt} = 0$ for all t. I call this line the *interest rate – exchange rate frontier* in the sense that the monetary authority cannot alter it.

4 Sample periods for the VARs were one year after the outbreak of the crises: 12/1/1997–11/30/1998 for Korea and 7/1/1997–6/30/1998 for Thailand and the Philippines. Ten lagged variables, or approximately two weeks, were included in the VAR, and the exchange rate was put first in the Cholesky decomposition. Differenced data were used in estimation, but the impulse responses were calculated for the levels. Dotted lines indicate 95 percent confidence bands in each graph.

5 The legal introduction of inflation targeting in 1998 might have served to raise Korea's monetary policy credibility but this does not seem to be the major factor behind the success in exchange rate stabilization. Inflation targeting had not yet become standard practice in 1998, and many international investors were worried about the possibility of deflation rather than inflation.

6 The new Bank of Korea Act (passed by the National Assembly in December 1997 and which took effect on April 1, 1988) declares that the primary goal of monetary policy is price stability instead of multiple, obscure objectives such as the soundness of the banking system and economic growth. Since 1999, the Bank of Korea has announced the next year's inflation target at the end of every year, and the Board of Governors convenes every month to set up the policy directions (mostly the level of call rate as the operating target) in accordance with the announced inflation target.

7 In fact, Ball (1999) proposes a policy rule that considers the short-term effect of the lagged exchange rate, but I did not include this effect for two reasons. First, this rule appears to be sensitive to an *ad hoc* specification about economic structures. Second, I applied this part in the calibration exercises, but the results did not change much.

8 Strictly speaking, Equation (6) is not a formula describing the optimal interest rate rule in the sense that the right hand side includes an endogenous variable, e: when i changes, e changes too.

9 Since the data frequency is quarterly, the expected annual inflation rate needs forecast values of up to four quarters ahead.

10 As for the application of the Blanchard and Quah (1989) methodology to the Korean data, Kim (1996) already reported detailed estimation results. The most critical identification assumption of this technique is that the demand shock does not change the output level in the long run, while the supply shock does. The only deviation of this paper's estimation from Kim (1996) is that I used the core CPI instead of the GDP deflator.

11 Cho (2002) shows that this simple index is similar to a far more complex index based on 16 trading partners' currencies using the relative portions of trading volumes as the respective currencies' weights.

References

Ball, Laurence, 1999. "Policy Rules for Open Economies," in *Monetary Policy Rules*, edited by John B. Taylor, Chicago: University of Chicago Press, pp. 127–156.

Barsurto, Gabriela and Atish Ghosh, 2000, "The Interest Rate-Exchange Rate Nexus in Currency Crises," *IMF Working Paper* 00–19, Washington, DC.

Blanchard, Olivier J. and Danny Quah, 1989. "The Dynamic Effects of Aggregate Demand and Supply Disturbances," *American Economic Review*, 79, pp. 655–673.

Cho, Dongchul, 2002. "Post-Crisis Structural Changes and Monetary Policy Scheme in Korea," *manuscript*, Korea Development Institute, Seoul.

Cho, Dongchul and Kenneth D. West, 2000. "Interest Rates and Exchange Rates in the Korean, Philippines, and Thai Exchange Rate Crises," forthcoming in *Management of Currency Crisis*, edited by Jeffrey Frenkel and Michael Dooley. Cambridge, MA: NBER.

Cho, Dongchul and Kenneth D. West, 2001. "The Effect of Monetary Policy in Exchange Rate Stabilization in Post-Crisis Korea," in *The Korean Crisis: Before and After*, edited by Inseok Shin, pp. 257–286. Seoul: Korea Development Institute.

Dekle, Robert, Cheng Hsiao, and Siyan Wang, 1999. "Interest Rate Stabilization of Exchange Rates and Contagion in the Asian Crisis Countries," *manuscript*, University of Southern California, Los Angeles.

Freedman, Charles, 1994. "The Use of Indicators and of the Monetary Conditions Index in Canada," in *Frameworks for Monetary Stability: Policy Issues and Country Experiences*, edited by Tomas J. T. Balino and Carlo Cottarelli, pp. 458–476. Washington, DC: International Monetary Fund.

Furman, Jason and Joseph E. Stiglitz, 1998. "Economic Crises: Evidence and Insights from East Asia," *Brookings Papers on Economic Activity*, 2, pp. 1–135.

Gerlach, Stefan and Frank Smets, 2000. "MCIs and Monetary Policy," *European Economic Review*, 44, pp. 1677–1700.

Goldfajn, Ilan and Taimur Baig, 1998. "Monetary Policy in the Aftermath of Currency Crises: The Case of Asia," *IMF Working Paper* 99–42, Washington, DC.

Goldfajn, Ilan and Poonam Gupta, 1999. "Does Monetary Policy Stabilize the Exchange Rate Following a Currency Crisis?" *IMF Working Paper* 99–42, Washington, DC.

Gould, David M. and Steven B. Kamin, 2000. "The Impact of Monetary Policy on Exchange Rates During Financial Crises," *Board of Governors of the Federal Reserve System International Financial Discussion paper* no. 669, Washington, DC.

Kim, June-Il, 1996. "Business Cycles and GDP Gap," *KDI Policy Studies*, Spring, pp. 217–270 (in Korean).

Kraay, Aart, 2000. "Do High Interest Rates Defend Currencies during Speculative Attacks?" *World Bank Working Paper* no. 2267, Washington, DC.

Park, Daekeun, and In Choi, 1999. "Was the High Interest Rate Policy Effective to the Exchange Rate Stabilization?" *Analysis of the Korean Economy*, December, pp. 63–119 (in Korean).

Tanner, Evan, 1999. "Exchange Market Pressures and Monetary Policy: Asia and Latin America in the 1990s," *IMF Working Paper* no. 99–114, Washington, DC.

15 Responses of the Korean economy to the global crisis
Another currency crisis?*

1. Introduction

The crisis during the 2008–2009 period was truly *global*. Enormous impacts were spread throughout the whole world. Reinhart and Rogoff (2009, Box 16.1), for example, identified the recent crisis as one of the two *global* crises (the other being the Great Depression) from the past two centuries of financial data.

It was no surprise that Korea, too, was severely hit by the crisis. Korea was particularly susceptible to global shocks since its financial and export sectors were opened. Asset prices plummeted and exports collapsed. A drastic economic contraction followed and even a trauma from the financial crisis in 1997 resurfaced. Sentiments in the market were propelled to the extreme and the *Economist* (2009) ranked Korea at the fourth (following after South Africa, Hungary and Poland) on the list of most likely emerging economies to become the next victim of the global crisis. Yet, Korea managed to recover relatively early at a relatively strong pace.

In these respects, Korea is an interesting country to study: it is an open economy subject to global shocks and has the experience of a comparable crisis in its past to the recent one. By examining Korea's adjustment to the recent global crisis, this chapter seeks some clues to the transmission mechanism of global shocks to emerging economies and the critical factors of host countries for either mitigating or amplifying the effects of external shocks.

The chapter is organized as follows. Section 2 sketches development of the recent crisis in Korea and compares it with the 1997–1998 crisis. Section 3 examines the two transmission channels, financial and export markets. Section 4 explains Korea's macro-policy reactions to the crisis and compares them with those during the 1997–1998 crisis. Section 5 concludes with an emphasis on the roles of fundamentals in mitigating the effects of external shocks.

2. The Korean economy during the global crisis period

2.1 Crisis and recovery: a brief sketch

The Korean economy had maintained a reasonable pace of stable growth until the third quarter of 2008. Domestic demand had somewhat slowed due to the soaring oil prices and the resulting loss of purchasing power but exports had maintained a solid expansion. In fact, the third quarter's exports increased by 27 percent compared to that in the same quarter of the previous year, despite the global slowdown since the sub-prime mortgage crisis in the US.

However, the Lehman Brothers bankruptcy filing in September and the subsequent panic in the global financial market changed the whole environment. Enormous shocks hit Korea through the open doors of financial and export markets. The exchange rate depreciated from around 1,100 won/dollar to more than 1,500 won/dollar, and foreign reserves declined from $240 billion at the end of September to $201 billion at the end of December. Other asset markets also responded. For example, stock values collapsed by approximately 30 percent by the end of the year 2008 (see Figure 15.1).

Korea's export also collapsed at an incredible pace. The year-on-year growth rate of export declined from 27.6 percent in September to 7.8 percent (−2.6 percent, month-to-month) in October and further to −19.5 percent (−22.3 percent, month-to-month) in November. (See Figure 15.2) This collapse in export revenue

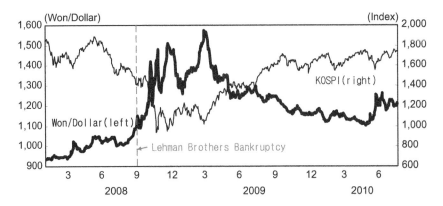

Figure 15.1 Exchange rate and stock price index

Source: Bank of Korea.

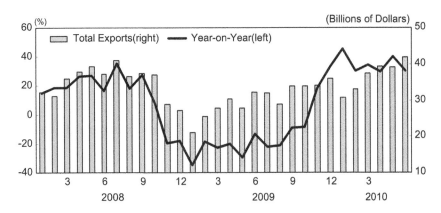

Figure 15.2 Exports

Source: Korea Customs Service.

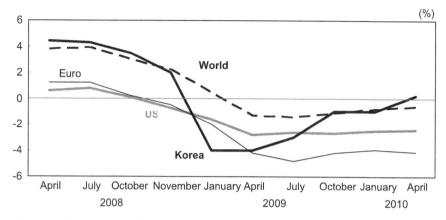

Figure 15.3 Revisions of IMF forecasts on 2009 growth rates
Source: IMF World Economic Outlook.

raised concerns over the Korea's capability to earn hard currency and aggravated investor sentiments in the currency market that was already unstable.

International forecasting institutions rushed to join the march of downgrading Korea's outlook. For example, the IMF revised its forecast on Korea's 2009 growth from +2.5 percent in November 2008 to –4.0 percent in January 2009 – a 6.5 percent drop within just two months! (See Figure 15.3) However, this was not particularly dramatic at that moment, compared to the revisions of major investment banks. And most of these forecasts shared a common prediction that Korea (as well as other East Asian economies) would contract more than crisis-originating countries such as the US.

To the surprise of many commentators, however, the Korean economy began to recover from the second quarter of 2009. After final jitters in March, the financial market began to stabilize. Also in trade sectors, some recovery signals of export demand were detected. Having paused in the first quarter, the Korean economy began to recover at a relatively rapid pace, achieving more than 8 percent growth in just a one-year period until the first quarter 2010. Whenever relevant statistics were released, international institutions continued to revise their "forecasts" upward, until Korea's official annual growth rate of 2009 was finally announced as 0.2 percent in February 2010.

2.2   Comparison with the 1997–1998 crisis: a first look

The early recovery of Korea may have been a surprise to many forecasters, particularly those who had memories of the deep and painful crisis triggered in 1997. On the surface, the two crises looked alike: asset values and GDP collapsed simultaneously, though the recent crisis was slightly less severe in terms of magnitude and duration. The initial adjustments in the currency value, stock price index and GDP during the recent crisis were approximately two-thirds of those in 1997 (see Figure 15.4). The duration of crisis – though the definition of "crisis" is always elusive – was also shorter this time: it took six months this time, compared to 12 months during the previous crisis, until the currency was restored to the value of 20 percent lower than its pre-crisis level and also for the stock price index to restore to its pre-crisis level; and it took four quarters this time, compared to six quarters during the previous crisis, until GDP restored to its pre-crisis level.

The fundamental difference between the two crises, however, can be found from the responses of aggregate demand components (see Figure 15.5). During the 1997–1998 period, domestic demand drove the collapse of GDP, while export demand continued to expand. This time, in contrast, it was external demand that triggered the crisis, while the contraction in domestic demand was relatively mild. This stark contrast in the responses of aggregate demand components clearly demonstrates that the sources of the crises were different. Whereas

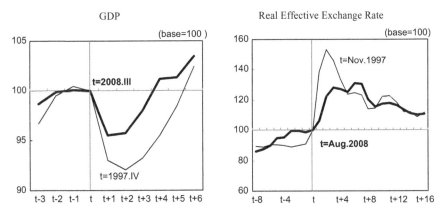

Figure 15.4 Similarities of the recent crisis with the 1997–1998 crisis

Source: Bank of Korea.

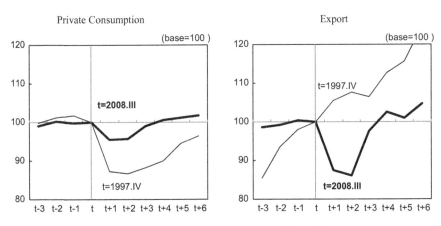

Figure 15.5 Differences of the recent crisis from the 1997–1998 crisis

Source: Bank of Korea.

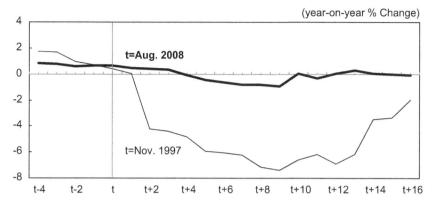

Figure 15.6 Employment growth rate: recent crisis and the 1997–1998 crisis
Source: National Statistics Office of Korea.

the 1997–1998 crisis was triggered by the *implosion* of domestic markets, the recent crisis was mainly triggered by the *explosion* of foreign markets.

This difference in the two crises was translated into the difference in job loss statistics – probably the most direct single indicator of society's suffering from an economic crisis (see Figure 15.6). It has been shown that most short-term employment fluctuation in Korea is driven by domestic demand rather than exports.[1] As consistent with this finding, the job-loss rate during the recent crisis was contained within 1 percent (on a year-on-year basis) at its peak, May 2009, which was far milder than the 7.4 percent in August 1998.

In short, the two crises of Korea appeared similar, but their sources and impacts were quite different. The foreign-driven crisis in 2008 ended up incurring less pain than the 1997–1998 crisis that was caused by weak domestic fundamentals, particularly in financial markets.

3.   Two channels of crisis transmission

3.1   *Financial market: currency crisis but not a banking crisis*

3.1.1   *Currency and domestic credit markets*

The financial market was the first channel that directly transmitted the global crisis. Immediately after the Lehman Brothers bankruptcy, panicked financial institutions rushed out to secure liquidity from anywhere possible in the world. Korea, which had accumulated short-term foreign debts since 2005, was particularly susceptible to this liquidity shock (see Figure 15.7). Despite having the sixth largest foreign reserves in the world, Korea's ratio of short-term foreign debt-to-reserves exceeded those of other emerging economies in September 2008.[2] Being an emerging economy with no hard currency, Korea was swept into the strong current of global financial panic and experienced an abrupt and massive capital outflow. The size of financial capital withdrawn on net for just one month of October 2008 was $25.5 billion (more than 3 percent of annual GDP), which was far larger than $6.4 billion in December 1997, the worst month during the 1997–1998 crisis.[3] As a result, the Korean won lost its value *vis-à-vis* the US dollar by more than 30 percent and foreign reserves were reduced by approximately 20 percent during the three-month period from September to December 2008. By any working definition of the literature, this event should be classified as a currency crisis.[4] The stock market's adjustment

A. Trends

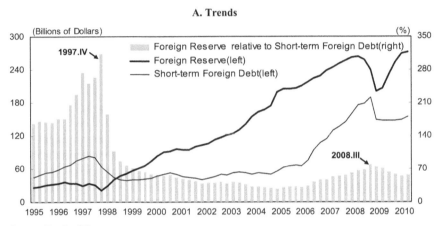

Source: Bank of Korea.

B. Comparison with Other Countries

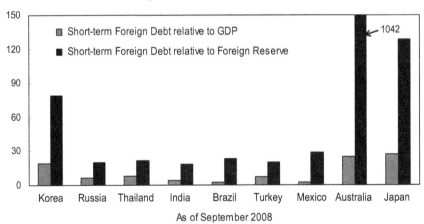

Source: BIS, IMF, World Bank, Global insight.

Figure 15.7 Short-term foreign debts and foreign reserves

during the same period, more than 20 percent, can also be classified as a crisis by some definitions.[5]

Despite the crises in asset markets, however, Korea's credit market was not greatly affected by, or largely immune to, the global crisis. Bank credits continued to increase and no evident spikes were observed in either the ratio of non-performing loans or the dishonored ratio of promissory notes (see Figure 15.8). No

A. Loan Growth Rates of Depository Banks

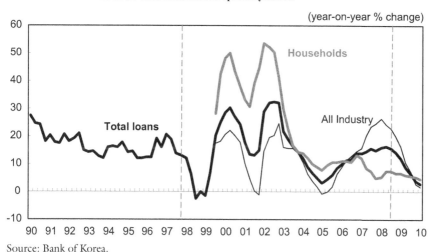

Source: Bank of Korea.

B. Default Rates

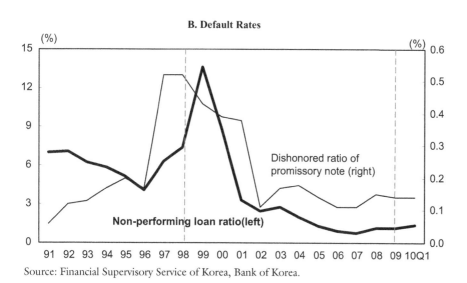

Source: Financial Supervisory Service of Korea, Bank of Korea.

Figure 15.8 Domestic credit market

major banks were bailed out by the government and no symptoms of bank-runs were detected. By any working definition of the literature, it was far from a banking crisis.[6] In fact, this was the most marked difference from the 1997–1998 crisis period, when the whole financial system melted down.[7]

3.1.2 Financial policy reactions

Many efforts of the government contributed to relieving the tensions in the financial market. First, the government announced a measure to provide temporary guarantees (until the end of June 2009, later extended to the end of December 2009) on rolled-over short-term foreign debts of commercial banks, as many other governments did at that time. Although no banks ended up relying on government money, this policy must have helped mitigate concerns of international investors. The government also raised 10 trillion won (1 percent of GDP) of funds for stabilizing bond markets (though only 5 trillion won was used until dissolved) and increased capital bases of public agencies for credit guarantees. In many instances, the government allegedly relied even on moral suasions for commercial banks to roll-over the loans to small- and medium-sized enterprises. The Bank of Korea also kept pace with the government by extending its operating instruments to risky assets such as commercial bank debentures.

However, it is noteworthy that a similar menu of policies was taken in response to the 1997–1998 crisis, but Korea nonetheless plunged into a severe banking crisis. In this respect, critical factors that protected the Korea's banking system must have lied somewhere else.

3.1.3 Buffers to absorb the shocks

Typically, a currency crisis is transmitted into a banking crisis – a twin crisis – through the following channels:

1   sudden reversal of foreign currency liquidity flow →
2   shrinkage of bank assets in public (when the exchange rate is pegged) or private sector (when the exchange rate is floated) →
3   decrease in credit supply and a surge in default →
4   deterioration of banks' capital bases →
5   vicious cycles of credit crunch between banks and borrowers.

Every single step toward a twin crisis was observed during the 1997–1998 crisis, but the Korean economy in 2008 was equipped with better buffers at most junctures.

First, an ample amount of foreign reserves helped dampen the impacts of a sudden reversal in capital flows on private banks' assets. Although the massively accumulated short-term foreign debts made the Korean economy fragile to a foreign liquidity shock, the amount of foreign reserves was still large enough to cover the whole short-term foreign debt. For example, the aforementioned government guarantee on foreign debts would not have been regarded as credible by the market had foreign reserves not been sufficient as in 1997.

The way to supply foreign reserves was also improved. Unlike in 1997, the government did not waste foreign reserves this time by committing to a certain level of *price* (i.e. the exchange rate). Instead, the government secured additional liquidity via currency swaps with the US and other countries and supplied a manageable *quantity* of reserves within a closed circuit of the banking sector by auction. That is, instead of fighting the market to protect the currency value, the government concentrated its efforts on protecting the banking system by supplying foreign currency liquidity required to reduce the accumulated leverage. It was not a sheer coincidence that the amount of decrease in foreign reserves during the crisis period from September to December 2008, approximately $40 billion, was almost the same as that of short-term foreign debts.[8] This approach to the foreign exchange market seems to have been effective in dampening the adverse impacts of capital outflows on the banking sector, while honoring the automatic stabilizing role of the exchange rate (see the following).

Second, the sound financial positions of firms, particularly large corporations (or *chaebols*), were crucial in absorbing the impacts from the banking system to real economy. Since the 1997–1998 crisis, Korean firms had carried out drastic restructuring and their financial stability had been significantly improved.[9] As an example, the average debt-to-equity ratio of the corporate sector fell from more than 400 percent in 1997 to around 100 percent in 2008 and the interest coverage ratio rose from barely more than 100 percent in 1997 to more than 500 percent in 2008 (see Figure 15.9). This improvement in financial buffers greatly helped Korean firms to weather the credit constraints and demand contraction posed by the global crisis.

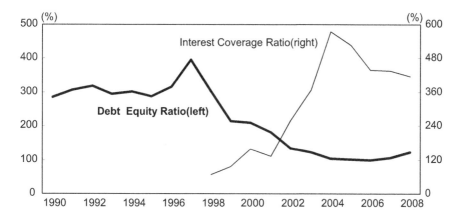

Figure 15.9 Financial buffers of Korean firms

Source: Bank of Korea.

There was a concern about households' debt-leverage. As in many advanced countries, Korean households had substantially increased debts in relation to housing investment since the 1997–1998 crisis. An important difference, however, was that the magnitude of house price hikes in Korea was far milder than those in advanced countries during the run-up to the crisis (see Figure 15.10). To the extent that the debts were backed by less bubbly assets, the associated risks were likely to be smaller. In fact, Korea's house prices were almost immune to the crisis, and household debts did not trigger any significant troubles during the crisis period.

Third, banks also have secured far better capacities to absorb shocks in 2008 than in 1997. Based on the improved Bank for International Settlement (BIS) capital adequacy ratio and return on equity, the banking sector would have been able to avoid a critical situation even if a certain degree of defaults had taken place (see Figure 15.11).

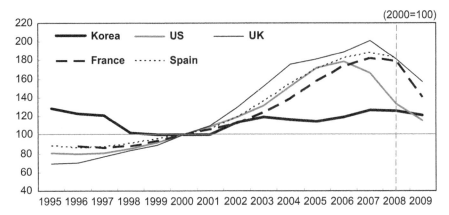

Figure 15.10 (Real) House price hikes during the run-up to the crisis

Source: Kookmin Bank (Korea), Standard & Poor's/Shiller Case (US), National Institute for Statistics and Economic Studies (France), Banco de Espana (Spain), Nationwide (UK).

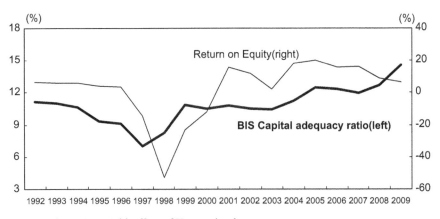

Figure 15.11 Financial buffers of Korean banks

Source: Financial Supervisory Service of Korea.

All in all, the financial buffers of each sector played critical roles in protecting Korea from plaguing the currency crisis to a banking crisis. This must have helped save domestic demand, hence employment, during the recent crisis, despite enormous additional shocks that flooded into Korea through the trade channel.[10]

3.2 Export market: faster recovery than other countries

3.2.1 Fall and rise of Korea's exports

The magnitude of the shock through the trade channel was no smaller than that through the financial channel: approximately 40 percent of export demand evaporated during the three-month period from September to December 2008.[11] This dramatic collapse in export was a worldwide phenomenon but served as the main grounds for the extremely gloomy forecasts on the Korean economy (as well as other East Asian economies) that heavily relied on manufacturing export sectors.[12]

Having passed the trough in January 2009, however, Korea's exports began to recover along with global trade. This recovery must have been benefited by the global policy coordination and demand recovery. But it is still notable that the recovery pace of Korea's export was faster than those of other economies. By the second quarter 2010, Korea was fully recovered to the pre-crisis level, while most of other countries have not recovered (see Figure 15.12) For the entire year of 2009, Korea's export went through a relatively milder correction, –13.8 percent, than that of global trade, –22.9 percent, raising its market share in global trade to 3.1 percent from 2.8 percent in 2008.

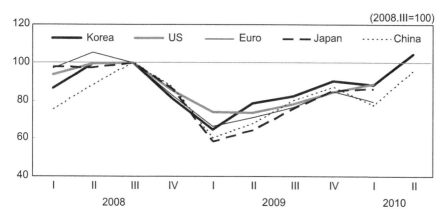

Figure 15.12 Fall and rise of exports

Source: Eurostat, Korea Customs Service, Trade Statistics of Japan, National Bureau of Statistics of China, US Census Bureau.

3.2.2   *China, the biggest trading partner of Korea*

One of the reasons for the relatively fast recovery of Korea's export was its structure concentrating on China's market: the share of China in Korea's export market was 24 percent (almost 30 percent including Hong Kong) in 2008, while those of the US, EU, and Japan were 10 percent, 13 percent, and 6 percent, respectively. Therefore, Korea's export market was likely to recover faster if China's imports recovered faster than other regions, which in turn was a natural implication of the global rebalancing: the unwinding of global imbalance should imply a relatively small correction of final demand (domestic absorption, to be precise) in China compared to that in the US. As far as Korea's exports to China did not entirely rely on final demand induced by the US, or to the extent that it depended on China's autonomous domestic absorption, a relatively small correction of Korea's exports was required in the process of global rebalancing.

This composition effect thanks to China's faster recovery alone, however, cannot fully explain the differential between the growth rate of Korea's exports and that of global trade. If Korea's market shares in China and other regions had remained the same, the growth rate of Korea's exports in 2009 would have recorded –20.8 percent (a weighted average of the import growth rates of China, –11.3 percent, and the other regions, –23.8 percent), still falling short of the realized rate, –13.8 percent. In fact, Korea's market shares did increase in both China and other regions, implying that macro-factors in addition to the China factor must have worked (see Table 15.1).

3.2.3   *Exchange rate, an automatic stabilizer*

The most likely macro-factor was the huge depreciation of the Korean won that occurred during the crisis period. Though it is always difficult to precisely quantify the effects of exchange rates on exports, the following result from a simple regression (for monthly data from January 2000 to April 2010) can provide a first approximation:

$$EX_{Korea} = -3.28 + 0.37\,IM_{US} + 0.33\,IM_{Euro} + 0.20\,IM_{Japan} + 0.25\,IM_{China}$$
$$\quad (-4.31) \quad (2.25) \quad\quad (3.48) \quad\quad\quad (1.90) \quad\quad\quad (8.35)$$

$$-0.03\,ER_0 - 0.38\,ER_{-1} + 0.13\,ER_{-2} + 0.56\,ER_{-3} + residual$$
$$(-0.14) \quad (-0.90) \quad\quad (0.31) \quad\quad (2.21)$$

Table 15.1 Korea's exports and global imports

	Korea's Export Growth Rate	Import Growth Rate			Share of Korea's Exports		
		World	China	Others	World	China[1]	Others[2]
2008	–	–	–	–	2.7	9.9	2.2
2009	–13.8	–22.9	–11.3	–23.8	3.0	10.2	2.4

Source: Global Insight, Bloomberg.

where EX_{Korea} is log-export (in US$) of Korea, IM_i is log-import (in US$) of region i, and ER_t is log of real effective exchange rate of the Korean won.[13] A noticeable result is that the effect of IM_{China} appears smaller than that of IM_{US} or IM_{Euro}, despite a larger portion of China than that of the US or Euro in terms of Korea's export destination. This result suggests that a substantial portion of China's imports is induced by other regions' final demand. In fact, the relative magnitudes of the coefficients for each region appear to be similar to the relative sizes of GDP.

As for the exchange rate, it appears to take several months until its effects kick in, which seems to explain why Korea's exports began to recover from the second quarter 2009, several months after the exchange rate shock in the fourth quarter 2008. Yet, the accumulated elasticity with respect to the exchange rate is calculated at 0.28, with due consideration to the unpolished regression specification.[14] Applying this rough estimate, more than 20 percent of exchange rate depreciation that occurred during the crisis period could generate at least 5–6 percent of export increase, accounting for two-thirds of the differential in growth rates between Korea's exports and global trade in 2009.

In this regard, the "currency crisis," not accompanied with a banking crisis, contributed to the faster recovery of export sectors in Korea. To put it elegantly, Korea's experience confirmed the textbook prediction that a flexible exchange rate system would help automatically stabilize the economy. And this role of the exchange rate was particularly necessary in an economy opened to capricious international capital flows, such as Korea.

4. Macro-policy reactions

4.1 Monetary policy

Among many policy reactions to the crisis, the most contrasting in 2008 to those in 1997 was the monetary policy. The policy interest rate was raised in 1997 to the level (almost 30 percent) above twice the pre-crisis rate (approximately 12 percent), but it was lowered to the level (2.00 percent) below half the pre-crisis rate (5.25 percent) in response to the recent crisis (see Figure 15.13). No doubt the monetary easing in 2008 was crucial in guarding domestic economy from the external storm, whereas the monetary tightening in 1997 aggravated the domestic banking crisis.

More interesting than the policy effects, however, were the environments that led to different policies.[15] Most advanced countries aggressively lowered interest rates to cope with their own financial crises in 2008, while they did not in 1997. This trend in international policies lightened the Bank of Korea's burden associated with the monetary easing in 2008, despite the exchange rate depreciation.

The most critical difference, however, was the foreign currency liquidity situation when the crisis was triggered. Given foreign reserves were almost depleted, the high interest rate policy in December 1997 may have been inevitable, but Korea in 2008 reserved rooms to maneuver on this front.[16] And the most important factor that led to different foreign reserve situations was the government's approach to the foreign exchange market. In 1997, the government believed that it could, and should, control the foreign exchange market and actually did attempt to engineer a "smooth

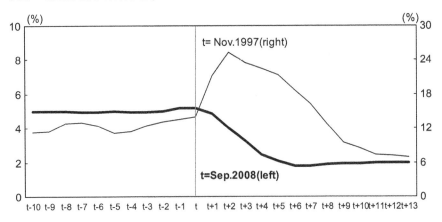

Figure 15.13 Inter-bank overnight call rate

Source: Bank of Korea.

and orderly" depreciation from the beginning of 1997. This approach only invited currency speculation and catalyzed reserve depletion in the end. In 2008, in contrast, the government let the exchange rate adjust to the shock instead of wasting foreign reserves, which eventually saved the flexibility of monetary policy as well as the aforementioned automatic stabilizing role of the exchange rate.

4.2. Fiscal policy

Fiscal policy reactions were not as contrasting as monetary policy reactions. In both periods, expansionary fiscal stances were assumed. The sizes of budget deficits, approximately 3 percent of GDP, were also similar.

However, the processes to similar results, *ex post*, were different. In 1997, the IMF initially recommended the Korean government to maintain a budget balance in December 1997 when fiscal stimulus was most needed. Only after the severe recession was realized was a budget deficit allowed in 1998 and gradually expanded as the recession deepened.[17] This time, in contrast, the Korean government announced fiscal expansion as soon as the global crisis was set off and injected the necessary stimulus. A supplementary budget of 10 trillion won (approximately 1 percent of GDP) was implemented in November 2008, and an additional supplementary budget of 28.4 trillion won (approximately 2.8 percent of GDP) was drawn up by March 2009. Considering time lags common to fiscal policy effects, the early execution of fiscal spending must have contributed to stabilizing the economy.

5.   Conclusion: putting the pieces together

The recent crisis and subsequent recovery of Korea may have been a surprise to many forecasters. But it was a relief to most Koreans who still had vivid memories of the 1997–1998 crisis. There were many factors that contributed to mitigating the effects of shocks on Korea. Some factors worked in protecting the domestic banking system and others operated to induce relatively fast export recovery (see Figure 15.14).

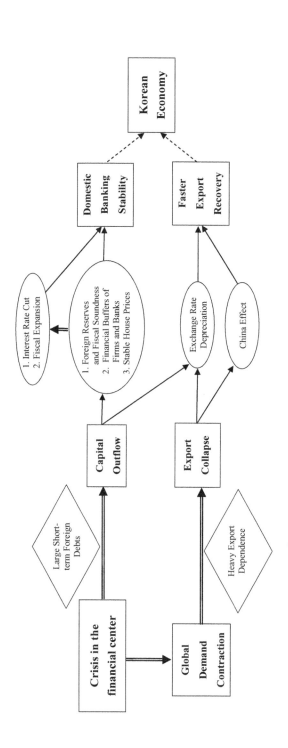

Figure 15.14 Transmission of the global crisis to Korea

These factors can be broadly classified into two categories: pre-crisis fundamentals and post-crisis macro-policy reactions. The former includes a large amount of foreign reserves, improved financial structures of firms and banks, relatively mild house price hikes, and the tradition of sound government budgets, while the latter includes the foreign exchange policy that honored market forces, monetary policy that stabilizes the domestic economy, and fiscal policy that was carried out on time. Between the two categories, however, inextricable relationships exist. Sound fundamentals are necessary, though not sufficient, conditions for flexible macro-policy reactions.[18] In reverse, prolonged expansionary policies erode the soundness of fundamentals, which will eventually restrict the flexibility of macro-policies.

Korea could successfully recover this time, thanks to the relatively sound pre-crisis fundamentals achieved by the restructuring processes since the 1997–1998 crisis, along with consistent macro-policies. However, if the emergency policies are not normalized on time and necessary restructuring is delayed, the recent success can become an ominous prelude to another crisis in the future.

Notes

* This chapter is reprinted from *Global Economic Crisis: Impacts, Transmission, and Recovery*, edited by Maurice Obstfeld, Dongchul Cho and Andrew Mason, Edward Elgar Publishing Inc., pp. 57–77, 2012.

1 Shin and Kim (2008), for example, find that domestic demand, particularly private consumption, is significantly correlated with employment. This finding, though subject to simultaneity bias critiques, makes sense in that export (or manufacturing) industries are mostly capital intensive, while service industries are labor intensive.

2 Lee and Song (2011) in this volume explain in detail how Korea's short-term foreign debt had accumulated since 2005.

3 More than 90 percent of this capital outflow, $25.5 billion, was accounted for by the reduction in short-term debts, while equity market exhibited net capital inflow.

4 The empirical literature's definition of "currency crisis" ranges from a narrow one focusing on devaluations of nominal exchange rates (Edwards and Montiel, 1989, and Frankel and Rose, 1996, among others) to a broader one that also considers reductions in foreign reserves and hikes in interest rates (Eichengreen, Rose and Wyplosz, 1996, and Sachs, Tornell and Velasco, 1996, among others).

5 See, for example, Reinhart and Rogoff (2009).

6 Caprio and Klingebiel (1996) define a period of "financial distress" as 'when a significant fraction of the banking sector is insolvent but remains open', and Calomiris and Gorton (1991) define a "financial panic" as 'when bank debt holders suddenly demand their debt claims into cash to an extent that the banks are forced to suspend the convertibility of their debt into cash'. Demirguc-Kunt and Detragiache (1998) define "systemic crisis" as the one in which: (1) non-performing loans (NPLs) were at least 10 percent of total assets; (2) cost of rescue operations was greater than 2 percent of GDP; (3) banking problems resulted in a large-scale nationalization of banks; and (4) emergency measures, such as deposit freeze, prolonged bank holidays, generalized deposit guarantees were introduced.

7 After the 1997–1998 crisis, five out of 33 major banks were closed and 10 were merged until the end of 2004. A more drastic restructuring was carried out for small banks (called "merchant bank corporations"), as a result of which only two

out of 30 survived, while 22 were closed and seven were merged, during the same period. For this restructuring, 64 trillion won (almost 13 percent of GDP) of public money was mobilized in 1998 and 40 trillion won (almost 7 percent of GDP) was added in 2000. See the Korea's Committee for Public Fund Management (2001).

8 From September to December in 2008, short-term debts were reduced by $39.7 billion (from $186.6 billion to $149.9 billon) and foreign reserves were reduced by $38.5 billion (from $239.7 billion to $201.2 billion).

9 Using micro-data for Korea's listed companies, Lim (2011) in this volume analyzes in detail how Korean firms have changed their financial positions since 1998 and how they could cope with the recent crisis without significant disruptions.

10 See Bernanke (1983), Bernanke and Gertler (1989), Kiyotaki and Moor (1997), among others, for the literature emphasizing the importance of credit markets on economic fluctuations. Similarly to Kaminsky and Reinhart (1999), Cerra and Saxena (2008) recently documented that the output impact of a banking crisis was nearly twice as large as a currency crisis, using a wide set of data covering 190 countries.

11 See Lee (2011) for cross-country analyses of the drastic collapse in global trade volume during this period of time.

12 A leading example was the IMF's position note by Martin Sommer (2009), which established a strong negative cross-country relationship between the growth rate of the fourth quarter 2008 and the portion of manufacturing industries in GDP. It is obvious that an economy more dependent on exports should be more affected by the global trade shock. However, contrary to a casual argument, this never implies that crisis-affected regions (e.g. East Asia) should contract more than crisis-originating countries (e.g. the US) through trade channels. See Kato (2009) and Cho (2009) for more discussion on this point.

13 The real effective exchange rate was constructed by taking an average of nominal exchange rates deflated by CPI for 12 countries (Australia, China, Japan, France, Germany, Italy, Hong Kong, Netherlands, Singapore, Taiwan, U.K., and US), weighted by the trade portion of respective country.

14 Estimates of the accumulated elasticity from different specifications range from 0.15 to 0.35.

15 Kim (2011) in this volume discusses Korea's monetary and fiscal policies before and after the crisis in detail, and thus this section emphasizes the differences from the macro-policies during the 1997–1998 crisis period.

16 At the verge of national default in December 1997, all of the policy measures including monetary policy were lined up to secure foreign currency liquidity rather than economic stabilization. See Fischer (1988) and Krueger (2000) for example. Under this policy priority, it was necessary, or probably inevitable, to impose a high interest rate policy. It was particularly so given that the penalty interest rate was charged on the foreign currency loans of the Bank of Korea to commercial banks. Otherwise, commercial banks desperate of foreign currency liquidity would have rushed to borrow domestic currency at relatively low interest rates and converted it into foreign currency to pay back their existing borrowings to the Bank of Korea, which could have further deteriorated foreign exchange situation. See Lee (2010) and Cho (2010) for details of the financial market situation in Korea during the crisis period.

17 The recommended budget deficit of the IMF was expanded to 0.8 percent of GDP in the fifth agreement on February 7; 1.75 percent of GDP in the sixth agreement on May 2; 4 percent of GDP in the seventh agreement on July 24; and finally 5 percent of GDP in in eighth agreement on October 27. See Chopra et al. (2002) for details.

18 The monetary policy of Korea in 1997 and the recent fiscal policy of Greece may be leading examples.

References

Bernanke, Ben S., 1983. "Nonmonetary Effects of the Financial Crisis in the Propagation of the Great Depression," *American Economic Review*, 73(3), pp. 257–276.

Bernanke, Ben S., and Mark Gertler, 1989. "Agency Costs, Net Worth, and Business Fluctuations," *American Economic Review*, 79(1), pp. 14–31.

Calomiris, Charles W., and Gary Gorton, 1991. "The Origins of Banking Panics: Models, Facts, and Bank Regulation," in *Financial Markets and Financial Crises*, edited by R. Glenn Hubbard, pp. 109–174. Chicago: University of Chicago Press.

Caprio, Gerard, Jr., and Klingebiel, Daniela, 1996. "Bank Insolvencies: Cross-Country Experience," *Policy Research Working Paper* no. 1620, World Bank, Washington, DC.

Cerra, Valerie, and Sweta Chaman Saxena, 2008. "Growth Dynamics: The Myth of Economic Recovery," *American Economic Review*, 98(1), pp. 439–457.

Cho, Dongchul, 2009. "The Republic of Korea's Economy in the Swirl of Global Crisis," *ADBI Working Paper Series* 147, Asia Development Bank Institute, Tokyo.

———, 2010. "Overcoming the 1997–98 Crisis: Macroeconomic Policy Adjustments," manuscript, Korea Development Institute., Seoul.

Chopra, Ajai, Kenneth Kang, Meral Karasulu, Hong Liang, Henry Ma, and Anthony Richards, 2002. "From Crisis to Recovery in Korea: Strategy, Achievements, and Lessons," in *Korean Crisis and Recovery*, edited by David T. Coe and Se-jik Kim, pp. 13–104. Washington, DC: International Monetary Fund and Korea Institute for International Economic Policy.

Demirgüç-Kunt, Asli, and Enrica Detragiache, 1998. "The Determinants of Banking Crises in Developing and Developed Countries," *IMF Staff Papers*, 45, IMF, Washington, DC.

Economist, The, 2009. "Domino Theory: Where Could Emerging Market Contagion Spread Next?" Economics Focus, February 26, http://www.economist.com/node/13184631.

Edwards, Sebastian, and Peter Montiel, 1989. "Devaluation Crises and the Macroeconomic Consequences of Postponed Adjustment," *IMF Staff Papers,* 366(4), pp. 875–903.

Eichengreen, Barry, Andrew Rose, and Charles Wyplosz, 1996. "Contagious Currency Crises: First Tests," *The Scandinavian Journal of Economics*, 98(4), pp. 463–484.

Fischer, Stanley. 1998. "The Asian Crisis: A View from the IMF," IMF, Washington, DC, www.imf.org/external/np/speeches/1998/012298.htm.

Frankel, Jeffrey, and Andrew Rose, 1996. "Currency Crashes in Emerging Markets: Empirical Indicators," *Journal of International Economics*, 41(3–4), pp. 351–366.

International Monetary Fund, 2008, 2009. *World Economic Outlook*. IMF, Washington, DC.

Kaminsky, Graciela L. and Carmen M. Reinhart, 1999. "The Twin Crises: The Causes of Banking and Balance of Payments Problems," *American Economic Review*, 89, pp. 473–500.

Kato, Takatoshi, 2009. "Implications for Asia from the Global Financial Crisis and Policy Perspectives," Harvard Asia Business Conference, February, pp. 14–15.

Kim, Hyeon-Wook, 2011. "Macroeconomic Policies of Korea to Cope with the Crisis." this volume.

Kiyotaki, Nobuhiro, and John Moore, 1997. "Credit Cycles," *Journal of Political Economy*, 105, pp. 211–248.

Korea's Committee for Public Fund Management. 2001. *White Paper*. www.pbfunds. go.kr. (in Korean).

Krueger, Anne O. 2000. "Conflicting Demands on the International Monetary Funds," *American Economic Review*, 90(2), pp. 38–42.

Lee, Hangyong and Min-Kyu Song, 2011. "The International Spillover of the Financial Disruption," this volume.

Lee, Hangyu, 2011. "The Great Trade Collapse and Contraction of Exports," this volume.

Lee, Kyu-sung, 2010. *Korea's Financial Crisis: Onset, Turnaround and Thereafter*. Forthcoming, World Bank.

Lim, Kyung-Mook, 2011. "Structural Fundamentals of Korean Corporations: This Time Was Different," in *Global Economic Crisis: Impacts, Transmission, and Recovery*, edited by Maurice Obstfeld, Dongchul Cho, and Andrew Mason, pp. 250–272. Cheltenham, UK: Edward Elgar Press.

Reinhart, Carmen, and Kenneth S. Rogoff, 2009. *This Time is Different: Eight Centuries of Financial Folly*. Princeton, NJ: Princeton University Press.

Sachs, Jeffrey, Aaron Tornell and Andres Velascom, 1996. "Financial Crises in Emerging Markets: The Lessons form 1995", NBER Working Paper No. 5576, May.

Shin, Sukha, and Heesam Kim, 2008. "An Analysis on the Recent Slowdown of Employment," *KDI Economic Outlook*, 25(1), pp. 153–164 (in Korean).

Sommer, Martin, 2009. "Why Has Japan Been So Hard by the Global Recession?" *IMF Staff Position Note*, SPN/09/05, March 18, Washington, DC.

Index

Page numbers in italic indicate figures and tables.

For Product Safety Concerns and Information please contact our EU
representative GPSR@taylorandfrancis.com Taylor & Francis Verlag GmbH,
Kaufingerstraße 24, 80331 München, Germany

Printed and bound by CPI Group (UK) Ltd, Croydon, CR0 4YY
08/05/2025
01864345-0002